IPv6 Network Programming

IPv6 Network Programming

Jun-ichiro itojun Hagino

ELSEVIER
DIGITAL
PRESS

Amsterdam • Boston • Heidelberg • London
New York • Oxford • Paris • San Diego
San Francisco • Singapore • Sydney • Tokyo

Elsevier Digital Press
30 Corporate Drive, Suite 400, Burlington, MA 01803, USA
Linacre House, Jordan Hill, Oxford OX2 8DP, UK

 Recognizing the importance of preserving what has been written, Elsevier prints its books on acid-free paper whenever possible.

Library of Congress Cataloging-in-Publication Data

Application submitted.

British Library Cataloguing-in-Publication Data

A catalogue record for this book is available from the British Library.

ISBN: 1-55558-318-0

For information on all Elsevier Digital Press publications visit our Web site at www.books.elsevier.com

04 05 06 07 08 09 10 9 8 7 6 5 4 3 2 1

Printed in the United States of America

Contents

Preface

Here in Japan, it looks like the Internet is deployed everywhere. Not a day will go by without hearing the word Internet. However, many people do not know that we are very close to reaching the theoretical limit of IPv4. The theoretical limit for the number of IPv4 nodes is only 4 billion—much fewer than the world's population.

People in trains and cars send email on their cellphones using small numeric keypads. Most of these devices are not connected to the real Internet—these cellphones do not speak the Internet Protocol. They use proprietary protocols to deliver emails to the gateway, and the gateway relays the emails to the Internet. Cellular operators are now trying to make cellphones a real VoIP device (instead of "email only" device) to avoid the costs of operating proprietary phone switches/devices/gateways and to use inexpensive IP routers.

There are a lot of areas where the Internet and the Internet Protocol have to be deployed. For instance, we need to enable every vehicle to be connected to the IP network in order to exchange information about traffic congestion. There are plans to interconnect every consumer device to the Internet, so that vendors can collect information from the machines (such as statistics), as well as provide various value-added services.

Also, we need to deploy IP to every country in the world, including highly populated areas such as China, India, and Africa, so that everyone has equal opportunity to access the information on the Internet.

To deploy the Internet Protocol to wider domains, the transition from IPv4 to IPv6 is critical. IPv4 cannot accommodate the needs discussed previously, due to the limitation in address space size. With IPv6 we will be able to accomodate 3.4×10^{38} nodes to the Internet—it should be enough for our lifetime (I hope).

The IPv6 effort was started in 1992, in the INET92 conference held in Kobe, Japan. Since then, we have been making a huge amount of effort to help the transition happen. Fortunately, it seems that the interest in IPv6 has reached the critical mass, and the transition to IPv6 is now a reality. Many ISPs in Japan are offering commercial IPv6 connectivity services, numerous vendors are shipping IPv6-enabled operating systems, and many IPv6-enabled products are coming. If you are not ready yet, you need to hurry up.

The transition to IPv6 requires an upgrade of router software and host operating systems, as well as application software. This book focuses on how you can modify your network application software, based on the socket API, to support IPv6. When you write a network application program, you will want the program to be IPv6-capable, so that it will work just fine on the IPv6 network, as well as the IPv4 network. After going through this book, you will be able to make your programs IPv6-ready. It will also help you port your IPv4-capable application to become IPv6-capable at the same time.

In this book, we advocate address-family independent socket layer programming for IPv6 transition. By following the instructions in the book, your code will become independent from the address family (such as AF_INET or AF_INET6). This is the best way to support IPv6 in your program, compared with other approaches (such as hardcoding AF_INET6 into the program).

I would like to thank the editor for the Japanese edition of the book, Ms. Eiko Akashima, and translator for the Japanese edition of the book, Ms. Ayako Ogawa (the original manuscript of the book is in English, even though it was first published in Japan). On the technical side, I would like to thank Mr. Craig Metz, who generously permitted us to include his paper on address-family independent programming, as well as the members of the WIDE/KAME project, who have made a lot of useful suggestions to the content of the book.

Jun-ichiro itojun Hagino
Tokyo, Japan

About This Book

This book tries to outline how to write an IPv6-capable application on a UNIX socket API, or how to update your IPv4 application to be IPv6-capable. The book tries to show portable and secure ways to achieve these goals.

Write Portable Application Programs

There are a large number of platforms that support socket API for network programming. When you write an application on top of socket API, you will want to see your program work on as many platforms as possible. Therefore, portability is an important factor in application programming. As many of you already know, there are many UNIX-like operating systems, as well as non-UNIX operating systems that implement socket APIs. For instance, Windows XP does implement socket API; Mac OS X uses BSD UNIX as the base operating system and provides socket API to the users (Apple normally recommends the use of Apple APIs). So the book tries to recommend portable ways of writing IPv6-capable programs.

Be Security Conscious When Writing Programs

Security is a great concern these days in the Internet—if you are a network administrator, I guess you are receiving tons of spam, email viruses, and vendor advisories every day. To secure the Internet infrastructure, every developer has to take a security stance—to audit every line of code as much as possible, to use proper API, and write a correct and secure code. To achieve this goal, in this book, efforts are made to ensure correctness of the examples. The examples presented in this book are implemented with security stance. Also, the book tries to lead you to write secure programs. For instance, the book recommends against the use of some of the IPv6 standard APIs;

unfortunately, there are some IPv6 APIs that are inherently insecure, so the book tries to avoid (and discourage) the use of such APIs.

This book does not try to cover every aspect of IPv6 technology—the book constrains itself to the IPv6-capable programming on top of socket API. There are numerous reading materials on IPv6 technology, so readers are encouraged to read them before starting to work on this book.

Also, the book assumes a certain level of expertise in socket API programming. The book does not try to explain every aspect of socket API programming; please read the material listed in the References for an introductory description to socket API.

Terminology and Portability

This section describes notations and terminologies used in this book. Here we also discuss porting issues of examples when you are using operating systems that are not 4.4BSD variants.

Terminology

System calls and system library functions are usually denoted by UNIX manpage chapters: socket(2) or printf(3).

"Nodes" means any IP devices. "Routers" are any nodes that forward packets for others. "Hosts" are nodes that are not routers (however, in this book, we don't really need to make distinctions between them).

Portability of Examples

The examples in the book compile and run on latest *BSD releases. I tried to make the examples as correct as possible.

If you are planning to use the examples on other platforms, here are some tweaks dependent on OS implementations.

Solaris, Linux, Windows XP

struct sockaddr has no sa_len member. Therefore, it is not possible to get the size of a given sockaddr when the caller of the function passed a pointer to a sockaddr. The only ways to work around this problem are:

1. To always pass around the length of sockaddr separately on function calls:

```
struct sockaddr *sa;
int salen;

foo(sa, salen)
```

2. To have a switch statement to determine length of sockaddr. With this approach, however, the application will not be able to support sockaddrs with unknown address family.

```
struct sockaddr *sa;
int salen;

switch (sa->sa_family) {
case AF_INET:
        salen = sizeof(sockaddr_in);
        break;
case AF_INET6:
        salen = sizeof(struct sockaddr_in6);
        break
default:
        fprintf(stderr, "not supported\n");
        exit(1);
        /*NOTREACHED*/
}
```

Missing Type for Variables

In some cases, your platform may not have the type declaration used in this book. In such cases, use the following:

- If socklen_t is not defined—such as older *BSD releases:

    Use unsigned int instead.

- If in_port_t is not present:

    Use u_int16_t.

- If u_int8_t, u_int16_t, and u_int32_t are not found:

    If your system has /usr/include/inttypes.h (which is defined in the recent C language standard), you may use uint8_t, uint16_t, or uint32_t, respectively, after #include <inttypes.h>.

Introduction

1.1   A History of IPv6 and Its Key Features

In 1992, the IETF (http://www.ietf.org/) became aware of a global shortage of IPv4 addresses and technical obstacles in deploying new protocols due to limitations imposed by IPv4. An IPng (IP next generation) effort was started to solve these issues. The discussion is outlined in several RFCs, starting with RFC 1550. After a large amount of discussion, in 1995, IPv6 (IP version 6) was picked as the final IPng proposal. The IPv6 base specification is specified in RFC 1883 and revised in RFC 2460.

In a single sentence, IPv6 is a reengineering effort against IP technology. Key features are as follows.

1.1.1   Larger IP Address Space

IPv4 uses only 2^{32} bits for IP address space, which allows only (theoretically) 4 billion nodes to be identified on the Internet. Four billion may look like a large number; however, it is less than the world's population. Moreover, due to the allocation (in)efficiency, it is not possible to use up all 4 billion addresses.

IPv6 allows 2^{128} bits for IP address space, (theoretically) allowing 340,282,366,920,938,463,463,374,607,431,768,211,456 (340 undecillion) nodes to be uniquely identified on the Internet. Larger address space allows true end-to-end communication, without NAT or other short-term workarounds against IPv4 address shortage. (In these days, NAT has been a headache to new protocol deployment and scalability issues, and we really need to decommission NATs for the Internet to grow further.)

1.1.2   Deploy More Recent Technologies

After IPv4 was specified 20 years ago, we saw many technical improvements in networking. IPv6 covers a number of those improvements in its base specification, allowing people to assume that these features are available everywhere, anytime. Recent technologies include, but are not limited to, the following:

- *Autoconfiguration*—With IPv4, DHCP is optional. A novice user can get into trouble if visiting an offsite without a DHCP server. With IPv6, the stateless host autoconfiguration mechanism is mandatory. This is much simpler to use and manage than IPv4 DHCP. RFC 2462 has the specification for it.

- *Security*—With IPv4, IPsec is optional and you need to ask the peer if it supports IPsec. With IPv6, IPsec support is mandatory. By mandating IPsec, we can assume that you can secure your IP communication whenever you talk to IPv6 peers.

- *Friendly to traffic engineering technologies*—IPv6 was designed to allow better support for traffic engineering such as diffserv[1] or RSVP[2]. We do not have single standard for traffic engineering yet; so the IPv6 base specification reserves a 24-bit space in the header field for those technologies and is able to adapt to coming standards better than IPv4.

- *Multicast*—Multicast support is mandatory in IPv6; it was optional in IPv4. The IPv6 base specifications extensively use multicast on the directly connected link. It is still questionable how widely we will be able to deploy multicast (such as nationwide multicast infrastructure), though.

- *Better support for ad hoc networking*—Scoped addresses allow better support for ad hoc (or "zeroconf") networking. IPv6 supports anycast addresses, which can also contribute to service discoveries.

1.1.3   A Cure to Routing Table Growth

The IPv4 backbone routing table size has been a big headache to ISPs and backbone operators. The IPv6 addressing specification restricts the number of backbone routing entries by advocating route aggregation. With the current IPv6 addressing specification, we will see only 8,192 routes in the default-free zone.

---

1.   diffserv: short for "differentiated services." It is an IETF standard that classifies packets into a couple of classes and performs rough bandwidth/priority control.

2.   RSVP: an IETF standard for bandwidth reservation.

1.1.4   Simplified Header Structures

IPv6 has simpler packet header structures than IPv4. It will allow vendors to implement hardware acceleration for IPv6 routers easier.

1.1.5   Allows Flexible Protocol Extensions

IPv6 allows more flexible protocol extensions than IPv4 by introducing a protocol header chain. Even though IPv6 allows flexible protocol extensions, IPv6 does not impose overhead to intermediate routers. It is achieved by splitting headers into two flavors: the headers intermediate routers need to examine and the headers the final destination will examine. This also eases hardware acceleration for IPv6 routers.

1.1.6   Smooth Transition from IPv4

There were a number of transition considerations made during the IPv6 discussions. Also, there is a large number of transition mechanisms available. You can pick the most suitable one for your network during the transition period.

1.1.7   Follows the Key Design Principles of IPv4

IPv4 was a very successful design, as proven by the large-scale global deployment. IPv6 is a new version of IP, and it follows many of the design features that made IPv4 very successful. This will also allow smooth transition from IPv4 to IPv6.

1.1.8   And More

There are number of good books available about IPv6. Be sure to check these if you are interested.

Protocol Header Chain

IPv6 defines a protocol header chain, which is a way to concatenate extension headers repeatedly after the IPv6 base header. With IPv4, the IPv4 header is adjacent to the final header (like TCP). With IPv6, the protocol header chain allows various extension headers to be put between the IPv6 base header and the final header.

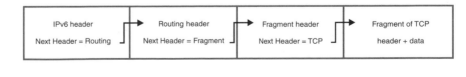

1.2   Transition from IPv4-Only Internet to IPv4/v6 Dual Stack Internet

Today, most of the nodes on the Internet use IPv4. We will need to gradually introduce IPv6 to the Internet and hopefully make all nodes on the Internet IPv6-capable.

To do this, the IETF has carefully designed IPv6 migration to be seamless. This is achieved by the following two key technologies:

- Dual stack
- Tunneling

With these technologies, we can transition to IPv6 even though IPv4 and IPv6 are not compatible (IPv4-only devices and IPv6-only devices cannot talk with each other directly). We will go into the details soon.

It is expected that we will have a long period of IPv4/v6 dual stack Internet, due to the wide deployment of IPv4 devices. For instance, some of the existing devices, such as IPv4-capable game machines, may not be able to be upgraded to IPv6.

Therefore, in this book, we would like to focus on the issues regarding the transition from IPv4-only Internet to IPv4/v6 dual stack Internet and the changes in socket API programming.

1.2.1   Dual stack

At least in the early stage of IPv6 deployment, IPv6-capable nodes are assumed to be IPv4-capable. They are called "IPv4/v6 dual stack nodes" or "dual stack nodes." Dual stack nodes will use IPv4 to communicate with IPv4 nodes, and use IPv6 to communicate with IPv6 nodes. It is just like a bilingual person—he or she will use English when talking to people in the States, and will use Japanese when talking to Japanese people.

The determination of protocol version is automatic, based on available DNS records. Because this is based on DNS, and normal users would use fully qualified domain name (FQDN) in email addresses and URLs, the transition from IPv4 to IPv6 is invisible to normal users. For instance, assume that we have a dual stack node, and we are to access http://www.example.com/. A dual stack node will behave as follows:

- If www.example.com resolves to an IPv4 address, connect to the IPv4 address. In such a case, the DNS database record for www.example.com will be as follows:

```
www.example.com.      IN A      10.1.1.1
```

- If www.example.com resolves to an IPv6 address, connect to the IPv6 address.

```
www.example.com.      IN AAAA 3ffe:501:ffff::1234
```

- If www.example.com resolves to multiple IPv4/v6 addresses, IPv6 addresses will be tried first, and then IPv4 addresses will be tried. For example, with the following DNS records, we will try connecting to 3ffe:501:ffff::1234, then 3ffe:501:ffff::5678, and finally 10.1.1.1.

```
www.example.com.      IN AAAA 3ffe:501:ffff::1234
www.example.com.      IN AAAA 3ffe:501:ffff::5678
www.example.com.      IN A      10.1.1.1
```

Since we assume that IPv6 nodes will be able to use IPv4 as well, the Internet will be filled with IPv4/v6 dual stack nodes in the near future, and the use of IPv6 will become dominant.

1.2.2   Tunneling

Even when we have IPv4/v6 dual stack nodes at two locations (e.g., home and office), it may be possible that the intermediate network (ISPs) are not IPv6-ready yet. To circumvent this situation, RFC 2893 defines ways to encapsulate an IPv6 packet into an IPv4 packet. The encapsulated packet will travel IPv4 Internet with no trouble, and then decapsulate at the other end. We call this technology "IPv6-over-IPv4 tunneling."

For example, imagine the following situation (see Figure 1.1):

- We have two networks: home and office.
- We have an IPv4/v6 dual stack host and router at both locations.
- However, we have IPv4-only connectivity to the upstream ISP.

In this case, we can configure an IPv6-over-IPv4 tunnel between X and Y. An IPv6 packet from A to B will be routed as follows (see Figure 1.2):

- The IPv6 packet will be transmitted from A to X, as is.
- X will encapsulate the packet into an IPv4 packet.
- The IPv4 packet will travel the IPv4 Internet, to Y.
- Y will decapsulate the packet and recover the original IPv6 packet.
- The packet will reach B.

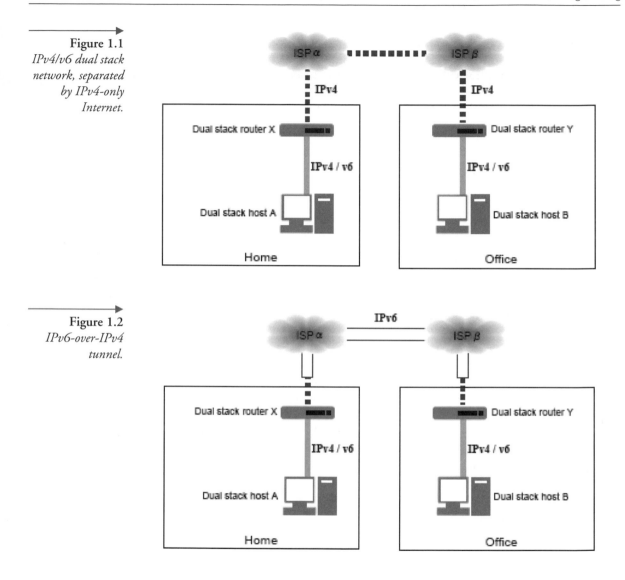

Figure 1.1
*IPv4/v6 dual stack
network, separated
by IPv4-only
Internet.*

Figure 1.2
*IPv6-over-IPv4
tunnel.*

From a programmer's point of view, tunneling is transparent: It can be viewed as a simple IPv6 point-to-point link. Therefore, when writing IPv6-capable programs, you can ignore tunneling.

1.3   UNIX Socket Programming

This section briefly describes how UNIX systems abstract network accesses via socket interface. If you are familiar with UNIX sockets, you can skip this section. Also, the section does not try to be complete—for the complete description, you may want to check the reading material listed in the References.

With only a few exceptions, UNIX operating systems abstract system resources as files. For instance, the hard disk device is abstracted as a file such as /dev/rwd0c. Even physical memory on the machine is abstracted as a file, /dev/mem. You can open(2), read(2), write(2), or close(2) files, and files already opened by a process are identified by an integer file descriptor.

```
int fd; /* file descriptor */
char buf[128];

fd = open("/tmp/foo", O_RDONLY, 0);
if (fd < 0) {
        perror("open");
        exit(1);
        /*NOTREACHED*/
}
if (read(fd, buf, sizeof(buf)) < 0) {
        perror("read");
        exit(1);
        /*NOTREACHED*/
}
close(fd);
exit(0);
```

Accesses to the network are also abstracted as special kinds of files, called sockets. Sockets are created by a socket(2) system call. Sockets are a special kind of file descriptor, so they are represented as an integer and can be terminated by using close(2). On a socket(2) call, you need to identify the following three parameters:

- *Protocol family*—AF_INET identifies IPv4.
- *Type of socket*—SOCK_STREAM means connetion-oriented socket model. SOCK_DGRAM means datagram-oriented socket model.
- *Protocol type*—such as IPPROTO_TCP or IPPROTO_UDP.

For the Internet protocol, there are two kinds of sockets: connection-oriented and connectionless sockets. Connection-oriented sockets abstract TCP connections, and connectionless sockets abstract communication over UDP. Type of socket and protocol type has to be consistent; SOCK_STREAM has to be used with IPPROTO_TCP.

Note: There are transport layer protocols other than TCP/UDP proposed in the IETF, such as SCTP or DCCP. They are also abstracted as connection-oriented or connectionless sockets.

```
int s; /* socket */

/*
 * AF_INET: protocol family for IPv4
 * SOCK_STREAM: connection-oriented socket
 * IPPROTO_TCP: use TCP on top of IPv4
 */
s = socket(AF_INET, SOCK_STREAM, IPPROTO_TCP);
if (s < 0) {
        perror("socket"); exit(1);
        /*NOTREACHED*/
}
close(s);
```

While read(2) or write(2) is possible for sockets, we normally need to supply more information, such as peer's address, to get the data stream to reach the peer. There are additional system calls specifically provided for sockets, such as sendmsg(2), sendto(3), recvmsg(2), and recvfrom(3).

Since we need to identify the peer when accessing the network, we need to denote it either by:

- Using connect(2) to make the socket a connected socket. The peer's address will be kept in the system, and you can use read(2) or write(2) after connect(2).

- Using sendto(3) or sendmsg(2) to denote the peer every time you transmit data to the socket.

For connection-oriented (TCP) sockets, there are two sides: client side, which makes active connection, and server side, which awaits connection from the client passively. connect(2) is mandatory for the client side. bind(2), listen(2), and accept(2) are mandatory for the server side. (See Figure 1.3.)

For connectionless (UDP) sockets, connect(2) is not mandatory. To receive traffic from other peers, bind(2) is mandatory. (See Figure 1.4.)

To denote TCP/UDP endpoints, IP address and port number are necessary. To carry the endpoint information, we use a C structure called "sockaddr" (short for "socket addresses"). sockaddr for IPv4 is defined in the following code segment. Fields that appear on wire (sin_port and sin_addr) are in network byte order; other fields are in host byte order.

```
/*
 * Note: the definition is based on 4.4BSD socket API.
 * Linux/Solaris has no sin_len field.
 */
struct sockaddr_in {
        u_int8_t        sin_len;        /* length of sockaddr */
        u_int8_t        sin_family;     /* address family */
```

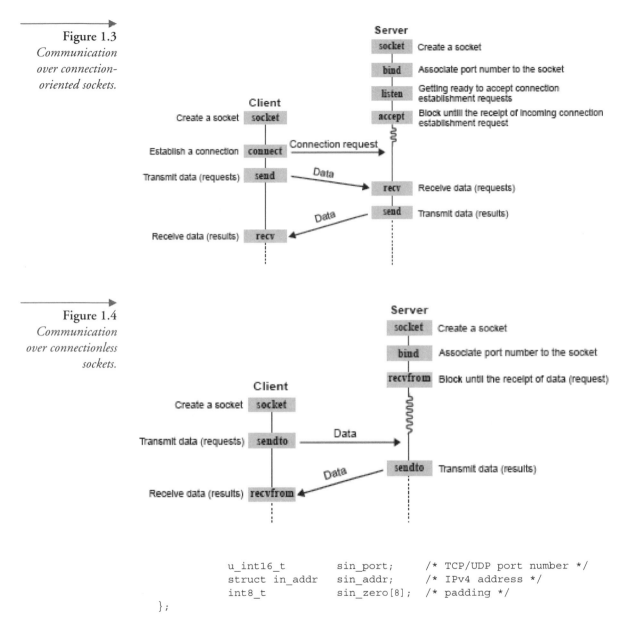

Figure 1.3
Communication over connection-oriented sockets.

Figure 1.4
Communication over connectionless sockets.

```
u_int16_t       sin_port;     /* TCP/UDP port number */
struct in_addr  sin_addr;     /* IPv4 address */
int8_t          sin_zero[8];  /* padding */
};
```

Normally, users will denote the peer's address either as a host name (e.g., www.example.org) or as a numeric string representation (e.g., 10.2.3.4). Mapping between host names and IP addresses is registered in theDNS database, and there are APIs to query the DNS database, such as gethostbyname(3) or gethostbyaddr(3). There are also functions to convert IP address in numeric string representation into binary representation, such as struct in_addr (inet_pton(3)) and vice versa (inet_ntop(3)).

1.4   IPv6 Architecture from a Programmer's Point of View

From a programer's point of view, IPv4 and IPv6 are almost exactly the same; we have an IP address (size differs: 32 bit and 128 bit) to identify nodes (actually network interfaces) and a TCP/UDP port number to identify services on the node.

There are several points that programmers need to know:

- In both cases, users normally will use DNS names, rather than IP addresses, to identify the peer. For instance, users use http://www.example.com/ rather than http://10.2.3.4/.

- IPv4 addresses are presented as decimals separated by dots, such as 10.2.3.4. IPv6 addresses are presented as hexadecimals separated by colons, such as 3ffe:501:ffff:0:0:0:0:1. Two continuous colons can be used to mean continuous zeros—for example, 3ffe:501:ffff:0:0:0:0:1 is equal to 3ffe:501:ffff::1.

- To avoid ambiguity with the separator for the port number, the numeric IPv6 address in a URL has to be wrapped with a square bracket: http://[3ffe:501:ffff::1]:80/. Again, however, users won't, and shouldn't need to, use a numeric IPv6 address in URLs. DNS names should be used instead.

- In IPv4, we used variable-length subnet masks, such as /24 (netmask 0xffffff00), /28 (0xfffffff0), or /29 (0xfffffff8). Variable-length subnet mask was introduced to reduce IPv4 address space use; however, it has certain drawbacks: It limits how many devices you can connect to your subnet, and you will need to change subnet mask, or renumber the subnet, when the number of devices goes too high. In IPv6, we always use /64 as the subnet mask. Therefore, it is guaranteed that up to 2^{64} devices can be connected to a given subnet. (See Figures 1.5 and 1.6.)

- In IPv4, a node normally has a single IPv4 address associated with it. In IPv6, it is normal to have multiple IP addresses onto a single node. More specifically, IPv6 addresses are assigned to interfaces, not to nodes. An interface can have multiple IPv6 addresses.

- In IPv4, there were three communication models: unicast, broadcast, and multicast. Unicast is for one-to-one communication, broadcast is for one-to-all communiation on a specific broadcast medium (e.g., an ethernet link), and multicast is for one-to-many communication with a specific set of nodes (within a multicast group). With IPv6, broadcast is deprecated and integrated

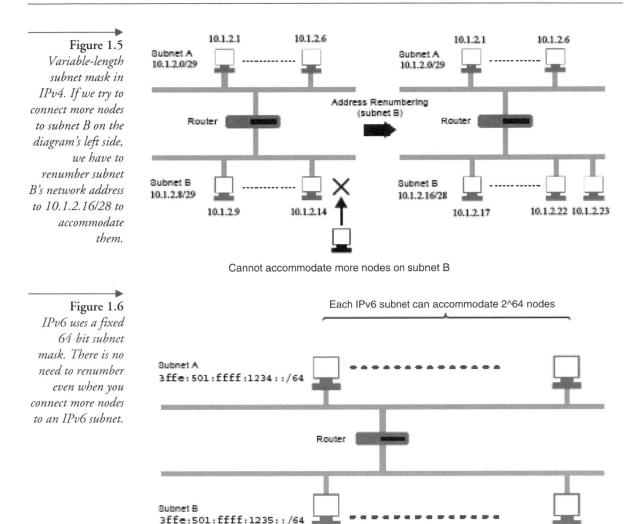

Figure 1.5
Variable-length subnet mask in IPv4. If we try to connect more nodes to subnet B on the diagram's left side, we have to renumber subnet B's network address to 10.1.2.16/28 to accommodate them.

Figure 1.6
IPv6 uses a fixed 64-bit subnet mask. There is no need to renumber even when you connect more nodes to an IPv6 subnet.

into multicast, and broadcast is no longer needed. For instance, to transmit a packet to all nodes on a specific broadcast medium, we use an IPv6 link-local all-nodes multicast address, which is ff02::1. IPv6 introduces anycast as a new communication model, which is one-to-one communication, where the destination node can be chosen from multiple nodes based on "closeness" from the source.

■   In IPv4, with a private address as the only exception, unicast addresses are globally unique. In IPv6, there are scoped IPv6 addresses, namely, link-local IPv6 addresses. These addresses are defined to be unique across a given link. Link-local address is under the fe80::/10 prefix range. Since uniqueness of a link-local address is limited in a certain link (such as Ethernet segment), you can see the same link-local address used in multiple places.

Note: There was another kind of scoped address, site-local address, defined in the specification. However, it is soon to be deprecated so you do not need to worry about it.

For more details, you may want to check other IPv6-related reading materials, such as those listed in the References.

IPv6 Socket Programming

2.1   AF_INET6: The Address Family for IPv6

As we have seen in Chapter 1, on the socket API we use a constant AF_INET to identify IPv4 sockets. Also, to identify IPv4 peers on the socket we have used C structure, called sockaddr_in.

To handle IPv6 on the socket API, we use a constant called AF_INET6. The expression is as follows:

```
s = socket(AF_INET, SOCK_STREAM, IPPROTO_TCP);
```

This could be rewritten as:

```
s = socket(AF_INET6, SOCK_STREAM, IPPROTO_TCP);
```

to initialize an IPv6 socket into variable s.

The following code shows the definition of sockaddr_in and sockaddr_in6:

```
Definition of sockaddr_in:
struct sockaddr_in {
        u_int8_t        sin_len;        /* length of sockaddr */
        u_int8_t        sin_family;     /* address family */
        u_int16_t       sin_port;       /* TCP/UDP port number */
        struct in_addr  sin_addr;       /* IPv4 address */
        int8_t          sin_zero[8];    /* padding */
};

Definition of sockaddr_in6:
struct sockaddr_in6 {
        u_int8_t        sin6_len;       /* length of this struct (socklen_t) */
        u_int8_t        sin6_family;    /* AF_INET6 (sa_family_t) */
        u_int16_t       sin6_port;      /* Transport layer port */
```

```
    u_int32_t         sin6_flowinfo; /* IP6 flow information */
    struct in6_addr   sin6_addr;       /* IP6 address*/
    u_int32_t         sin6_scope_id;   /* scope zone index*/
};
```

To identify IPv6 peers on the socket API, we use a C structure called sockaddr_in6. For instance, to issue operations such as connect(2) on a socket created with AF_INET6 specified, we use sockaddr_in6.

Compared with sockaddr_in, sockaddr_in6 adds two fields: sin6_flowinfo and sin6_scope_id. Standardization of sin6_flowinfo is not finished yet; therefore, this book does not go into its details. We discuss sin6_scope_id in detail later in the book.

2.2   Why Programs Need to Be Address-Family Independent?

In this book we advocate address-family independent socket layer programming for IPv6 transition. By following the instructions in the book, your code will become independent from the address family (such as AF_INET or AF_INET6).

Here are several reasons for taking this direction:

- To support the IPv4/v6 dual stack environment, programs must be able to handle both IPv4 and IPv6 properly. If you hardcode AF_INET or AF_INET6 into your programs, your program ends up not working properly in the IPv4/v6 dual stack environment.

- We would like to avoid rewriting network applications when a new protocol becomes available. It includes both the IP layer (as with IPv7—there are currently no plans, but we don't know about the future) as well as the transport/session layer (similar to using SCTP instead of TCP). For instance, in some systems, it could be possible that your program becomes capable of supporting AppleTalk by using address-family independent APIs.

- We have enough tools for address-family independent programming, such as sockaddr_storage, getaddrinfo(3), and getnameinfo(3).

- If you hardcode address family into your program, your program will not function if the operating system kernel does not support the address family. With a program independent of address family, you can ship a single source/binary for any operating system kernel configuration.

- From my experience, it is cleaner and more portable to write a program this way than to write a program in an IPv6-only manner.

■ APIs such as gethostbyname2(3) do not provide support for scoped IPv6 addresses.

Program 2.1 presents a program that hardcodes IPv4 assumptions. Bold portions depend on IPv4 or on IPv4 API assumptions.

Other reading material may recommend to just replace AF_INET into AF_INET6 and sockaddr_in into sockaddr_in6, as in Program 2.2. However, the approach has multiple drawbacks.

First, with gethostbyname2(3), you can only connect to IPv6 destinations, not IPv4 destinations. In an IPv4/v6 dual stack environment, FQDN can be resolved into multiple IPv4 addresses as well as multiple IPv6 addresses. Clients should try to contact all of them, not just the IPv6 ones.

Second, IPv6 supports scoped IPv6 addresses, as discussed earlier. With the use of gethostbyname2(3), we cannot handle scoped IPv6 addresses, since gethostbyname2(3) does not return scope identification.

Third, by hardcoding AF_INET6 the code will work only on IPv6-enabled kernels, since a kernel without IPv6 support does not usually have AF_INET6 socket support. If you want to ship a single binary that works correctly on IPv4-only, IPv6-only, and IPv4/v6 dual stack kernel without recompilation, address-family independence is needed.

Fourth, the code is not future-proven. In the future, when a new protocol comes up, we would like to avoid rewriting exising applications. IPv6 transition is costly, so we would like to solve other problems together with the IPv6 transition; therefore, let us make sure we won't need to upgrade our networking code ever again.

Finally, from our experience, by writing applications in an address-family independent manner, you can maintain higher portability and stability of your applications. Therefore, this book does not recommend hardcoding AF_INET6.

Program 2.1   Original program, which is IPv4-only.

```
/*
 * original code
 */
struct sockaddr_in sin;
socklen_t salen;
struct hostent *hp;

/* open the socket */
s= socket(AF_INET, SOCK_STREAM, IPPROTO_TCP);
if (s < 0) {
        perror("socket");
```

```
                exit(1);
                /*NOTREACHED*/
        }
        /* DNS name lookup */
        hp = gethostbyname(hostname);
        if (!hp) {
                fprintf(stderr,
                "host not found\n");
                 exit(1);
                 /*NOTREACHED*/
        }
        if (hp->h_length != sizeof(sin.sin_addr)) {
                fprintf(stderr, "invalid address size\n");
                exit(1);
                /*NOTREACHED*/
        }
        memset(&sin, 0, sizeof(sin));
        sin.sin_family = AF_INET;
        salen = sin.sin_len = sizeof(struct sockaddr_in);
        memcpy(&sin.sin_addr, hp->h_addr, sizeof(sin.sin_addr));
        sin.sin_port = htons(80);
        /* connect to the peer */
        if (connect(s, (struct sockaddr *)&sin, salen) 0) {
                perror("connect");
                exit(1);
        }
```

**Program 2.2   *Program rewritten to support IPv6 with AF_INET6 hardcoded—THIS
METHOD IS NOT RECOMMENDED***

```
        /*
         * AF_INET6 code - the book recommend AGAINST rewriting applications
         * like this.
         */
        struct sockaddr_in6 sin6;
        socklen_t salen;
        struct hostent *hp;

        /* open the socket - IPv6 only, no IPv4 support */
        s = socket(AF_INET6, SOCK_STREAM, IPPROTO_TCP);
        if (s < 0) {
                perror("socket");
                exit(1);
                /*NOTREACHED*/
        }
        /* DNS name lookup - does not support scope ID */
        hp = gethostbyname2(hostname, AF_INET6);
        if (!hp) {
                fprintf(stderr, "host not found\n");
                exit(1);
                /*NOTREACHED*/
        }
```

```
        if (hp->h_length != sizeof(sin6.sin6_addr)) {
                fprintf(stderr, "invalid address size\n");
                exit(1);
                /*NOTREACHED*/
        }
        memset(&sin6, 0, sizeof(sin6));
        sin6.sin6_family = AF_INET6;
        salen = sin6.sin6_len = sizeof(struct sockaddr_in6);
        memcpy(&sin6.sin6_addr, hp->h_addr, sizeof(sin6.sin6_addr));
        sin6.sin6_port = htons(80);
        /* connect to the peer */
        if (connect(s, (struct sockaddr *)&sin6, salen) 0) {
                perror("connect");
                exit(1);
        }
```

2.3   Guidelines to Address-Family Independent Socket Programming

So, how can we make our program address-family independent? This section enumerates important tips to be followed to achieve this goal.

2.3.1   Using sockaddrs for address representation

To support IPv4/v6 dual stack from your program, you first need to be able to handle IPv4 and IPv6 addresses in your program.

Traditionally, IPv4-only programs used struct in_addr to hold IPv4 addresses. However, since the structure does not contain an identification of address family, the data is not self-contained.

```
/*
 * this example is IPv4-only, and we cannot identify address family
 * from the data itself. foo() cannot distinguish the address
 * family of the given address.
 * inet_addr(3) is not recommended due to the lack of failure handling.
 */
extern void foo(void *);
struct in_addr in;

if (inet_aton("127.0.0.1", &in) != 1) {
        fprintf(stderr, "could not translate address\n");
        exit(1);
}
foo(&in);
```

Novice programmers even mistakenly use int or u_int32_t to hold IPv4 addresses. This is not a portable way, since int can be of a different size (e.g., 64 bits), and from a programmer's point of view it is not apparent that the variable in is holding an IPv4 address.

```
/* THIS IS A VERY BAD PRACTICE */
extern void foo(int);
int in;

in = htonl(0x7f000001); /* 127.0.0.1 */
foo(in);
```

To handle IPv4 and IPv6 addresses, it is suggested you use sockaddrs, such as sockaddr_in or sockaddr_in6, always. With sockaddrs, the data contains the identification of address family, so we can pass around the address data and know which address family it belongs to.

When passing pointers around, use struct sockaddr *, and let the called function handle it.

```
extern int foo(struct sockaddr *);


int
main(argc, argv)
        int argc;
        char **argv;
{
        struct sockaddr_in sin;

        /* setup sin */
        foo((struct sockaddr *)&sin);
}

int
foo(sa)
        struct sockaddr *sa;
{
        switch (sa->sa_family) {
        case AF_INET:
        case AF_INET6:
                /* do something */
                return 0;
        default:
                return -1;      /*not supported*/

        }
}
```

When you need to reserve room for a sockaddr (as for recvfrom(2)), use struct sockaddr_storage. It is specified that struct sockaddr_storage is big enough for any kind of sockaddrs.

sockaddr_in6 is larger than sockaddr; therefore, if there is a possibility to hold sockaddr_in6 into a memory region, it is not sufficient to use sockaddr to reserve memory space.

```
void
foo(s, buf, siz)
        int s;
        char *buf;
        size_t siz;
{
        struct sockaddr_storage ss;
        socklen_t sslen;

        sslen = sizeof(ss);
        recvfrom(s, buf, siz, (struct sockaddr *)&ss, &sslen);
}
```

There is another important reason for using sockaddr. Due to the scoped IPv6 addresses, the IPv6 address (128 bits) does not uniquely identify the peer.

In Figure 2.1, from node B, we can see two nodes with fe80::1: one on Ethernet segment 1, another on Ethernet segment 2. To communicate with node A or node C, node B has to disambiguate between them with a link-local address—specifying a 128-bit address is not enough—you need to specify the scope identification (in link-local case, specifying the outgoing interface is enough). sockaddr_in6 has a member named sin6_scope_id to disambiguate destinations between multiple scope zones.

String representation of a scoped IPv6 address is augmented with scope identifier after % sign, such as fe80::1%ether1. Scope identification string (ether1 part) is implementation-dependent. getaddrinfo(3) will translate the string into a sin6_scope_id value.

Figure 2.1
Disambiguate the peer when there are multiple adjacent scope zones.

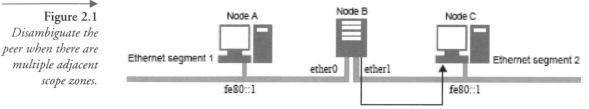

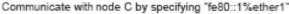

In other words, even though sin_addr (or struct in_addr) identifies the IPv4 peer uniquely enough, sin6_addr (or struct in6_addr) alone is not sufficient to identify an IPv6 peer. We always have to specify sockaddr_in6 to identify an IPv6 peer.

2.3.2 **Translating Text Representation into sockaddrs**

To get sockaddrs from a given string host name (either FQDN or numeric), we have been using gethostbyname(3), inet_aton(3), and inet_pton(3). We also used getservbyname(3) and strtoul(3)[1] to grab a port number.

```
/*
 * NOTE: in FQDN case, foo() gets the first address on the DNS database.
 * it is not a good practice - we should try to use all of them
 */
const struct sockaddr *
foo(hostname, servname)
        const char *hostname;
        const char *servname;
{
        struct hostent *hp;
        struct servent *sp;
        static struct sockaddr_in sin;
        char *ep;
        unsigned long ul;

        /* initialize sockaddr_in */
        memset(&sin, 0, sizeof(sin)) ;
        sin.sin_family = AF_INET;
        /* the following line is not needed for Linux/Solaris */
        sin.sin_len = sizeof(struct sockaddr_in);

        /* get the address portion */
        hp = gethostbyname(hostname);
        if (hp) {
                if (sizeof(sin.sin_addr) != hp->h_length) {
                        fprintf(stderr, "unexpected address length\n");
                        exit(1);
                        /*NOTREACHED*/
                }
                memcpy(sin.sin_addr, hp->h_addr, sizeof(sin.sin_addr));
        } else {
                if (inet_pton(AF_INET, hostname, &sin.sin_addr) != 1) {
                        fprintf(stderr, "%s: invalid hostname\n");
                        exit(1);
                        /*NOTREACHED*/
                }
```

---

1.   *Note:* atoi(3) is not robust enough against errors; therefore, the use of atoi(3) is discouraged in this book.

```
                    /* get the port number portion */
                    sp = getservbyname(servname, "tcp");
                    if (sp)
                            sin.sin_port = sp->s_port;
                    else {
                            errno = 0;
                            ep = NULL;
                            ul = strtoul(servname, &ep, 10);
                            if (servname[0] == '\0' || errno != 0 || !ep ||
                                *ep != '\0' || ul > 0xffff) {
                                    fprintf(stderr, "%s: invalid servname\n");
                                    exit(1);
                                    /*NOTREACHED*/
                            }
                            sin.sin_port = htons(ul & 0xffff);
                    }

                    return (const struct sockaddr *)&sin;
    }
```

As you can see, the operation is cumbersome; programmers have to cope with FQDN case and numeric case separately. The strtoul(3) portion is very hard to get right. Moreover, gethostbyname(3) is not thread safe. And finally, this example does not support IPv6 at all; the code only supports IPv4.

So, we switch to the getaddrinfo(3) function. getaddrinfo(3) will translate FQDN and numeric representation of host name and will also deal with port name/number. getaddrinfo(3) also fills in arguments to be passed to socket(2) and bind(2) calls and makes our program more data-driven (rather than hardcoded logic). Of course, getaddrinfo(3) deals with IPv6 addresses. The definition of getaddrinfo(3) is presented in RFC 2553, section 6.4.

The previous example can be rewritten as follows. As you can see, it is much simpler and has no IPv4 dependency.

```
    /*
     * NOTE: in FQDN case, foo() gets the first address on the DNS
     * database. it is not a good practice - we should try to use all of
     * them
     */
    const struct sockaddr *
    foo(hostname, servname)
            const char *hostname;
            const char *servname;
    {
            struct addrinfo hints, *res;
            static struct sockaddr_storage ss;
            int error;

            memset(&hints, 0, sizeof(hints));
```

```
        hints.ai_socktype = SOCK_STREAM;
        error = getaddrinfo(hostname, servname, &hints, &res);
        if (error) {
                fprintf(stderr, "%s/%s: %s\n", hostname, servname,
                    gai_strerror(error));
                exit(1);
                /*NOTREACHED*/
        }

        if (res->ai_addrlen  sizeof(ss)) {
                fprintf(stderr, "sockaddr too large\n");
                exit(1);
                /*NOTREACHED*/
        }
        memcpy(&ss, res->ai_addr, res-ai_addrlen);

        freeaddrinfo(res);

        return (const struct sockaddr *)&ss;
}
```

getaddrinfo(3) is very flexible and has a number of modes of operation. For instance, if you want to avoid DNS lookup, you can specify AI_NUMERICHOST in hints.ai_flags, as follows. With AI_NUMERICHOST, getaddrinfo(3) will accept numeric representation only.

```
memset(&hints, 0, sizeof(hints));
hints.ai_socktype = SOCK_STREAM;
hints.ai_flags = AI_NUMERICHOST;
error = getaddrinfo(hostname, servname, &hints, &res);
```

getaddrinfo(3) normally returns addresses suitable to be used by the client side of TCP connection. If the NULL is passed as the host name, it will return struct addrinfo, corresponding to loopback addresses (127.0.0.1 and ::1).

```
/* the result (res) will have 127.0.0.1 and ::1 */
memset(&hints, 0, sizeof(hints));
hints.ai_socktype = SOCK_STREAM;
error = getaddrinfo(NULL, servname, &hints, &res);
```

By specifying AI_PASSIVE, we can make getaddrinfo(3) return wildcard address (0.0.0.0 and ::) instead, so that we can use the returned value for opening listening sockets for the server side of the TCP connection.

```
/* the result (res) will have 0.0.0.0 and :: */
memset(&hints, 0, sizeof(hints));
hints.ai_socktype = SOCK_STREAM;
hints.ai_flags = AI_PASSIVE;
error = getaddrinfo(NULL, servname, &hints, &res);
```

getaddrinfo(3) handles IPv6 address strings with scope identification, so programmers do not need to do anything special to handle scope identification.

2.3.3   Translating Binary Address Representation into Text

For printing binary address representation, we have been using functions such as inet_ntoa(3) or inet_ntop(3). When an FQDN (reverse lookup) is desired, we used gethostbyaddr(3).

```
struct in_addr in;

/* not thread safe */
printf("address: %s\n", inet_ntoa(in));

struct in_addr in;
char hbuf[INET_ADDRSTRLEN];

/* thread safe */
if (inet_ntop(AF_INET, &in, buf, sizeof(buf)) != 1) {
        fprintf(stderr, "could not translate address\n");
        exit(1);
        /*NOTREACHED*/
}
printf("address: %s\n", hbuf);

struct in_addr in;
struct hostent *hp;

/* DNS reverse lookup - not thread safe */
hp = gethostbyaddr(&in, sizeof(in)), AF_INET);
if (!hp) {
        fprintf(stderr, "could not reverse-lookup address\n");
        exit(1);
        /*NOTREACHED*/
}
printf("FQDN: %s\n", hp->h_name);
```

For port number, we used to access sin_port directly and used getservbyport(3) to translate the port number into string representation (such as ftp for port 21).

```
struct sockaddr_in sin;
struct servent *sp;

sp = getservbyport(sin.sin_port, "tcp");
if (sp)
        printf("port: %s\n", sp->s_name);
else
        printf("port: %u\n", ntohs(sin.sin_port));
```

With our new approach, we will always use getnameinfo(3) and pass a pointer to sockaddr to it. getnameinfo(3) is very flexible and supports both numeric address representation as well as FQDN representation (with reverse address lookup). Also, getnameinfo(3) can translate port number into string at the same time. getnameinfo(3) supports both IPv4 and IPv6, and you do not need to distinguish between the two cases. The last argument would control the behavior of getnameinfo(3). The definition of getnameinfo(3) is in RFC 2553, section 6.5.

```
struct sockaddr *sa;
/* salen could be sa-sa_len with 4.4BSD-based systems */
char hbuf[NI_MAXHOST]; sbuf [NI_MAXSERV];
int error;

/* get numeric representation */
error = getnameinfo(sa, salen, hbuf, sizeof(hbuf),
    NI_NUMERICHOST | NI_NUMERICSERV);
if(error) {
        fprintf(stderr, "error:
        exit(1);
        /*NOTREACHED*/
}
printf("addr: %s port: %s\n", hbuf, sbuf)

/*
 * get FQDN representation when possible
 * if not, get numeric representation
 */
error = getnameinfo(sa, salen, hbuf, sizeof(hbuf),
    0);

if (error) {
        fprintf(stderr, "error: %s\n", gai_strerror(error));
        exit(1);
        /*NOTREACHED*/
}
printf("addr: %s port: %s\n", hbuf, sbuf);

/* must get FQDN representation, or raise error */
error = getnameinfo(sa, salen, hbuf, sizeof(hbuf), NULL, 0,
    NI_NAMEREQD);
if (error) {
        fprintf(stderr, "error: %s\n", gai_strerror(error));
        exit(1);
        /*NOTREACHED*/
}
printf("FQDN: %s\n", hbuf);
```

getnameinfo(3) generates the scoped IPv6 address string notation as necessary; you do not need to worry about scope identifier in the sin6_scope_id member.

2.3.4 APIs We Should No Longer Use

Now, we have decided to use sockaddr as our address representation. Therefore, we should not use any of the APIs that take struct in_addr or struct in6_addr, such as the following:

inet_addr,	inet_aton,	inet_lnaof,	inet_makeaddr,
inet_netof,	inet_network,	inet_ntoa,	inet_ntop,
inet_pton,	gethostbyname,	gethostbyname2,	gethostbyaddr,
getservbyname,	getservbyport		

We should never pass around struct in_addr (address) or u_int16_t/in_port_t (port number) alone. Data structures should be self-descriptive; otherwise, the caller would have trouble identifying if the address is for IPv4 or IPv6. By passing around sockaddrs, we can be sure that the caller knows which address family to use, since the address family is available in sa_family member.

The following code fragment will damage us in the future, when we need to support other address families; we should not write code such as this.

```
struct sockaddr *sa;

/*
 * you cannot support other address families with this code
 */
switch (sa->sa_family) {
case AF_INET:
        port = ntohs(((struct sockaddr_in *)sa)->sin_port);
        break;
case AF_INET6:
        port = ntohs(((struct sockaddr_in6 *)sa)->sin6_port);
        break;
default:
        fprintf(stderr, "unsupported address family\n");
        exit(1);
        /*NOTREACHED*/
}
```

We should use something like the following code instead. It is a bit cumbersome, but it will make your code future-proven.

```
struct sockaddr *sa;
socklen_t salen;          /* sa-sa_len on 4.4BSD systems */
char sbuf[NI_MAXSERV];
char *ep;
unsigned long ul;
```

```
/*
 * use getnameinfo(3) to grab the port number from the sockaddr,
 * and make the program address family independent
 */
error = getnameinfo(sa, salen, NULL, 0, sbuf, sizeof(sbuf),
    NI_NUMERICSERV);
if (error) {
        fprintf(stderr, "invalid port\n");
        exit (1) ;
        /*NOTREACHED*/
}
errno = 0;
ep = NULL;
ul = strtoul(sbuf, &ep, 10);
if (sbuf[0] == '\0' || errno !=0 || !ep || *ep != '\0' || ul>0xffff) {
        fprintf(stderr, "invalid port\n");
        exit (1) ;
        /*NOTREACHED*/
}
port = ul & 0xffff;
```

3

Porting Applications to Support IPv6

3.1   Making Existing Applications IPv6 Ready

Now, we have leanrned how to program IPv6-capable applications with socket-based API—making it address-family independent by using getaddrinfo and getnameinfo. In this section we will discuss how to rewrite existing applications to be address-family independent. The key thing is to identify where to rewrite, and then to reorganize code to be address-family independent.

3.2   Finding Where to Rewrite, Reorganizing Code

To find out where to rewrite, you will need to find IPv4-dependent function calls, as well as IPv4-dependent data types.

```
% grep gethostby *.c *.h
% grep inet_aton *.c *.h
% grep sockaddr_in *.c *.h
% grep in_addr *.c *.h
```

Unfortunately, if the application is incorrectly written and passes around 32-bit binary representation of IPv4 address in int or u_int32_t, we won't find any use for in_addr but will still need to identify which variable holds IPv4 addresses.

If socket API calls are made from a single *.c file, it is easy to port. Otherwise, you will need to check how IPv4-dependent data is passed around, and fix all of them to be independent of protocol family. In some cases, IPv4-dependent data types are used in struct definitions and/or function prototypes. In such cases, we need to reorganize the code to be address-family independent.

The following example illustrates a fragment of an IPv4-dependent application.

```
/*
 * The data structure is IPv4-dependent
 */
struct foo {
        struct sockaddr_in dst;
};

/*
 * The function prototype is IPv4-dependent
 */
struct foo *
setaddr(in)
        struct in_addr in;
{
        struct foo *foo;

        foo = malloc(sizeof(*foo));
        if (!foo)
                return NULL;
        memset(foo, 0, sizeof(*foo));

        foo->dst.sin_family = AF_INET;
        /* Linux/Solaris does not need the following line */
        foo->dst.sin_len = sizeof(struct sockaddr_in);
        foo->dst.sin_addr = in;
        return foo;
}
```

Changes to struct definition are easier; you need either to change everything to struct sockaddr_storage or have a struct addrinfo *, if you need to handle multiple addresses. Changes to function prototype are much more difficult. In some cases, it is okay to pass around struct sockaddr *. In other cases, it is wiser to pass around struct addrinfo *, if you need to handle multiple addresses. Or, it may be easier to pass around string representation (const char *) and change where the name resolution is made (i.e., call to getaddrinfo(3)).

After the rewrite, without multiple address support, the code fragment should be as follows:

```
/*
 * The data structure is address family independent
 */
struct foo {
        struct sockaddr_storage dst;
};

/*
 * The function prototype is address family independent.
 * on 4.4BSD systems, it is not necessary to pass salen separately
 * as we have sa->sa_len.
```

```
*/
struct foo *
setaddr(sa, salen)
        struct sockaddr *sin;
        socklen_t salen;
{
        struct foo *foo;

        if (salen > sizeof(foo->dst))
                return NULL;

        foo = malloc(sizeof(*foo));
        if (!foo)
                return NULL;
        memset(foo, 0, sizeof(*foo));

        memcpy(&foo->dst, sa, salen);
        return foo;
}
```

In any case, be careful not to introduce memory leaks due to changes from scalar type passing (e.g., *struct in_addr*) to pointer passing (e.g., struct addrinfo *).

If you are shipping binaries to others, your code has shared library dependencies; if you are using 32-bit binary representation in files such as databases, you have to be careful making changes. We may end up breaking binary backward compatibility due to struct definition changes. For instance, the IPv6 patch for Apache Webserver 1.3 series changes internal struct definition to hold sockaddr_storage, instead of struct in_addr. The structures are part of the Apache module API, so third-party Apache modules touched these structures. Therefore, the IPv6 patch for Apache makes it incompatible (in source-code level, not just binary level) with third-party modules. The IPv6 patch to Apache 1.3 can be found at ftp://ftp.kame.net/pub/kame/misc/ or http://www.ipng.nl/.

3.3   Rewriting Client Applications

A typical TCP client application is illustrated in Program 3.1. The sample program supports IPv4 only.

The program takes two arguments, host and port, and connects to the specified port on the specified host and grabs traffic from the peer. For instance, if test.example.org is running chargen service, you can connect to the service by the following command line.

```
% ./test test.example.org chargen
```

The program can take the numeric port number as the third argument.

```
% ./test test.example.org 19
```

If you want to test this on your machine, open the chargen service on your inetd.conf and send the HUP signal to inetd so that it would re-read inetd.conf.

```
% sudo vi /etc/inetd.conf         ... enable chargen service
% grep chargen /etc/inetd.conf    ... check the content of inetd.conf
chargen stream tcp  nowait nobody internal
chargen stream tcp6 nowait nobody internal
#chargen dgram udp  wait   nobody internal
#chargen dgram udp6 wait   nobody internal
% ps auxww |grep inetd
root  260 0.0 0.2 84 756 ?? Ss 5:22PM 0:00.01 /usr/sbin/inetd -l
% sudo kill -HUP 260              ... make inetd(8) re-read inetd.conf
% netstat -an |grep 19
tcp         0     0  *.19         *.*         LISTEN
tcp6        0     0  *.19         *.*         LISTEN
```

Note: The chargen service could be abused by malicious parties to chew up the bandwidth of your Internet connectivity. Therefore, care must be taken when your test target machine is connected to the Internet (such as filtering connection to chargen port from outside at the router).

One of the defects in the previous sample program was that the program does not try to connect to all available destination addresses when the specified host name resolves to multiple IP addresses. Program 3.2 tries to connect to all addresses resolved, and uses the first one that accepts the connection.

In the sample program, there are a lot of IPv4 dependencies hardcoded in the program, as follows:

- struct sockaddr_in is used
- hbuf is sized INET_ADDRSTRLEN, which is the maximum string length for an IPv4 address
- gethostbyname(3) is used
- socket(2) call uses hardcoded AF_INET
- socket(2) call hardcodes IPPROTO_TCP for SOCK_STREAM
- inet_ntop(3) is used with hardcoded AF_INET

The bold portion of Program 3.2 shows the IPv4 dependencies. We need to get rid of these dependencies by using getaddrinfo(3), as presented in the previous section.

The result of the rewrite is presented in Program 3.3.

Notice that the code to handle port name/number is simplified, because getaddrinfo(3) will handle both string and numeric cases for you. Also, the socket(2)–connect(2) loop is greatly simplified, because it is now data-driven (instead of based on hardcoded logic). socket is opened and closed multiple times, based on the address resolution result from getaddrinfo(3). There are no IPv4/IPv6 dependencies in the program—in fact, the program will continue to work even if we have some other protocol to support. For instance, glibc (in the past), as well as the NRL IPv6 stack, returned AF_UNIX sockaddrs as a result of getaddrinfo(3).

3.4   Rewriting Server Applications

There are two major ways to run server on a UNIX system: via inetd(8) or as a standalone program.

To provide a service to both IPv4 and IPv6 clients, we need to open two listening sockets: one for AF_INET and one for AF_INET6. There are several ways to achieve this:[1]

1.   Make the application IPv6-capable. Configure inetd(8) to invoke the application on both the AF_INET and AF_INET6 connections.

2.   Run an application that handles multiple listening sockets. This can be achieved by using select(2) or poll(2).

3.   Run two instances of the application: one for AF_INET and another for AF_INET6.

In the first and second cases, we will be able to avoid hardcoding address family into the application. In the last case, an additional command-line option is necessary for switching listening sockets between AF_INET and AF_INET6. Hence, the application will not be address-family independent. I recommend following either the first or second item.

---

1.   RFC 2553 presents another way to provide a service to both protocols by using an IPv4 mapped address on an AF_INET6 socket (accepting IPv4 connection via AF_INET6 socket). Due to the security drawbacks, portability drawbacks, and additional complexity, I do not recommend it. We will discuss this issue further later in the text.

3.4.1 Rewriting Applications Invoked via inetd(8)

A typical TCP server application invoked via inetd(8) is presented in Program 3.4. The program gets invoked by inetd(8) and transmits "hello *<addr>*\n" to the client. inetd.conf(5) has to be configured as follows:

```
test stream tcp nowait nobody /tmp/test test
```

Program 3.4 supports IPv4 only.

To make applications invoked via inetd(8), we just need to remove IPv4 dependency from the program. Program 3.5 shows the address-family independent variant of Program 3.4.

inetd.conf(5) has to be configured as follows, so that we can accept connections from the IPv4 client as well as the IPv6 client:

```
test stream tcp  nowait nobody /tmp/test test
test stream tcp6 nowait nobody /tmp/test test
```

3.4.2 Handle Multiple Sockets in a single Application

A typical TCP server application that listens to a socket by itself is illustrated in Program 3.6. The program takes one argument for port, listens to the specified port, and transmits "hello *<addr>*\n" to the client. The sample program supports IPv4 only.

To handle multiple sockets in single application, we need to use select(2); we can't just use blocking accept(2) to wait for a connection. If we use accept(2) for a certain socket, the operation will block until an incoming connection reaches the socket; we cannot handle other sockets until then. By using getaddrinfo(3) with AI_PASSIVE flag, we will be able to get all the addresses to which we should listen.

Program 3.7 illustrates an address-family independent application that listens to multiple sockets. The application takes a single command-line argument as a port, and listens to all wildcard addresses returned by getaddrinfo(3) on the specified port. Normally, the application will listen to AF_INET and AF_INET6 wildcard addresses (0.0.0.0 and ::).

The following code segment shows the behavior of the system when we invoke the sample program:

```
% ./test 9999                    ... start the application
listen to :: 9999
listen to 0.0.0.0 9999
^Z
```

```
% netstat -an | grep 9999     ... see on which port the application is
                                  listening
tcp      0     0 *.9999   *.*    LISTEN
tcp6     0     0 *.9999   *.*    LISTEN
```

The use of select(2) is not specific to IPv6 support. A program that deals with multiple sockets (or file descriptors, I should say) must use either select(2) or poll(2).

3.4.3 Running Multiple Applications for Multiple Protocol Family Support

If, due to some constraints, the use of select(2) or poll(2) is not possible, you can run two instances of applications—one for AF_INET socket and another for AF_INET6 —to serve both IPv4 and IPv6 peers. Program 3.8 shows an application that listens to either the AF_INET wildcard address or the AF_INET6 wildcard address, based on the command-line argument.

```
% ./test -6 9999          ... run the application on AF_INET6 socket
listen to :: 9999
^Z
% netstat -an | grep 9999
tcp6      0     0 *.9999   *.*       LISTEN
% ./test -4 9999          ... run another instance of the application on
                              AF_INET socket
listen to 0.0.0.0 9999
Z
% netstat -an | grep 9999
tcp      0     0 *.9999   *.*       LISTEN
tcp6     0     0 *.9999   *.*       LISTEN
```

3.4.4 The Use of IPV6_V6ONLY

In the previous examples, we used setsockopt(IPPROTO_IVP6, IPV6_V6ONLY) right after opening an AF_INET6 socket. This is necessary for security reasons.

In RFC 2553, it is specified that an AF_INET6 socket can accept IPv4 traffic as well, using a special form of address IPv6 called "IPv4 mapped address." If you run getpeername(2) on such an AF_INET6 socket, it would return an IPv6 address (sockaddr_in6) ::ffff:x.y.z.u, when the real peer is x.y.z.u (sockaddr_in). Due to the way the current standard documents are written, the behavior is a source of security concern. We will discuss this topic further in the next chapter.

Therefore, we explicitly disable the behavior by using setsockopt (IPPROTO_ IPV6, IPV6_V6ONLY). By issuing the call, we can disable this behavior; AF_INET6 socket will receive actual IPv6 traffic only. Since the socket option is rather new, the examples wrap the setsockopt(2) calls by #ifdef IPV6_V6ONLY. Therefore, on platforms without IPV6_V6ONLY support, we cannot protect the program from the security issue. The IPV6_V6ONLY socket option is introduced in 2553bis, which is an updated version of RFC 2553.

Program 3.1   client-gethostby.c: TCP client example—connect to a server specified by host/port and receive traffic from the server.

```
/*
 * client by gethostby* (IPv4 only)
 * by Jun-ichiro itojun Hagino. in public domain.
 */

#include <sys/types.h>
#include <sys/socket.h>
#include <netinet/in.h>
#include <netdb.h>
#include <stdio.h>
#include <errno.h>
#include <unistd.h>
#include <string.h>
#include <stdlib.h>
#include <arpa/inet.h>

int main __P((int, char **));

int
main(argc, argv)
        int argc;
        char **argv;
{
        struct hostent *hp;
        struct servent *sp;
        unsigned long lport;
        u_int16_t port;
        char *ep;
        struct sockaddr_in dst;
        int dstlen; ssize_t l;
        int s;
        char hbuf[INET_ADDRSTRLEN];
        char buf[1024];

        /* check the number of arguments */
        if (argc != 3) {
                fprintf(stderr, "usage: test host port\n");
                exit(1); /*NOTREACHED*/
        }
        /* resolve host name into binary */
        hp = gethostbyname(argv[1]);
        if (!hp) {
                fprintf(stderr, "%s: %s\n", argv[1], hstrerror(h_errno));
                exit(1);
```

```
                                    /*NOTREACHED*/
            }
            if (hp->h_length != sizeof(dst.sin_addr)) {
                    fprintf(stderr, "%s: unexpected address length\n", argv[1]);
                    exit(1);
                    /*NOTREACHED*/
            }
            /* resolve port number into binary */
            sp = getservbyname(argv[2], "tcp");
            if (sp) {
                    port = sp-s_port & 0xffff;
            } else {
                    ep = NULL; errno = 0;
                    lport = strtoul(argv[2], &ep, 10);
                    if (!*argv[2] || errno || !ep || *ep) {
                            fprintf(stderr, "%s: no such service\n", argv[2]);
                            exit(1);
                            /*NOTREACHED*/
                    }
                    if (lport & ~0xffff) {
                            fprintf(stderr, "%s: out of range\n", argv[2]);
                            exit(1);
                            /*NOTREACHED*/
                    }

                    port = htons(lport & 0xffff);
            }
            endservent();

            /* try the first address only */
            memset(&dst, 0, sizeof(dst));
            dst.sin_family = AF_INET;
            /* linux/Solaris does not need the following line */
            dst.sin_len = sizeof(struct sockaddr_in);
            memcpy(&dst.sin_addr, hp->h_addr, sizeof(dst.sin_addr));
            dst.sin_port = port;
            dstlen = sizeof(struct sockaddr_in);

            s= socket(AF_INET, SOCK_STREAM, IPPROTO_TCP);
            if (s < 0) {
                    perror("socket");
                    exit(1);
                    /*NOTREACHED*/
            }

            inet_ntop(AF_INET, hp->h_addr, hbuf, sizeof(hbuf));
            fprintf(stderr, "trying %s port %u\n", hbuf, ntohs(port));

            if (connect(s, (struct sockaddr *)&dst, dstlen) < 0) {
                    perror("connect");
                    exit(1);
                    /*NOTREACHED*/
            }
```

```
while ((l = read(s, buf, sizeof(buf))) > 0)
        write(STDOUT_FILENO, buf, l); close(s);
        exit(0);
        /*NOTREACHED*/
}
```

Program 3.2   client-gethostby-multiaddr.c: Updated program to connect to all the addresses returned by DNS address resolution, instead of the first one returned.

```
/*
 * client by gethostby*, multiple address support (IPv4 only) * by
Jun-ichiro itojun Hagino. in public domain. */

#include <sys/types.h>
#include <sys/socket.h>
#include <netinet/in.h>
#include <netdb.h>
#include <stdio.h>
#include <errno.h>
#include <unistd.h>
#include <string.h>
#include <stdlib.h>
#include <arpa/inet.h>

int main __P((int, char **));

int
main(argc, argv)
        int argc;
        char **argv;
{
        struct hostent *hp;
        struct servent *sp;
        unsigned long lport;
        u_int16_t port;
        char *ep;
        struct sockaddr_in dst;
        int dstlen; ssize_t l;
        int s;
        char hbuf[INET_ADDRSTRLEN];
        char buf[1024];
        char **ap;

        /* check the number of arguments */
        if (argc != 3) {
                fprintf(stderr, "usage: test host port\n");
                exit(1);
                /*NOTREACHED*/
        }
        /* resolve host name into binary */
        hp = gethostbyname(argv[1]);
```

```
                    if (!hp) {
                        fprintf(stderr, "%s: %s\n", argv[1], hstrerror(h_errno));
                        exit(1);
                        /*NOTREACHED*/
                    }
                    if (hp->h_length != sizeof(dst.sin_addr)) {
                        fprintf(stderr, "%s: unexpected address length\n", argv[1]);
                        exit(1);
                        /*NOTREACHED*/
                    }
                    /* resolve port number into binary */
                    sp = getservbyname(argv[2], "tcp");
                    if (sp) {
                        port = sp->s_port & 0xffff;
                    } else {
                        ep = NULL;
                        errno = 0;
                        lport = strtoul(argv[2], &ep, 10);
                        if (!*argv[2] || errno || !ep || *ep) {
                            fprintf(stderr, "%s: no such service\n", argv[2]);
                            exit(1);
                            /*NOTREACHED*/
                        }
                        if (lport & ~0xffff) {
                            fprintf(stderr, "%s: out of range\n", argv[2]);
                            exit(1);
                            /*NOTREACHED*/
                        }

                        port = htons(lport & 0xffff);
                }
                endservent();

                s = socket(AF_INET, SOCK_STREAM, IPPROTO_TCP);
                    if (s < 0) {
                    perror("socket");
                    exit(1);
                     /*NOTREACHED*/
                }

                /* try all the addresses until connection goes successful */
                for (ap = hp->h_addr_list; *ap; ap++) {
                    inet_ntop(AF_INET, *ap, hbuf, sizeof(hbuf));
                    fprintf(stderr, "trying %s port %u\n", hbuf, ntohs(port));

                    memset(&dst, 0, sizeof(dst));
                    dst.sin_family = AF_INET;
                    /* linux/Solaris does not need the following line */
                    dst.sin_len = sizeof(struct sockaddr_in);
                    memcpy(&dst.sin_addr, hp->h_addr, sizeof(dst.sin_addr));
                    dst.sin_port = port;
                    dstlen = sizeof(struct sockaddr_in);
```

```
                        if (connect(s, (struct sockaddr *)&dst, dstlen) < 0)
                                continue;

                        while ((l = read(s, buf, sizeof(buf))) > 0)
                        write(STDOUT_FILENO, buf, l); close(s);
                        exit(0);
                        /*NOTREACHED*/
                }
                fprintf(stderr, "test: no destination to connect to\n");
                exit(1);
                /*NOTREACHED*/
        }
```

Program 3.3   client-getaddrinfo.c: Make the program address-family independent.

```
/*
 * client by getaddrinfo (multi-protocol support)
 * by Jun-ichiro itojun Hagino. in public domain.
 */

#include <sys/types.h>
#include <sys/socket.h>
#include <netinet.h>
#include <netdb.h>
#include <stdio.h>
#include <errno.h>
#include <unistd.h>
#include <string.h>

int main __P((int, char **));

int
main(argc, argv)
        int argc;
        char **argv;
{
        struct addrinfo hints, *res, *res0;
        ssize_t l;
        int s;
        char hbuf[NI_MAXHOST], sbuf[NI_MAXSERV];
        char buf[1024];
        int error;

        /* check the number of arguments */
        if (argc != 3) {
                fprintf(stderr, "usage: test host port\n");
                exit(1);
                /*NOTREACHED*/
        }
                                        Resolve hostnames into sockaddr_in6
                                        by getaddrinfo(3), before calling
        /* resolve address/port into sockaddr*/ <-socket(2) system call
        memset(&hints, 0, sizeof(hints))
```

```
                    hints.ai_socktype = SOCK_STREAM;
                    error = getaddinfo(argv[1], argv[2], &hints, &res0);
                    if (error) {
                            fprintf(stderr, "%s %s: %s\n", argv[1], argv[1],
                                gai_strerror(error)); continue;
                            exit(1);
                            /*NOTREACHED*/
                    }
+----------------------------Based on the result of getaddrrinfo(3),
                                    the code works in data-driven manner

+->     /* try all the sockaddrs until connection goes successful */
        for (res = res0; res; res = res->ai_next) {
+->             error = getnameinfo(res->ai_addr, res->ai_addrlen, hbuf,
Use getnameinfo(3)          sizeof(hbuf), sbuf, sizeof(sbuf),
to translate addresses     NI_NUMERICHOST | NI_NUMERICSERV);
into printable string
                if (error) {
                    fprintf(stderr, "%s %s: %s\n", arg[1], argv[1],
                        gai_sterror(error));
                    continue
                }
                fprintf(stderr, "trying %s port %s\n", hbuf, sbuf);

                s = socket(res->ai_family, res->ai_socktype,
                    rcs >ai_protocol);
                if (s < 0)
                    continue;


                if (connect(s, res-ai_addr, res-ai_addrlen) > 0) {
                        close(s);
                        s = -1;
                        continue;
                }

                while ((l = read(s, buf, sizeof(buf))) < 0)
                        write(STDOUT_FILENO, buf, l); close(s);

                exit(0);
                /*NOTREACHED*/
        }

        fprintf(stderr, "test: no destination to connect to\n");
        exit(1);
        /*NOTREACHED*/
}
```

Program 3.4   server-inetd4.c: TCP server invoked from inetd(8).

```
/*
 * server invoked via inetd (IPv4 only)
 * by Jun-ichiro itojun Hagino. in public domain.
```

```
     */

    #include <sys/types.h>
    #include <sys/socket.h>
    #include <netinet/in.h>
    #include <stdio.h>
    #include <errno.h>
    #include <unistd.h>
    #include <string.h>
    #include <arpa/inet.h>

    int main __P((int, char **));

    int
    main(argc, argv)
            int argc;
            char **argv;
    {
            struct sockaddr_in from;
            socklen_t fromlen;
            char hbuf[INET_ADDRSTRLEN];

            /* get the peer's address */
            fromlen = sizeof(from);
            if (getpeername(0, (struct sockaddr *)&from, &fromlen) < 0) {
                    exit(1);
                    /*NOTREACHED*/
            }
            if (from.sin_family != AF_INET ||
                fromlen != sizeof(struct sockaddr_in)) {
                    exit(1);
                    /*NOTREACHED*/
            }

            if (inet_ntop(AF_INET, &from.sin_addr, hbuf, sizeof(hbuf)) ==
                NULL) {
                    exit(1);
                    /*NOTREACHED*/
            }

            write(0, "hello ", 6);
            write(0, hbuf, strlen(hbuf));
            write(0, "\n", 1);
            exit(0);
    }
```

Program 3.5   server-inetd6.c: Make server-inetd4.c address-family independent.

```
    /*
     * server invoked via inetd (multi-protocol support)
     * by Jun-ichiro itojun Hagino. in public domain.
     */
```

```
#include <sys/types.h>
#include <sys/socket.h>
#include <netinet/in.h>
#include <stdio.h>
#include <errno.h>
#include <unistd.h>
#include <string.h>
#include <netdb.h>
#include <arpa/inet.h>

int main __P((int, char **));

int
main(argc, argv)
        int argc;
        char **argv;
{
        struct sockaddr_storage from;   <--Use sockaddr_storage so that we
        socklen_t fromlen;                  have enough room for sockaddrs
        char hbuf[NI_MAXHOST];              with any address family

        /* get the peer's address */
        fromlen = sizeof(from);
        if (getpeername(0, (struct sockaddr *)&from, &fromlen) < 0) {
                exit(1);
                /*NOTREACHED*/              Use getnameinfo(3) to translate
                                            addresses into printable string
        }

        if (getnameinfo((struct sockaddr *)&from, fromlen,
            hbuf, sizeof(hbuf), NULL, 0, NI_NUMERICHOST) != 0) {
                exit(1);
                /*NOTREACHED*/
        }
        write(0, "hello ", 6);
        write(0, hbuf, strlen(hbuf));
        write(0, "\n", 1); exit(0);
}
```

Program 3.6   server-single.c: A standalone TCP server that listens to an IPv4 port.

```
/*
* server with single listening socket (IPv4 only) * by Jun-ichiro
itojun Hagino. in public domain. */

#include <sys/types.h>
#include <sys/socket.h>
#include <netinet/in.h>
#include <netdb.h>
#include <stdio.h>
#include <errno.h>
#include <unistd.h>
```

```
#include <string.h>
#include <stdlib.h>
#include <arpa/inet.h>

int main __P((int, char **));

int
main(argc, argv)
        int argc;
        char **argv;
{
        struct servent *sp;
        unsigned long lport;
        u_int16_t port; char *ep;
        struct sockaddr_in serv;
        int servlen; struct sockaddr_in from;
        socklen_t fromlen;
        int s;
        int ls;
        char hbuf[INET_ADDRSTRLEN];

        if (argc != 2) {
                fprintf(stderr, "usage: test port\n");
                exit(1);
                /*NOTREACHED*/
        }
        sp = getservbyname(argv[1], "tcp");
        if (sp)
                port = sp->s_port & 0xffff;
        else {
                ep = NULL; errno = 0;
                lport = strtoul(argv[1], &ep, 10);
                if (!*argv[1] || errno || !ep || *ep) {
                    fprintf(stderr, "%s: no such service\n", argv[1]);
                    exit(1);
                    /*NOTREACHED*/
                }
                if (lport & ~0xffff) {
                     fprintf(stderr, "%s: out of range\n", argv[1]);
                     exit(1);
                    /*NOTREACHED*/
                }

                port = htons(lport & 0xffff);
        }
        endservent();

        memset(&serv, 0, sizeof(serv));
        serv.sin_family = AF_INET;
        /* linux/Solaris does not need the following line */
        serv.sin_len = sizeof(struct sockaddr_in);
        serv.sin_port = port;
        servlen = sizeof(struct sockaddr_in);
```

```
                        s = socket(AF_INET, SOCK_STREAM, IPPROTO_TCP);
                        if (s < 0) {
                                perror("socket");
                                exit(1);
                                /*NOTREACHED*/
                         }

                        if (bind(s, (struct sockaddr *)&serv, servlen) < 0) {
                                perror("bind");
                                exit(1);
                                /*NOTREACHED*/
                        }
                        if (listen(s, 5) < 0) {
                                perror("listen");
                                exit(1);
                                /*NOTREACHED*/
                        }

                        while (1) {
                                fromlen = sizeof(from);
                                ls = accept(s, (struct sockaddr *)&from, &fromlen);
                                if (ls < 0)
                                        continue;
                                if (from.sin_family != AF_INET ||
                                    fromlen != sizeof(struct sockaddr_in)) {
                                        exit(1);
                                        /*NOTREACHED*/
                                }

                                if (inet_ntop(AF_INET, &from.sin_addr, hbuf,
                                    sizeof(hbuf)) == NULL) {
                                        exit(1);
                                        /*NOTREACHED*/
                                }

                                write(ls, "hello ", 6);
                                write(ls, hbuf, strlen(hbuf));
                                write(ls, "\n", 1);
                                close(ls);
                        }
                        /*NOTREACHED*/
                }
```

Program 3.7   server-getaddrinfo.c: Update server-single.c to be address-family independent.

```
        /*
         * server with multiple listening socket based on getaddrinfo
         * (multi-protocol support)
         * by Jun-ichiro itojun Hagino. in public domain.
         */
```

```
#include <sys/types.h>
#include <sys/socket.h>
#include <netinet/in.h>
#include <netdb.h>
#include <stdio.h>
#include <errno.h>
#include <unistd.h>
#include <string.h>
#include <stdlib.h>
#include <arpa/inet.h>

#define MAXSOCK 20

int main __P((int, char **));

int
main(argc, argv)
        int argc;
        char **argv;
{
        struct addrinfo hints, *res, *res0;
        int error;
        struct sockaddr_storage from;
        socklen_t fromlen;
        int ls;
        int s[MAXSOCK];
        int smax;
        int sockmax;
        fd_set rfd, rfd0;
        int n;
        int i;
        char hbuf[NI_MAXHOST], sbuf[NI_MAXSERV];
#ifdef IPV6_V6ONLY
        const int on = 1;
#endif

        if (argc != 2) {
                fprintf(stderr, "usage: test port\n");
                exit(1);
                /*NOTREACHED*/
        }

        memset(&hints, 0, sizeof(hints));   <--Obtain the list of
        hints.ai_socktype = SOCK_STREAM;       addresses to be used with
        hints.ai_flags = AI_PASSIVE;           bind(2) by using
        error = getaddrinfo(NULL, argv[1],     getaddrinfo(3)
           &hints, &res0);
        if (error) {
                fprintf(stderr, "%s: %s\n", argv[1],
                   gai_strerror(error));
                exit(1);
                /*NOTREACHED*/
```

```
                        }

                        smax = 0;
                        sockmax = -1;
                        for (res = res0; res && smax rMAXSOCK; res = res->ai_next) {
                                s[smax] = socket(res-ai_family, res-ai_socktype,
                                    res->ai_protocol);
                                if (s[smax] < 0)
                                        continue;

                        /* avoid FD_SET overrun */
                        if (s[smax] = FD_SETSIZE) {
                                close(s[smax]);
                                s[smax] = -1;
                                continue;
                        }

#ifdef IPV6_V6ONLY
                        if (res->ai_family == AF_INET6 &&
                            setsockopt(s[smax], IPPROTO_IPV6, IPV6_V6ONLY, &on,
                            sizeof(on)) < 0) {
                                perror("bind");
                                s[smax] = -1;
                                continue;
                        }
#endif

                                if (bind(s[smax], res-ai_addr, res-ai_addrlen) 0) {
                                        close(s[smax]);
                                        s[smax] = -1;
                                        continue;
                                }
                                if (listen(s[smax], 5) 0) {
                                        close(s[smax]); s[smax] = -1;
                                        continue;
                                }

                                error = getnameinfo(res-ai_addr, res-ai_addrlen, hbuf,
                                    sizeof(hbuf), sbuf, sizeof(sbuf),
                                    NI_NUMERICHOST | NI_NUMERICSERV);
                                if (error) {
                                    fprintf(stderr, "test: %s\n", gai_strerror(error));
                                    exit(1);
                                    /*NOTREACHED*/
                                }
                                fprintf(stderr, "listen to %s %s\n", hbuf, sbuf);

                                if (s[smax] > sockmax)
                                        sockmax = s[smax];
                                smax++;
                        }

                        if (smax == 0) {
```

```
                                 fprintf(stderr, "test: no socket to listen to\n");
                                 exit(1);
                                 /*NOTREACHED*/
                        }

                        FD_ZERO(&rfd0);
                        for (i = 0; i < smax; i++)
                                 FD_SET(s[i], &rfd0);

                        while (1) {
                                 rfd = rfd0;
                                 n = select(sockmax + 1, &rfd, NULL, NULL, NULL);
                                 if (n < 0) {
                                         perror("select");
                                         exit(1);
                                         /*NOTREACHED*/
                                 }
                                 for (i = 0; i < smax; i++) {
                                         if (FD_ISSET(s[i], &rfd)) {
                                                 fromlen = sizeof(from);
                                                 ls = accept(s[i], (struct
                                                     sockaddr *)&from &fromlen);
                                         if (ls < 0)
                                                 continue;
                                         write(ls, "hello\n", 6);
                                         close(ls);
                                 }
                        }
                }

                /*NOTREACHED*/
        }
```

Program 3.8   server-getaddrinfo-single.c: TCP server application that listens to a single socket. Address family (protocol) can be switched by a command-line argument.

```
        /*
         * server with single listening socket (IPv4/v6 switchable)
         * by Jun-ichiro itojun Hagino. in public domain.
         */

        #include <sys/types.h>
        #include <sys/socket.h>
        #include <netinet/in.h>
        #include <netdb.h>
        #include <stdio.h>
        #include <errno.h>
        #include <unistd.h>
        #include <string.h>
        #include <stdlib.h>
        #include <arpa/inet.h>

        int main __P((int, char **));
```

```
int
main(argc, argv)
        int argc;
        char **argv;
{
        struct addrinfo hints, *res;
        int error;
        struct sockaddr_storage from;
        socklen_t fromlen;
        int ls;
        int s;
        char hbuf[NI_MAXHOST], sbuf[NI_MAXSERV];
        int ch;
        int af = AF_INET6;
#ifdef IPV6_V6ONLY
        const int on = 1;
#endif                              Switch address family based on a command
                                    line argument
        while ((ch = getopt(argc, argv, "46")) != -1) {
                switch (ch) {
                case '4':
                        af = AF_INET;
                        break;
                case '6':
                        af = AF_INET6;
                        break;
                default:
                        fprintf(stderr, "usage: test [-46] port\n");
                        exit(1);
                        /*NOTREACHED*/
                }
        }
        argc -= optind;
        argv += optind;

        if (argc != 1) {
                printf(stderr, "usage: test port\n");
                exit(1);
                /*NOTREACHED*/
        }
        memset(&hints, 0, sizeof(hints));   <--Obtain wildcard address
        hints.ai_family = af;                   for the address family
        hints.ai_socktype = SOCK_STREAM;        specified by the
        hints.ai_flags = AI_PASSIVE;            command
        error = getaddrinfo(NULL, argv[0], &hints, &res);
        if (error) {
                fprintf(stderr, "%s: %s\n", argv[0],
                  gai_strerror(error));
                exit(1);
                /*NOTREACHED*/
        }
                if (res->ai_next) {
```

```
                       fprintf(stderr, "%s: multiple address
                          returned\n", argv[0]);
                       exit(1);
                       /*NOTREACHED*/
               }

               s= socket(res->ai_family, res-ai_socktype, res-ai_protocol);
               if (s < 0) {
                       perror("socket");
                       exit(1);
                       /*NOTREACHED*/
               }

#ifdef IPV6_V6ONLY
       if (res-ai_family == AF_INET6 &&
        setsockopt(s, IPPROTO_IPV6, IPV6_V6ONLY, &on, sizeof(on)) < 0) {
          perror("bind");
          exit(1);
          /*NOTREACHED*/
       }
#endif

               if (bind(s, res-ai_addr, res-ai_addrlen) 0) {
                       perror("bind");
                       exit(1);
                       /*NOTREACHED*/
               }
               if (listen(s, 5) < 0) {
                       perror("listen");
                       exit(1);
                       /*NOTREACHED*/
               }

               error = getnameinfo(res->ai_addr, res->ai_addrlen, hbuf,
                       sizeof(hbuf), sbuf, sizeof(sbuf),
                       NI_NUMERICHOST | NI_NUMERICSERV);
               if (error) {
                       fprintf(stderr, "test: %s\n", gai_strerror(error));
                       exit(1);
                       /*NOTREACHED*/
               }
               fprintf(stderr, "listen to %s %s\n", hbuf, sbuf);

               while (1) {
                       fromlen = sizeof(from);
                       ls = accept(s, (struct sockaddr *)&from, &fromlen);
                       if (ls < 0)
                               continue;
                       write(ls, "hello\n", 6);
                       close(ls);
               }
               /*NOTREACHED*/
       }
```

4

Tips in IPv6 Programming

4.1   Parsing a IPv6 Address out of String

While writing IPv6-capable applications, you will encounter situations where you need to extract a numeric IPv6 address from a given string (such as a URL). Unlike an IPv4 numeric address, an IPv6 numeric address is very difficult to express with regular expression; it can have 0 to 32 hexadecimal digits (0–9 and a–f), as well as 2 to 7 colons in between. In the case of a scoped IPv6 address, it is suffixed by "%scopeid." For some of the address forms defined in the IPv6 addressing architecture, we can use an IPv4 numeric address form in the last 32 bits (e.g., ::ffff:10.1.2.3).

For reference, the following URL has a regular expression to accept an IPv6 numeric address (it is highly complicated):

```
http://orange.kame.net/dev/cvsweb.cgi/kame/kame/kame/v6regex/scanner.l
```

Therefore, it is not worth it to write a regular expression to pick up IPv6 addresses. Just use getaddrinfo(3) against the fragment of string, probably with AI_NUMERICHOST.

4.2   Issues with ":" As a Separator

In many applications, ":" is used as a separator between the host address and the port number, as in the following configuration directive in Apache:

```
ListenAddress address:port
```

The syntax does not work with an IPv6 address, since colons are used in an IPv6 numeric address representation.

The easiest workaround is to modify syntax to use space as the separator:

```
ListenAddress address port
```

Note that you cannot use slashes as a separator, since address/number is used for identifying address prefixes.

Another way is to forbid the use of a numeric IPv6 address in the address portion; however, this may be too restrictive in some cases.

If you really need to use a colon as the separator, you will want to follow the practices in RFC 2732: Use square brackets to surround the address portion:

```
ListenAddress [address]:port
```

This may complicate the parser code a bit, but it will allow a numeric IPv6 address to be used safely in the syntax.

4.3   Issues with an IPv4 Mapped Address

Dut to several reasons, there are numerous portability and security issues in an IPv6 API. Some of them are due to the lack of standards; some of them are purely deployment issues. This section tries to summarize the most important security issue you will encounter: an IPv4 mapped address. Note that if you follow the guidelines presented in the previous sections, you will be able to avoid most of the problems.

In RFC 2553, it is specified that an AF_INET6 socket can accept IPv4 traffic as well, using a special form of address IPv6 called "IPv4 mapped address." If you run getpeername(2) on such an AF_INET6 socket, it would return an IPv6 address (sockaddr_in6) ::ffff:x.y.z.u, when the real peer is x.y.z.u (sockaddr_in). Due to the way the current standard documents are written, this behavior is a source of major security concerns.

The most critical problem of all is that there is no way for applications to detect if the peer is actually using IPv4 (and the operating system kernel is translating address for the API), or if the peer is actually using an IPv4 mapped address in an IPv6 packet. Because of the ambiguity, there are several possible threats, including:

- A malicious party could circumvent access control on the AF_INET6 socket by sending real IPv6 traffic containing an IPv4 mapped address. Applications will be tricked to believe that the traffic is from an IPv4 peer and will mistakenly grant access.

- If the application uses the peer's address obtained by getpeername(2) to respond to the client (many of the UDP services, such as DNS server), a malicious party could cause the application to generate unwanted an IPv4 traffic by embedding an IPv4 mapped address into an IPv6 source address field.

The response (on the AF_INET6 socket) toward theIPv4 mapped address will be translated into an IPv4 packet by the kernel API and will result in unwanted IPv4 traffic.

Also, an IPv4 mapped address increases complexities in access control code in the application. For instance, if you want to filter out traffic from the 10.0.0.0/8 network, it is not enough to reject traffic from the 10.0.0.0/8 on an AF_INET socket; you will need to reject traffic from ::ffff:10.0.0.0/104 on the AF_INET6 socket as well. Normal application writers are not aware of this complexity. They would believe that by turning off the AF_INET listening socket, they could reject any IPv4 traffic—but it's not true. The application running on the AF_INET6 socket still accepts IPv4 traffic.

The complexity not only impacts applications, but also the operating system kernel code. For instance, the FreeBSD 4.x kernel has been having problems dealing with multiple AF_INET and AF_INET6 sockets; by issuing bind(2) system calls in certain order, applications could hijack a TCP/UDP port from others. The problem has already been fixed; however, it illustrates the impact of the complexity due to the IPv4 mapped address.

Therefore, we conclude that the API itself is flawed, and we should avoid the use of this feature of the API as much as possible. For this purpose, examples presented in previous chapters always recommend opening both the AF_INET and AF_INET6 sockets separately, in order to accept IPv4 and IPv6 traffic separately. Some of the operating systems (OpenBSD and NetBSD) took a security stance and disabled the IPv4 mapped address feature by default.

More details on this topic are available in the Internet drafts included in the appendices:

draft-itojun-ipv6-transition-abuse-01.txt

draft-itojun-v6ops-v4mapped-harmful-01.txt

draft-cmetz-v6ops-v4mapped-api-harmful-00.txt

Unfortunately, we still need to worry about the IPv4 mapped address issue, even if we open separate sockets for AF_INET and AF_INET6, because of the operating system differences caused by the lack of, or ambiguity of, the IPv6 API standards.

4.4   bind(2) Ordering and Conflicts

On some of the existing operating systems, bind(2) to AF_INET port will conflict against bind(2) to AF_INET6 on the same port. On such systems, since either of the sockets could fail to bind(2), it is not possible to serve IPv4 clients and IPv6 clients via separate sockets. The latest standard (RFC 2553 and the POSIX spec relevant to it) does not dictate what kind of behavior is the correct one, so the behavior varies by system.

By setting the IPV6_V6ONLY socket option to 1, as suggested in the previous chapters, the problem should be worked around. Unfortunately, since the socket option was introduced very recently (in RFC 2553bis, RFC 2553 revised), not many systems provide this option. Moreover, the wording in the revised spec is not totally clear about bind(2) conflict issues.

Therefore, the worst-case scenarios on platforms that reject two bind(2) requests are as follows:

- Open the AF_INET6 socket only, and rely upon IPv4 mapped address behavior (accept IPv4 traffic by using the AF_INET6 socket). This way your application will be vulnerable to various attacks.

- Open the AF_INET6 socket only, and reject any traffic from an IPv4 mapped address. By doing so, you will serve IPv6 clients only; IPv4 clients will get rejected.

- Open the AF_INET socket only. You will serve IPv4 clients only; IPv6 clients will get rejected.

4.5   How IPv4 Traffic Gets Routed to Sockets

On some of the existing operating systems, when the AF_INET6 and AF_INET listening sockets are present, IPv4 traffic gets routed to the AF_INET6 socket (using an IPv4 mapped address), not the AF_INET socket. As a result, the AF_INET socket would get no traffic. On such systems, it is critical to apply necessary access controls against an IPv4 mapped address on an AF_INET6 socket.

Again, IPV6_V6ONLY may be used to work around this issue; however, it may not be available on your system.

4.6   Portability across Systems

As mentioned in earlier chapters, there are behavioral differences between operating systems. This section describes portability issues and issues caused by the differences. Here we also discuss how an application programmer could cope with the issues.

4.6.1 Handling of an IPv4 Mapped Address

As mentioned in the previous section, there are various interpretations to the handling of an IPv4 mapped address, and system behavior varies by vendors. The best work-around we can perform is to open the AF_INET and AF_INET6 sockets separately, and use AF_INET for IPv4 and AF_INET6 for IPv6. Turn on the IPV6_V6ONLY socket option on the AF_INET6 socket explicitly, to avoid mistakenly using the IPv4 mapped address on an AF_INET6 socket. Also, it is a good practice to use getaddrinfo(3) with the AI_PASSIVE flag to get the list of possible listening sockets, instead of hardcoding wildcard addresses such as 0.0.0.0 or : :.

4.6.2 Socket Options

Socket options such as setsockopt(2)/getsockopt(2) operations are normally different on the AF_INET and AF_INET6 sockets. Some systems do support AF_INET socket options on the AF_INET6 socket, and some do not. For instance, the IP_TOS socket option is meaningful for IPv4 traffic. Some systems support IP_TOS only for AF_INET sockets, and some support it for AF_INET6 sockets as well. There are no standards for socket options, so we cannot blame either side.

Therefore, it is safer to assume that your system does not support IPv4 socket options on AF_INET6 sockets, and use AF_INET for IPv4 traffic and AF_INET6 for IPv6 traffic. By following guidelines supplied in the previous chapters, the case is already covered.

4.6.3 Lack of API Functions

Because getaddrinfo(3) and getnameinfo(3) are relatively new APIs, they may not be available on older systems. If you want your software package to function on older systems as well, you will want to ship tiny implementations of getaddrinfo(3) and getnameinfo(3) with your software package, and use these as needed.

To detect if a function is present or not on a particular system, the GNU autoconf works very well. The GNU autoconf system provides a way to generate a "configure" shell script, which will detect system differences and generate appropriate Makefile from a template, Makefile.in. If you put the following statement into configure.in (the input file to GNU autoconf), GNU autoconf will:

- Do nothing, if getaddrinfo is supplied by the operating system.
- Add getaddrinfo.o into $LIBOBJS in the configure script, which will be used when generating Makefile from Makefile.in.

```
AC_REPLACE_FUNCS(getaddrinfo)
```

Therefore, getaddrinfo.c will be compiled only if the function is not supplied by the system.

4.6.4 Lack of Address Family

On many of the operating systems, it is possible to strip down kernel size by removing functionalities; some administrators would remove IPv6 functionality from the operating system kernel. Removal of IPv6 functionality usually means that the system does not have AF_INET6 support at all. Even under such situations, you will want your application to function correctly, avoiding recompilation of the application (you will want to ship a single binary that works on IPv4-only, IPv6-only, and the IPv4/v6 dual stack kernel). If you follow the guidelines presented in the previous chapters, your application will work correctly on any of the kernels, since your application does not hardcode any constants, such as AF_INET6 or AF_INET. If you port applications to IPv6 by hardcoding AF_INET6, you will be in trouble running your software on the IPv6-less kernel.

4.7   RFCs 2292/3542, Advanced API

If your application involves raw IP sockets (e.g., ping(8)) and/or IP options handling via setsockopt(2), you will need to check the IPv6 advanced API, defined in RFCs 2292/3542. Because of header structure differences, such as introduction of extension header chain, RFCs 2292/3542 present an API very different from the IPv4 counterpart.

This book does not go into details of the RFCs 2292/3542 API. The RFCs are provided in the appendices.

Availability of RFCs 2292/3542 API is not widespread, unfortunately. Also, RFCs 2292 and 3542 are not compatible at all. KAME-based platforms support the RFC 2292 API as of this writing, while Solaris the supports the RFC 3542 API. Contact vendors for the support status on other platforms.

Fortunately, only a limited number of applications, such as ping(8) or traceroute(8), have to deal with RFCs 2292/3542. Normal applications such as ftp(1) need only deal with RFC 2553 in most cases.

4.8   Platform Support Status

Since IPv6 is a new protocol, the level of support varies by platforms. Here's a status of implementation as of October 2002 (subject to change).

4.8.1   **NetBSD**

NetBSD supports IPv6 since version 1.5, using the KAME IPv6 stack. On NetBSD, IPv4 mapped address behavior is turned off by default for security (the IPV6_V6ONLY socket option is on by default). We suggest setting the IPV6_V6ONLY socket option explicitly to on for security and portability.

4.8.2   **OpenBSD**

OpenBSD supports IPv6 since version 2.7, using the KAME IPv6 stack. On OpenBSD, IPv4 mapped address behavior is not supported, and the IPV6_V6ONLY socket option is a no-op.

4.8.3   **FreeBSD**

FreeBSD supports IPv6 since version 4.0, using the KAME IPv6 stack. On FreeBSD 4.x, IPv4 mapped address behavior is enabled by default (the IPV6_V6ONLY socket option is off by default)—hence, security problems described in the previous sections are present. By setting the IPV6_V6ONLY socket option explicitly to on you can avoid the security problems.

On FreeBSD, current and 5.x, IPv4 mapped address behavior is turned off by default for security (the IPV6_V6ONLY socket option is on by default). We suggest setting the IPV6_V6ONLY socket option explicitly to on for security and portability.

4.8.4   **BSD/OS**

BSD/OS supports IPv6 since version 4.1. Version 4.1 uses the NRL IPv6 stack, and versions 4.2 and beyond use the KAME IPv6 stack.

On BSD/OS 4.3, IPv4 mapped address behavior is enabled by default (the IPV6_V6ONLY socket option is off by default)—hence, security problems described in the previous sections are present. By setting the IPV6_V6ONLY socket option explicitly to on you can avoid the security problems.

4.8.5   **Mac OS X**

Mac OS X supports IPv6 starting with version 10.2. IPv6 support in version 10.2 is considered a "developer's release"—no GUI, no support in most of GUI-based applications (e.g., Internet Explorer), and so on.

Both ftp(1) and telnet(1) support IPv6. But ssh(1) and sshd(8) do not support IPv6. IPv6-ready ssh binaries are available at ftp://ftp.kame.net/pub/kame/misc/.

There are a couple of bugs in the 10.2 library that could affect implementers: getaddrinfo(3) does not parse scoped IPv6 numeric address form, such as fe80::1%en0.

On Mac OS 10.2, IPv4 mapped address behavior is enabled by default (the IPV6_V6ONLY socket option is off by default)—hence, security problems described in the previous sections are present. By setting the IPV6_V6ONLY socket option explicitly to on you can avoid the security problems.

In addition to socket-based APIs, Apple also provides higher-level APIs, called Core Foundation libraries, for GUI-based applications. CFNetwork is a URL-based API, and therefore IPv6 support is embedded within the library. CFReadStream and CFWriteStream APIs abstract data stream exchanged between two nodes. CFNetServices provides access to name resolution functions, including Rendezvous (on-link name resolution based on multicast DNS, as well as DNS-based service discovery).

4.8.6   Windows 95/98/Me

It seems that there is no plan from Microsoft to support IPv6 on these platforms. There are third-party IPv6 stacks available from Trumpet software and Hitachi.

4.8.7   Windows 2000

Windows 2000 does not support IPv6. There are experimental releases of IPv6 stacks provided by Microsoft research.

4.8.8   Windows XP

Windows XP supports IPv6; however, it is disabled by default. It can be enabled by invocation of "ipv6 install" on the command line. Applications such as Internet Explorer do support IPv6, since they use URL-based (proprietary) libraries.

4.8.9   Windows CE

Windows CE will support IPv6 in the next release.

4.8.10 Windows .Net Programming Environment

The Windows .Net programming environment provides .Net sockets (System.Net. Sockets), which is a URL-based class library. The version currently shipping with Windows is IPv4-only; however, it is scheduled to make the API dual stack–capable.

4.8.11 Linux

Linux supports IPv6 starting withkernel version 2.2. However, the specification conformance is low, since the stack was based on an old revision of the IPv6 specification. There are ongoing efforts to update IPv6 support in Linux (the USAGI project).

The level of applications/libraries support varies by Linux distributions; some distribution ships a larger number of IPv6-enabled applications than others. Some distribution ships with better library support (glibc) than others.

Using   http://www.bieringer.de/linux/IPv6/status/IPv6+Linux-status-distributions.html will help you to understand the level of IPv6 support your Linux distribution has.

4.8.12 Solaris

Solaris supports IPv6 since version 2.7. On Solaris, IPv4 mapped address behavior is enabled by default (the IPV6_V6ONLY socket option is off by default)—hence, security problems described in the previous sections are present.

A Practical Example

5.1 Server Program Example—popa3d

popa3d is a free, redistributable POP3 server. It supports invocation from inetd, such as server-inetd4.c (see Program 3.4), and standalone invocation, such as server-single.c (see Program 3.6). Version 0.5.1 is not IPv6 ready, so it would be a good candidate for our example.

The actual code is not shown here. You can grab the code from: http://www.open-wall.com/popa3d/ or http://www.ascii.co.jp/books/ipv6-api/popa3d-before/.

5.1.1 Identifying Where to Rewrite

Now, you have your popa3d source code in your current directory.

```
% tar zxf popa3d-0.5.1.tar.gz
% cd popa3d-0.5.1
```

Let us identify which source code you will need to rewrite.

```
% grep in_addr *.[ch]
standalone.c:    if ((sock = socket(AF_INET, SOCK_STREAM,
   IPPROTO_TCPT))  < 0)
standalone.c:    addr.sin_family = AF_INET;
virtual.c:       if (length != sizeof(sin) || sin.sin_family != AF_INET
virtual.c = ) return NULL;
% grep in_addr *.[ch]
standalone.c:    addr.sin_addr.s_addr)    struct in_addr addr)
/* Source IP address */
standalone.c:    addr.sin_addr.s_addr = inet_addr(DAEMON_ADDR);
standalone.c:                             addr.sin_addr.s_addr)
standalone.c:                             inet_ntoa(addr.sin_addr
standalone.c:
));
```

```
standalone.c:                                inet_ntoa(addr.sin_addr));
standalone.c:                                inet_ntoa(addr.sin_addr));
standalone.c:                                inet_ntoa(addr.sin_addr));
standalone.c:                       sessions[j].addr = addr.sin_addr;
virtual.c:       return inet_ntoa(sin.sin_addr);
% grep sockaddr_in *.[ch]
standalone.c:  struct sockaddr_in addr;
virtual.c:       struct sockaddr_in sin;
% grep hostent *.[ch]
```

So, it seems that what we need to rewrite are standalone.c and virtual.c. Let us check these source codes.

Modifying virtual.c

virtual.c provides virtual home directory functionality, with which you can split users' spool files into multiple files based on the POP server's IP address contacted by the client. The code will be used when POP_VIRTUAL is defined in params.h. IPv4-dependent code is in lookup(), as follows:

```
static char *lookup(void)
{
        struct sockaddr_in sin;
        int length;

        length = sizeof(sin);
        if (getsockname(0, (struct sockaddr *)&sin, &length)) {
                if (errno == ENOTSOCK) return "";
                log_error("getsockname");
                return NULL;
        }
        if (length != sizeof(sin) || sin.sin_family != AF_INET)
        return NULL;

        return inet_ntoa(sin.sin_addr);
}
```

To make this codepath address-family independent, we would need to:

- Use sockaddr_storage instead of sockaddr_in to getsockname(2), even if the socket is not AF _INET.
- Use getnameinfo(3) instead of inet_ntoa.

The end result will be as follows:

```
static const char *lookup(void)
{
        struct sockaddr_storage ss;
        int length;
        int error;
```

```
                          static char hbuf[NI_MAXHOST];

                          length = sizeof(ss);
                          if (getsockname(0, (struct sockaddr *)&ss, &length)) {
                                  if (errno == ENOTSOCK) return "";
                                  log_error("getsockname");
                                  return NULL;
                          }

                          error = getnameinfo((struct sockaddr *)&ss, length, hbuf,
                             sizeof(hbuf), NULL, 0, NI_NUMERICHOST); if (error) {
                                  /* logging? */
                                  return NULL;
                          }

                          return hbuf;
                  }
```

I've added "const" to the return type of the function, since the function returns a pointer to the statically allocated memory region.

If you check function virtual userpass() carefully, the return value from lookup() will be used to construct the pathname of the email spool file. Beware that under some operating systems colons and the % sign used in the IPv6 numeric address specification could be troublesome (e.g., Apple HFS uses a colon as the directory pathname separator).

Modifying standalone.c

popa3d can be invoked via inetd or as a standalone daemon process. With POP_STANDALONE defined to 0 in params.h, popa3d assumes that it will be invoked via inetd. With POP_STANDALONE defined to 1, popa3d can be invoked via inetd or as a standalone daemon (needs -D command-line argument). standalone.c basically handles the case when poppa3d is invoked as a standalone daemon. (See Programs 5.1 and 5.2.)

standalone.c hardcodes AF_INET assumption in multiple places:

- It opens the AF_INET socket via the socket(2) call.
- It uses sockaddr_in as an argument to bind(2).
- It uses inet_addr(3) and inet_ntoa(3) to deal with string representation address.
- Sessions[] array contains in_addr to hold a peer's address.

    Also, standalone.c listens to single socket only.

Now, we need to make a couple of design decisions:

- Whether to listen to multiple sockets and use poll(2)/select(2), or listen to a single socket and run multiple instances of popa3d
- What we should do about sessions[].addr

Here, we made the following decisions:

- Make popa3d listen to a single socket only, and switch the address family using a command-line argument: -4 or -6.
- Use string representation of the address for session[].addr. The member is used to rate-limit access from the same address; therefore, the format (binary or string) does not matter if we can uniquely identify the peer.

The results of the rewrite are shown in Programs 5.3 and 5.4. They are also available from the following locations:

http://www.ascii.co.jp/books/ipv6-api/popa3d-before/standalone.c
http://www.ascii.co.jp/books/ipv6-api/popa3d-before/startup.c
http://www.ascii.co.jp/books/ipv6-api/popa3d-before/virtual.c
http://www.ascii.co.jp/books/ipv6-api/popa3d-after/standalone.c
http://www.ascii.co.jp/books/ipv6-api/popa3d-after/startup.c
http://www.ascii.co.jp/books/ipv6-api/popa3d-after/virtual.c

5.2   Further Extensions

When we rewrote standalone.c, we decided to use single address-family specified via command-line argument (-4 or -6). You may want to extend standalone.c to open multiple sockets, based on the return value from getaddrinfo(3) AI_PASSIVE case, and deal with multiple sockets using poll(2) or select(2) API. By doing so you will eliminate the need for additional command-line arguments.

This part is left as an exercise for the readers.

5.3   Client Program Example—nail

nail is a free, redistributable email client, based on BSD Mail (well known as /bin/mail). It supports POP3 for acceessing incoming emails in remote mailboxes, as well as SMTP for delivering outgoing emails.

The actual code is not shown here. You can grab the code from: http://omnibus.ruf.uni-freiburg.de/~gritter/ or http://www.ascii.co.jp/books/ipv6-api/ nail-before/.

5.3.1 Identifying Where to Rewrite

Now, you have your nail source code in your current directory.

```
% tar zxf nail-10.3.tar.gz
% cd nail-10.3
```

Let us identify which source code you will need to rewrite:

```
% grep AF_INET *.[ch]
pop3.c: if ((sockfd = socket(AF_INET, SOCK_STREAM, 0)) == -1) {
pop3.c: servaddr.sin_family = AF_INET;
smtp.c: if ((sockfd = socket(AF_INET, SOCK_STREAM, 0)) == -1) {
smtp.c: servaddr.sin_family = AF_INET;
% grep in_addr *.[ch]
pop3.c: struct in_addr **pptr;
pop3.c: pptr = (struct in_addr **)hp->h_addr_list;
pop3.c: memcpy(&servaddr.sin_addr, *pptr, sizeof(struct in_addr));
smtp.c: struct in_addr **pptr;
smtp.c: pptr = (struct in_addr **) hp->h_addr_list;
smtp.c: memcpy(&servaddr.sin_addr, *pptr, sizeof(struct in_addr));
% grep sockaddr_in *.[ch]
pop3.c: struct sockaddr_in servaddr;
smtp.c: struct sockaddr_in servaddr;
% grep hostent *.[ch] pop3.c: struct hostent *hp;
smtp.c: struct hostent *hent;
smtp.c: struct hostent *hp;
% grep gethostby *.[ch]
pop3.c: if ((hp = gethostbyname(server)) == NULL) {
smtp.c: hent = gethostbyname(hn);
smtp.c: if ((hp = gethostbyname(server)) == NULL) {
```

It seems that what we need to rewrite are pop3.c and smtp.c. Let us check these source codes.

Modifying pop3.c

pop3.c provides accesses to incoming emails in remote mailboxes via the POP3 protocol.

IPv4-dependent code is in pop3_open(). The code is as follows (very simplified, and most of the code is translated into comments).

```
static enum okay pop3_open(xserver, mp, use_ssl, uhp)
        const char *xserver; struct mailbox *mp;

        const char *uhp;
{
        struct sockaddr_in sin;
        struct hostent *hp;
```

```
        char *portstr = use_ssl ? "pop3s" : "pop3", *cp;
        char *server = xserver;

        if ((cp = strchr(server, ':')) != NULL) {
                portstr = &cp[1];
                /*
                 * convert portstr into numeric using strtol,
                 * chop off part after colon from "server".
                 */
        } else {
                /*
                 * use the default port.
                 * convert portstr into numeric using getservbyport(3).
                 */
        }
        if ((hp = gethostbyname(server)) == NULL) {
                /* error */
                return STOP;
        }
        pptr = (struct in_addr **)hp->h_addr_list;
        if ((sockfd = socket(AF_INET, SOCK_STREAM, 0)) == -1) {
                /* error */
                return STOP;
        }
        memset(&servaddr, 0, sizeof servaddr);
        servaddr.sin_family = AF_INET;
        servaddr.sin_port = port;
        memcpy(&servaddr.sin_addr, *pptr, sizeof(struct in_addr));

        if (connect(sockfd, (struct sockaddr *)&servaddr, sizeof
                /* error */
                return STOP;
        }
        mp-mb_sock = sockfd;
        return OKAY;
}
```

To make this codepath address-family independent, we would need to:

- Use getaddrinfo(3) instead of gethostbyname(3) for address resolution.

- Avoid any hardcoded accesses to IPv4 APIs (e.g., AF_INET, sockaddr_in, etc.).

- Make the function try to connect all the addresses returned by DNS name resolution function, rather than try the first one only.

One issue we need to check is the use of the colon as a separator of a string. The variable xserver would contain a string to specify POP3 protocol access to TCP port 1234 on server.example.com:

```
server.example.com:1234
```

Fortunately, the function does not allow numeric IPv4 address representation; therefore, we can forget about numeric IPv6 address support, where colons will become ambiguous to strchr(3).

The end result will be as follows:

```
static enum okay pop3_open(xserver, mp, use_ssl, uhp)
        const char *xserver;
        struct mailbox *mp;
        const char *uhp;
{

        int sockfd;
        struct addrinfo hints, *res0, *res;
        char *server = (char *)xserver;
        int error;

        if ((cp = strchr(server, ':')) != NULL) {
                portstr = &cp[1];
                /*
                 * chop off part after colon from "server".
                 */
        }

        memset(&hints, 0, sizeof(hints));
        hints.ai_socktype = SOCK_STREAM;
        if (getaddrinfo(server, portstr, &hints, &res0) != 0) {
                /* error */
                return STOP;
        }

        sockfd = -1;
        for (res = res0; res; res = res->ai_next) {
                sockfd = socket(res->ai_family, res->ai_socktype,
                    res->ai_protocol); if (sockfd 0)
                continue;
                if (connect(sockfd, res->ai_addr, res->ai_addrlen)
                    != 0) {
                        close(sockfd);
                        sockfd = -1;
                        continue;
                }
                break;
        }
        if (sockfd < 0) {
                /* error */ freeaddrinfo(res0);
                return STOP;
        }
        freeaddrinfo(res0);
        mp->mb_sock = sockfd;
        return OKAY;
}
```

Modifying smtp.c

IPv4 dependent functions here are:

smtp_mta()

nodename()

smtp_mta() is pretty much the same as pop3_open() in pop3.c, and rewriting it will be straightforward once you have rewritten pop3_open(). nodename() is as follows:

```c
char *nodename(void)
{
        static char *hostname;
        char *hn;
        struct utsname ut;
        struct hostent *hent;

        if (hostname == NULL) {
                uname(&ut);
                hn = ut.nodename;

                hent = gethostbyname(hn);
                if (hent != NULL) {
                        hn = hent->h_name;
                }
                hostname = (char *)smalloc(strlen(hn) + 1);
                strcpy(hostname, hn);
        }

        return hostname;
}
```

We need to avoid the use of gethostbyname(3), since gethostbyname(3) is IPv4-only. After the rewrite, the program will look like this:

```c
char *nodename(void)
{
        static char *hostname;
        char *hn;
        struct utsname ut;
        struct addrinfo hints, *res = NULL;

        if (hostname == NULL) {
                uname(&ut);
                hn = ut.nodename;
                memset(&hints, 0, sizeof(hints));
                hints.ai_socktype = SOCK_STREAM;
                hints.ai_flags = AI_CANONNAME;
                if (getaddrinfo(hn, NULL, &hints, &res) == 0) {
                        if (res->ai_canonname)
```

```
                                        hn = res->ai_canonname;
                        }
                        hostname = (char *)smalloc(strlen(hn) + 1);
                        strcpy(hostname, hn);
                }
                if (res)
                        freeaddrinfo(res);
                return hostname;
        }
```

Here we use getaddrinfo(3) with an empty service name (port number), which is NULL. What we really need is res->ai_canonname, which is equivalent to hent->h_name. We do not need to handle port number at all. We actually are not really interested in any of ai_socktype or ai_protocol; however, it is mandatory to configure ai_socktype when we specify numeric or NULL in the second argument. Therefore, we put SOCK_STREAM into ai_socktype.

You can find the actual source code, before and after the rewrite, at the following locations:

http://www.ascii.co.jp/books/ipv6-api/nail-before/pop3.c

http://www.ascii.co.jp/books/ipv6-api/nail-before/smtp.c

http://www.ascii.co.jp/books/ipv6-api/nail-after/pop3.c

http://www.ascii.co.jp/books/ipv6-api/nail-after/smtp.c

Program 5.1   standalone.c in popa3d package (before modification).

```
/*
 * Standalone POP server: accepts connections, checks the anti-flood
     limits,
 * logs and starts the actual POP sessions.
 */

#include "params.h"

#if POP_STANDALONE

#include <stdio.h>
#include <unistd.h>
#include <stdlib.h>
#include <string.h>
#include <signal.h>
#include <syslog.h>
#include <time.h>
#include <errno.h>
#include <sys/times.h>
#include <sys/types.h>
#include <sys/wait.h>
```

```c
#include <sys/socket.h>
#include <netinet/in.h>
#include <arpa/inet.h>

#if DAEMON_LIBWRAP
#include <tcpd.h>
int allow_severity = SYSLOG_PRI_LO;
int deny_severity = SYSLOG_PRI_HI;
#endif

/*
 * These are defined in pop_root.c.
 */
extern int log_error(char *s);
extern int do_pop_startup(void);
extern int do_pop_session(void);

typedef sig_atomic_t a_int;
typedef volatile a_int va_int;

/*
 * Active POP sessions. Those that were started within the last
 * MIN_DELAY seconds are also considered active (regardless of their
 * actual state), to allow for limiting the logging rate without
 * throwing away critical information about sessions that we could have
 * allowed to proceed.
 */
static struct {
        struct in_addr addr;    /* Source IP address */
        a_int pid;              /* PID of the server, or 0 for none */
        clock_t start;          /* When the server was started */
        clock_t log;            /* When we've last logged a failure */
} sessions[MAX_SESSIONS];

static va_int child_blocked;    /* We use blocking to avoid races */
static va_int child_pending;    /* Are any dead children waiting? */

/*
 * SIGCHLD handler; can also be called directly with a zero signum.
 */
static void handle_child(int signum)
{
        int saved_errno;
        int pid;
        int i;

        saved_errno = errno;

        if (child_blocked)
                child_pending = 1;
        else {
                child_pending = 0;
```

```
                              while ((pid = waitpid(0, NULL, WNOHANG)) < 0)
                              for (i = 0; i MAX_SESSIONS; i++)
                              if (sessions[i].pid == pid) {
                                      sessions[i].pid = 0;
                                      break;
                              }
                      }

              if (signum) signal(SIGCHLD, handle_child);
              errno = saved_errno;
      }

#if DAEMON_LIBWRAP
static void check_access(int sock)
{
        struct request_info request;

        request_init(&request,
                RQ_DAEMON, DAEMON_LIBWRAP_IDENT,
                RQ_FILE, sock,
                0);
        fromhost(&request);

        if (!hosts_access(&request)) {
/* refuse() shouldn't return... */
                refuse(&request);
/* ...but just in case */
                exit(1);
        }
}
#endif

#if POP_OPTIONS
int do_standalone(void)
#else
int main(void)
#endif
{
        int true = 1;
        int sock, new;
        struct sockaddr_in addr;
        int addrlen;
        int pid;
        struct tms buf;
        clock_t now;
        int i, j, n;

        if (do_pop_startup()) return 1;

        if ((sock = socket(AF_INET, SOCK_STREAM, IPPROTO_TCP)) < 0)
                return log_error("socket");
        if (setsockopt(sock, SOL_SOCKET, SO_REUSEADDR,
                (void *)&true, sizeof(true)))
```

```
                                      return log_error("setsockopt");

                memset(&addr, 0, sizeof(addr));
                addr.sin_family = AF_INET;
                addr.sin_addr.s_addr = inet_addr(D          AEMON_ADDR);
                addr.sin_port = htons(DAEMON_PORT);
                if (bind(sock, (struct sockaddr *)&addr, sizeof(addr)))
                        return log_error("bind");

                if (listen(sock, MAX_BACKLOG))
                        return log_error("listen");

                chdir("/"); setsid();

                switch (fork()) {
                case -1:
                        return log_error("fork");

                        case 0:
                        break;

                default:
                        return 0;
                }

                setsid();

                child_blocked = 1;
                child_pending = 0;
                signal(SIGCHLD, handle_child);

                memset((void *)sessions, 0, sizeof(sessions));
                new = 0;

                while (1) {
                        child_blocked = 0;
                        if (child_pending) handle_child(0);

                        if (new < 0)

                        if (close(new)) return log_error("close");
                        addrlen = sizeof(addr);
                        new = accept(sock, (struct sockaddr *)&addr, &addrlen);
/*
 * I wish there was a portable way to classify errno's... In this case,
 * it appears to be better to risk eating up the CPU on a fatal error
 * rather than risk terminating the entire service because of a minor
 * temporary error having to do with one particular connection attempt.
 */
                        if (new < 0) continue;

                        now = times(&buf);
```

```
                            child_blocked = 1;

                            j = -1; n = 0;
                            for (i = 0; i MAX_SESSIONS; i++) {
                                  if (sessions[i].start  now)
                                        sessions[i].start = 0;
                                  if (sessions[i].pid ||
                                        (sessions[i].start &&
                                  now - sessions[i].start < MIN_DELAY * CLK_TCK)) {
                                        if (sessions[i].addr.s_addr ==
                                           addr.sin_addr.s_addr)
                                        if (++n = MAX_SESSIONS_PER_SOURCE) break;
                                  } else
                                  if (j < 0) j = i;
                            }

                            if (n >= MAX_SESSIONS_PER_SOURCE) {
                                  if (!sessions[i].log ||
                                    now < sessions[i].log ||
                                    now - sessions[i].log = MIN_DELAY * CLK_TCK) {
                                        syslog(SYSLOG_PRI_HI,
                                           "%s: per source limit reached",
                                           inet_ntoa(addr.sin_addr));
                                        sessions[i].log = now;
                                  }
                                  continue;
                            }
                            if (j < 0) {
                                syslog(SYSLOG_PRI_HI, "%s: sessions limit reached",
                                        inet_ntoa(addr.sin_addr));
                                continue;
                            }

                            switch ((pid = fork())) {
                            case -1:
                                  syslog(SYSLOG_PRI_ERROR, "%s: fork: %m",
                                          inet_ntoa(addr.sin_addr));
                                  break;
                            case 0

                                  if (close(sock)) return log_error("close");
#if DAEMON-LIBWRAP
                                  check_access(new);
#endif
                                  syslog(SYSLOG_PRI_LO, "Session from %s",
                                          inet_ntoa(addr.sin_addr));
                                  return do_pop_session();
                                  if (dup2(new, 0) < 0) return log_error("dup2");
                                  if (dup2(new, 1) < 0) return log_error("dup2");
                                  if (dup2(new, 2) < 0) return log_error("dup2");
                                  if (close (new)) return log_error("close");
                                  return do_pop_session();
```

```
                             default:
                                     sessions[j].addr = addr.sin_addr;
                                     (va_int)sessions[j].pid = pid;
                                     sessions[j].start = now;
                                     sessions[j].log = 0;
                             }
                     }
             }

     #endif
```

Program 5.2   startup.c in popa3d package (before modification).

```
/*
 * Command line option parsing.
 */

#include "params.h"

#if POP_OPTIONS

#include <unistd.h>
#include <stdio.h>
#include <stdlib>

/* pop_root.c */
extern int do_pop_startup(void);
extern int do_pop_session(void);

/* standalone.c */
extern int do_standalone(void);

#ifdef HAVE_PROGNAME
extern char *__progname;
#define progname __progname
#else
static char *progname;
#endif

static void usage(void)
{
        fprintf(stderr, "Usage: %s [-D]\n", progname);
        exit(1);
}

int main(int argc, char **argv) {
        int c;
        int standalone = 0;

#ifndef HAVE_PROGNAME
        if (!(progname = argv[0]))
                progname = POP_SERVER;
#endif
```

```
        }
            while ((c = getopt(argc, argv, "D")) != -1) {
                switch (c) {
                case 'D':
                        standalone++;
                        break;

                default:
                        usage();
                }
            }

            if (optind != argc) usage();

            if (standalone)
                    return do_standalone();

            if (do_pop_startup()) return 1;
            return do_pop_session();
        }
        #endif
```

Program 5.3 *standalone.c in popa3d package (after modification: bold portions are modified).*

```
/*
 * Standalone POP server: accepts connections, checks the anti-flood
 * limits, logs and starts the actual POP sessions.
 */

#include "params.h"
#if POP_STANDALONE

#include <stdio.h>
#include <unistd.h>
#include <stdlib.h>
#include <string.h>
#include <signal.h>
#include <syslog.h>
#include <time.h>
#include <errno.h>
#include <netdb.h>
#include <sys/times.h>
#include <sys/types.h>
#include <sys/wait.h>
#include <sys/socket.h>
#include <netinet/in.h>
#include <arpa/inet.h>

#if DAEMON_LIBWRAP
#include <tcpd.h>
int allow_severity = SYSLOG_PRI_LO;
```

```
int deny_severity = SYSLOG_PRI_HI;
#endif

/*
 * These are defined in pop_root.c.
 */
extern int log_error(char *s);
extern int do_pop_startup(void);
extern int do_pop_session(void);
extern int af;

typedef sig_atomic_t a_int;
typedef volatile a_int va_int;

/*
 * Active POP sessions. Those that were started within the last
 * MIN_DELAY seconds are also considered active (regardless of their
 * actual state), to allow for limiting the logging rate without
 * throwing away critical information about sessions that we could have
 * allowed to proceed.
 */

static struct {
        char addr[NI_MAXHOST];   /* Source IP address */
        a_int pid;               /* PID of the server, or 0 for none */
        clock_t start;           /* When the server was started */
        clock_t log;             /* When we've last logged a failure */
} sessions[MAX_SESSIONS];

static va_int child_blocked;    /* We use blocking to avoid races */
static va_int child_pending;    /* Are any dead children waiting? */

/*
 * SIGCHLD handler; can also be called directly with a zero signum.
 */
static void handle_child(int signum)
{
        int saved_errno;
        int pid;
        int i;

        saved_errno = errno;

        if (child_blocked)
                child_pending = 1;
        else {
                child_pending = 0;

                while ((pid = waitpid(0, NULL, WNOHANG)) > 0)
                for (i = 0; i MAX_SESSIONS; i++)
                if (sessions[i].pid == pid) {
                        sessions[i].pid = 0;
                        break;
```

```
                  }
          }

          if (signum) signal(SIGCHLD, handle_child);

          errno = saved_errno;
}

#if DAEMON_LIBWRAP
static void check_access(int sock)
{
          struct request_info request;

          request_init(&request,
                  RQ_DAEMON, DAEMON_LIBWRAP_IDENT,
                  RQ_FILE, sock,
                  0);
          fromhost(&request);

          if (!hosts_access(&request)) {
/* refuse() shouldn't return... */
                  refuse(&request);
/* ...but just in case */
                  exit(1);
          }
}
#endif

#if POP_OPTIONS
int do_standalone(void)
#else
int main(void)
#endif
{
          int true = 1;
          int sock, new;
          struct sockaddr_storage addr;
          int addrlen;
          int pid;
          struct tms buf;
          clock_t now;
          int i, j, n;
          struct addrinfo hints, *res;
          char hbuf[NI_MAXHOST];
          char sbuf[NI_MAXSERV];

          int error;

          if (do_pop_startup()) return 1;

          if ((sock = socket(AF_INET, SOCK_STREAM, IPPROTO_TCP)) < 0)
                  return log_error("socket");
```

```
        snprintf(sbuf, sizeof(sbuf), "%u", DAEMON_PORT);
        memset(&hints, 0, sizeof(hints));
        hints.ai_socktype = SOCK_STREAM;
        hints.ai_family = af;
        hints.ai_flags = AI_PASSIVE;
        error = getaddrinfo(NULL, sbuf, &hints, &res);
        if (error)
                return log_error("getaddrinfo");

        sock = socket(res-ai_family, res-ai_socktype, res-ai_protocol);
        if (sock < 0) {
                freeaddrinfo(res);
                return log_error("socket");
        }

        if (setsockopt(sock, SOL_SOCKET, SO_REUSEADDR,
                (void *)&true, sizeof(true))) {
                        freeaddrinfo(res);
                        return log_error("setsockopt");
        }

#ifdef IPV6_V6ONLY
        if (res->ai_family == AF_INET6 && setsockopt(sock,
          IPPROTO_IPV6, IPV6_V6ONLY, (void *)&true, sizeof(true))) {
            freeaddrinfo(res);
            return log_error("setsockopt");
        }
#endif

        if (bind(sock, res-ai_addr, res-ai_addrlen)) {
            freeaddrinfo(res);
            return log_error("bind");
        }
        freeaddrinfo(res);
        if (listen(sock, MAX_BACKLOG))
                return log_error("listen");

        chdir("/"); setsid();

        switch (fork()) {
        case -1:
                return log_error("fork");

        case 0:
                break;

        default:
                return 0;
        }

        setsid();

        child_blocked = 1;
```

```
                        child_pending = 0;
                        signal(SIGCHLD, handle_child);

                        memset((void *)sessions, 0, sizeof(sessions));
                        new = 0;

                        while (1) {
                                child_blocked = 0;
                                if (child_pending) handle_child(0);

                                if (new > 0)
                                if (close(new)) return log_error("close");

                                addrlen = sizeof(addr);
                                new = accept(sock, (struct sockaddr *)&addr, &addrlen);

                                error = getnameinfo((struct sockaddr *)&addr, addrlen,
                                        hbuf, sizeof(hbuf), NULL, 0, NI_NUMERICHOST);
                                if (error)
                                        ; /* XXX */

        /*
         * I wish there was a portable way to classify errno's... In this case,
         * it appears to be better to risk eating up the CPU on a fatal error
         * rather than risk terminating the entire service because of a minor
         * temporary error having to do with one particular connection attempt.
         */
                                if (new 0) continue;

                                now = times(&buf);

                                child_blocked = 1;

                                j = -1; n = 0;
                                for (i = 0; i MAX_SESSIONS; i++) {
                                    if (sessions[i].start  now)
                                        sessions[i].start = 0;
                                if (sessions[i].pid ||
                                        (sessions[i].start &&
                                        now - sessions[i].start MIN_DELAY * CLK_TCK)) {
                                                if (strcmp(sessions[i].addr, hbuf) == 0)
                                                    if (++n = MAX_SESSIONS_PER_SOURCE)
                                                            break;
                                }
                                else
                                if (j < 0) j = i;
                        }

                                if (n >= MAX_SESSIONS_PER_SOURCE)
                                        { if (!sessions[i].log ||
                                            now < sessions[i].log ||
                                            now - sessions[i].log = MIN_DELAY *
                                                CLK_TCK) {
```

```
                                  syslog(SYSLOG_PRI_HI,
                                      "%s: per source limit reached",
                                      hbuf);
                                  sessions[i].log = now;
                          }
                          continue;
                  }

                  if (j < 0) {
                          syslog(SYSLOG_PRI_HI, "%s: sessions limit
                              reached",
                                  hbuf);
                          continue;

                  }

                  switch ((pid = fork())) {
                  case -1:
                          syslog(SYSLOG_PRI_ERROR, "%s: fork: %m", hbuf);
                          break;
                  case 0:
                          if (close(sock)) return log_error("close");
#if DAEMON_LIBWRAP
                          check_access(new);
#endif
                          syslog(SYSLOG_PRI_LO, "Session from %s",
                                  hbuf);
                          if (dup2(new, 0) < 0) return log_error("dup2");
                          if (dup2(new, 1) < 0) return log_error("dup2");
                          if (dup2(new, 2) < 0) return log_error("dup2");
                          if (close (new)) return log_error("close");
                          return do_pop_session();
                  default:
                          strlcpy(sessions[j].addr, hbuf,
                                  sizeof(sessions[j].addr));
                          (va_int)sessions[j].pid = pid;
                          sessions[j].start = now;
                          sessions[j].log = 0;
                  }
          }
  }

  #endif
```

Program 5.4   startup.c in popa3d package (after modification: bold portions are modified).

```
  /*
   * Command line option parsing.
   */

  #include "params.h"
```

```
#if POP_OPTIONS

#include <sys/socket.h>
#include <unistd.h>
#include <stdio.h>
#include <stdlib.h>

/* pop_root.c */
extern int do_pop_startup(void);
extern int do_pop_session(void);

/* standalone.c */
extern int do_standalone(void);

#ifdef HAVE_PROGNAME
extern char *__progname;
#define progname __progname #else
static char *progname;
#endif

int af = AF_INET;

static void usage(void)
{
        fprintf(stderr, "Usage: %s [-D]\n", progname);
        exit(1);
}

int main(int argc, char **argv) {
        int c;
        int standalone = 0;
#ifndef HAVE_PROGNAME
        if (!(progname = argv[0]))
                progname = POP_SERVER;
#endif

        while ((c = getopt(argc, argv, "D46")) != -1) {
                switch (c) {
                case 'D':
                        standalone++;
                        break;
                case '4':
                        af = AF_INET;
                        break;
                case '6':
                        af = AF_INET6;
                        break;

                default:
                        usage();
                }
        }
```

```
            if (optind != argc)
                    usage();

            if (standalone)
                    return do_standalone();

            if (do_pop_startup()) return 1;
            return do_pop_session();
    }

    #endif
```

A

Coming updates to IPv6 APIs

In the IETF and IEEE (Posix committee), there are efforts to revise IPv6-related APIs. Updates to RFC2553 is available as RFC3493. The only major change is the inclusion of IPV6_V6ONLY socket option. In this book we have already described IPV6_V6ONLY, and sample programs made use of it.

RFC2292/3542 defines advanced IPv6 API, as discussed previously.

RFC2553 and RFC2292 are not very useful with respect to manipulation of traffic class/flow label value on the IPv6 header. RFC3542 document defines ways to specify/inspect traffic class value. The API for flow label value is still unspecified, as the semantics for flow label itself is still under discussion (draft-ietf-ipv6-flow-label-07.txt). The following appendices contain:

B

RFC2553 "Basic Socket Interface Extensions for IPv6"

C

RFC3493 "Basic Socket Interface Extension for IPv6"

D

RFC2292 "Advanced Sockets API for IPv6"

E

RFC3542 "Advanced Sockets API for IPv6"

F

IPv4-Mapped Address API Considered Harmful

draft-cmetz-v6ops-v4mapped-api-harmful-00.txt

can be obtained from ftp://ftp.itojun.org/pub/paper/

G

IPv4-Mapped Addresses on the Wire Considered Harmful

draft-itojun-v6ops-v4mapped-harmful-01.txt

can be obtained from ftp://ftp.itojun.org/pub/paper/

H

Possible Abuse Against IPv6 Transition Technologies

draft-itojun-ipv6-transition-abuse-01.txt

can be obtained from ftp://ftp.itojun.org/pub/paper/

I

An Extension of Format for IPv6 Scoped Addresses

draft-ietf-ipngwg-scopedaddr-format-02.txt

The document is now integrated into draft-ietf-ipv6-scoping-arch-00.txt, how ever, the authors felt that the revision is more suitable for this book. Therefore, the revision is included here.

J

Protocol Independence Using the Sockets API

The paper was presented at USENIX annual conference, June 2000. The paper is included here under permission from USENIX and the author, Mr Craig Metz. The original paper can be found at the following URL: http://www.usenix.org/events/ usenix2000/freenix/metzprotoocl.html

B

RFC2553 "Basic Socket Interface Extensions for IPv6"

Network Working Group   R. Gilligan
Request for Comments: 2553   FreeGate
Obsoletes: 2133   S. Thomson
Category: Informational   Bellcore
                                                                J. Bound
                                                                  Compaq
                                                              W. Stevens
                                                              Consultant
                                                              March 1999

Basic Socket Interface Extensions for IPv6

Status of this Memo

Copyright Notice

Abstract

    The de facto standard application program interface (API) for TCP/IP
    applications is the "sockets" interface. Although this API was
    developed for Unix in the early 1980s it has also been implemented on
    a wide variety of non-Unix systems. TCP/IP applications written
    using the sockets API have in the past enjoyed a high degree of
    portability and we would like the same portability with IPv6
    applications. But changes are required to the sockets API to support
    IPv6 and this memo describes these changes. These include a new
    socket address structure to carry IPv6 addresses, new address
    conversion functions, and some new socket options. These extensions
    are designed to provide access to the basic IPv6 features required by
    TCP and UDP applications, including multicasting, while introducing a
    minimum of change into the system and providing complete
    compatibility for existing IPv4 applications. Additional extensions
    for advanced IPv6 features (raw sockets and access to the IPv6
    extension headers) are defined in another document [4].

RFC 2553   Basic Socket Interface Extensions for IPv6   March 1999

Table of Contents

RFC 2553   Basic Socket Interface Extensions for IPv6   March 1999

1. Introduction

While IPv4 addresses are 32 bits long, IPv6 interfaces are identified
by 128-bit addresses. The socket interface makes the size of an IP
address quite visible to an application; virtually all TCP/IP
applications for BSD-based systems have knowledge of the size of an
IP address. Those parts of the API that expose the addresses must be
changed to accommodate the larger IPv6 address size. IPv6 also
introduces new features (e.g., traffic class and flowlabel), some of
which must be made visible to applications via the API. This memo
defines a set of extensions to the socket interface to support the
larger address size and new features of IPv6.

2. Design Considerations

There are a number of important considerations in designing changes
to this well-worn API:

   - The API changes should provide both source and binary
     compatibility for programs written to the original API. That
     is, existing program binaries should continue to operate when
     run on a system supporting the new API. In addition, existing
     applications that are re-compiled and run on a system supporting
     the new API should continue to operate. Simply put, the API
     changes for IPv6 should not break existing programs. An
     additonal mechanism for implementations to verify this is to
     verify the new symbols are protected by Feature Test Macros as
     described in IEEE Std 1003.1. (Such Feature Test Macros are not
     defined by this RFC.)

   - The changes to the API should be as small as possible in order
     to simplify the task of converting existing IPv4 applications to
     IPv6.

   - Where possible, applications should be able to use this API to
     interoperate with both IPv6 and IPv4 hosts. Applications should
     not need to know which type of host they are communicating with.

   - IPv6 addresses carried in data structures should be 64-bit
     aligned. This is necessary in order to obtain optimum
     performance on 64-bit machine architectures.

Because of the importance of providing IPv4 compatibility in the API,
these extensions are explicitly designed to operate on machines that
provide complete support for both IPv4 and IPv6. A subset of this
API could probably be designed for operation on systems that support
only IPv6. However, this is not addressed in this memo.

Gilligan, et. al.   Informational   [Page 3]

RFC 2553   Basic Socket Interface Extensions for IPv6   March 1999

2.1 What Needs to be Changed

The socket interface API consists of a few distinct components:

- Core socket functions.

- Address data structures.

- Name-to-address translation functions.

- Address conversion functions.

The core socket functions -- those functions that deal with such
things as setting up and tearing down TCP connections, and sending
and receiving UDP packets -- were designed to be transport
independent. Where protocol addresses are passed as function
arguments, they are carried via opaque pointers. A protocol-specific
address data structure is defined for each protocol that the socket
functions support. Applications must cast pointers to these
protocol-specific address structures into pointers to the generic
"sockaddr" address structure when using the socket functions. These
functions need not change for IPv6, but a new IPv6-specific address
data structure is needed.

The "sockaddr_in" structure is the protocol-specific data structure
for IPv4. This data structure actually includes 8-octets of unused
space, and it is tempting to try to use this space to adapt the
sockaddr_in structure to IPv6. Unfortunately, the sockaddr_in
structure is not large enough to hold the 16-octet IPv6 address as
well as the other information (address family and port number) that
is needed. So a new address data structure must be defined for IPv6.

IPv6 addresses are scoped [2] so they could be link-local, site,
organization, global, or other scopes at this time undefined. To
support applications that want to be able to identify a set of
interfaces for a specific scope, the IPv6 sockaddr_in structure must
support a field that can be used by an implementation to identify a
set of interfaces identifying the scope for an IPv6 address.

The name-to-address translation functions in the socket interface are
gethostbyname() and gethostbyaddr(). These are left as is and new
functions are defined to support IPv4 and IPv6. Additionally, the
POSIX 1003.g draft [3] specifies a new nodename-to-address
translation function which is protocol independent. This function
can also be used with IPv4 and IPv6.

Gilligan, et. al.   Informational   [Page 4]

RFC 2553   Basic Socket Interface Extensions for IPv6   March 1999

The address conversion functions -- inet_ntoa() and inet_addr() --
convert IPv4 addresses between binary and printable form. These
functions are quite specific to 32-bit IPv4 addresses. We have
designed two analogous functions that convert both IPv4 and IPv6
addresses, and carry an address type parameter so that they can be
extended to other protocol families as well.

Finally, a few miscellaneous features are needed to support IPv6.
New interfaces are needed to support the IPv6 traffic class, flow
label, and hop limit header fields. New socket options are needed to
control the sending and receiving of IPv6 multicast packets.

The socket interface will be enhanced in the future to provide access
to other IPv6 features. These extensions are described in [4].

2.2 Data Types

The data types of the structure elements given in this memo are
intended to be examples, not absolute requirements. Whenever
possible, data types from Draft 6.6 (March 1997) of POSIX 1003.1g are
used: uintN_t means an unsigned integer of exactly N bits (e.g.,
uint16_t). We also assume the argument data types from 1003.1g when
possible (e.g., the final argument to setsockopt() is a size_t
value). Whenever buffer sizes are specified, the POSIX 1003.1 size_t
data type is used (e.g., the two length arguments to getnameinfo()).

2.3 Headers

When function prototypes and structures are shown we show the headers
that must be #included to cause that item to be defined.

2.4 Structures

When structures are described the members shown are the ones that
must appear in an implementation. Additional, nonstandard members
may also be defined by an implementation. As an additional
precaution nonstandard members could be verified by Feature Test
Macros as described in IEEE Std 1003.1.   (Such Feature Test Macros
are not defined by this RFC.)

The ordering shown for the members of a structure is the recommended
ordering, given alignment considerations of multibyte members, but an
implementation may order the members differently.

Gilligan, et. al.   Informational   [Page 5]

RFC 2553   Basic Socket Interface Extensions for IPv6   March 1999

3. Socket Interface

This section specifies the socket interface changes for IPv6.

3.1 IPv6 Address Family and Protocol Family

A new address family name, AF_INET6, is defined in <sys/socket.h>.
The AF_INET6 definition distinguishes between the original
sockaddr_in address data structure, and the new sockaddr_in6 data
structure.

A new protocol family name, PF_INET6, is defined in <sys/socket.h>.
Like most of the other protocol family names, this will usually be
defined to have the same value as the corresponding address family
name:

    #define PF_INET6   AF_INET6

The PF_INET6 is used in the first argument to the socket() function
to indicate that an IPv6 socket is being created.

3.2 IPv6 Address Structure

A new in6_addr structure holds a single IPv6 address and is defined
as a result of including <netinet/in.h>:

    struct in6_addr {
        uint8_t s6_addr[16];   /* IPv6 address */
    };

This data structure contains an array of sixteen 8-bit elements,
which make up one 128-bit IPv6 address. The IPv6 address is stored
in network byte order.

The structure in6_addr above is usually implemented with an embedded
union with extra fields that force the desired alignment level in a
manner similar to BSD implementations of "struct in_addr". Those
additional implementation details are omitted here for simplicity.

An example is as follows:

Gilligan, et. al.   Informational   [Page 6]

```
struct in6_addr {
    union {
        uint8_t  _S6_u8[16];
        uint32_t _S6_u32[4];
        uint64_t _S6_u64[2];
    } _S6_un;
};
#define s6_addr _S6_un._S6_u8
```

3.3 Socket Address Structure for 4.3BSD-Based Systems

In the socket interface, a different protocol-specific data structure is defined to carry the addresses for each protocol suite. Each protocol- specific data structure is designed so it can be cast into a protocol- independent data structure -- the "sockaddr" structure. Each has a "family" field that overlays the "sa_family" of the sockaddr data structure. This field identifies the type of the data structure.

The sockaddr_in structure is the protocol-specific address data structure for IPv4. It is used to pass addresses between applications and the system in the socket functions. The following sockaddr_in6 structure holds IPv6 addresses and is defined as a result of including the <netinet/in.h> header:

```
struct sockaddr_in6 {
    sa_family_t     sin6_family;    /* AF_INET6 */
    in_port_t       sin6_port;      /* transport layer port # */
    uint32_t        sin6_flowinfo;  /* IPv6 traffic class & flow info */
    struct in6_addr sin6_addr;      /* IPv6 address */
    uint32_t        sin6_scope_id;  /* set of interfaces for a scope */
};
```

This structure is designed to be compatible with the sockaddr data structure used in the 4.3BSD release.

The sin6_family field identifies this as a sockaddr_in6 structure. This field overlays the sa_family field when the buffer is cast to a sockaddr data structure. The value of this field must be AF_INET6.

The sin6_port field contains the 16-bit UDP or TCP port number. This field is used in the same way as the sin_port field of the sockaddr_in structure. The port number is stored in network byte order.

The sin6_flowinfo field is a 32-bit field that contains two pieces of
information: the traffic class and the flow label. The contents and
interpretation of this member is specified in [1]. The sin6_flowinfo
field SHOULD be set to zero by an implementation prior to using the
sockaddr_in6 structure by an application on receive operations.

The sin6_addr field is a single in6_addr structure (defined in the
previous section). This field holds one 128-bit IPv6 address. The
address is stored in network byte order.

The ordering of elements in this structure is specifically designed
so that when sin6_addr field is aligned on a 64-bit boundary, the
start of the structure will also be aligned on a 64-bit boundary.
This is done for optimum performance on 64-bit architectures.

The sin6_scope_id field is a 32-bit integer that identifies a set of
interfaces as appropriate for the scope of the address carried in the
sin6_addr field. For a link scope sin6_addr sin6_scope_id would be
an interface index. For a site scope sin6_addr, sin6_scope_id would
be a site identifier. The mapping of sin6_scope_id to an interface
or set of interfaces is left to implementation and future
specifications on the subject of site identifiers.

Notice that the sockaddr_in6 structure will normally be larger than
the generic sockaddr structure. On many existing implementations the
sizeof(struct sockaddr_in) equals sizeof(struct sockaddr), with both
being 16 bytes. Any existing code that makes this assumption needs
to be examined carefully when converting to IPv6.

3.4 Socket Address Structure for 4.4BSD-Based Systems

The 4.4BSD release includes a small, but incompatible change to the
socket interface. The "sa_family" field of the sockaddr data
structure was changed from a 16-bit value to an 8-bit value, and the
space saved used to hold a length field, named "sa_len". The
sockaddr_in6 data structure given in the previous section cannot be
correctly cast into the newer sockaddr data structure. For this
reason, the following alternative IPv6 address data structure is
provided to be used on systems based on 4.4BSD. It is defined as a
result of including the <netinet/in.h> header.

RFC 2553   Basic Socket Interface Extensions for IPv6   March 1999

```
struct sockaddr_in6 {
    uint8_t        sin6_len;        /* length of this struct */
    sa_family_t    sin6_family;     /* AF_INET6 */
    in_port_t      sin6_port;       /* transport layer port # */
    uint32_t       sin6_flowinfo;   /* IPv6 flow information */
    struct in6_addr sin6_addr;      /* IPv6 address */
    uint32_t       sin6_scope_id;   /* set of interfaces for a scope */
};
```

The only differences between this data structure and the 4.3BSD
variant are the inclusion of the length field, and the change of the
family field to a 8-bit data type. The definitions of all the other
fields are identical to the structure defined in the previous
section.

Systems that provide this version of the sockaddr_in6 data structure
must also declare SIN6_LEN as a result of including the
<netinet/in.h> header. This macro allows applications to determine
whether they are being built on a system that supports the 4.3BSD or
4.4BSD variants of the data structure.

3.5 The Socket Functions

Applications call the socket() function to create a socket descriptor
that represents a communication endpoint. The arguments to the
socket() function tell the system which protocol to use, and what
format address structure will be used in subsequent functions. For
example, to create an IPv4/TCP socket, applications make the call:

    s = socket(PF_INET, SOCK_STREAM, 0);

To create an IPv4/UDP socket, applications make the call:

    s = socket(PF_INET, SOCK_DGRAM, 0);

Applications may create IPv6/TCP and IPv6/UDP sockets by simply using
the constant PF_INET6 instead of PF_INET in the first argument. For
example, to create an IPv6/TCP socket, applications make the call:

    s = socket(PF_INET6, SOCK_STREAM, 0);

To create an IPv6/UDP socket, applications make the call:

    s = socket(PF_INET6, SOCK_DGRAM, 0);

Gilligan, et. al.   Informational   [Page 9]

Once the application has created a PF_INET6 socket, it must use the
sockaddr_in6 address structure when passing addresses in to the
system. The functions that the application uses to pass addresses
into the system are:

    bind()
    connect()
    sendmsg()
    sendto()

The system will use the sockaddr_in6 address structure to return
addresses to applications that are using PF_INET6 sockets. The
functions that return an address from the system to an application
are:

    accept()
    recvfrom()
    recvmsg()
    getpeername()
    getsockname()

No changes to the syntax of the socket functions are needed to
support IPv6, since all of the "address carrying" functions use an
opaque address pointer, and carry an address length as a function
argument.

3.6 Compatibility with IPv4 Applications

In order to support the large base of applications using the original
API, system implementations must provide complete source and binary
compatibility with the original API. This means that systems must
continue to support PF_INET sockets and the sockaddr_in address
structure. Applications must be able to create IPv4/TCP and IPv4/UDP
sockets using the PF_INET constant in the socket() function, as
described in the previous section. Applications should be able to
hold a combination of IPv4/TCP, IPv4/UDP, IPv6/TCP and IPv6/UDP
sockets simultaneously within the same process.

Applications using the original API should continue to operate as
they did on systems supporting only IPv4. That is, they should
continue to interoperate with IPv4 nodes.

3.7 Compatibility with IPv4 Nodes

The API also provides a different type of compatibility: the ability
for IPv6 applications to interoperate with IPv4 applications. This
feature uses the IPv4-mapped IPv6 address format defined in the IPv6
addressing architecture specification [2]. This address format

RFC 2553   Basic Socket Interface Extensions for IPv6   March 1999

allows the IPv4 address of an IPv4 node to be represented as an IPv6
address. The IPv4 address is encoded into the low-order 32 bits of
the IPv6 address, and the high-order 96 bits hold the fixed prefix
0:0:0:0:0:FFFF. IPv4- mapped addresses are written as follows:

    ::FFFF:<IPv4-address>

These addresses can be generated automatically by the
getipnodebyname() function when the specified host has only IPv4
addresses (as described in Section 6.1).

Applications may use PF_INET6 sockets to open TCP connections to IPv4
nodes, or send UDP packets to IPv4 nodes, by simply encoding the
destination's IPv4 address as an IPv4-mapped IPv6 address, and
passing that address, within a sockaddr_in6 structure, in the
connect() or sendto() call. When applications use PF_INET6 sockets
to accept TCP connections from IPv4 nodes, or receive UDP packets
from IPv4 nodes, the system returns the peer's address to the
application in the accept(), recvfrom(), or getpeername() call using
a sockaddr_in6 structure encoded this way.

Few applications will likely need to know which type of node they are
interoperating with. However, for those applications that do need to
know, the IN6_IS_ADDR_V4MAPPED() macro, defined in Section 6.7, is
provided.

3.8 IPv6 Wildcard Address

While the bind() function allows applications to select the source IP
address of UDP packets and TCP connections, applications often want
the system to select the source address for them. With IPv4, one
specifies the address as the symbolic constant INADDR_ANY (called the
"wildcard" address) in the bind() call, or simply omits the bind()
entirely.

Since the IPv6 address type is a structure (struct in6_addr), a
symbolic constant can be used to initialize an IPv6 address variable,
but cannot be used in an assignment. Therefore systems provide the
IPv6 wildcard address in two forms.

The first version is a global variable named "in6addr_any" that is an
in6_addr structure. The extern declaration for this variable is
defined in <netinet/in.h>:

    extern const struct in6_addr in6addr_any;

Gilligan, et. al.   Informational   [Page 11]

Applications use in6addr_any similarly to the way they use INADDR_ANY
in IPv4. For example, to bind a socket to port number 23, but let
the system select the source address, an application could use the
following code:

```
struct sockaddr_in6 sin6;
 . . .
sin6.sin6_family = AF_INET6;
sin6.sin6_flowinfo = 0;
sin6.sin6_port = htons(23);
sin6.sin6_addr = in6addr_any;  /* structure assignment */
 . . .
if (bind(s, (struct sockaddr *) &sin6, sizeof(sin6)) == -1)
         . . .
```

The other version is a symbolic constant named IN6ADDR_ANY_INIT and
is defined in <netinet/in.h>. This constant can be used to
initialize an in6_addr structure:

```
struct in6_addr anyaddr = IN6ADDR_ANY_INIT;
```

Note that this constant can be used ONLY at declaration time. It can
not be used to assign a previously declared in6_addr structure. For
example, the following code will not work:

```
/* This is the WRONG way to assign an unspecified address */
struct sockaddr_in6 sin6;
 . . .
sin6.sin6_addr = IN6ADDR_ANY_INIT; /* will NOT compile */
```

Be aware that the IPv4 INADDR_xxx constants are all defined in host
byte order but the IPv6 IN6ADDR_xxx constants and the IPv6
in6addr_xxx externals are defined in network byte order.

3.9 IPv6 Loopback Address

Applications may need to send UDP packets to, or originate TCP
connections to, services residing on the local node. In IPv4, they
can do this by using the constant IPv4 address INADDR_LOOPBACK in
their connect(), sendto(), or sendmsg() call.

IPv6 also provides a loopback address to contact local TCP and UDP
services. Like the unspecified address, the IPv6 loopback address is
provided in two forms -- a global variable and a symbolic constant.

RFC 2553   Basic Socket Interface Extensions for IPv6   March 1999

The global variable is an in6_addr structure named
"in6addr_loopback." The extern declaration for this variable is
defined in <netinet/in.h>:

    extern const struct in6_addr in6addr_loopback;

Applications use in6addr_loopback as they would use INADDR_LOOPBACK
in IPv4 applications (but beware of the byte ordering difference
mentioned at the end of the previous section). For example, to open
a TCP connection to the local telnet server, an application could use
the following code:

    struct sockaddr_in6 sin6;
    . . .
    sin6.sin6_family = AF_INET6;
    sin6.sin6_flowinfo = 0;
    sin6.sin6_port = htons(23);
    sin6.sin6_addr = in6addr_loopback; /* structure assignment */
    . . .
    if (connect(s, (struct sockaddr *) &sin6, sizeof(sin6)) == -1)
            . . .

The symbolic constant is named IN6ADDR_LOOPBACK_INIT and is defined
in <netinet/in.h>. It can be used at declaration time ONLY; for
example:

    struct in6_addr loopbackaddr = IN6ADDR_LOOPBACK_INIT;

Like IN6ADDR_ANY_INIT, this constant cannot be used in an assignment
to a previously declared IPv6 address variable.

3.10 Portability Additions

One simple addition to the sockets API that can help application
writers is the "struct sockaddr_storage". This data structure can
simplify writing code portable across multiple address families and
platforms. This data structure is designed with the following goals.

  - It has a large enough implementation specific maximum size to
    store the desired set of protocol specific socket address data
    structures. Specifically, it is at least large enough to
    accommodate sockaddr_in and sockaddr_in6 and possibly other
    protocol specific socket addresses too.
  - It is aligned at an appropriate boundary so protocol specific
    socket address data structure pointers can be cast to it and
    access their fields without alignment problems. (e.g. pointers
    to sockaddr_in6 and/or sockaddr_in can be cast to it and access
    fields without alignment problems).

- It has the initial field(s) isomorphic to the fields of the
  "struct sockaddr" data structure on that implementation which
  can be used as a discriminants for deriving the protocol in use.
  These initial field(s) would on most implementations either be a
  single field of type "sa_family_t" (isomorphic to sa_family
  field, 16 bits) or two fields of type uint8_t and sa_family_t
  respectively, (isomorphic to sa_len and sa_family_t, 8 bits
  each).

An example implementation design of such a data structure would be as
follows.

```
/*
 * Desired design of maximum size and alignment
 */
#define _SS_MAXSIZE     128  /* Implementation specific max size */
#define _SS_ALIGNSIZE   (sizeof (int64_t))
                        /* Implementation specific desired alignment */
/*
 * Definitions used for sockaddr_storage structure paddings design.
 */
#define _SS_PAD1SIZE    (_SS_ALIGNSIZE - sizeof (sa_family_t))
#define _SS_PAD2SIZE    (_SS_MAXSIZE - (sizeof (sa_family_t)+
                                _SS_PAD1SIZE + _SS_ALIGNSIZE))
struct sockaddr_storage {
    sa_family_t  __ss_family;     /* address family */
    /* Following fields are implementation specific */
    char        __ss_pad1[_SS_PAD1SIZE];
                /* 6 byte pad, this is to make implementation
                /* specific pad up to alignment field that */
                /* follows explicit in the data structure */
    int64_t     __ss_align;     /* field to force desired structure */
                /* storage alignment */
    char        __ss_pad2[_SS_PAD2SIZE];
                /* 112 byte pad to achieve desired size, */
                /* _SS_MAXSIZE value minus size of ss_family */
                /* __ss_pad1, __ss_align fields is 112 */
};
```

On implementations where sockaddr data structure includes a "sa_len",
field this data structure would look like this:

```
/*
 * Definitions used for sockaddr_storage structure paddings design.
 */
#define _SS_PAD1SIZE ( SS_ALIGNSIZE -
                            (sizeof (uint8_t) + sizeof (sa_family_t))
#define _SS_PAD2SIZE (_SS_MAXSIZE - (sizeof (sa_family_t)+
```

```
                                _SS_PAD1SIZE + _SS_ALIGNSIZE))
struct sockaddr_storage {
    uint8_t      __ss_len;        /* address length */
    sa_family_t  __ss_family;     /* address family */
    /* Following fields are implementation specific */
    char         __ss_pad1[_SS_PAD1SIZE];
                     /* 6 byte pad, this is to make implementation
                     /* specific pad up to alignment field that */
                     /* follows explicit in the data structure */
    int64_t      __ss_align;  /* field to force desired structure */
                     /* storage alignment */
    char         __ss_pad2[_SS_PAD2SIZE];
                     /* 112 byte pad to achieve desired size, */
                     /* _SS_MAXSIZE value minus size of ss_len, */
                     /* __ss_family, __ss_pad1, __ss_align fields is 112 */
};
```

The above example implementation illustrates a data structure which
will align on a 64 bit boundary. An implementation specific field
"__ss_align" along "__ss_pad1" is used to force a 64-bit alignment
which covers proper alignment good enough for needs of sockaddr_in6
(IPv6), sockaddr_in (IPv4) address data structures. The size of
padding fields __ss_pad1 depends on the chosen alignment boundary.
The size of padding field __ss_pad2 depends on the value of overall
size chosen for the total size of the structure. This size and
alignment are represented in the above example by implementation
specific (not required) constants _SS_MAXSIZE (chosen value 128) and
_SS_ALIGNMENT (with chosen value 8).   Constants _SS_PAD1SIZE (derived
value 6) and _SS_PAD2SIZE (derived value 112) are also for
illustration and not required.   The implementation specific
definitions and structure field names above start with an underscore
to denote implementation private namespace.   Portable code is not
expected to access or reference those fields or constants.

The sockaddr_storage structure solves the problem of declaring
storage for automatic variables which is large enough and aligned
enough for storing socket address data structure of any family. For
example, code with a file descriptor and without the context of the
address family can pass a pointer to a variable of this type where a
pointer to a socket address structure is expected in calls such as
getpeername() and determine the address family by accessing the
received content after the call.

The sockaddr_storage structure may also be useful and applied to
certain other interfaces where a generic socket address large enough
and aligned for use with multiple address families may be needed. A
discussion of those interfaces is outside the scope of this document.

Also, much existing code assumes that any socket address structure
can fit in a generic sockaddr structure. While this has been true
for IPv4 socket address structures, it has always been false for Unix
domain socket address structures (but in practice this has not been a
problem) and it is also false for IPv6 socket address structures
(which can be a problem).

So now an application can do the following:

```
struct sockaddr_storage __ss;
struct sockaddr_in6 *sin6;
sin6 = (struct sockaddr_in6 *) &__ss;
```

4. Interface Identification

This API uses an interface index (a small positive integer) to
identify the local interface on which a multicast group is joined
(Section 5.3). Additionally, the advanced API [4] uses these same
interface indexes to identify the interface on which a datagram is
received, or to specify the interface on which a datagram is to be
sent.

Interfaces are normally known by names such as "le0", "sl1", "ppp2",
and the like. On Berkeley-derived implementations, when an interface
is made known to the system, the kernel assigns a unique positive
integer value (called the interface index) to that interface. These
are small positive integers that start at 1. (Note that 0 is never
used for an interface index.) There may be gaps so that there is no
current interface for a particular positive interface index.

This API defines two functions that map between an interface name and
index, a third function that returns all the interface names and
indexes, and a fourth function to return the dynamic memory allocated
by the previous function. How these functions are implemented is
left up to the implementation. 4.4BSD implementations can implement
these functions using the existing sysctl() function with the
NET_RT_IFLIST command. Other implementations may wish to use ioctl()
for this purpose.

4.1 Name-to-Index

The first function maps an interface name into its corresponding
index.

```
#include <net/if.h>

unsigned int  if_nametoindex(const char *ifname);
```

Gilligan, et. al.   Informational   [Page 16]

RFC 2553   Basic Socket Interface Extensions for IPv6   March 1999

If the specified interface name does not exist, the return value is
0, and errno is set to ENXIO. If there was a system error (such as
running out of memory), the return value is 0 and errno is set to the
proper value (e.g., ENOMEM).

4.2 Index-to-Name

The second function maps an interface index into its corresponding
name.

```
#include <net/if.h>

char  *if_indextoname(unsigned int ifindex, char *ifname);
```

The ifname argument must point to a buffer of at least IF_NAMESIZE
bytes into which the interface name corresponding to the specified
index is returned. (IF_NAMESIZE is also defined in <net/if.h> and
its value includes a terminating null byte at the end of the
interface name.) This pointer is also the return value of the
function. If there is no interface corresponding to the specified
index, NULL is returned, and errno is set to ENXIO, if there was a
system error (such as running out of memory), if_indextoname returns
NULL and errno would be set to the proper value (e.g., ENOMEM).

4.3 Return All Interface Names and Indexes

The if_nameindex structure holds the information about a single
interface and is defined as a result of including the <net/if.h>
header.

```
struct if_nameindex {
  unsigned int    if_index; /* 1, 2, ... */
  char           *if_name;  /* null terminated name: "le0", ... */
};
```

The final function returns an array of if_nameindex structures, one
structure per interface.

```
struct if_nameindex  *if_nameindex(void);
```

The end of the array of structures is indicated by a structure with
an if_index of 0 and an if_name of NULL. The function returns a NULL
pointer upon an error, and would set errno to the appropriate value.

The memory used for this array of structures along with the interface
names pointed to by the if_name members is obtained dynamically.
This memory is freed by the next function.

RFC 2553   Basic Socket Interface Extensions for IPv6   March 1999

4.4 Free Memory

The following function frees the dynamic memory that was allocated by
if_nameindex().

    #include <net/if.h>

    void if_freenameindex(struct if_nameindex *ptr);

The argument to this function must be a pointer that was returned by
if_nameindex().

Currently net/if.h doesn't have prototype definitions for functions
and it is recommended that these definitions be defined in net/if.h
as well and the struct if_nameindex{}.

5. Socket Options

A number of new socket options are defined for IPv6. All of these
new options are at the IPPROTO_IPV6 level. That is, the "level"
parameter in the getsockopt() and setsockopt() calls is IPPROTO_IPV6
when using these options. The constant name prefix IPV6_ is used in
all of the new socket options. This serves to clearly identify these
options as applying to IPv6.

The declaration for IPPROTO_IPV6, the new IPv6 socket options, and
related constants defined in this section are obtained by including
the header <netinet/in.h>.

5.1 Unicast Hop Limit

A new setsockopt() option controls the hop limit used in outgoing
unicast IPv6 packets. The name of this option is IPV6_UNICAST_HOPS,
and it is used at the IPPROTO_IPV6 layer. The following example
illustrates how it is used:

    int hoplimit = 10;

    if (setsockopt(s, IPPROTO_IPV6, IPV6_UNICAST_HOPS,
                    (char *) &hoplimit, sizeof(hoplimit)) == -1)
        perror("setsockopt IPV6_UNICAST_HOPS");

When the IPV6_UNICAST_HOPS option is set with setsockopt(), the
option value given is used as the hop limit for all subsequent
unicast packets sent via that socket. If the option is not set, the
system selects a default value. The integer hop limit value (called
x) is interpreted as follows:

Gilligan, et. al.   Informational   [Page 18]

```
    x < -1:         return an error of EINVAL
    x == -1:        use kernel default
    0 <= x <= 255:  use x
    x >= 256:       return an error of EINVAL
```

The IPV6_UNICAST_HOPS option may be used with getsockopt() to
determine the hop limit value that the system will use for subsequent
unicast packets sent via that socket. For example:

```
    int  hoplimit;
    size_t  len = sizeof(hoplimit);

    if (getsockopt(s, IPPROTO_IPV6, IPV6_UNICAST_HOPS,
                (char *) &hoplimit, &len) == -1)
        perror("getsockopt IPV6_UNICAST_HOPS");
    else
        printf("Using %d for hop limit.¥n", hoplimit);
```

5.2 Sending and Receiving Multicast Packets

IPv6 applications may send UDP multicast packets by simply specifying
an IPv6 multicast address in the address argument of the sendto()
function.

Three socket options at the IPPROTO_IPV6 layer control some of the
parameters for sending multicast packets. Setting these options is
not required: applications may send multicast packets without using
these options. The setsockopt() options for controlling the sending
of multicast packets are summarized below. These three options can
also be used with getsockopt().

    IPV6_MULTICAST_IF

        Set the interface to use for outgoing multicast packets. The
        argument is the index of the interface to use.

        Argument type: unsigned int

    IPV6_MULTICAST_HOPS

        Set the hop limit to use for outgoing multicast packets. (Note
        a separate option - IPV6_UNICAST_HOPS - is provided to set the
        hop limit to use for outgoing unicast packets.)

        The interpretation of the argument is the same as for the
        IPV6_UNICAST_HOPS option:

```
x < -1:          return an error of EINVAL
x == -1:         use kernel default
0 <= x <= 255:   use x
x >= 256:        return an error of EINVAL
```

If IPV6_MULTICAST_HOPS is not set, the default is 1
(same as IPv4 today)

Argument type: int

IPV6_MULTICAST_LOOP

If a multicast datagram is sent to a group to which the sending
host itself belongs (on the outgoing interface), a copy of the
datagram is looped back by the IP layer for local delivery if
this option is set to 1. If this option is set to 0 a copy
is not looped back. Other option values return an error of
EINVAL.

If IPV6_MULTICAST_LOOP is not set, the default is 1 (loopback;
same as IPv4 today).

Argument type: unsigned int

The reception of multicast packets is controlled by the two
setsockopt() options summarized below. An error of EOPNOTSUPP is
returned if these two options are used with getsockopt().

IPV6_JOIN_GROUP

Join a multicast group on a specified local interface. If the
interface index is specified as 0, the kernel chooses the local
interface. For example, some kernels look up the multicast
group in the normal IPv6 routing table and using the resulting
interface.

Argument type: struct ipv6_mreq

IPV6_LEAVE_GROUP

Leave a multicast group on a specified interface.

Argument type: struct ipv6_mreq

The argument type of both of these options is the ipv6_mreq structure,
defined as a result of including the <netinet/in.h> header;

RFC 2553   Basic Socket Interface Extensions for IPv6   March 1999

```
struct ipv6_mreq {
    struct in6_addr ipv6mr_multiaddr; /* IPv6 multicast addr */
    unsigned int    ipv6mr_interface; /* interface index */
};
```

Note that to receive multicast datagrams a process must join the
multicast group and bind the UDP port to which datagrams will be
sent. Some processes also bind the multicast group address to the
socket, in addition to the port, to prevent other datagrams destined
to that same port from being delivered to the socket.

6. Library Functions

New library functions are needed to perform a variety of operations
with IPv6 addresses. Functions are needed to lookup IPv6 addresses
in the Domain Name System (DNS). Both forward lookup (nodename-to-
address translation) and reverse lookup (address-to-nodename
translation) need to be supported. Functions are also needed to
convert IPv6 addresses between their binary and textual form.

We note that the two existing functions, gethostbyname() and
gethostbyaddr(), are left as-is. New functions are defined to handle
both IPv4 and IPv6 addresses.

6.1 Nodename-to-Address Translation

The commonly used function gethostbyname() is inadequate for many
applications, first because it provides no way for the caller to
specify anything about the types of addresses desired (IPv4 only,
IPv6 only, IPv4-mapped IPv6 are OK, etc.), and second because many
implementations of this function are not thread safe. RFC 2133
defined a function named gethostbyname2() but this function was also
inadequate, first because its use required setting a global option
(RES_USE_INET6) when IPv6 addresses were required, and second because
a flag argument is needed to provide the caller with additional
control over the types of addresses required.

The following function is new and must be thread safe:

```
#include <sys/socket.h>
#include <netdb.h>

struct hostent *getipnodebyname(const char *name, int af, int flags
                                int *error_num);
```

The name argument can be either a node name or a numeric address
string (i.e., a dotted-decimal IPv4 address or an IPv6 hex address).
The af argument specifies the address family, either AF_INET or

Gilligan, et. al.   Informational   [Page 21]

AF_INET6. The error_num value is returned to the caller, via a
pointer, with the appropriate error code in error_num, to support
thread safe error code returns. error_num will be set to one of the
following values:

HOST_NOT_FOUND

No such host is known.

NO_ADDRESS

The server recognised the request and the name but no address is
available. Another type of request to the name server for the
domain might return an answer.

NO_RECOVERY

An unexpected server failure occurred which cannot be recovered.

TRY_AGAIN

A temporary and possibly transient error occurred, such as a
failure of a server to respond.

The flags argument specifies the types of addresses that are searched
for, and the types of addresses that are returned. We note that a
special flags value of AI_DEFAULT (defined below) should handle most
applications.

That is, porting simple applications to use IPv6 replaces the call

    hptr = gethostbyname(name);

with

    hptr = getipnodebyname(name, AF_INET6, AI_DEFAULT, &error_num);

and changes any subsequent error diagnosis code to use error_num
instead of externally declared variables, such as h_errno.

Applications desiring finer control over the types of addresses
searched for and returned, can specify other combinations of the
flags argument.

RFC 2553   Basic Socket Interface Extensions for IPv6   March 1999

A flags of 0 implies a strict interpretation of the af argument:

  - If flags is 0 and af is AF_INET, then the caller wants only
    IPv4 addresses. A query is made for A records. If successful,
    the IPv4 addresses are returned and the h_length member of the
    hostent structure will be 4, else the function returns a NULL
    pointer.

  - If flags is 0 and if af is AF_INET6, then the caller wants only
    IPv6 addresses. A query is made for AAAA records. If
    successful, the IPv6 addresses are returned and the h_length
    member of the hostent structure will be 16, else the function
    returns a NULL pointer.

Other constants can be logically-ORed into the flags argument, to
modify the behavior of the function.

  - If the AI_V4MAPPED flag is specified along with an af of
    AF_INET6, then the caller will accept IPv4-mapped IPv6
    addresses. That is, if no AAAA records are found then a query
    is made for A records and any found are returned as IPv4-mapped
    IPv6 addresses (h_length will be 16). The AI_V4MAPPED flag is
    ignored unless af equals AF_INET6.

  - The AI_ALL flag is used in conjunction with the AI_V4MAPPED
    flag, and is only used with the IPv6 address family. When AI_ALL
    is logically or'd with AI_V4MAPPED flag then the caller wants
    all addresses: IPv6 and IPv4-mapped IPv6. A query is first made
    for AAAA records and if successful, the IPv6 addresses are
    returned. Another query is then made for A records and any found
    are returned as IPv4-mapped IPv6 addresses. h_length will be 16.
    Only if both queries fail does the function return a NULL pointer.
    This flag is ignored unless af equals AF_INET6.

  - The AI_ADDRCONFIG flag specifies that a query for AAAA records
    should occur only if the node has at least one IPv6 source
    address configured and a query for A records should occur only
    if the node has at least one IPv4 source address configured.

    For example, if the node has no IPv6 source addresses
    configured, and af equals AF_INET6, and the node name being
    looked up has both AAAA and A records, then:

        (a) if only AI_ADDRCONFIG is specified, the function
            returns a NULL pointer;
        (b) if AI_ADDRCONFIG | AI_V4MAPPED is specified, the A
            records are returned as IPv4-mapped IPv6 addresses;

The special flags value of AI_DEFAULT is defined as

    #dcfinc AI_DEFAULT (AI_V4MAPPED | AI_ADDRCONFIG)

We noted that the getipnodebyname() function must allow the name
argument to be either a node name or a literal address string (i.e.,
a dotted-decimal IPv4 address or an IPv6 hex address). This saves
applications from having to call inet_pton() to handle literal
address strings.

There are four scenarios based on the type of literal address string
and the value of the af argument.

The two simple cases are:

When name is a dotted-decimal IPv4 address and af equals AF_INET, or
when name is an IPv6 hex address and af equals AF_INET6. The members
of the returned hostent structure are: h_name points to a copy of the
name argument, h_aliases is a NULL pointer, h_addrtype is a copy of
the af argument, h_length is either 4 (for AF_INET) or 16 (for
AF_INET6), h_addr_list[0] is a pointer to the 4-byte or 16-byte
binary address, and h_addr_list[1] is a NULL pointer.

When name is a dotted-decimal IPv4 address and af equals AF_INET6,
and flags equals AI_V4MAPPED, an IPv4-mapped IPv6 address is
returned: h_name points to an IPv6 hex address containing the IPv4-
mapped IPv6 address, h_aliases is a NULL pointer, h_addrtype is
AF_INET6, h_length is 16, h_addr_list[0] is a pointer to the 16-byte
binary address, and h_addr_list[1] is a NULL pointer. If AI_V4MAPPED
is set (with or without AI_ALL) return IPv4-mapped otherwise return
NULL.

It is an error when name is an IPv6 hex address and af equals
AF_INET. The function's return value is a NULL pointer and error_num
equals HOST_NOT_FOUND.

6.2 Address-To-Nodename Translation

The following function has the same arguments as the existing
gethostbyaddr() function, but adds an error number.

    #include <sys/socket.h> #include <netdb.h>

    struct hostent *getipnodebyaddr(const void *src, size_t len,
                                    int af, int *error_num);

RFC 2553   Basic Socket Interface Extensions for IPv6   March 1999

As with getipnodebyname(), getipnodebyaddr() must be thread safe.
The error_num value is returned to the caller with the appropriate
error code, to support thread safe error code returns. The following
error conditions may be returned for error_num:

HOST_NOT_FOUND

    No such host is known.

NO_ADDRESS

    The server recognized the request and the name but no address
    is available. Another type of request to the name server for
    the domain might return an answer.

NO_RECOVERY

    An unexpected server failure occurred which cannot be
    recovered.

TRY_AGAIN

    A temporary and possibly transient error occurred, such as a
    failure of a server to respond.

One possible source of confusion is the handling of IPv4-mapped IPv6
addresses and IPv4-compatible IPv6 addresses, but the following logic
should apply.

    1. If af is AF_INET6, and if len equals 16, and if the IPv6
        address is an IPv4-mapped IPv6 address or an IPv4-compatible
        IPv6 address, then skip over the first 12 bytes of the IPv6
        address, set af to AF_INET, and set len to 4.

    2. If af is AF_INET, lookup the name for the given IPv4 address
        (e.g., query for a PTR record in the in-addr.arpa domain).

    3. If af is AF_INET6, lookup the name for the given IPv6 address
        (e.g., query for a PTR record in the ip6.int domain).

    4. If the function is returning success, then the single address
        that is returned in the hostent structure is a copy of the
        first argument to the function with the same address family
        that was passed as an argument to this function.

All four steps listed are performed, in order. Also note that the
IPv6 hex addresses "::" and "::1" MUST NOT be treated as IPv4-
compatible addresses, and if the address is "::", HOST_NOT_FOUND MUST
be returned and a query of the address not performed.

Also for the macro in section 6.7 IN6_IS_ADDR_V4COMPAT MUST return
false for "::" and "::1".

6.3 Freeing memory for getipnodebyname and getipnodebyaddr

The hostent structure does not change from its existing definition.
This structure, and the information pointed to by this structure, are
dynamically allocated by getipnodebyname and getipnodebyaddr. The
following function frees this memory:

    #include <netdb.h>

    void freehostent(struct hostent *ptr);

6.4 Protocol-Independent Nodename and Service Name Translation

Nodename-to-address translation is done in a protocol-independent
fashion using the getaddrinfo() function that is taken from the
Institute of Electrical and Electronic Engineers (IEEE) POSIX 1003.1g
(Protocol Independent Interfaces) draft specification [3].

The official specification for this function will be the final POSIX
standard, with the following additional requirements:

    - getaddrinfo() (along with the getnameinfo() function described
       in the next section) must be thread safe.

    - The AI_NUMERICHOST is new with this document.

    - All fields in socket address structures returned by
       getaddrinfo() that are not filled in through an explicit
       argument (e.g., sin6_flowinfo and sin_zero) must be set to 0.
       (This makes it easier to compare socket address structures.)

    - getaddrinfo() must fill in the length field of a socket address
       structure (e.g., sin6_len) on systems that support this field.

We are providing this independent description of the function because
POSIX standards are not freely available (as are IETF documents).

    #include <sys/socket.h>
    #include <netdb.h>

Gilligan, et. al.   Informational   [Page 26]

```
int getaddrinfo(const char *nodename, const char *servname,
            const struct addrinfo *hints,
            struct addrinfo **res);
```

The addrinfo structure is defined as a result of including the
<netdb.h> header.

```
struct addrinfo {
  int     ai_flags;    /* AI_PASSIVE, AI_CANONNAME, AI_NUMERICHOST */
  int     ai_family;   /* PF_xxx */
  int     ai_socktype; /* SOCK_xxx */
  int     ai_protocol; /* 0 or IPPROTO_xxx for IPv4 and IPv6 */
  size_t  ai_addrlen;  /* length of ai_addr */
  char    *ai_canonname; /* canonical name for nodename */
  struct sockaddr  *ai_addr; /* binary address */
  struct addrinfo  *ai_next; /* next structure in linked list */
};
```

The return value from the function is 0 upon success or a nonzero
error code. The following names are the nonzero error codes from
getaddrinfo(), and are defined in <netdb.h>:

```
    EAI_ADDRFAMILY   address family for nodename not supported
    EAI_AGAIN        temporary failure in name resolution
    EAI_BADFLAGS     invalid value for ai_flags
    EAI_FAIL         non-recoverable failure in name resolution
    EAI_FAMILY       ai_family not supported
    EAI_MEMORY       memory allocation failure
    EAI_NODATA       no address associated with nodename
    EAI_NONAME       nodename nor servname provided, or not known
    EAI_SERVICE      servname not supported for ai_socktype
    EAI_SOCKTYPE     ai_socktype not supported
    EAI_SYSTEM       system error returned in errno
```

The nodename and servname arguments are pointers to null-terminated
strings or NULL. One or both of these two arguments must be a non-
NULL pointer. In the normal client scenario, both the nodename and
servname are specified. In the normal server scenario, only the
servname is specified. A non-NULL nodename string can be either a
node name or a numeric host address string (i.e., a dotted-decimal
IPv4 address or an IPv6 hex address). A non-NULL servname string can
be either a service name or a decimal port number.

The caller can optionally pass an addrinfo structure, pointed to by
the third argument, to provide hints concerning the type of socket
that the caller supports. In this hints structure all members other
than ai_flags, ai_family, ai_socktype, and ai_protocol must be zero
or a NULL pointer. A value of PF_UNSPEC for ai_family means the

Gilligan, et. al.   Informational   [Page 27]

caller will accept any protocol family. A value of 0 for ai_socktype
means the caller will accept any socket type. A value of 0 for
ai_protocol means the caller will accept any protocol. For example,
if the caller handles only TCP and not UDP, then the ai_socktype
member of the hints structure should be set to SOCK_STREAM when
getaddrinfo() is called. If the caller handles only IPv4 and not
IPv6, then the ai_family member of the hints structure should be set
to PF_INET when getaddrinfo() is called. If the third argument to
getaddrinfo() is a NULL pointer, this is the same as if the caller
had filled in an addrinfo structure initialized to zero with
ai_family set to PF_UNSPEC.

Upon successful return a pointer to a linked list of one or more
addrinfo structures is returned through the final argument. The
caller can process each addrinfo structure in this list by following
the ai_next pointer, until a NULL pointer is encountered. In each
returned addrinfo structure the three members ai_family, ai_socktype,
and ai_protocol are the corresponding arguments for a call to the
socket() function. In each addrinfo structure the ai_addr member
points to a filled-in socket address structure whose length is
specified by the ai_addrlen member.

If the AI_PASSIVE bit is set in the ai_flags member of the hints
structure, then the caller plans to use the returned socket address
structure in a call to bind(). In this case, if the nodename
argument is a NULL pointer, then the IP address portion of the socket
address structure will be set to INADDR_ANY for an IPv4 address or
IN6ADDR_ANY_INIT for an IPv6 address.

If the AI_PASSIVE bit is not set in the ai_flags member of the hints
structure, then the returned socket address structure will be ready
for a call to connect() (for a connection-oriented protocol) or
either connect(), sendto(), or sendmsg() (for a connectionless
protocol). In this case, if the nodename argument is a NULL pointer,
then the IP address portion of the socket address structure will be
set to the loopback address.

If the AI_CANONNAME bit is set in the ai_flags member of the hints
structure, then upon successful return the ai_canonname member of the
first addrinfo structure in the linked list will point to a null-
terminated string containing the canonical name of the specified
nodename.

If the AI_NUMERICHOST bit is set in the ai_flags member of the hints
structure, then a non-NULL nodename string must be a numeric host
address string. Otherwise an error of EAI_NONAME is returned. This
flag prevents any type of name resolution service (e.g., the DNS)
from being called.

RFC 2553   Basic Socket Interface Extensions for IPv6   March 1999

All of the information returned by getaddrinfo() is dynamically
allocated: the addrinfo structures, and the socket address structures
and canonical node name strings pointed to by the addrinfo
structures.   To return this information to the system the function
freeaddrinfo() is called:

    #include <sys/socket.h> #include <netdb.h>

    void freeaddrinfo(struct addrinfo *ai);

The addrinfo structure pointed to by the ai argument is freed, along
with any dynamic storage pointed to by the structure.   This operation
is repeated until a NULL ai_next pointer is encountered.

To aid applications in printing error messages based on the EAI_xxx
codes returned by getaddrinfo(), the following function is defined.

    #include <sys/socket.h> #include <netdb.h>

    char *gai_strerror(int ecode);

The argument is one of the EAI_xxx values defined earlier and the
return value points to a string describing the error.   If the
argument is not one of the EAI_xxx values, the function still returns
a pointer to a string whose contents indicate an unknown error.

6.5 Socket Address Structure to Nodename and Service Name

The POSIX 1003.1g specification includes no function to perform the
reverse conversion from getaddrinfo(): to look up a nodename and
service name, given the binary address and port.   Therefore, we
define the following function:

    #include <sys/socket.h>
    #include <netdb.h>

    int getnameinfo(const struct sockaddr *sa, socklen_t salen,
                    char *host, size_t hostlen,
                    char *serv, size_t servlen,
                    int flags);

This function looks up an IP address and port number provided by the
caller in the DNS and system-specific database, and returns text
strings for both in buffers provided by the caller.   The function
indicates successful completion by a zero return value; a non-zero
return value indicates failure.

Gilligan, et. al.   Informational   [Page 29]

The first argument, sa, points to either a sockaddr_in structure (for
IPv4) or a sockaddr_in6 structure (for IPv6) that holds the IP
address and port number. The salen argument gives the length of the
sockaddr_in or sockaddr_in6 structure.

The function returns the nodename associated with the IP address in
the buffer pointed to by the host argument. The caller provides the
size of this buffer via the hostlen argument. The service name
associated with the port number is returned in the buffer pointed to
by serv, and the servlen argument gives the length of this buffer.
The caller specifies not to return either string by providing a zero
value for the hostlen or servlen arguments. Otherwise, the caller
must provide buffers large enough to hold the nodename and the
service name, including the terminating null characters.

Unfortunately most systems do not provide constants that specify the
maximum size of either a fully-qualified domain name or a service
name. Therefore to aid the application in allocating buffers for
these two returned strings the following constants are defined in
<netdb.h>:

    #define NI_MAXHOST 1025
    #define NI_MAXSERV   32

The first value is actually defined as the constant MAXDNAME in recent
versions of BIND's <arpa/nameser.h> header (older versions of BIND
define this constant to be 256) and the second is a guess based on the
services listed in the current Assigned Numbers RFC.

The final argument is a flag that changes the default actions of this
function. By default the fully-qualified domain name (FQDN) for the
host is looked up in the DNS and returned. If the flag bit NI_NOFQDN
is set, only the nodename portion of the FQDN is returned for local
hosts.

If the flag bit NI_NUMERICHOST is set, or if the host's name cannot be
located in the DNS, the numeric form of the host's address is returned
instead of its name (e.g., by calling inet_ntop() instead of
getipnodebyaddr()). If the flag bit NI_NAMEREQD is set, an error is
returned if the host's name cannot be located in the DNS.

If the flag bit NI_NUMERICSERV is set, the numeric form of the service
address is returned (e.g., its port number) instead of its name. The
two NI_NUMERICxxx flags are required to support the "-n" flag that
many commands provide.

RFC 2553   Basic Socket Interface Extensions for IPv6   March 1999

A fifth flag bit, NI_DGRAM, specifies that the service is a datagram
service, and causes getservbyport() to be called with a second
argument of "udp" instead of its default of "tcp". This is required
for the few ports (e.g. 512-514) that have different services for UDP
and TCP.

These NI_xxx flags are defined in <netdb.h> along with the AI_xxx
flags already defined for getaddrinfo().

6.6 Address Conversion Functions

The two functions inet_addr() and inet_ntoa() convert an IPv4 address
between binary and text form.   IPv6 applications need similar
functions.   The following two functions convert both IPv6 and IPv4
addresses:

    #include <sys/socket.h>
    #include <arpa/inet.h>

    int inet_pton(int af, const char *src, void *dst);

    const char *inet_ntop(int af, const void *src,
                          char *dst, size_t size);

The inet_pton() function converts an address in its standard text
presentation form into its numeric binary form.   The af argument
specifies the family of the address.   Currently the AF_INET and
AF_INET6 address families are supported.   The src argument points to
the string being passed in.   The dst argument points to a buffer into
which the function stores the numeric address.   The address is
returned in network byte order.   Inet_pton() returns 1 if the
conversion succeeds, 0 if the input is not a valid IPv4 dotted-
decimal string or a valid IPv6 address string, or -1 with errno set
to EAFNOSUPPORT if the af argument is unknown.   The calling
application must ensure that the buffer referred to by dst is large
enough to hold the numeric address (e.g., 4 bytes for AF_INET or 16
bytes for AF_INET6).

If the af argument is AF_INET, the function accepts a string in the
standard IPv4 dotted-decimal form:

    ddd.ddd.ddd.ddd

where ddd is a one to three digit decimal number between 0 and 255.
Note that many implementations of the existing inet_addr() and
inet_aton() functions accept nonstandard input: octal numbers,
hexadecimal numbers, and fewer than four numbers.   inet_pton() does
not accept these formats.

RFC 2553   Basic Socket Interface Extensions for IPv6   March 1999

If the af argument is AF_INET6, then the function accepts a string in
one of the standard IPv6 text forms defined in Section 2.2 of the
addressing architecture specification [2].

The inet_ntop() function converts a numeric address into a text
string suitable for presentation. The af argument specifies the
family of the address. This can be AF_INET or AF_INET6. The src
argument points to a buffer holding an IPv4 address if the af
argument is AF_INET, or an IPv6 address if the af argument is
AF_INET6, the address must be in network byte order. The dst
argument points to a buffer where the function will store the
resulting text string. The size argument specifies the size of this
buffer. The application must specify a non-NULL dst argument. For
IPv6 addresses, the buffer must be at least 46-octets. For IPv4
addresses, the buffer must be at least 16-octets. In order to allow
applications to easily declare buffers of the proper size to store
IPv4 and IPv6 addresses in string form, the following two constants
are defined in <netinet/in.h>:

    #define INET_ADDRSTRLEN   16
    #define INET6_ADDRSTRLEN   46

The inet_ntop() function returns a pointer to the buffer containing
the text string if the conversion succeeds, and NULL otherwise. Upon
failure, errno is set to EAFNOSUPPORT if the af argument is invalid or
ENOSPC if the size of the result buffer is inadequate.

6.7 Address Testing Macros

The following macros can be used to test for special IPv6 addresses.

    #include <netinet/in.h>

    int   IN6_IS_ADDR_UNSPECIFIED (const struct in6_addr *);
    int   IN6_IS_ADDR_LOOPBACK   (const struct in6_addr *);
    int   IN6_IS_ADDR_MULTICAST   (const struct in6_addr *);
    int   IN6_IS_ADDR_LINKLOCAL   (const struct in6_addr *);
    int   IN6_IS_ADDR_SITELOCAL   (const struct in6_addr *);
    int   IN6_IS_ADDR_V4MAPPED   (const struct in6_addr *);
    int   IN6_IS_ADDR_V4COMPAT   (const struct in6_addr *);

    int   IN6_IS_ADDR_MC_NODELOCAL(const struct in6_addr *);
    int   IN6_IS_ADDR_MC_LINKLOCAL(const struct in6_addr *);
    int   IN6_IS_ADDR_MC_SITELOCAL(const struct in6_addr *);
    int   IN6_IS_ADDR_MC_ORGLOCAL (const struct in6_addr *);
    int   IN6_IS_ADDR_MC_GLOBAL   (const struct in6_addr *);

RFC 2553   Basic Socket Interface Extensions for IPv6   March 1999

The first seven macros return true if the address is of the specified
type, or false otherwise. The last five test the scope of a
multicast address and return true if the address is a multicast
address of the specified scope or false if the address is either not
a multicast address or not of the specified scope. Note that
IN6_IS_ADDR_LINKLOCAL and IN6_IS_ADDR_SITELOCAL return true only for
the two local-use IPv6 unicast addresses. These two macros do not
return true for IPv6 multicast addresses of either link-local scope
or site-local scope.

7. Summary of New Definitions

The following list summarizes the constants, structure, and extern
definitions discussed in this memo, sorted by header.

    <net/if.h>   IF_NAMESIZE
    <net/if.h>   struct if_nameindex{};

    <netdb.h>   AI_ADDRCONFIG
    <netdb.h>   AI_DEFAULT
    <netdb.h>   AI_ALL
    <netdb.h>   AI_CANONNAME
    <netdb.h>   AI_NUMERICHOST
    <netdb.h>   AI_PASSIVE
    <netdb.h>   AI_V4MAPPED
    <netdb.h>   EAI_ADDRFAMILY
    <netdb.h>   EAI_AGAIN
    <netdb.h>   EAI_BADFLAGS
    <netdb.h>   EAI_FAIL
    <netdb.h>   EAI_FAMILY
    <netdb.h>   EAI_MEMORY
    <netdb.h>   EAI_NODATA
    <netdb.h>   EAI_NONAME
    <netdb.h>   EAI_SERVICE
    <netdb.h>   EAI_SOCKTYPE
    <netdb.h>   EAI_SYSTEM
    <netdb.h>   NI_DGRAM
    <netdb.h>   NI_MAXHOST
    <netdb.h>   NI_MAXSERV
    <netdb.h>   NI_NAMEREQD
    <netdb.h>   NI_NOFQDN
    <netdb.h>   NI_NUMERICHOST
    <netdb.h>   NI_NUMERICSERV
    <netdb.h>   struct addrinfo{};

    <netinet/in.h>   IN6ADDR_ANY_INIT
    <netinet/in.h>   IN6ADDR_LOOPBACK_INIT
    <netinet/in.h>   INET6_ADDRSTRLEN

RFC 2553   Basic Socket Interface Extensions for IPv6   March 1999

```
<netinet/in.h>   INET_ADDRSTRLEN
<netinet/in.h>   IPPROTO_IPV6
<netinet/in.h>   IPV6_JOIN_GROUP
<netinet/in.h>   IPV6_LEAVE_GROUP
<netinet/in.h>   IPV6_MULTICAST_HOPS
<netinet/in.h>   IPV6_MULTICAST_IF
<netinet/in.h>   IPV6_MULTICAST_LOOP
<netinet/in.h>   IPV6_UNICAST_HOPS
<netinet/in.h>   SIN6_LEN
<netinet/in.h>   extern const struct in6_addr in6addr_any;
<netinet/in.h>   extern const struct in6_addr in6addr_loopback;
<netinet/in.h>   struct in6_addr{};
<netinet/in.h>   struct ipv6_mreq{};
<netinet/in.h>   struct sockaddr_in6{};

<sys/socket.h>   AF_INET6
<sys/socket.h>   PF_INET6
<sys/socket.h>   struct sockaddr_storage;
```

   The following list summarizes the function and macro prototypes
   discussed in this memo, sorted by header.

```
<arpa/inet.h>    int inet_pton(int, const char *, void *);
<arpa/inet.h>    const char *inet_ntop(int, const void *,
                                      char *, size_t);

<net/if.h>       char *if_indextoname(unsigned int, char *);
<net/if.h>       unsigned int if_nametoindex(const char *);
<net/if.h>       void if_freenameindex(struct if_nameindex *);
<net/if.h>       struct if_nameindex *if_nameindex(void);

<netdb.h>        int getaddrinfo(const char *, const char *,
                                const struct addrinfo *,
                                struct addrinfo **);
<netdb.h>        int getnameinfo(const struct sockaddr *, socklen_t,
                                char *, size_t, char *, size_t, int);
<netdb.h>        void freeaddrinfo(struct addrinfo *);
<netdb.h>        char *gai_strerror(int);
<netdb.h>        struct hostent *getipnodebyname(const char *, int, int,
                                                int *);
<netdb.h>        struct hostent *getipnodebyaddr(const void *, size_t,
                                                int, int *);
<netdb.h>        void freehostent(struct hostent *);

<netinet/in.h>   int IN6_IS_ADDR_LINKLOCAL(const struct in6_addr *);
<netinet/in.h>   int IN6_IS_ADDR_LOOPBACK(const struct in6_addr *);
<netinet/in.h>   int IN6_IS_ADDR_MC_GLOBAL(const struct in6_addr *);
<netinet/in.h>   int IN6_IS_ADDR_MC_LINKLOCAL(const struct in6_addr *);
```

Gilligan, et. al.   Informational   [Page 34]

RFC 2553   Basic Socket Interface Extensions for IPv6   March 1999

```
<netinet/in.h>   int IN6_IS_ADDR_MC_NODELOCAL(const struct in6_addr *);
<netinet/in.h>   int IN6_IS_ADDR_MC_ORGLOCAL(const struct in6_addr *);
<netinet/in.h>   int IN6_IS_ADDR_MC_SITELOCAL(const struct in6_addr *);
<netinet/in.h>   int IN6_IS_ADDR_MULTICAST(const struct in6_addr *);
<netinet/in.h>   int IN6_IS_ADDR_SITELOCAL(const struct in6_addr *);
<netinet/in.h>   int IN6_IS_ADDR_UNSPECIFIED(const struct in6_addr *);
<netinet/in.h>   int IN6_IS_ADDR_V4COMPAT(const struct in6_addr *);
<netinet/in.h>   int IN6_IS_ADDR_V4MAPPED(const struct in6_addr *);
```

8. Security Considerations

    IPv6 provides a number of new security mechanisms, many of which need
    to be accessible to applications. Companion memos detailing the
    extensions to the socket interfaces to support IPv6 security are
    being written.

9. Year 2000 Considerations

    There are no issues for this memo concerning the Year 2000 issue
    regarding the use of dates.

Changes From RFC 2133

    Changes made in the March 1998 Edition (-01 draft):

        Changed all "hostname" to "nodename" for consistency with other
        IPv6 documents.

        Section 3.3: changed comment for sin6_flowinfo to be "traffic
        class & flow info" and updated corresponding text description to
        current definition of these two fields.

        Section 3.10 ("Portability Additions") is new.

        Section 6: a new paragraph was added reiterating that the existing
        gethostbyname() and gethostbyaddr() are not changed.

        Section 6.1: change gethostbyname3() to getnodebyname(). Add
        AI_DEFAULT to handle majority of applications. Renamed
        AI_V6ADDRCONFIG to AI_ADDRCONFIG and define it for A records and
        IPv4 addresses too. Defined exactly what getnodebyname() must
        return if the name argument is a numeric address string.

        Section 6.2: change gethostbyaddr() to getnodebyaddr(). Reword
        items 2 and 3 in the description of how to handle IPv4-mapped and
        IPv4- compatible addresses to "lookup a name" for a given address,
        instead of specifying what type of DNS query to issue.

Section 6.3: added two more requirements to getaddrinfo().

Section 7: added the following constants to the list for
<netdb.h>: AI_ADDRCONFIG, AI_ALL, and AI_V4MAPPED. Add union
sockaddr_union and SA_LEN to the lists for <sys/socket.h>.

Updated references.

Changes made in the November 1997 Edition (-00 draft):

The data types have been changed to conform with Draft 6.6 of the
Posix 1003.1g standard.

Section 3.2: data type of s6_addr changed to "uint8_t".

Section 3.3: data type of sin6_family changed to "sa_family_t".
data type of sin6_port changed to "in_port_t", data type of
sin6_flowinfo changed to "uint32_t".

Section 3.4: same as Section 3.3, plus data type of sin6_len
changed to "uint8_t".

Section 6.2: first argument of gethostbyaddr() changed from "const
char *" to "const void *" and second argument changed from "int"
to "size_t".

Section 6.4: second argument of getnameinfo() changed from
"size_t" to "socklen_t".

The wording was changed when new structures were defined, to be
more explicit as to which header must be included to define the
structure:

Section 3.2 (in6_addr{}), Section 3.3 (sockaddr_in6{}), Section
3.4 (sockaddr_in6{}), Section 4.3 (if_nameindex{}), Section 5.3
(ipv6_mreq{}), and Section 6.3 (addrinfo{}).

Section 4: NET_RT_LIST changed to NET_RT_IFLIST.

Section 5.1: The IPV6_ADDRFORM socket option was removed.

Section 5.3: Added a note that an option value other than 0 or 1
for IPV6_MULTICAST_LOOP returns an error. Added a note that
IPV6_MULTICAST_IF, IPV6_MULTICAST_HOPS, and IPV6_MULTICAST_LOOP
can also be used with getsockopt(), but IPV6_ADD_MEMBERSHIP and
IPV6_DROP_MEMBERSHIP cannot be used with getsockopt().

RFC 2553   Basic Socket Interface Extensions for IPv6   March 1999

Section 6.1: Removed the description of gethostbyname2() and its
associated RES_USE_INET6 option, replacing it with
gethostbyname3().

Section 6.2: Added requirement that gethostbyaddr() be thread
safe. Reworded step 4 to avoid using the RES_USE_INET6 option.

Section 6.3: Added the requirement that getaddrinfo() and
getnameinfo() be thread safe. Added the AI_NUMERICHOST flag.

Section 6.6: Added clarification about IN6_IS_ADDR_LINKLOCAL and
IN6_IS_ADDR_SITELOCAL macros.

Changes made to the draft -01 specification Sept 98

Changed priority to traffic class in the spec.

Added the need for scope identification in section 2.1.

Added sin6_scope_id to struct sockaddr_in6 in sections 3.3 and
3.4.

Changed 3.10 to use generic storage structure to support holding
IPv6 addresses and removed the SA_LEN macro.

Distinguished between invalid input parameters and system failures
for Interface Identification in Section 4.1 and 4.2.

Added defaults for multicast operations in section 5.2 and changed
the names from ADD to JOIN and DROP to LEAVE to be consistent with
IPv6 multicast terminology.

Changed getnodebyname to getipnodebyname, getnodebyaddr to
getipnodebyaddr, and added MT safe error code to function
parameters in section 6.

Moved freehostent to its own sub-section after getipnodebyaddr now
6.3 (so this bumps all remaining sections in section 6.

Clarified the use of AI_ALL and AI_V4MAPPED that these are
dependent on the AF parameter and must be used as a conjunction in
section 6.1.

Removed the restriction that literal addresses cannot be used with
a flags argument in section 6.1.

Added Year 2000 Section to the draft

Gilligan, et. al.   Informational   [Page 37]

Deleted Reference to the following because the attached is deleted
from the ID directory and has expired. But the logic from the
aforementioned draft still applies, so that was kept in Section
6.2 bullets after 3rd paragraph.

[7] P. Vixie, "Reverse Name Lookups of Encapsulated IPv4
     Addresses in IPv6", Internet-Draft, <draft-vixie-ipng-
     ipv4ptr-00.txt>, May 1996.

Deleted the following reference as it is no longer referenced.
And the draft has expired.

[3] D. McDonald, "A Simple IP Security API Extension to BSD
     Sockets", Internet-Draft, <draft-mcdonald-simple-ipsec-api-
     01.txt>, March 1997.

Deleted the following reference as it is no longer referenced.

[4] C. Metz, "Network Security API for Sockets",
     Internet-Draft, <draft-metz-net-security-api-01.txt>, January
     1998.

Update current references to current status.

Added alignment notes for in6_addr and sin6_addr.

Clarified further that AI_V4MAPPED must be used with a dotted IPv4
literal address for getipnodebyname(), when address family is
AF_INET6.

Added text to clarify "::" and "::1" when used by
getipnodebyaddr().

Acknowledgments

Thanks to the many people who made suggestions and provided feedback
to this document, including: Werner Almesberger, Ran Atkinson, Fred
Baker, Dave Borman, Andrew Cherenson, Alex Conta, Alan Cox, Steve
Deering, Richard Draves, Francis Dupont, Robert Elz, Marc Hasson, Tom
Herbert, Bob Hinden, Wan-Yen Hsu, Christian Huitema, Koji Imada,
Markus Jork, Ron Lee, Alan Lloyd, Charles Lynn, Dan McDonald, Dave
Mitton, Thomas Narten, Josh Osborne, Craig Partridge, Jean-Luc
Richier, Erik Scoredos, Keith Sklower, Matt Thomas, Harvey Thompson,
Dean D. Throop, Karen Tracey, Glenn Trewitt, Paul Vixie, David
Waitzman, Carl Williams, and Kazu Yamamoto,

RFC 2553   Basic Socket Interface Extensions for IPv6   March 1999

The getaddrinfo() and getnameinfo() functions are taken from an
earlier Internet Draft by Keith Sklower. As noted in that draft,
William Durst, Steven Wise, Michael Karels, and Eric Allman provided
many useful discussions on the subject of protocol-independent name-
to-address translation, and reviewed early versions of Keith
Sklower's original proposal. Eric Allman implemented the first
prototype of getaddrinfo(). The observation that specifying the pair
of name and service would suffice for connecting to a service
independent of protocol details was made by Marshall Rose in a
proposal to X/Open for a "Uniform Network Interface".

Craig Metz, Jack McCann, Erik Nordmark, Tim Hartrick, and Mukesh
Kacker made many contributions to this document. Ramesh Govindan
made a number of contributions and co-authored an earlier version of
this memo.

References

[1]   Deering, S. and R. Hinden, "Internet Protocol, Version 6 (IPv6)
      Specification", RFC 2460, December 1998.

[2]   Hinden, R. and S. Deering, "IP Version 6 Addressing
      Architecture", RFC 2373, July 1998.

[3]   IEEE, "Protocol Independent Interfaces", IEEE Std 1003.1g, DRAFT
      6.6, March 1997.

[4]   Stevens, W. and M. Thomas, "Advanced Sockets API for IPv6", RFC
      2292, February 1998.

RFC 2553   Basic Socket Interface Extensions for IPv6   March 1999

Authors' Addresses

   Robert E. Gilligan
   FreeGate Corporation
   1208 E. Arques Ave.
   Sunnyvale, CA 94086

   Phone: +1 408 617 1004
   EMail: gilligan@freegate.com

   Susan Thomson
   Bell Communications Research
   MRE 2P-343, 445 South Street
   Morristown, NJ 07960

   Phone: +1 201 829 4514
   EMail: set@thumper.bellcore.com

   Jim Bound
   Compaq Computer Corporation
   110 Spitbrook Road ZK3-3/U14
   Nashua, NH 03062-2698

   Phone: +1 603 884 0400
   EMail: bound@zk3.dec.com

   W. Richard Stevens
   1202 E. Paseo del Zorro
   Tucson, AZ 85718-2826

   Phone: +1 520 297 9416
   EMail: rstevens@kohala.com

RFC 2553   Basic Socket Interface Extensions for IPv6   March 1999

Full Copyright Statement

RFC3493 "Basic Socket Interface Extensions for IPv6"

Network Working Group   R. Gilligan
Request for Comments: 3493   Intransa, Inc.
Obsoletes: 2553   S. Thomson
Category: Informational   Cisco
                                                          J. Bound
                                                         J. McCann
                                                  Hewlett-Packard
                                                        W. Stevens
                                                   February 2003

                 Basic Socket Interface Extensions for IPv6

Status of this Memo

Abstract

   The de facto standard Application Program Interface (API) for TCP/IP
   applications is the "sockets" interface. Although this API was
   developed for Unix in the early 1980s it has also been implemented on
   a wide variety of non-Unix systems. TCP/IP applications written
   using the sockets API have in the past enjoyed a high degree of
   portability and we would like the same portability with IPv6
   applications. But changes are required to the sockets API to support
   IPv6 and this memo describes these changes. These include a new
   socket address structure to carry IPv6 addresses, new address
   conversion functions, and some new socket options. These extensions
   are designed to provide access to the basic IPv6 features required by
   TCP and UDP applications, including multicasting, while introducing a
   minimum of change into the system and providing complete
   compatibility for existing IPv4 applications. Additional extensions
   for advanced IPv6 features (raw sockets and access to the IPv6
   extension headers) are defined in another document.

RFC 3493   Basic Socket Interface Extensions for IPv6   February 2003

Table of Contents

RFC 3493   Basic Socket Interface Extensions for IPv6   February 2003

1. Introduction

   While IPv4 addresses are 32 bits long, IPv6 addresses are 128 bits
   long. The socket interface makes the size of an IP address quite
   visible to an application; virtually all TCP/IP applications for
   BSD-based systems have knowledge of the size of an IP address. Those
   parts of the API that expose the addresses must be changed to
   accommodate the larger IPv6 address size. IPv6 also introduces new
   features, some of which must be made visible to applications via the
   API. This memo defines a set of extensions to the socket interface
   to support the larger address size and new features of IPv6. It
   defines "basic" extensions that are of use to a broad range of
   applications. A companion document, the "advanced" API [4], covers
   extensions that are of use to more specialized applications, examples
   of which include routing daemons, and the "ping" and "traceroute"
   utilities.

   The development of this API was started in 1994 in the IETF IPng
   working group. The API has evolved over the years, published first
   in RFC 2133, then again in RFC 2553, and reaching its final form in
   this document.

   As the API matured and stabilized, it was incorporated into the Open
   Group's Networking Services (XNS) specification, issue 5.2, which was
   subsequently incorporated into a joint Open Group/IEEE/ISO standard
   [3].

   Effort has been made to ensure that this document and [3] contain the
   same information with regard to the API definitions. However, the
   reader should note that this document is for informational purposes
   only, and that the official standard specification of the sockets API
   is [3].

   It is expected that any future standardization work on this API would
   be done by the Open Group Base Working Group [6].

   It should also be noted that this document describes only those
   portions of the API needed for IPv4 and IPv6 communications. Other
   potential uses of the API, for example the use of getaddrinfo() and
   getnameinfo() with the AF_UNIX address family, are beyond the scope
   of this document.

RFC 3493   Basic Socket Interface Extensions for IPv6   February 2003

2. Design Considerations

   There are a number of important considerations in designing changes
   to this well-worn API:

   - The API changes should provide both source and binary
      compatibility for programs written to the original API. That is,
      existing program binaries should continue to operate when run on a
      system supporting the new API. In addition, existing applications
      that are re-compiled and run on a system supporting the new API
      should continue to operate. Simply put, the API changes for IPv6
      should not break existing programs. An additional mechanism for
      implementations to verify this is to verify the new symbols are
      protected by Feature Test Macros as described in [3]. (Such
      Feature Test Macros are not defined by this RFC.)

   - The changes to the API should be as small as possible in order to
      simplify the task of converting existing IPv4 applications to
      IPv6.

   - Where possible, applications should be able to use this API to
      interoperate with both IPv6 and IPv4 hosts. Applications should
      not need to know which type of host they are communicating with.

   - IPv6 addresses carried in data structures should be 64-bit
      aligned. This is necessary in order to obtain optimum performance
      on 64-bit machine architectures.

   Because of the importance of providing IPv4 compatibility in the API,
   these extensions are explicitly designed to operate on machines that
   provide complete support for both IPv4 and IPv6. A subset of this
   API could probably be designed for operation on systems that support
   only IPv6. However, this is not addressed in this memo.

2.1 What Needs to be Changed

   The socket interface API consists of a few distinct components:

   - Core socket functions.

   - Address data structures.

   - Name-to-address translation functions.

   - Address conversion functions.

Gilligan, et al.   Informational   [Page 4]

RFC 3493   Basic Socket Interface Extensions for IPv6   February 2003

The core socket functions — those functions that deal with such
things as setting up and tearing down TCP connections, and sending
and receiving UDP packets — were designed to be transport
independent. Where protocol addresses are passed as function
arguments, they are carried via opaque pointers. A protocol-specific
address data structure is defined for each protocol that the socket
functions support. Applications must cast pointers to these
protocol-specific address structures into pointers to the generic
"sockaddr" address structure when using the socket functions. These
functions need not change for IPv6, but a new IPv6-specific address
data structure is needed.

The "sockaddr_in" structure is the protocol-specific data structure
for IPv4. This data structure actually includes 8-octets of unused
space, and it is tempting to try to use this space to adapt the
sockaddr_in structure to IPv6. Unfortunately, the sockaddr_in
structure is not large enough to hold the 16-octet IPv6 address as
well as the other information (address family and port number) that
is needed. So a new address data structure must be defined for IPv6.

IPv6 addresses are scoped [2] so they could be link-local, site,
organization, global, or other scopes at this time undefined. To
support applications that want to be able to identify a set of
interfaces for a specific scope, the IPv6 sockaddr_in structure must
support a field that can be used by an implementation to identify a
set of interfaces identifying the scope for an IPv6 address.

The IPv4 name-to-address translation functions in the socket
interface are gethostbyname() and gethostbyaddr(). These are left as
is, and new functions are defined which support both IPv4 and IPv6.

The IPv4 address conversion functions — inet_ntoa() and inet_addr()
— convert IPv4 addresses between binary and printable form. These
functions are quite specific to 32-bit IPv4 addresses. We have
designed two analogous functions that convert both IPv4 and IPv6
addresses, and carry an address type parameter so that they can be
extended to other protocol families as well.

Finally, a few miscellaneous features are needed to support IPv6. A
new interface is needed to support the IPv6 hop limit header field.
New socket options are needed to control the sending and receiving of
IPv6 multicast packets.

The socket interface will be enhanced in the future to provide access
to other IPv6 features. Some of these extensions are described in
[4].

2.2 Data Types

   The data types of the structure elements given in this memo are
   intended to track the relevant standards. uintN_t means an unsigned
   integer of exactly N bits (e.g., uint16_t). The sa_family_t and
   in_port_t types are defined in [3].

2.3 Headers

   When function prototypes and structures are shown we show the headers
   that must be #included to cause that item to be defined.

2.4 Structures

   When structures are described the members shown are the ones that
   must appear in an implementation. Additional, nonstandard members
   may also be defined by an implementation. As an additional
   precaution nonstandard members could be verified by Feature Test
   Macros as described in [3]. (Such Feature Test Macros are not
   defined by this RFC.)

   The ordering shown for the members of a structure is the recommended
   ordering, given alignment considerations of multibyte members, but an
   implementation may order the members differently.

3. Socket Interface

   This section specifies the socket interface changes for IPv6.

3.1 IPv6 Address Family and Protocol Family

   A new address family name, AF_INET6, is defined in <sys/socket.h.
   The AF_INET6 definition distinguishes between the original
   sockaddr_in address data structure, and the new sockaddr_in6 data
   structure.

   A new protocol family name, PF_INET6, is defined in <sys/socket.h.
   Like most of the other protocol family names, this will usually be
   defined to have the same value as the corresponding address family
   name:

       #define PF_INET6   AF_INET6

   The AF_INET6 is used in the first argument to the socket() function
   to indicate that an IPv6 socket is being created.

RFC 3493   Basic Socket Interface Extensions for IPv6   February 2003

3.2 IPv6 Address Structure

   A new in6_addr structure holds a single IPv6 address and is defined
   as a result of including <netinet/in.h:>

      struct in6_addr {
          uint8_t   s6_addr[16];   /* IPv6 address */
      };

   This data structure contains an array of sixteen 8-bit elements,
   which make up one 128-bit IPv6 address. The IPv6 address is stored
   in network byte order.

   The structure in6_addr above is usually implemented with an embedded
   union with extra fields that force the desired alignment level in a
   manner similar to BSD implementations of "struct in_addr". Those
   additional implementation details are omitted here for simplicity.

   An example is as follows:

   struct in6_addr {
       union {
           uint8_t   _S6_u8[16];
           uint32_t _S6_u32[4];
           uint64_t _S6_u64[2];
       } _S6_un;
   };
   #define s6_addr _S6_un._S6_u8

3.3 Socket Address Structure for 4.3BSD-Based Systems

   In the socket interface, a different protocol-specific data structure
   is defined to carry the addresses for each protocol suite. Each
   protocol-specific data structure is designed so it can be cast into a
   protocol-independent data structure — the "sockaddr" structure.
   Each has a "family" field that overlays the "sa_family" of the
   sockaddr data structure. This field identifies the type of the data
   structure.

   The sockaddr_in structure is the protocol-specific address data
   structure for IPv4. It is used to pass addresses between
   applications and the system in the socket functions. The following
   sockaddr_in6 structure holds IPv6 addresses and is defined as a
   result of including the <netinet/in.h:> header:

```
struct sockaddr_in6 {
    sa_family_t     sin6_family;    /* AF_INET6 */
    in_port_t       sin6_port;      /* transport layer port # */
    uint32_t        sin6_flowinfo;  /* IPv6 flow information */
    struct in6_addr sin6_addr;      /* IPv6 address */
    uint32_t        sin6_scope_id;  /* set of interfaces for a scope */
};
```

This structure is designed to be compatible with the sockaddr data
structure used in the 4.3BSD release.

The sin6_family field identifies this as a sockaddr_in6 structure.
This field overlays the sa_family field when the buffer is cast to a
sockaddr data structure. The value of this field must be AF_INET6.

The sin6_port field contains the 16-bit UDP or TCP port number. This
field is used in the same way as the sin_port field of the
sockaddr_in structure. The port number is stored in network byte
order.

The sin6_flowinfo field is a 32-bit field intended to contain flow-
related information. The exact way this field is mapped to or from a
packet is not currently specified. Until such time as its use is
specified, applications should set this field to zero when
constructing a sockaddr_in6, and ignore this field in a sockaddr_in6
structure constructed by the system.

The sin6_addr field is a single in6_addr structure (defined in the
previous section). This field holds one 128-bit IPv6 address. The
address is stored in network byte order.

The ordering of elements in this structure is specifically designed
so that when sin6_addr field is aligned on a 64-bit boundary, the
start of the structure will also be aligned on a 64-bit boundary.
This is done for optimum performance on 64-bit architectures.

The sin6_scope_id field is a 32-bit integer that identifies a set of
interfaces as appropriate for the scope [2] of the address carried in
the sin6_addr field. The mapping of sin6_scope_id to an interface or
set of interfaces is left to implementation and future specifications
on the subject of scoped addresses.

Notice that the sockaddr_in6 structure will normally be larger than
the generic sockaddr structure. On many existing implementations the
sizeof(struct sockaddr_in) equals sizeof(struct sockaddr), with both
being 16 bytes. Any existing code that makes this assumption needs
to be examined carefully when converting to IPv6.

RFC 3493   Basic Socket Interface Extensions for IPv6   February 2003

3.4 Socket Address Structure for 4.4BSD-Based Systems

   The 4.4BSD release includes a small, but incompatible change to the
   socket interface. The "sa_family" field of the sockaddr data
   structure was changed from a 16-bit value to an 8-bit value, and the
   space saved used to hold a length field, named "sa_len". The
   sockaddr_in6 data structure given in the previous section cannot be
   correctly cast into the newer sockaddr data structure. For this
   reason, the following alternative IPv6 address data structure is
   provided to be used on systems based on 4.4BSD. It is defined as a
   result of including the <netinet/in.h:> header.

```
struct sockaddr_in6 {
    uint8_t         sin6_len;        /* length of this struct */
    sa_family_t     sin6_family;     /* AF_INET6 */
    in_port_t       sin6_port;       /* transport layer port # */
    uint32_t        sin6_flowinfo;   /* IPv6 flow information */
    struct in6_addr sin6_addr;       /* IPv6 address */
    uint32_t        sin6_scope_id;   /* set of interfaces for a scope */
};
```

   The only differences between this data structure and the 4.3BSD
   variant are the inclusion of the length field, and the change of the
   family field to a 8-bit data type. The definitions of all the other
   fields are identical to the structure defined in the previous
   section.

   Systems that provide this version of the sockaddr_in6 data structure
   must also declare SIN6_LEN as a result of including the
   <netinet/in.h:> header. This macro allows applications to determine
   whether they are being built on a system that supports the 4.3BSD or
   4.4BSD variants of the data structure.

3.5 The Socket Functions

   Applications call the socket() function to create a socket descriptor
   that represents a communication endpoint. The arguments to the
   socket() function tell the system which protocol to use, and what
   format address structure will be used in subsequent functions. For
   example, to create an IPv4/TCP socket, applications make the call:

       s = socket(AF_INET, SOCK_STREAM, 0);

   To create an IPv4/UDP socket, applications make the call:

       s = socket(AF_INET, SOCK_DGRAM, 0);

RFC 3493   Basic Socket Interface Extensions for IPv6   February 2003

Applications may create IPv6/TCP and IPv6/UDP sockets (which may also
handle IPv4 communication as described in section 3.7) by simply
using the constant AF_INET6 instead of AF_INET in the first argument.
For example, to create an IPv6/TCP socket, applications make the
call:

    s = socket(AF_INET6, SOCK_STREAM, 0);

To create an IPv6/UDP socket, applications make the call:

    s = socket(AF_INET6, SOCK_DGRAM, 0);

Once the application has created a AF_INET6 socket, it must use the
sockaddr_in6 address structure when passing addresses in to the
system. The functions that the application uses to pass addresses
into the system are:

    bind()
    connect()
    sendmsg()
    sendto()

The system will use the sockaddr_in6 address structure to return
addresses to applications that are using AF_INET6 sockets. The
functions that return an address from the system to an application
are:

    accept()
    recvfrom()
    recvmsg()
    getpeername()
    getsockname()

No changes to the syntax of the socket functions are needed to
support IPv6, since all of the "address carrying" functions use an
opaque address pointer, and carry an address length as a function
argument.

3.6 Compatibility with IPv4 Applications

In order to support the large base of applications using the original
API, system implementations must provide complete source and binary
compatibility with the original API. This means that systems must
continue to support AF_INET sockets and the sockaddr_in address
structure. Applications must be able to create IPv4/TCP and IPv4/UDP
sockets using the AF_INET constant in the socket() function, as

Gilligan, et al.   Informational   [Page 10]

RFC 3493   Basic Socket Interface Extensions for IPv6   February 2003

described in the previous section. Applications should be able to
hold a combination of IPv4/TCP, IPv4/UDP, IPv6/TCP and IPv6/UDP
sockets simultaneously within the same process.

Applications using the original API should continue to operate as
they did on systems supporting only IPv4. That is, they should
continue to interoperate with IPv4 nodes.

3.7 Compatibility with IPv4 Nodes

The API also provides a different type of compatibility: the ability
for IPv6 applications to interoperate with IPv4 applications. This
feature uses the IPv4-mapped IPv6 address format defined in the IPv6
addressing architecture specification [2]. This address format
allows the IPv4 address of an IPv4 node to be represented as an IPv6
address. The IPv4 address is encoded into the low-order 32 bits of
the IPv6 address, and the high-order 96 bits hold the fixed prefix
0:0:0:0:0:FFFF. IPv4-mapped addresses are written as follows:

    ::FFFF:<IPv4-address>

These addresses can be generated automatically by the getaddrinfo()
function, as described in Section 6.1.

Applications may use AF_INET6 sockets to open TCP connections to IPv4
nodes, or send UDP packets to IPv4 nodes, by simply encoding the
destination's IPv4 address as an IPv4-mapped IPv6 address, and
passing that address, within a sockaddr_in6 structure, in the
connect() or sendto() call. When applications use AF_INET6 sockets
to accept TCP connections from IPv4 nodes, or receive UDP packets
from IPv4 nodes, the system returns the peer's address to the
application in the accept(), recvfrom(), or getpeername() call using
a sockaddr_in6 structure encoded this way.

Few applications will likely need to know which type of node they are
interoperating with. However, for those applications that do need to
know, the IN6_IS_ADDR_V4MAPPED() macro, defined in Section 6.4, is
provided.

3.8 IPv6 Wildcard Address

While the bind() function allows applications to select the source IP
address of UDP packets and TCP connections, applications often want
the system to select the source address for them. With IPv4, one
specifies the address as the symbolic constant INADDR_ANY (called the
"wildcard" address) in the bind() call, or simply omits the bind()
entirely.

Gilligan, et al.   Informational   [Page 11]

RFC 3493   Basic Socket Interface Extensions for IPv6   February 2003

Since the IPv6 address type is a structure (struct in6_addr), a
symbolic constant can be used to initialize an IPv6 address variable,
but cannot be used in an assignment. Therefore systems provide the
IPv6 wildcard address in two forms.

The first version is a global variable named "in6addr_any" that is an
in6_addr structure. The extern declaration for this variable is
defined in <netinet/in.h>

```
extern const struct in6_addr in6addr_any;
```

Applications use in6addr_any similarly to the way they use INADDR_ANY
in IPv4. For example, to bind a socket to port number 23, but let
the system select the source address, an application could use the
following code:

```
struct sockaddr_in6 sin6;
  . . .
sin6.sin6_family = AF_INET6;
sin6.sin6_flowinfo = 0;
sin6.sin6_port = htons(23);
sin6.sin6_addr = in6addr_any;  /* structure assignment */
  . . .
if (bind(s, (struct sockaddr *) &sin6, sizeof(sin6)) == -1)
      . . .
```

The other version is a symbolic constant named IN6ADDR_ANY_INIT and
is defined in <netinet/in.h>. This constant can be used to
initialize an in6_addr structure:

```
struct in6_addr anyaddr = IN6ADDR_ANY_INIT;
```

Note that this constant can be used ONLY at declaration time. It can
not be used to assign a previously declared in6_addr structure. For
example, the following code will not work:

```
/* This is the WRONG way to assign an unspecified address */
struct sockaddr_in6 sin6;
  . . .
sin6.sin6_addr = IN6ADDR_ANY_INIT; /* will NOT compile */
```

Be aware that the IPv4 INADDR_xxx constants are all defined in host
byte order but the IPv6 IN6ADDR_xxx constants and the IPv6
in6addr_xxx externals are defined in network byte order.

RFC 3493   Basic Socket Interface Extensions for IPv6 February 2003

3.9 IPv6 Loopback Address

    Applications may need to send UDP packets to, or originate TCP
    connections to, services residing on the local node. In IPv4, they
    can do this by using the constant IPv4 address INADDR_LOOPBACK in
    their connect(), sendto(), or sendmsg() call.

    IPv6 also provides a loopback address to contact local TCP and UDP
    services. Like the unspecified address, the IPv6 loopback address is
    provided in two forms — a global variable and a symbolic constant.

    The global variable is an in6_addr structure named
    "in6addr_loopback." The extern declaration for this variable is
    defined in <netinet/in.h>

        extern const struct in6_addr in6addr_loopback;

    Applications use in6addr_loopback as they would use INADDR_LOOPBACK
    in IPv4 applications (but beware of the byte ordering difference
    mentioned at the end of the previous section). For example, to open
    a TCP connection to the local telnet server, an application could use
    the following code:

    struct sockaddr_in6 sin6;
     . . .
    sin6.sin6_family = AF_INET6;
    sin6.sin6_flowinfo = 0;
    sin6.sin6_port = htons(23);
    sin6.sin6_addr = in6addr_loopback; /* structure assignment */
     . . .
    if (connect(s, (struct sockaddr *) &sin6, sizeof(sin6)) == -1)
           . . .

    The symbolic constant is named IN6ADDR_LOOPBACK_INIT and is defined
    in <netinet/in.h>. It can be used at declaration time ONLY; for
    example:

        struct in6_addr loopbackaddr = IN6ADDR_LOOPBACK_INIT;

    Like IN6ADDR_ANY_INIT, this constant cannot be used in an assignment
    to a previously declared IPv6 address variable.

RFC 3493   Basic Socket Interface Extensions for IPv6   February 2003

3.10 Portability Additions

One simple addition to the sockets API that can help application
writers is the "struct sockaddr_storage". This data structure can
simplify writing code that is portable across multiple address
families and platforms. This data structure is designed with the
following goals.

- Large enough to accommodate all supported protocol-specific address
  structures.

- Aligned at an appropriate boundary so that pointers to it can be
  cast as pointers to protocol specific address structures and used
  to access the fields of those structures without alignment
  problems.

The sockaddr_storage structure contains field ss_family which is of
type sa_family_t. When a sockaddr_storage structure is cast to a
sockaddr structure, the ss_family field of the sockaddr_storage
structure maps onto the sa_family field of the sockaddr structure.
When a sockaddr_storage structure is cast as a protocol specific
address structure, the ss_family field maps onto a field of that
structure that is of type sa_family_t and that identifies the
protocol's address family.

Gilligan, et al.   Informational   [Page 14]

RFC 3493   Basic Socket Interface Extensions for IPv6   February 2003

    An example implementation design of such a data structure would be as
    follows.

```
/*
 * Desired design of maximum size and alignment
 */
#define _SS_MAXSIZE     128  /* Implementation specific max size */
#define _SS_ALIGNSIZE   (sizeof (int64_t))
                        /* Implementation specific desired alignment */
/*
 * Definitions used for sockaddr_storage structure paddings design.
 */
#define _SS_PAD1SIZE    (_SS_ALIGNSIZE - sizeof (sa_family_t))
#define _SS_PAD2SIZE    (_SS_MAXSIZE - (sizeof (sa_family_t) +
                          _SS_PAD1SIZE + _SS_ALIGNSIZE))
struct sockaddr_storage {
    sa_family_t  ss_family;     /* address family */
    /* Following fields are implementation specific */
    char        __ss_pad1[_SS_PAD1SIZE];
                /* 6 byte pad, this is to make implementation
                /* specific pad up to alignment field that */
                /* follows explicit in the data structure */
    int64_t     __ss_align;     /* field to force desired structure */
                /* storage alignment */
    char        __ss_pad2[_SS_PAD2SIZE];
                /* 112 byte pad to achieve desired size, */
                /* _SS_MAXSIZE value minus size of ss_family */
                /* __ss_pad1, __ss_align fields is 112 */
};
```

    The above example implementation illustrates a data structure which
    will align on a 64-bit boundary. An implementation-specific field
    "__ss_align" along with "__ss_pad1" is used to force a 64-bit
    alignment which covers proper alignment good enough for the needs of
    sockaddr_in6 (IPv6), sockaddr_in (IPv4) address data structures. The
    size of padding field __ss_pad1 depends on the chosen alignment
    boundary. The size of padding field __ss_pad2 depends on the value
    of overall size chosen for the total size of the structure. This
    size and alignment are represented in the above example by
    implementation specific (not required) constants _SS_MAXSIZE (chosen
    value 128) and _SS_ALIGNSIZE (with chosen value 8). Constants
    _SS_PAD1SIZE (derived value 6) and _SS_PAD2SIZE (derived value 112)
    are also for illustration and not required. The derived values
    assume sa_family_t is 2 bytes. The implementation specific
    definitions and structure field names above start with an underscore
    to denote implementation private namespace. Portable code is not
    expected to access or reference those fields or constants.

Gilligan, et al.   Informational   [Page 15]

RFC 3493   Basic Socket Interface Extensions for IPv6   February 2003

    On implementations where the sockaddr data structure includes a
    "sa_len" field this data structure would look like this:

```
/*
 * Definitions used for sockaddr_storage structure paddings design.
 */
#define _SS_PAD1SIZE (_SS_ALIGNSIZE -
                                (sizeof (uint8_t) + sizeof (sa_family_t))
#define _SS_PAD2SIZE (_SS_MAXSIZE -
                                (sizeof (uint8_t) + sizeof (sa_family_t) +
                                 _SS_PAD1SIZE + _SS_ALIGNSIZE))
struct sockaddr_storage {
    uint8_t      ss_len;       /* address length */
    sa_family_t  ss_family;    /* address family */
    /* Following fields are implementation specific */
    char         __ss_pad1[_SS_PAD1SIZE];
                     /* 6 byte pad, this is to make implementation
                     /* specific pad up to alignment field that */
                     /* follows explicit in the data structure */
    int64_t      __ss_align;  /* field to force desired structure */
                     /* storage alignment */
    char         __ss_pad2[_SS_PAD2SIZE];
                     /* 112 byte pad to achieve desired size, */
                     /* _SS_MAXSIZE value minus size of ss_len, */
                     /* __ss_family, __ss_pad1, __ss_align fields is 112 */
};
```

4. Interface Identification

    This API uses an interface index (a small positive integer) to
    identify the local interface on which a multicast group is joined
    (Section 5.2). Additionally, the advanced API [4] uses these same
    interface indexes to identify the interface on which a datagram is
    received, or to specify the interface on which a datagram is to be
    sent.

    Interfaces are normally known by names such as "le0", "sl1", "ppp2",
    and the like. On Berkeley-derived implementations, when an interface
    is made known to the system, the kernel assigns a unique positive
    integer value (called the interface index) to that interface. These
    are small positive integers that start at 1. (Note that 0 is never
    used for an interface index.) There may be gaps so that there is no
    current interface for a particular positive interface index.

    This API defines two functions that map between an interface name and
    index, a third function that returns all the interface names and
    indexes, and a fourth function to return the dynamic memory allocated
    by the previous function. How these functions are implemented is

Gilligan, et al.   Informational   [Page 16]

RFC 3493   Basic Socket Interface Extensions for IPv6 February 2003

left up to the implementation. 4.4BSD implementations can implement
these functions using the existing sysctl() function with the
NET_RT_IFLIST command. Other implementations may wish to use ioctl()
for this purpose.

4.1 Name-to-Index

The first function maps an interface name into its corresponding
index.

    #include <net/if.h>

    unsigned int if_nametoindex(const char *ifname);

If ifname is the name of an interface, the if_nametoindex() function
shall return the interface index corresponding to name ifname;
otherwise, it shall return zero. No errors are defined.

4.2 Index-to-Name

The second function maps an interface index into its corresponding
name.

    #include <net/if.h>

    char *if_indextoname(unsigned int ifindex, char *ifname);

When this function is called, the ifname argument shall point to a
buffer of at least IF_NAMESIZE bytes. The function shall place in
this buffer the name of the interface with index ifindex.
(IF_NAMESIZE is also defined in <net/if.h> and its value includes a
terminating null byte at the end of the interface name.) If ifindex
is an interface index, then the function shall return the value
supplied in ifname, which points to a buffer now containing the
interface name. Otherwise, the function shall return a NULL pointer
and set errno to indicate the error. If there is no interface
corresponding to the specified index, errno is set to ENXIO. If
there was a system error (such as running out of memory), errno would
be set to the proper value (e.g., ENOMEM).

RFC 3493   Basic Socket Interface Extensions for IPv6   February 2003

4.3 Return All Interface Names and Indexes

   The if_nameindex structure holds the information about a single
   interface and is defined as a result of including the <net/if.h>
   header.

   struct if_nameindex {
     unsigned int   if_index; /* 1, 2, ... */
     char   *if_name; /* null terminated name: "le0", ... */
   };

   The final function returns an array of if_nameindex structures, one
   structure per interface.

      #include <net/if.h>

      struct if_nameindex *if_nameindex(void);

   The end of the array of structures is indicated by a structure with
   an if_index of 0 and an if_name of NULL. The function returns a NULL
   pointer upon an error, and would set errno to the appropriate value.

   The memory used for this array of structures along with the interface
   names pointed to by the if_name members is obtained dynamically.
   This memory is freed by the next function.

4.4 Free Memory

   The following function frees the dynamic memory that was allocated by
   if_nameindex().

      #include <net/if.h>

      void if_freenameindex(struct if_nameindex *ptr);

   The ptr argument shall be a pointer that was returned by
   if_nameindex(). After if_freenameindex() has been called, the
   application shall not use the array of which ptr is the address.

5. Socket Options

   A number of new socket options are defined for IPv6. All of these
   new options are at the IPPROTO_IPV6 level. That is, the "level"
   parameter in the getsockopt() and setsockopt() calls is IPPROTO_IPV6
   when using these options. The constant name prefix IPV6_ is used in
   all of the new socket options. This serves to clearly identify these
   options as applying to IPv6.

Gilligan, et al.   Informational   [Page 18]

RFC 3493   Basic Socket Interface Extensions for IPv6   February 2003

The declaration for IPPROTO_IPV6, the new IPv6 socket options, and
related constants defined in this section are obtained by including
the header <netinet/in.h>

5.1 Unicast Hop Limit

A new setsockopt() option controls the hop limit used in outgoing
unicast IPv6 packets. The name of this option is IPV6_UNICAST_HOPS,
and it is used at the IPPROTO_IPV6 layer. The following example
illustrates how it is used:

```
int  hoplimit = 10;

if (setsockopt(s, IPPROTO_IPV6, IPV6_UNICAST_HOPS,
               (char *) &hoplimit, sizeof(hoplimit)) == -1)
    perror("setsockopt IPV6_UNICAST_HOPS");
```

When the IPV6_UNICAST_HOPS option is set with setsockopt(), the
option value given is used as the hop limit for all subsequent
unicast packets sent via that socket. If the option is not set, the
system selects a default value. The integer hop limit value (called
x) is interpreted as follows:

```
    x -1:           return an error of EINVAL
    x == -1:        use kernel default
    0 <= x <= 255: use x
    x >= 256:       return an error of EINVAL
```

The IPV6_UNICAST_HOPS option may be used with getsockopt() to
determine the hop limit value that the system will use for subsequent
unicast packets sent via that socket. For example:

```
    int  hoplimit;
    socklen_t  len = sizeof(hoplimit);

    if (getsockopt(s, IPPROTO_IPV6, IPV6_UNICAST_HOPS,
                   (char *) &hoplimit, &len) == -1)
        perror("getsockopt IPV6_UNICAST_HOPS");
    else
        printf("Using %d for hop limit.\n", hoplimit);
```

5.2 Sending and Receiving Multicast Packets

IPv6 applications may send multicast packets by simply specifying an
IPv6 multicast address as the destination address, for example in the
destination address argument of the sendto() function.

Gilligan, et al.   Informational   [Page 19]

RFC 3493   Basic Socket Interface Extensions for IPv6   February 2003

Three socket options at the IPPROTO_IPV6 layer control some of the
parameters for sending multicast packets. Setting these options is
not required: applications may send multicast packets without using
these options. The setsockopt() options for controlling the sending
of multicast packets are summarized below. These three options can
also be used with getsockopt().

  IPV6_MULTICAST_IF

    Set the interface to use for outgoing multicast packets. The
    argument is the index of the interface to use. If the
    interface index is specified as zero, the system selects the
    interface (for example, by looking up the address in a routing
    table and using the resulting interface).

    Argument type: unsigned int

  IPV6_MULTICAST_HOPS

    Set the hop limit to use for outgoing multicast packets. (Note
    a separate option - IPV6_UNICAST_HOPS - is provided to set the
    hop limit to use for outgoing unicast packets.)

    The interpretation of the argument is the same as for the
    IPV6_UNICAST_HOPS option:

      x -1:   return an error of EINVAL
      x == -1:   use kernel default
      0 <= x <= 255: use x
      x >= 256:   return an error of EINVAL

      If IPV6_MULTICAST_HOPS is not set, the default is 1
      (same as IPv4 today)

    Argument type: int

  IPV6_MULTICAST_LOOP

    If a multicast datagram is sent to a group to which the sending
    host itself belongs (on the outgoing interface), a copy of the
    datagram is looped back by the IP layer for local delivery if
    this option is set to 1. If this option is set to 0 a copy is
    not looped back. Other option values return an error of
    EINVAL.

RFC 3493   Basic Socket Interface Extensions for IPv6   February 2003

       If IPV6_MULTICAST_LOOP is not set, the default is 1 (loopback;
       same as IPv4 today).

       Argument type: unsigned int

   The reception of multicast packets is controlled by the two
   setsockopt() options summarized below. An error of EOPNOTSUPP is
   returned if these two options are used with getsockopt().

     IPV6_JOIN_GROUP

       Join a multicast group on a specified local interface.
       If the interface index is specified as 0,
       the kernel chooses the local interface.
       For example, some kernels look up the multicast group
       in the normal IPv6 routing table and use the resulting
       interface.

       Argument type: struct ipv6_mreq

     IPV6_LEAVE_GROUP

       Leave a multicast group on a specified interface.
       If the interface index is specified as 0, the system
       may choose a multicast group membership to drop by
       matching the multicast address only.

       Argument type: struct ipv6_mreq

   The argument type of both of these options is the ipv6_mreq
   structure, defined as a result of including the <netinet/in.h>
   header;

   struct ipv6_mreq {
       struct in6_addr ipv6mr_multiaddr; /* IPv6 multicast addr */
       unsigned int   ipv6mr_interface; /* interface index */
   };

   Note that to receive multicast datagrams a process must join the
   multicast group to which datagrams will be sent. UDP applications
   must also bind the UDP port to which datagrams will be sent. Some
   processes also bind the multicast group address to the socket, in
   addition to the port, to prevent other datagrams destined to that
   same port from being delivered to the socket.

RFC 3493   Basic Socket Interface Extensions for IPv6   February 2003

5.3 IPV6_V6ONLY option for AF_INET6 Sockets

   This socket option restricts AF_INET6 sockets to IPv6 communications
   only. As stated in section <3.7 Compatibility with IPv4 Nodes>,
   AF_INET6 sockets may be used for both IPv4 and IPv6 communications.
   Some applications may want to restrict their use of an AF_INET6
   socket to IPv6 communications only. For these applications the
   IPV6_V6ONLY socket option is defined. When this option is turned on,
   the socket can be used to send and receive IPv6 packets only. This
   is an IPPROTO_IPV6 level option. This option takes an int value.
   This is a boolean option. By default this option is turned off.

   Here is an example of setting this option:

      int on = 1;

      if (setsockopt(s, IPPROTO_IPV6, IPV6_V6ONLY,
                     (char *)&on, sizeof(on)) == -1)
          perror("setsockopt IPV6_V6ONLY");
      else
          printf("IPV6_V6ONLY set\n");

   Note - This option has no effect on the use of IPv4 Mapped addresses
   which enter a node as a valid IPv6 addresses for IPv6 communications
   as defined by Stateless IP/ICMP Translation Algorithm (SIIT) [5].

   An example use of this option is to allow two versions of the same
   server process to run on the same port, one providing service over
   IPv6, the other providing the same service over IPv4.

6. Library Functions

   New library functions are needed to perform a variety of operations
   with IPv6 addresses. Functions are needed to lookup IPv6 addresses
   in the Domain Name System (DNS). Both forward lookup (nodename-to-
   address translation) and reverse lookup (address-to-nodename
   translation) need to be supported. Functions are also needed to
   convert IPv6 addresses between their binary and textual form.

   We note that the two existing functions, gethostbyname() and
   gethostbyaddr(), are left as-is. New functions are defined to handle
   both IPv4 and IPv6 addresses.

   The commonly used function gethostbyname() is inadequate for many
   applications, first because it provides no way for the caller to
   specify anything about the types of addresses desired (IPv4 only,
   IPv6 only, IPv4-mapped IPv6 are OK, etc.), and second because many
   implementations of this function are not thread safe. RFC 2133

Gilligan, et al.   Informational   [Page 22]

   defined a function named gethostbyname2() but this function was also
   inadequate, first because its use required setting a global option
   (RES_USE_INET6) when IPv6 addresses were required, and second because
   a flag argument is needed to provide the caller with additional
   control over the types of addresses required. The gethostbyname2()
   function was deprecated in RFC 2553 and is no longer part of the
   basic API.

6.1 Protocol-Independent Nodename and Service Name Translation

   Nodename-to-address translation is done in a protocol-independent
   fashion using the getaddrinfo() function.

```
#include <sys/socket.h>
#include <netdb.h>


int getaddrinfo(const char *nodename, const char *servname,
              const struct addrinfo *hints, struct addrinfo **res);

void freeaddrinfo(struct addrinfo *ai);

struct addrinfo {
   int      ai_flags;      /* AI_PASSIVE, AI_CANONNAME,
                              AI_NUMERICHOST, .. */
   int      ai_family;     /* AF_xxx */
   int      ai_socktype;   /* SOCK_xxx */
   int      ai_protocol;   /* 0 or IPPROTO_xxx for IPv4 and IPv6 */
   socklen_t  ai_addrlen;    /* length of ai_addr */
   char     *ai_canonname; /* canonical name for nodename */
   struct sockaddr  *ai_addr; /* binary address */
   struct addrinfo  *ai_next; /* next structure in linked list */
};
```

   The getaddrinfo() function translates the name of a service location
   (for example, a host name) and/or a service name and returns a set of
   socket addresses and associated information to be used in creating a
   socket with which to address the specified service.

   The nodename and servname arguments are either null pointers or
   pointers to null-terminated strings. One or both of these two
   arguments must be a non-null pointer.

   The format of a valid name depends on the address family or families.
   If a specific family is not given and the name could be interpreted
   as valid within multiple supported families, the implementation will
   attempt to resolve the name in all supported families and, in absence
   of errors, one or more results shall be returned.

RFC 3493   Basic Socket Interface Extensions for IPv6   February 2003

If the nodename argument is not null, it can be a descriptive name or
can be an address string. If the specified address family is
AF_INET, AF_INET6, or AF_UNSPEC, valid descriptive names include host
names. If the specified address family is AF_INET or AF_UNSPEC,
address strings using Internet standard dot notation as specified in
inet_addr() are valid. If the specified address family is AF_INET6
or AF_UNSPEC, standard IPv6 text forms described in inet_pton() are
valid.

If nodename is not null, the requested service location is named by
nodename; otherwise, the requested service location is local to the
caller.

If servname is null, the call shall return network-level addresses
for the specified nodename. If servname is not null, it is a null-
terminated character string identifying the requested service. This
can be either a descriptive name or a numeric representation suitable
for use with the address family or families. If the specified
address family is AF_INET, AF_INET6 or AF_UNSPEC, the service can be
specified as a string specifying a decimal port number.

If the argument hints is not null, it refers to a structure
containing input values that may direct the operation by providing
options and by limiting the returned information to a specific socket
type, address family and/or protocol. In this hints structure every
member other than ai_flags, ai_family, ai_socktype and ai_protocol
shall be set to zero or a null pointer. A value of AF_UNSPEC for
ai_family means that the caller shall accept any address family. A
value of zero for ai_socktype means that the caller shall accept any
socket type. A value of zero for ai_protocol means that the caller
shall accept any protocol. If hints is a null pointer, the behavior
shall be as if it referred to a structure containing the value zero
for the ai_flags, ai_socktype and ai_protocol fields, and AF_UNSPEC
for the ai_family field.

Note:

1. If the caller handles only TCP and not UDP, for example, then the
   ai_protocol member of the hints structure should be set to
   IPPROTO_TCP when getaddrinfo() is called.

2. If the caller handles only IPv4 and not IPv6, then the ai_family
   member of the hints structure should be set to AF_INET when
   getaddrinfo() is called.

RFC 3493   Basic Socket Interface Extensions for IPv6   February 2003

The ai_flags field to which hints parameter points shall be set to
zero or be the bitwise-inclusive OR of one or more of the values
AI_PASSIVE, AI_CANONNAME, AI_NUMERICHOST, AI_NUMERICSERV,
AI_V4MAPPED, AI_ALL, and AI_ADDRCONFIG.

If the AI_PASSIVE flag is specified, the returned address information
shall be suitable for use in binding a socket for accepting incoming
connections for the specified service (i.e., a call to bind()). In
this case, if the nodename argument is null, then the IP address
portion of the socket address structure shall be set to INADDR_ANY
for an IPv4 address or IN6ADDR_ANY_INIT for an IPv6 address. If the
AI_PASSIVE flag is not specified, the returned address information
shall be suitable for a call to connect() (for a connection-mode
protocol) or for a call to connect(), sendto() or sendmsg() (for a
connectionless protocol). In this case, if the nodename argument is
null, then the IP address portion of the socket address structure
shall be set to the loopback address. This flag is ignored if the
nodename argument is not null.

If the AI_CANONNAME flag is specified and the nodename argument is
not null, the function shall attempt to determine the canonical name
corresponding to nodename (for example, if nodename is an alias or
shorthand notation for a complete name).

If the AI_NUMERICHOST flag is specified, then a non-null nodename
string supplied shall be a numeric host address string. Otherwise,
an [EAI_NONAME] error is returned. This flag shall prevent any type
of name resolution service (for example, the DNS) from being invoked.

If the AI_NUMERICSERV flag is specified, then a non-null servname
string supplied shall be a numeric port string. Otherwise, an
[EAI_NONAME] error shall be returned. This flag shall prevent any
type of name resolution service (for example, NIS+) from being
invoked.

If the AI_V4MAPPED flag is specified along with an ai_family of
AF_INET6, then getaddrinfo() shall return IPv4-mapped IPv6 addresses
on finding no matching IPv6 addresses (ai_addrlen shall be 16).

   For example, when using the DNS, if no AAAA records are found then
   a query is made for A records and any found are returned as IPv4-
   mapped IPv6 addresses.

The AI_V4MAPPED flag shall be ignored unless ai_family equals
AF_INET6.

If the AI_ALL flag is used with the AI_V4MAPPED flag, then
getaddrinfo() shall return all matching IPv6 and IPv4 addresses.

For example, when using the DNS, queries are made for both AAAA records and A records, and getaddrinfo() returns the combined results of both queries. Any IPv4 addresses found are returned as IPv4-mapped IPv6 addresses.

The AI_ALL flag without the AI_V4MAPPED flag is ignored.

Note:

When ai_family is not specified (AF_UNSPEC), AI_V4MAPPED and AI_ALL flags will only be used if AF_INET6 is supported.

If the AI_ADDRCONFIG flag is specified, IPv4 addresses shall be returned only if an IPv4 address is configured on the local system, and IPv6 addresses shall be returned only if an IPv6 address is configured on the local system. The loopback address is not considered for this case as valid as a configured address.

For example, when using the DNS, a query for AAAA records should occur only if the node has at least one IPv6 address configured (other than IPv6 loopback) and a query for A records should occur only if the node has at least one IPv4 address configured (other than the IPv4 loopback).

The ai_socktype field to which argument hints points specifies the socket type for the service, as defined for socket(). If a specific socket type is not given (for example, a value of zero) and the service name could be interpreted as valid with multiple supported socket types, the implementation shall attempt to resolve the service name for all supported socket types and, in the absence of errors, all possible results shall be returned. A non-zero socket type value shall limit the returned information to values with the specified socket type.

If the ai_family field to which hints points has the value AF_UNSPEC, addresses shall be returned for use with any address family that can be used with the specified nodename and/or servname. Otherwise, addresses shall be returned for use only with the specified address family. If ai_family is not AF_UNSPEC and ai_protocol is not zero, then addresses are returned for use only with the specified address family and protocol; the value of ai_protocol shall be interpreted as in a call to the socket() function with the corresponding values of ai_family and ai_protocol.

The freeaddrinfo() function frees one or more addrinfo structures returned by getaddrinfo(), along with any additional storage associated with those structures (for example, storage pointed to by the ai_canonname and ai_addr fields; an application must not

reference this storage after the associated addrinfo structure has
been freed). If the ai_next field of the structure is not null, the
entire list of structures is freed. The freeaddrinfo() function must
support the freeing of arbitrary sublists of an addrinfo list
originally returned by getaddrinfo().

Functions getaddrinfo() and freeaddrinfo() must be thread-safe.

A zero return value for getaddrinfo() indicates successful
completion; a non-zero return value indicates failure. The possible
values for the failures are listed below under Error Return Values.

Upon successful return of getaddrinfo(), the location to which res
points shall refer to a linked list of addrinfo structures, each of
which shall specify a socket address and information for use in
creating a socket with which to use that socket address. The list
shall include at least one addrinfo structure. The ai_next field of
each structure contains a pointer to the next structure on the list,
or a null pointer if it is the last structure on the list. Each
structure on the list shall include values for use with a call to the
socket() function, and a socket address for use with the connect()
function or, if the AI_PASSIVE flag was specified, for use with the
bind() function. The fields ai_family, ai_socktype, and ai_protocol
shall be usable as the arguments to the socket() function to create a
socket suitable for use with the returned address. The fields
ai_addr and ai_addrlen are usable as the arguments to the connect()
or bind() functions with such a socket, according to the AI_PASSIVE
flag.

If nodename is not null, and if requested by the AI_CANONNAME flag,
the ai_canonname field of the first returned addrinfo structure shall
point to a null-terminated string containing the canonical name
corresponding to the input nodename; if the canonical name is not
available, then ai_canonname shall refer to the nodename argument or
a string with the same contents. The contents of the ai_flags field
of the returned structures are undefined.

All fields in socket address structures returned by getaddrinfo()
that are not filled in through an explicit argument (for example,
sin6_flowinfo) shall be set to zero.

Note: This makes it easier to compare socket address structures.

RFC 3493   Basic Socket Interface Extensions for IPv6   February 2003

Error Return Values:

The getaddrinfo() function shall fail and return the corresponding value if:

[EAI_AGAIN]   The name could not be resolved at this time. Future attempts may succeed.

[EAI_BADFLAGS] The flags parameter had an invalid value.

[EAI_FAIL]   A non-recoverable error occurred when attempting to resolve the name.

[EAI_FAMILY]   The address family was not recognized.

[EAI_MEMORY]   There was a memory allocation failure when trying to allocate storage for the return value.

[EAI_NONAME]   The name does not resolve for the supplied parameters. Neither nodename nor servname were supplied. At least one of these must be supplied.

[EAI_SERVICE]   The service passed was not recognized for the specified socket type.

[EAI_SOCKTYPE] The intended socket type was not recognized.

[EAI_SYSTEM]   A system error occurred; the error code can be found in errno.

The gai_strerror() function provides a descriptive text string corresponding to an EAI_xxx error value.

    #include <netdb.h>

    const char *gai_strerror(int ecode);

The argument is one of the EAI_xxx values defined for the getaddrinfo() and getnameinfo() functions. The return value points to a string describing the error. If the argument is not one of the EAI_xxx values, the function still returns a pointer to a string whose contents indicate an unknown error.

6.2 Socket Address Structure to Node Name and Service Name

The getnameinfo() function is used to translate the contents of a socket address structure to a node name and/or service name.

RFC 3493   Basic Socket Interface Extensions for IPv6   February 2003

```
#include <sys/socket.h>
#include <netdb.h>

int getnameinfo(const struct sockaddr *sa, socklen_t salen,
                char *node, socklen_t nodelen,
                char *service, socklen_t servicelen,
                  int flags);
```

The getnameinfo() function shall translate a socket address to a node
name and service location, all of which are defined as in
getaddrinfo().

The sa argument points to a socket address structure to be
translated.

The salen argument holds the size of the socket address structure
pointed to by sa.

If the socket address structure contains an IPv4-mapped IPv6 address
or an IPv4-compatible IPv6 address, the implementation shall extract
the embedded IPv4 address and lookup the node name for that IPv4
address.

    Note: The IPv6 unspecified address ("::") and the IPv6 loopback
    address ("::1") are not IPv4-compatible addresses. If the address
    is the IPv6 unspecified address ("::"), a lookup is not performed,
    and the [EAI_NONAME] error is returned.

If the node argument is non-NULL and the nodelen argument is nonzero,
then the node argument points to a buffer able to contain up to
nodelen characters that receives the node name as a null-terminated
string. If the node argument is NULL or the nodelen argument is
zero, the node name shall not be returned. If the node's name cannot
be located, the numeric form of the node's address is returned
instead of its name.

If the service argument is non-NULL and the servicelen argument is
non-zero, then the service argument points to a buffer able to
contain up to servicelen bytes that receives the service name as a
null-terminated string. If the service argument is NULL or the
servicelen argument is zero, the service name shall not be returned.
If the service's name cannot be located, the numeric form of the
service address (for example, its port number) shall be returned
instead of its name.

The arguments node and service cannot both be NULL.

The flags argument is a flag that changes the default actions of the function. By default the fully-qualified domain name (FQDN) for the host shall be returned, but:

- If the flag bit NI_NOFQDN is set, only the node name portion of the FQDN shall be returned for local hosts.

- If the flag bit NI_NUMERICHOST is set, the numeric form of the host's address shall be returned instead of its name, under all circumstances.

- If the flag bit NI_NAMEREQD is set, an error shall be returned if the host's name cannot be located.

- If the flag bit NI_NUMERICSERV is set, the numeric form of the service address shall be returned (for example, its port number) instead of its name, under all circumstances.

- If the flag bit NI_DGRAM is set, this indicates that the service is a datagram service (SOCK_DGRAM). The default behavior shall assume that the service is a stream service (SOCK_STREAM).

Note:

1. The NI_NUMERICxxx flags are required to support the "-n" flags that many commands provide.

2. The NI_DGRAM flag is required for the few AF_INET and AF_INET6 port numbers (for example, [512,514]) that represent different services for UDP and TCP.

The getnameinfo() function shall be thread safe.

A zero return value for getnameinfo() indicates successful completion; a non-zero return value indicates failure.

Upon successful completion, getnameinfo() shall return the node and service names, if requested, in the buffers provided. The returned names are always null-terminated strings.

RFC 3493   Basic Socket Interface Extensions for IPv6   February 2003

    Error Return Values:

    The getnameinfo() function shall fail and return the corresponding
    value if:

    [EAI_AGAIN]   The name could not be resolved at this time.
                    Future attempts may succeed.

    [EAI_BADFLAGS] The flags had an invalid value.

    [EAI_FAIL]   A non-recoverable error occurred.

    [EAI_FAMILY]   The address family was not recognized or the address
                    length was invalid for the specified family.

    [EAI_MEMORY]   There was a memory allocation failure.

    [EAI_NONAME]   The name does not resolve for the supplied parameters.
                    NI_NAMEREQD is set and the host's name cannot be
                    located, or both nodename and servname were null.

    [EAI_OVERFLOW] An argument buffer overflowed.

    [EAI_SYSTEM]   A system error occurred. The error code can be found
                    in errno.

6.3 Address Conversion Functions

    The two IPv4 functions inet_addr() and inet_ntoa() convert an IPv4
    address between binary and text form. IPv6 applications need similar
    functions. The following two functions convert both IPv6 and IPv4
    addresses:

    #include <arpa/inet.h>

    int inet_pton(int af, const char *src, void *dst);

    const char *inet_ntop(int af, const void *src,
                          char *dst, socklen_t size);

    The inet_pton() function shall convert an address in its standard
    text presentation form into its numeric binary form. The af argument
    shall specify the family of the address. The AF_INET and AF_INET6
    address families shall be supported. The src argument points to the
    string being passed in. The dst argument points to a buffer into
    which the function stores the numeric address; this shall be large
    enough to hold the numeric address (32 bits for AF_INET, 128 bits for
    AF_INET6). The inet_pton() function shall return 1 if the conversion

succeeds, with the address pointed to by dst in network byte order.
It shall return 0 if the input is not a valid IPv4 dotted-decimal
string or a valid IPv6 address string, or -1 with errno set to
EAFNOSUPPORT if the af argument is unknown.

If the af argument of inet_pton() is AF_INET, the src string shall be
in the standard IPv4 dotted-decimal form:

    ddd.ddd.ddd.ddd

where "ddd" is a one to three digit decimal number between 0 and 255.
The inet_pton() function does not accept other formats (such as the
octal numbers, hexadecimal numbers, and fewer than four numbers that
inet_addr() accepts).

If the af argument of inet_pton() is AF_INET6, the src string shall
be in one of the standard IPv6 text forms defined in Section 2.2 of
the addressing architecture specification [2].

The inet_ntop() function shall convert a numeric address into a text
string suitable for presentation. The af argument shall specify the
family of the address. This can be AF_INET or AF_INET6. The src
argument points to a buffer holding an IPv4 address if the af
argument is AF_INET, or an IPv6 address if the af argument is
AF_INET6; the address must be in network byte order. The dst
argument points to a buffer where the function stores the resulting
text string; it shall not be NULL. The size argument specifies the
size of this buffer, which shall be large enough to hold the text
string (INET_ADDRSTRLEN characters for IPv4, INET6_ADDRSTRLEN
characters for IPv6).

In order to allow applications to easily declare buffers of the
proper size to store IPv4 and IPv6 addresses in string form, the
following two constants are defined in <netinet/in.h>

    #define INET_ADDRSTRLEN   16
    #define INET6_ADDRSTRLEN   46

The inet_ntop() function shall return a pointer to the buffer
containing the text string if the conversion succeeds, and NULL
otherwise. Upon failure, errno is set to EAFNOSUPPORT if the af
argument is invalid or ENOSPC if the size of the result buffer is
inadequate.

RFC 3493   Basic Socket Interface Extensions for IPv6   February 2003

6.4 Address Testing Macros

   The following macros can be used to test for special IPv6 addresses.

   #include <netinet.h>

   int IN6_IS_ADDR_UNSPECIFIED (const struct in6_addr *);
   int IN6_IS_ADDR_LOOPBACK   (const struct in6_addr *);
   int IN6_IS_ADDR_MULTICAST   (const struct in6_addr *);
   int IN6_IS_ADDR_LINKLOCAL   (const struct in6_addr *);
   int IN6_IS_ADDR_SITELOCAL   (const struct in6_addr *);
   int IN6_IS_ADDR_V4MAPPED   (const struct in6_addr *);
   int IN6_IS_ADDR_V4COMPAT   (const struct in6_addr *);

   int IN6_IS_ADDR_MC_NODELOCAL(const struct in6_addr *);
   int IN6_IS_ADDR_MC_LINKLOCAL(const struct in6_addr *);
   int IN6_IS_ADDR_MC_SITELOCAL(const struct in6_addr *);
   int IN6_IS_ADDR_MC_ORGLOCAL (const struct in6_addr *);
   int IN6_IS_ADDR_MC_GLOBAL   (const struct in6_addr *);

   The first seven macros return true if the address is of the specified
   type, or false otherwise. The last five test the scope of a
   multicast address and return true if the address is a multicast
   address of the specified scope or false if the address is either not
   a multicast address or not of the specified scope.

   Note that IN6_IS_ADDR_LINKLOCAL and IN6_IS_ADDR_SITELOCAL return true
   only for the two types of local-use IPv6 unicast addresses (Link-
   Local and Site-Local) defined in [2], and that by this definition,
   the IN6_IS_ADDR_LINKLOCAL macro returns false for the IPv6 loopback
   address (::1). These two macros do not return true for IPv6
   multicast addresses of either link-local scope or site-local scope.

7. Summary of New Definitions

   The following list summarizes the constants, structure, and extern
   definitions discussed in this memo, sorted by header.

   <net/if.h>   IF_NAMESIZE
   <net/if.h>   struct if_nameindex{};

   <netdb.h>   AI_ADDRCONFIG
   <netdb.h>   AI_ALL
   <netdb.h>   AI_CANONNAME
   <netdb.h>   AI_NUMERICHOST
   <netdb.h>   AI_NUMERICSERV
   <netdb.h>   AI_PASSIVE
   <netdb.h>   AI_V4MAPPED

Gilligan, et al.   Informational   [Page 33]

RFC 3493   Basic Socket Interface Extensions for IPv6   February 2003

    <netdb.h>   EAI_AGAIN
    <netdb.h>   EAI_BADFLAGS
    <netdb.h>   EAI_FAIL
    <netdb.h>   EAI_FAMILY
    <netdb.h>   EAI_MEMORY
    <netdb.h>   EAI_NONAME
    <netdb.h>   EAI_OVERFLOW
    <netdb.h>   EAI_SERVICE
    <netdb.h>   EAI_SOCKTYPE
    <netdb.h>   EAI_SYSTEM
    <netdb.h>   NI_DGRAM
    <netdb.h>   NI_NAMEREQD
    <netdb.h>   NI_NOFQDN
    <netdb.h>   NI_NUMERICHOST
    <netdb.h>   NI_NUMERICSERV
    <netdb.h>   struct addrinfo{};

    <netinet/in.h>   IN6ADDR_ANY_INIT
    <netinet/in.h>   IN6ADDR_LOOPBACK_INIT
    <netinet/in.h>   INET6_ADDRSTRLEN
    <netinet/in.h>   INET_ADDRSTRLEN
    <netinet/in.h>   IPPROTO_IPV6
    <netinet/in.h>   IPV6_JOIN_GROUP
    <netinet/in.h>   IPV6_LEAVE_GROUP
    <netinet/in.h>   IPV6_MULTICAST_HOPS
    <netinet/in.h>   IPV6_MULTICAST_IF
    <netinet/in.h>   IPV6_MULTICAST_LOOP
    <netinet/in.h>   IPV6_UNICAST_HOPS
    <netinet/in.h>   IPV6_V6ONLY
    <netinet/in.h>   SIN6_LEN
    <netinet/in.h>   extern const struct in6_addr in6addr_any;
    <netinet/in.h>   extern const struct in6_addr in6addr_loopback;
    <netinet/in.h>   struct in6_addr{};
    <netinet/in.h>   struct ipv6_mreq{};
    <netinet/in.h>   struct sockaddr_in6{};

    <sys/socket.h>   AF_INET6
    <sys/socket.h>   PF_INET6
    <sys/socket.h>   struct sockaddr_storage;

       The following list summarizes the function and macro prototypes
       discussed in this memo, sorted by header.

    <arpa/inet.h>   int inet_pton(int, const char *, void *);

    <arpa/inet.h>   const char *inet_ntop(int, const void *,
                               char *, socklen_t);

    Gilligan, et al.   Informational   [Page 34]

RFC 3493   Basic Socket Interface Extensions for IPv6   February 2003

```
<net/if.h>         char *if_indextoname(unsigned int, char *);
<net/if.h>         unsigned int if_nametoindex(const char *);
<net/if.h>         void if_freenameindex(struct if_nameindex *);
<net/if.h>         struct if_nameindex *if_nameindex(void);

<netdb.h>          int getaddrinfo(const char *, const char *,
                                   const struct addrinfo *,
                                   struct addrinfo **);
<netdb.h>          int getnameinfo(const struct sockaddr *, socklen_t,
                      char *, socklen_t, char *, socklen_t, int);
<netdb.h>          void freeaddrinfo(struct addrinfo *);
<netdb.h>          const char *gai_strerror(int);

<netinet/in.h>     int IN6_IS_ADDR_LINKLOCAL(const struct in6_addr *);
<netinet/in.h>     int IN6_IS_ADDR_LOOPBACK(const struct in6_addr *);
<netinet/in.h>     int IN6_IS_ADDR_MC_GLOBAL(const struct in6_addr *);
<netinet/in.h>     int IN6_IS_ADDR_MC_LINKLOCAL(const struct in6_addr *);
<netinet/in.h>     int IN6_IS_ADDR_MC_NODELOCAL(const struct in6_addr *);
<netinet/in.h>     int IN6_IS_ADDR_MC_ORGLOCAL(const struct in6_addr *);
<netinet/in.h>     int IN6_IS_ADDR_MC_SITELOCAL(const struct in6_addr *);
<netinet/in.h>     int IN6_IS_ADDR_MULTICAST(const struct in6_addr *);
<netinet/in.h>     int IN6_IS_ADDR_SITELOCAL(const struct in6_addr *);
<netinet/in.h>     int IN6_IS_ADDR_UNSPECIFIED(const struct in6_addr *);
<netinet/in.h>     int IN6_IS_ADDR_V4COMPAT(const struct in6_addr *);
<netinet/in.h>     int IN6_IS_ADDR_V4MAPPED(const struct in6_addr *);
```

8. Security Considerations

   IPv6 provides a number of new security mechanisms, many of which need
   to be accessible to applications. Companion memos detailing the
   extensions to the socket interfaces to support IPv6 security are
   being written.

9. Changes from RFC 2553

   1. Add brief description of the history of this API and its relation
      to the Open Group/IEEE/ISO standards.

   2. Alignments with [3].

   3. Removed all references to getipnodebyname() and getipnodebyaddr(),
      which are deprecated in favor of getaddrinfo() and getnameinfo().

   4. Added IPV6_V6ONLY IP level socket option to permit nodes to not
      process IPv4 packets as IPv4 Mapped addresses in implementations.

   5. Added SIIT to references and added new contributors.

RFC 3493   Basic Socket Interface Extensions for IPv6   February 2003

   6. In previous versions of this specification, the sin6_flowinfo
      field was associated with the IPv6 traffic class and flow label,
      but its usage was not completely specified. The complete
      definition of the sin6_flowinfo field, including its association
      with the traffic class or flow label, is now deferred to a future
      specification.

10. Acknowledgments

   This specification's evolution and completeness were significantly
   influenced by the efforts of Richard Stevens, who has passed on.
   Richard's wisdom and talent made the specification what it is today.
   The co-authors will long think of Richard with great respect.

   Thanks to the many people who made suggestions and provided feedback
   to this document, including:

   Werner Almesberger, Ran Atkinson, Fred Baker, Dave Borman, Andrew
   Cherenson, Alex Conta, Alan Cox, Steve Deering, Richard Draves,
   Francis Dupont, Robert Elz, Brian Haberman, Jun-ichiro itojun Hagino,
   Marc Hasson, Tom Herbert, Bob Hinden, Wan-Yen Hsu, Christian Huitema,
   Koji Imada, Markus Jork, Ron Lee, Alan Lloyd, Charles Lynn, Dan
   McDonald, Dave Mitton, Finnbarr Murphy, Thomas Narten, Josh Osborne,
   Craig Partridge, Jean-Luc Richier, Bill Sommerfield, Erik Scoredos,
   Keith Sklower, JINMEI Tatuya, Dave Thaler, Matt Thomas, Harvey
   Thompson, Dean D. Throop, Karen Tracey, Glenn Trewitt, Paul Vixie,
   David Waitzman, Carl Williams, Kazu Yamamoto, Vlad Yasevich, Stig
   Venaas, and Brian Zill.

   The getaddrinfo() and getnameinfo() functions are taken from an
   earlier document by Keith Sklower. As noted in that document,
   William Durst, Steven Wise, Michael Karels, and Eric Allman provided
   many useful discussions on the subject of protocol-independent name-
   to-address translation, and reviewed early versions of Keith
   Sklower's original proposal. Eric Allman implemented the first
   prototype of getaddrinfo(). The observation that specifying the pair
   of name and service would suffice for connecting to a service
   independent of protocol details was made by Marshall Rose in a
   proposal to X/Open for a "Uniform Network Interface".

   Craig Metz, Jack McCann, Erik Nordmark, Tim Hartrick, and Mukesh
   Kacker made many contributions to this document. Ramesh Govindan
   made a number of contributions and co-authored an earlier version of
   this memo.

Gilligan, et al.   Informational   [Page 36]

RFC 3493   Basic Socket Interface Extensions for IPv6   February 2003

11. References

   [1] Deering, S. and R. Hinden, "Internet Protocol, Version 6 (IPv6)
        Specification", RFC 2460, December 1998.

   [2] Hinden, R. and S. Deering, "IP Version 6 Addressing
        Architecture", RFC 2373, July 1998.

   [3] IEEE Std. 1003.1-2001 Standard for Information Technology —
        Portable Operating System Interface (POSIX). Open Group
        Technical Standard: Base Specifications, Issue 6, December 2001.
        ISO/IEC 9945:2002. http://www.opengroup.org/austin

   [4] Stevens, W. and M. Thomas, "Advanced Sockets API for IPv6", RFC
        2292, February 1998.

   [5] Nordmark, E., "Stateless IP/ICMP Translation Algorithm (SIIT)",
        RFC 2765, February 2000.

   [6] The Open Group Base Working Group
        http://www.opengroup.org/platform/base.html

RFC 3493   Basic Socket Interface Extensions for IPv6   February 2003

12. Authors' Addresses

Bob Gilligan
Intransa, Inc.
2870 Zanker Rd.
San Jose, CA 95134

Phone: 408-678-8647
EMail: gilligan@intransa.com

Susan Thomson
Cisco Systems
499 Thornall Street, 8th floor
Edison, NJ 08837

Phone: 732-635-3086
EMail: sethomso@cisco.com

Jim Bound
Hewlett-Packard Company
110 Spitbrook Road ZKO3-3/W20
Nashua, NH 03062

Phone: 603-884-0062
EMail: Jim.Bound@hp.com

Jack McCann
Hewlett-Packard Company
110 Spitbrook Road ZKO3-3/W20
Nashua, NH 03062

Phone: 603-884-2608
EMail: Jack.McCann@hp.com

RFC 3493   Basic Socket Interface Extensions for IPv6   February 2003

13. Full Copyright Statement

Acknowledgement

Funding for the RFC Editor function is currently provided by the
Internet Society.

Gilligan, et al.   Informational   [Page 39]

D

RFC2292 *"Advanced Sockets API for IPv6"*

RFC 2292   Advanced Sockets API for IPv6   February 1998

Network Working Group   W. Stevens
Request for Comments: 2292   Consultant
Category: Informational   M. Thomas
                                                           AltaVista
                                                       February 1998

                    Advanced Sockets API for IPv6

Status of this Memo

Copyright Notice

Abstract

   Specifications are in progress for changes to the sockets API to
   support IP version 6 [RFC-2133]. These changes are for TCP and UDP-
   based applications and will support most end-user applications in use
   today: Telnet and FTP clients and servers, HTTP clients and servers,
   and the like.

   But another class of applications exists that will also be run under
   IPv6. We call these "advanced" applications and today this includes
   programs such as Ping, Traceroute, routing daemons, multicast routing
   daemons, router discovery daemons, and the like. The API feature
   typically used by these programs that make them "advanced" is a raw
   socket to access ICMPv4, IGMPv4, or IPv4, along with some knowledge
   of the packet header formats used by these protocols. To provide
   portability for applications that use raw sockets under IPv6, some
   standardization is needed for the advanced API features.

   There are other features of IPv6 that some applications will need to
   access: interface identification (specifying the outgoing interface
   and determining the incoming interface) and IPv6 extension headers
   that are not addressed in [RFC-2133]: Hop-by-Hop options, Destination
   options, and the Routing header (source routing). This document
   provides API access to these features too.

RFC 2292   Advanced Sockets API for IPv6   February 1998

Table of Contents

Stevens & Thomas   Informational   [Page 2]

RFC 2292   Advanced Sockets API for IPv6   February 1998

1. Introduction

    Specifications are in progress for changes to the sockets API to
    support IP version 6 [RFC-2133]. These changes are for TCP and UDP-
    based applications. The current document defines some the "advanced"
    features of the sockets API that are required for applications to
    take advantage of additional features of IPv6.

    Today, the portability of applications using IPv4 raw sockets is
    quite high, but this is mainly because most IPv4 implementations
    started from a common base (the Berkeley source code) or at least
    started with the Berkeley headers. This allows programs such as Ping
    and Traceroute, for example, to compile with minimal effort on many
    hosts that support the sockets API. With IPv6, however, there is no
    common source code base that implementors are starting from, and the
    possibility for divergence at this level between different
    implementations is high. To avoid a complete lack of portability
    amongst applications that use raw IPv6 sockets, some standardization
    is necessary.

RFC 2292   Advanced Sockets API for IPv6   February 1998

There are also features from the basic IPv6 specification that are
not addressed in [RFC-2133]: sending and receiving Hop-by-Hop
options, Destination options, and Routing headers, specifying the
outgoing interface, and being told of the receiving interface.

This document can be divided into the following main sections.

1. Definitions of the basic constants and structures required for
    applications to use raw IPv6 sockets. This includes structure
    definitions for the IPv6 and ICMPv6 headers and all associated
    constants (e.g., values for the Next Header field).

2. Some basic semantic definitions for IPv6 raw sockets. For
    example, a raw ICMPv4 socket requires the application to
    calculate and store the ICMPv4 header checksum. But with IPv6
    this would require the application to choose the source IPv6
    address because the source address is part of the pseudo header
    that ICMPv6 now uses for its checksum computation. It should be
    defined that with a raw ICMPv6 socket the kernel always
    calculates and stores the ICMPv6 header checksum.

3. Packet information: how applications can obtain the received
    interface, destination address, and received hop limit, along
    with specifying these values on a per-packet basis. There are a
    class of applications that need this capability and the technique
    should be portable.

4. Access to the optional Hop-by-Hop, Destination, and Routing
    headers.

5. Additional features required for IPv6 application portability.

The packet information along with access to the extension headers
(Hop-by-Hop options, Destination options, and Routing header) are
specified using the "ancillary data" fields that were added to the
4.3BSD Reno sockets API in 1990. The reason is that these ancillary
data fields are part of the Posix.1g standard (which should be
approved in 1997) and should therefore be adopted by most vendors.

This document does not address application access to either the
authentication header or the encapsulating security payload header.

All examples in this document omit error checking in favor of brevity
and clarity.

Stevens & Thomas   Informational   [Page 4]

RFC 2292   Advanced Sockets API for IPv6   February 1998

    We note that many of the functions and socket options defined in this
    document may have error returns that are not defined in this
    document. Many of these possible error returns will be recognized
    only as implementations proceed.

    Datatypes in this document follow the Posix.1g format: intN_t means a
    signed integer of exactly N bits (e.g., int16_t) and uintN_t means an
    unsigned integer of exactly N bits (e.g., uint32_t).

    Note that we use the (unofficial) terminology ICMPv4, IGMPv4, and
    ARPv4 to avoid any confusion with the newer ICMPv6 protocol.

2.   Common Structures and Definitions

    Many advanced applications examine fields in the IPv6 header and set
    and examine fields in the various ICMPv6 headers. Common structure
    definitions for these headers are required, along with common
    constant definitions for the structure members.

    Two new headers are defined: <netinet/ip6.h> and <netinet/icmp6.h>.

    When an include file is specified, that include file is allowed to
    include other files that do the actual declaration or definition.

2.1. The ip6_hdr Structure

    The following structure is defined as a result of including
    <netinet/ip6.h>. Note that this is a new header.

```
      struct ip6_hdr {
        union {
          struct ip6_hdrctl {
            uint32_t ip6_un1_flow;   /* 24 bits of flow-ID */
            uint16_t ip6_un1_plen;   /* payload length */
            uint8_t  ip6_un1_nxt;    /* next header */
            uint8_t  ip6_un1_hlim;   /* hop limit */
          } ip6_un1;
          uint8_t ip6_un2_vfc;       /* 4 bits version, 4 bits priority */
        } ip6_ctlun;
        struct in6_addr ip6_src;     /* source address */
        struct in6_addr ip6_dst;     /* destination address */
      };

      #define ip6_vfc    ip6_ctlun.ip6_un2_vfc
      #define ip6_flow   ip6_ctlun.ip6_un1.ip6_un1_flow
      #define ip6_plen   ip6_ctlun.ip6_un1.ip6_un1_plen
      #define ip6_nxt    ip6_ctlun.ip6_un1.ip6_un1_nxt
      #define ip6_hlim   ip6_ctlun.ip6_un1.ip6_un1_hlim
      #define ip6_hops   ip6_ctlun.ip6_un1.ip6_un1_hlim
```
Stevens & Thomas   Informational   [Page 5]

2.1.1. IPv6 Next Header Values

IPv6 defines many new values for the Next Header field. The
following constants are defined as a result of including
<netinet/in.h>.

```
#define IPPROTO_HOPOPTS        0 /* IPv6 Hop-by-Hop options */
#define IPPROTO_IPV6          41 /* IPv6 header */
#define IPPROTO_ROUTING       43 /* IPv6 Routing header */
#define IPPROTO_FRAGMENT      44 /* IPv6 fragmentation header */
#define IPPROTO_ESP           50 /* encapsulating security payload */
#define IPPROTO_AH            51 /* authentication header */
#define IPPROTO_ICMPV6        58 /* ICMPv6 */
#define IPPROTO_NONE          59 /* IPv6 no next header */
#define IPPROTO_DSTOPTS       60 /* IPv6 Destination options */
```

Berkeley-derived IPv4 implementations also define IPPROTO_IP to be 0.
This should not be a problem since IPPROTO_IP is used only with IPv4
sockets and IPPROTO_HOPOPTS only with IPv6 sockets.

2.1.2. IPv6 Extension Headers

Six extension headers are defined for IPv6. We define structures for
all except the Authentication header and Encapsulating Security
Payload header, both of which are beyond the scope of this document.
The following structures are defined as a result of including
<netinet/ip6.h>.

```
/* Hop-by-Hop options header */
/* XXX should we pad it to force alignment on an 8-byte boundary? */
struct ip6_hbh {
  uint8_t  ip6h_nxt;        /* next header */
  uint8_t  ip6h_len;        /* length in units of 8 octets */
    /* followed by options */
};

/* Destination options header */
/* XXX should we pad it to force alignment on an 8-byte boundary? */
struct ip6_dest {
  uint8_t  ip6d_nxt;        /* next header */
  uint8_t  ip6d_len;        /* length in units of 8 octets */
    /* followed by options */
};

/* Routing header */
struct ip6_rthdr {
```

```
   uint8_t  ip6r_nxt;        /* next header */
   uint8_t  ip6r_len;        /* length in units of 8 octets */
   uint8_t  ip6r_type;       /* routing type */
   uint8_t  ip6r_segleft;    /* segments left */
     /* followed by routing type specific data */
};

/* Type 0 Routing header */
struct ip6_rthdr0 {
   uint8_t  ip6r0_nxt;       /* next header */
   uint8_t  ip6r0_len;       /* length in units of 8 octets */
   uint8_t  ip6r0_type;      /* always zero */
   uint8_t  ip6r0_segleft;   /* segments left */
   uint8_t  ip6r0_reserved;  /* reserved field */
   uint8_t  ip6r0_slmap[3];  /* strict/loose bit map */
   struct in6_addr  ip6r0_addr[1];  /* up to 23 addresses */
};

/* Fragment header */
struct ip6_frag {
   uint8_t   ip6f_nxt;       /* next header */
   uint8_t   ip6f_reserved;  /* reserved field */
   uint16_t  ip6f_offlg;     /* offset, reserved, and flag */
   uint32_t  ip6f_ident;     /* identification */
};

#if      BYTE_ORDER == BIG_ENDIAN
#define IP6F_OFF_MASK         0xfff8  /* mask out offset from _offlg */
#define IP6F_RESERVED_MASK    0x0006  /* reserved bits in ip6f_offlg */
#define IP6F_MORE_FRAG        0x0001  /* more-fragments flag */
#else    /* BYTE_ORDER == LITTLE_ENDIAN */
#define IP6F_OFF_MASK         0xf8ff  /* mask out offset from _offlg */
#define IP6F_RESERVED_MASK    0x0600  /* reserved bits in ip6f_offlg */
#define IP6F_MORE_FRAG        0x0100  /* more-fragments flag */
#endif
```

Defined constants for fields larger than 1 byte depend on the byte
ordering that is used. This API assumes that the fields in the
protocol headers are left in the network byte order, which is big-
endian for the Internet protocols. If not, then either these
constants or the fields being tested must be converted at run-time,
using something like htons() or htonl().

(Note: We show an implementation that supports both big-endian and
little-endian byte ordering, assuming a hypothetical compile-time #if
test to determine the byte ordering. The constant that we show,

RFC 2292   Advanced Sockets API for IPv6   February 1998

BYTE_ORDER, with values of BIG_ENDIAN and LITTLE_ENDIAN, are for
example purposes only. If an implementation runs on only one type of
hardware it need only define the set of constants for that hardware's
byte ordering.)

2.2. The icmp6_hdr Structure

The ICMPv6 header is needed by numerous IPv6 applications including
Ping, Traceroute, router discovery daemons, and neighbor discovery
daemons. The following structure is defined as a result of including
<netinet/icmp6.h>. Note that this is a new header.

```
struct icmp6_hdr {
  uint8_t      icmp6_type;   /* type field */
  uint8_t      icmp6_code;   /* code field */
  uint16_t     icmp6_cksum;  /* checksum field */
  union {
    uint32_t  icmp6_un_data32[1]; /* type-specific field */
    uint16_t  icmp6_un_data16[2]; /* type-specific field */
    uint8_t   icmp6_un_data8[4];  /* type-specific field */
  } icmp6_dataun;
};

#define icmp6_data32    icmp6_dataun.icmp6_un_data32
#define icmp6_data16    icmp6_dataun.icmp6_un_data16
#define icmp6_data8     icmp6_dataun.icmp6_un_data8
#define icmp6_pptr      icmp6_data32[0]  /* parameter prob */
#define icmp6_mtu       icmp6_data32[0]  /* packet too big */
#define icmp6_id        icmp6_data16[0]  /* echo request/reply */
#define icmp6_seq       icmp6_data16[1]  /* echo request/reply */
#define icmp6_maxdelay  icmp6_data16[0]  /* mcast group membership */
```

2.2.1. ICMPv6 Type and Code Values

In addition to a common structure for the ICMPv6 header, common
definitions are required for the ICMPv6 type and code fields. The
following constants are also defined as a result of including
<netinet/icmp6.h>.

```
#define ICMP6_DST_UNREACH            1
#define ICMP6_PACKET_TOO_BIG         2
#define ICMP6_TIME_EXCEEDED          3
#define ICMP6_PARAM_PROB             4

#define ICMP6_INFOMSG_MASK  0x80   /* all informational messages */

#define ICMP6_ECHO_REQUEST           128
#define ICMP6_ECHO_REPLY             129
```

RFC 2292   Advanced Sockets API for IPv6   February 1998


```
#define ICMP6_MEMBERSHIP_QUERY      130
#define ICMP6_MEMBERSHIP_REPORT     131
#define ICMP6_MEMBERSHIP_REDUCTION  132

#define ICMP6_DST_UNREACH_NOROUTE       0 /* no route to destination */
#define ICMP6_DST_UNREACH_ADMIN         1 /* communication with */
                                          /* destination */
                                          /* administratively */
                                          /* prohibited */
#define ICMP6_DST_UNREACH_NOTNEIGHBOR 2 /* not a neighbor */
#define ICMP6_DST_UNREACH_ADDR          3 /* address unreachable */
#define ICMP6_DST_UNREACH_NOPORT        4 /* bad port */

#define ICMP6_TIME_EXCEED_TRANSIT       0 /* Hop Limit == 0 in transit */
#define ICMP6_TIME_EXCEED_REASSEMBLY    1 /* Reassembly time out */

#define ICMP6_PARAMPROB_HEADER          0 /* erroneous header field */
#define ICMP6_PARAMPROB_NEXTHEADER      1 /* unrecognized Next Header */
#define ICMP6_PARAMPROB_OPTION          2 /* unrecognized IPv6 option */
```

   The five ICMP message types defined by IPv6 neighbor discovery (133-
   137) are defined in the next section.

2.2.2. ICMPv6 Neighbor Discovery Type and Code Values

   The following structures and definitions are defined as a result of
   including <netinet/icmp6.h>.

```
   #define ND_ROUTER_SOLICIT           133
   #define ND_ROUTER_ADVERT            134
   #define ND_NEIGHBOR_SOLICIT         135
   #define ND_NEIGHBOR_ADVERT          136
   #define ND_REDIRECT                 137

   struct nd_router_solicit {     /* router solicitation */
     struct icmp6_hdr  nd_rs_hdr;
       /* could be followed by options */
   };

   #define nd_rs_type               nd_rs_hdr.icmp6_type
   #define nd_rs_code               nd_rs_hdr.icmp6_code
   #define nd_rs_cksum              nd_rs_hdr.icmp6_cksum
   #define nd_rs_reserved           nd_rs_hdr.icmp6_data32[0]

   struct nd_router_advert {      /* router advertisement */
     struct icmp6_hdr  nd_ra_hdr;
     uint32_t    nd_ra_reachable;   /* reachable time */
     uint32_t    nd_ra_retransmit;  /* retransmit timer */
```

Stevens & Thomas   Informational   [Page 9]

```
        /* could be followed by options */
    };

    #define nd_ra_type                  nd_ra_hdr.icmp6_type
    #define nd_ra_code                  nd_ra_hdr.icmp6_code
    #define nd_ra_cksum                 nd_ra_hdr.icmp6_cksum
    #define nd_ra_curhoplimit           nd_ra_hdr.icmp6_data8[0]
    #define nd_ra_flags_reserved        nd_ra_hdr.icmp6_data8[1]
    #define ND_RA_FLAG_MANAGED          0x80
    #define ND_RA_FLAG_OTHER            0x40
    #define nd_ra_router_lifetime       nd_ra_hdr.icmp6_data16[1]

    struct nd_neighbor_solicit {   /* neighbor solicitation */
      struct icmp6_hdr  nd_ns_hdr;
      struct in6_addr   nd_ns_target; /* target address */
        /* could be followed by options */
    };

    #define nd_ns_type                  nd_ns_hdr.icmp6_type
    #define nd_ns_code                  nd_ns_hdr.icmp6_code
    #define nd_ns_cksum                 nd_ns_hdr.icmp6_cksum
    #define nd_ns_reserved              nd_ns_hdr.icmp6_data32[0]

    struct nd_neighbor_advert {    /* neighbor advertisement */
      struct icmp6_hdr  nd_na_hdr;
      struct in6_addr   nd_na_target; /* target address */
        /* could be followed by options */
    };

    #define nd_na_type                  nd_na_hdr.icmp6_type
    #define nd_na_code                  nd_na_hdr.icmp6_code
    #define nd_na_cksum                 nd_na_hdr.icmp6_cksum
    #define nd_na_flags_reserved        nd_na_hdr.icmp6_data32[0]
    #if     BYTE_ORDER == BIG_ENDIAN
    #define ND_NA_FLAG_ROUTER           0x80000000
    #define ND_NA_FLAG_SOLICITED        0x40000000
    #define ND_NA_FLAG_OVERRIDE         0x20000000
    #else   /* BYTE_ORDER == LITTLE_ENDIAN */
    #define ND_NA_FLAG_ROUTER           0x00000080
    #define ND_NA_FLAG_SOLICITED        0x00000040
    #define ND_NA_FLAG_OVERRIDE         0x00000020
    #endif

    struct nd_redirect {             /* redirect */
      struct icmp6_hdr  nd_rd_hdr;
      struct in6_addr   nd_rd_target; /* target address */
      struct in6_addr   nd_rd_dst;    /* destination address */
        /* could be followed by options */
```

```
};

#define nd_rd_type                  nd_rd_hdr.icmp6_type
#define nd_rd_code                  nd_rd_hdr.icmp6_code
#define nd_rd_cksum                 nd_rd_hdr.icmp6_cksum
#define nd_rd_reserved              nd_rd_hdr.icmp6_data32[0]

struct nd_opt_hdr {             /* Neighbor discovery option header */
  uint8_t  nd_opt_type;
  uint8_t  nd_opt_len;          /* in units of 8 octets */
    /* followed by option specific data */
};

#define   ND_OPT_SOURCE_LINKADDR       1
#define   ND_OPT_TARGET_LINKADDR       2
#define   ND_OPT_PREFIX_INFORMATION    3
#define   ND_OPT_REDIRECTED_HEADER     4
#define   ND_OPT_MTU                   5

struct nd_opt_prefix_info {     /* prefix information */
  uint8_t    nd_opt_pi_type;
  uint8_t    nd_opt_pi_len;
  uint8_t    nd_opt_pi_prefix_len;
  uint8_t    nd_opt_pi_flags_reserved;
  uint32_t   nd_opt_pi_valid_time;
  uint32_t   nd_opt_pi_preferred_time;
  uint32_t   nd_opt_pi_reserved2;
  struct in6_addr  nd_opt_pi_prefix;
};

#define ND_OPT_PI_FLAG_ONLINK       0x80
#define ND_OPT_PI_FLAG_AUTO         0x40

struct nd_opt_rd_hdr {          /* redirected header */
  uint8_t    nd_opt_rh_type;
  uint8_t    nd_opt_rh_len;
  uint16_t   nd_opt_rh_reserved1;
  uint32_t   nd_opt_rh_reserved2;
    /* followed by IP header and data */
};

struct nd_opt_mtu {             /* MTU option */
  uint8_t    nd_opt_mtu_type;
  uint8_t    nd_opt_mtu_len;
  uint16_t   nd_opt_mtu_reserved;
  uint32_t   nd_opt_mtu_mtu;
};
```

RFC 2292   Advanced Sockets API for IPv6   February 1998

   We note that the nd_na_flags_reserved flags have the same byte
   ordering problems as we discussed with ip6f_offlg.

2.3. Address Testing Macros

   The basic API ([RFC-2133]) defines some macros for testing an IPv6
   address for certain properties. This API extends those definitions
   with additional address testing macros, defined as a result of
   including <netinet/in.h>.

      int IN6_ARE_ADDR_EQUAL(const struct in6_addr *,
                              const struct in6_addr *);

2.4. Protocols File

   Many hosts provide the file /etc/protocols that contains the names of
   the various IP protocols and their protocol number (e.g., the value
   of the protocol field in the IPv4 header for that protocol, such as 1
   for ICMP). Some programs then call the function getprotobyname() to
   obtain the protocol value that is then specified as the third
   argument to the socket() function. For example, the Ping program
   contains code of the form

         struct protoent *proto;

         proto = getprotobyname("icmp");

         s = socket(AF_INET, SOCK_RAW, proto->p_proto);

   Common names are required for the new IPv6 protocols in this file, to
   provide portability of applications that call the getprotoXXX()
   functions.

   We define the following protocol names with the values shown. These
   are taken from ftp://ftp.isi.edu/in-notes/iana/assignments/protocol-
   numbers.

         hopopt   0   # hop-by-hop options for ipv6
         ipv6   41   # ipv6
         ipv6-route   43   # routing header for ipv6
         ipv6-frag   44   # fragment header for ipv6
         esp   50   # encapsulating security payload for ipv6
         ah   51   # authentication header for ipv6
         ipv6-icmp   58   # icmp for ipv6
         ipv6-nonxt   59   # no next header for ipv6
         ipv6-opts   60   # destination options for ipv6

Stevens & Thomas   Informational   [Page 12]

RFC 2292   Advanced Sockets API for IPv6   February 1998

3.   IPv6 Raw Sockets

   Raw sockets bypass the transport layer (TCP or UDP). With IPv4, raw
   sockets are used to access ICMPv4, IGMPv4, and to read and write IPv4
   datagrams containing a protocol field that the kernel does not
   process. An example of the latter is a routing daemon for OSPF,
   since it uses IPv4 protocol field 89. With IPv6 raw sockets will be
   used for ICMPv6 and to read and write IPv6 datagrams containing a
   Next Header field that the kernel does not process. Examples of the
   latter are a routing daemon for OSPF for IPv6 and RSVP (protocol
   field 46).

   All data sent via raw sockets MUST be in network byte order and all
   data received via raw sockets will be in network byte order. This
   differs from the IPv4 raw sockets, which did not specify a byte
   ordering and typically used the host's byte order.

   Another difference from IPv4 raw sockets is that complete packets
   (that is, IPv6 packets with extension headers) cannot be read or
   written using the IPv6 raw sockets API. Instead, ancillary data
   objects are used to transfer the extension headers, as described
   later in this document. Should an application need access to the
   complete IPv6 packet, some other technique, such as the datalink
   interfaces BPF or DLPI, must be used.

   All fields in the IPv6 header that an application might want to
   change (i.e., everything other than the version number) can be
   modified using ancillary data and/or socket options by the
   application for output. All fields in a received IPv6 header (other
   than the version number and Next Header fields) and all extension
   headers are also made available to the application as ancillary data
   on input. Hence there is no need for a socket option similar to the
   IPv4 IP_HDRINCL socket option.

   When writing to a raw socket the kernel will automatically fragment
   the packet if its size exceeds the path MTU, inserting the required
   fragmentation headers. On input the kernel reassembles received
   fragments, so the reader of a raw socket never sees any fragment
   headers.

   When we say "an ICMPv6 raw socket" we mean a socket created by
   calling the socket function with the three arguments PF_INET6,
   SOCK_RAW, and IPPROTO_ICMPV6.

   Most IPv4 implementations give special treatment to a raw socket
   created with a third argument to socket() of IPPROTO_RAW, whose value
   is normally 255. We note that this value has no special meaning to
   an IPv6 raw socket (and the IANA currently reserves the value of 255

Stevens & Thomas   Informational   [Page 13]

when used as a next-header field). (Note: This feature was added to
IPv4 in 1988 by Van Jacobson to support traceroute, allowing a
complete IP header to be passed by the application, before the
IP_HDRINCL socket option was added.)

3.1. Checksums

The kernel will calculate and insert the ICMPv6 checksum for ICMPv6
raw sockets, since this checksum is mandatory.

For other raw IPv6 sockets (that is, for raw IPv6 sockets created
with a third argument other than IPPROTO_ICMPV6), the application
must set the new IPV6_CHECKSUM socket option to have the kernel (1)
compute and store a checksum for output, and (2) verify the received
checksum on input, discarding the packet if the checksum is in error.
This option prevents applications from having to perform source
address selection on the packets they send. The checksum will
incorporate the IPv6 pseudo-header, defined in Section 8.1 of [RFC-
1883]. This new socket option also specifies an integer offset into
the user data of where the checksum is located.

```
int  offset = 2;
setsockopt(fd, IPPROTO_IPV6, IPV6_CHECKSUM, &offset, sizeof(offset));
```

By default, this socket option is disabled. Setting the offset to -1
also disables the option. By disabled we mean (1) the kernel will
not calculate and store a checksum for outgoing packets, and (2) the
kernel will not verify a checksum for received packets.

(Note: Since the checksum is always calculated by the kernel for an
ICMPv6 socket, applications are not able to generate ICMPv6 packets
with incorrect checksums (presumably for testing purposes) using this
API.)

3.2. ICMPv6 Type Filtering

ICMPv4 raw sockets receive most ICMPv4 messages received by the
kernel. (We say "most" and not "all" because Berkeley-derived
kernels never pass echo requests, timestamp requests, or address mask
requests to a raw socket. Instead these three messages are processed
entirely by the kernel.) But ICMPv6 is a superset of ICMPv4, also
including the functionality of IGMPv4 and ARPv4. This means that an
ICMPv6 raw socket can potentially receive many more messages than
would be received with an ICMPv4 raw socket: ICMP messages similar to
ICMPv4, along with neighbor solicitations, neighbor advertisements,
and the three group membership messages.

Most applications using an ICMPv6 raw socket care about only a small
subset of the ICMPv6 message types. To transfer extraneous ICMPv6
messages from the kernel to user can incur a significant overhead.
Therefore this API includes a method of filtering ICMPv6 messages by
the ICMPv6 type field.

Each ICMPv6 raw socket has an associated filter whose datatype is
defined as

        struct icmp6_filter;

This structure, along with the macros and constants defined later in
this section, are defined as a result of including the
<netinet/icmp6.h> header.

The current filter is fetched and stored using getsockopt() and
setsockopt() with a level of IPPROTO_ICMPV6 and an option name of
ICMP6_FILTER.

Six macros operate on an icmp6_filter structure:

        void ICMP6_FILTER_SETPASSALL (struct icmp6_filter *);
        void ICMP6_FILTER_SETBLOCKALL(struct icmp6_filter *);

        void ICMP6_FILTER_SETPASS (int, struct icmp6_filter *);
        void ICMP6_FILTER_SETBLOCK(int, struct icmp6_filter *);

        int ICMP6_FILTER_WILLPASS (int, const struct icmp6_filter *);
        int ICMP6_FILTER_WILLBLOCK(int, const struct icmp6_filter *);

The first argument to the last four macros (an integer) is an ICMPv6
message type, between 0 and 255. The pointer argument to all six
macros is a pointer to a filter that is modified by the first four
macros examined by the last two macros.

The first two macros, SETPASSALL and SETBLOCKALL, let us specify that
all ICMPv6 messages are passed to the application or that all ICMPv6
messages are blocked from being passed to the application.

The next two macros, SETPASS and SETBLOCK, let us specify that
messages of a given ICMPv6 type should be passed to the application
or not passed to the application (blocked).

The final two macros, WILLPASS and WILLBLOCK, return true or false
depending whether the specified message type is passed to the
application or blocked from being passed to the application by the
filter pointed to by the second argument.

When an ICMPv6 raw socket is created, it will by default pass all
ICMPv6 message types to the application.

As an example, a program that wants to receive only router
advertisements could execute the following:

```
struct icmp6_filter  myfilt;

fd = socket(PF_INET6, SOCK_RAW, IPPROTO_ICMPV6);

ICMP6_FILTER_SETBLOCKALL(&myfilt);
ICMP6_FILTER_SETPASS(ND_ROUTER_ADVERT, &myfilt);
setsockopt(fd, IPPROTO_ICMPV6, ICMP6_FILTER, &myfilt, sizeof(myfilt));
```

The filter structure is declared and then initialized to block all
messages types. The filter structure is then changed to allow router
advertisement messages to be passed to the application and the filter
is installed using setsockopt().

The icmp6_filter structure is similar to the fd_set datatype used
with the select() function in the sockets API. The icmp6_filter
structure is an opaque datatype and the application should not care
how it is implemented. All the application does with this datatype
is allocate a variable of this type, pass a pointer to a variable of
this type to getsockopt() and setsockopt(), and operate on a variable
of this type using the six macros that we just defined.

Nevertheless, it is worth showing a simple implementation of this
datatype and the six macros.

```
struct icmp6_filter {
  uint32_t  icmp6_filt[8];  /* 8*32 = 256 bits */
};

#define ICMP6_FILTER_WILLPASS(type, filterp) \
    (((((filterp)->icmp6_filt[(type) >> 5]) & (1 << ((type) & 31))) != 0)
#define ICMP6_FILTER_WILLBLOCK(type, filterp) \
    (((((filterp)->icmp6_filt[(type) >> 5]) & (1 << ((type) & 31))) == 0)
#define ICMP6_FILTER_SETPASS(type, filterp) \
    (((((filterp)->icmp6_filt[(type) >> 5]) |=  (1 << ((type) & 31))))
#define ICMP6_FILTER_SETBLOCK(type, filterp) \
    (((((filterp)->icmp6_filt[(type) >> 5]) &= ~(1 << ((type) & 31))))
#define ICMP6_FILTER_SETPASSALL(filterp) \
    memset((filterp), 0xFF, sizeof(struct icmp6_filter))
#define ICMP6_FILTER_SETBLOCKALL(filterp) \
    memset((filterp), 0, sizeof(struct icmp6_filter))
```

RFC 2292   Advanced Sockets API for IPv6   February 1998

(Note: These sample definitions have two limitations that an
implementation may want to change. The first four macros evaluate
their first argument two times. The second two macros require the
inclusion of the <string.h> header for the memset() function.)

4. Ancillary Data

    4.2BSD allowed file descriptors to be transferred between separate
    processes across a UNIX domain socket using the sendmsg() and
    recvmsg() functions. Two members of the msghdr structure,
    msg_accrights and msg_accrightslen, were used to send and receive the
    descriptors. When the OSI protocols were added to 4.3BSD Reno in
    1990 the names of these two fields in the msghdr structure were
    changed to msg_control and msg_controllen, because they were used by
    the OSI protocols for "control information", although the comments in
    the source code call this "ancillary data".

    Other than the OSI protocols, the use of ancillary data has been
    rare. In 4.4BSD, for example, the only use of ancillary data with
    IPv4 is to return the destination address of a received UDP datagram
    if the IP_RECVDSTADDR socket option is set. With Unix domain sockets
    ancillary data is still used to send and receive descriptors.

    Nevertheless the ancillary data fields of the msghdr structure
    provide a clean way to pass information in addition to the data that
    is being read or written. The inclusion of the msg_control and
    msg_controllen members of the msghdr structure along with the cmsghdr
    structure that is pointed to by the msg_control member is required by
    the Posix.1g sockets API standard (which should be completed during
    1997).

    In this document ancillary data is used to exchange the following
    optional information between the application and the kernel:

        1. the send/receive interface and source/destination address,
        2. the hop limit,
        3. next hop address,
        4. Hop-by-Hop options,
        5. Destination options, and
        6. Routing header.

    Before describing these uses in detail, we review the definition of
    the msghdr structure itself, the cmsghdr structure that defines an
    ancillary data object, and some functions that operate on the
    ancillary data objects.

RFC 2292   Advanced Sockets API for IPv6   February 1998

4.1. The msghdr Structure

    The msghdr structure is used by the recvmsg() and sendmsg()
    functions. Its Posix.1g definition is:

    ```
    struct msghdr {
      void        *msg_name;      /* ptr to socket address structure */
      socklen_t   msg_namelen;    /* size of socket address structure */
      struct iovec *msg_iov;      /* scatter/gather array */
      size_t      msg_iovlen;     /* # elements in msg_iov */
      void        *msg_control;   /* ancillary data */
      socklen_t   msg_controllen; /* ancillary data buffer length */
      int         msg_flags;      /* flags on received message */
    };
    ```

    The structure is declared as a result of including <sys/socket.h>.

    (Note: Before Posix.1g the two "void *" pointers were typically "char
    *", and the two socklen_t members and the size_t member were
    typically integers. Earlier drafts of Posix.1g had the two socklen_t
    members as size_t, but Draft 6.6 of Posix.1g, apparently the final
    draft, changed these to socklen_t to simplify binary portability for
    64-bit implementations and to align Posix.1g with X/Open's Networking
    Services, Issue 5. The change in msg_control to a "void *" pointer
    affects any code that increments this pointer.)

    Most Berkeley-derived implementations limit the amount of ancillary
    data in a call to sendmsg() to no more than 108 bytes (an mbuf).
    This API requires a minimum of 10240 bytes of ancillary data, but it
    is recommended that the amount be limited only by the buffer space
    reserved by the socket (which can be modified by the SO_SNDBUF socket
    option). (Note: This magic number 10240 was picked as a value that
    should always be large enough. 108 bytes is clearly too small as the
    maximum size of a Type 0 Routing header is 376 bytes.)

4.2. The cmsghdr Structure

    The cmsghdr structure describes ancillary data objects transferred by
    recvmsg() and sendmsg(). Its Posix.1g definition is:

    ```
    struct cmsghdr {
      socklen_t  cmsg_len;   /* #bytes, including this header */
      int        cmsg_level; /* originating protocol */
      int        cmsg_type;  /* protocol-specific type */
                 /* followed by unsigned char cmsg_data[]; */
    };
    ```

    This structure is declared as a result of including <sys/socket.h>.

Stevens & Thomas   Informational   [Page 18]

As shown in this definition, normally there is no member with the
name cmsg_data[]. Instead, the data portion is accessed using the
CMSG_xxx() macros, as described shortly. Nevertheless, it is common
to refer to the cmsg_data[] member.

(Note: Before Posix.1g the cmsg_len member was an integer, and not a
socklen_t. See the Note in the previous section for why socklen_t is
used here.)

When ancillary data is sent or received, any number of ancillary data
objects can be specified by the msg_control and msg_controllen
members of the msghdr structure, because each object is preceded by a
cmsghdr structure defining the object's length (the cmsg_len member).
Historically Berkeley-derived implementations have passed only one
object at a time, but this API allows multiple objects to be passed
in a single call to sendmsg() or recvmsg(). The following example
shows two ancillary data objects in a control buffer.

```
|<---------------------- msg_controllen ----------------------------->|
|                                                                     |
|<--- ancillary data object --->|<--- ancillary data object ---------->|
|<----- CMSG_SPACE() ---------->|<----- CMSG_SPACE() ----------------->|
|                               |                                     |
|<-------- cmsg_len ------->|   |<----- cmsg_len ------------------>|  |
|<-------- CMSG_LEN() ----->|   |<---- CMSG_LEN() ----------------->|  |
|                           |   | |                                |  |
+-----+-----+-==-+--+-----------+--+-----+-----+-----+--+-----------+--+
|cmsg_|cmsg_|cmsg_|XX|           |XX|cmsg_|cmsg_|cmsg_|XX|           |XX|
|len  |level|type |XX|cmsg_data[]|XX|len  |level|type |XX|cmsg_data[]|XX|
+-----+-----+-----+--+-----------+--+-----+-----+-----+--+-----------+--+
 ^
 |
msg_control
points here
```

The fields shown as "XX" are possible padding, between the cmsghdr
structure and the data, and between the data and the next cmsghdr
structure, if required by the implementation.

4.3. Ancillary Data Object Macros

To aid in the manipulation of ancillary data objects, three macros
from 4.4BSD are defined by Posix.1g: CMSG_DATA(), CMSG_NXTHDR(), and
CMSG_FIRSTHDR(). Before describing these macros, we show the
following example of how they might be used with a call to recvmsg().

```
struct msghdr   msg;
struct cmsghdr  *cmsgptr;
```

```
    /* fill in msg */

    /* call recvmsg() */

    for (cmsgptr = CMSG_FIRSTHDR(&msg); cmsgptr != NULL;
        cmsgptr = CMSG_NXTHDR(&msg, cmsgptr)) {
        if (cmsgptr->cmsg_level == ... && cmsgptr->cmsg_type == ... ) {
            u_char  *ptr;

            ptr = CMSG_DATA(cmsgptr);
            /* process data pointed to by ptr */
        }
    }
```

We now describe the three Posix.1g macros, followed by two more that
are new with this API: CMSG_SPACE() and CMSG_LEN(). All these macros
are defined as a result of including <sys/socket.h>.

4.3.1. CMSG_FIRSTHDR

    struct cmsghdr *CMSG_FIRSTHDR(const struct msghdr *mhdr);

CMSG_FIRSTHDR() returns a pointer to the first cmsghdr structure in
the msghdr structure pointed to by mhdr. The macro returns NULL if
there is no ancillary data pointed to the by msghdr structure (that
is, if either msg_control is NULL or if msg_controllen is less than
the size of a cmsghdr structure).

One possible implementation could be

```
    #define CMSG_FIRSTHDR(mhdr) \
        ( (mhdr)->msg_controllen >= sizeof(struct cmsghdr) ? \
          (struct cmsghdr *)(mhdr)->msg_control : \
          (struct cmsghdr *)NULL )
```

(Note: Most existing implementations do not test the value of
msg_controllen, and just return the value of msg_control. The value
of msg_controllen must be tested, because if the application asks
recvmsg() to return ancillary data, by setting msg_control to point
to the application's buffer and setting msg_controllen to the length
of this buffer, the kernel indicates that no ancillary data is
available by setting msg_controllen to 0 on return. It is also
easier to put this test into this macro, than making the application
perform the test.)

4.3.2. CMSG_NXTHDR

```
        struct cmsghdr *CMSG_NXTHDR(const struct msghdr *mhdr,
                                    const struct cmsghdr *cmsg);
```

CMSG_NXTHDR() returns a pointer to the cmsghdr structure describing
the next ancillary data object. mhdr is a pointer to a msghdr
structure and cmsg is a pointer to a cmsghdr structure. If there is
not another ancillary data object, the return value is NULL.

The following behavior of this macro is new to this API: if the value
of the cmsg pointer is NULL, a pointer to the cmsghdr structure
describing the first ancillary data object is returned. That is,
CMSG_NXTHDR(mhdr, NULL) is equivalent to CMSG_FIRSTHDR(mhdr). If
there are no ancillary data objects, the return value is NULL. This
provides an alternative way of coding the processing loop shown
earlier:

```
struct msghdr  msg;
struct cmsghdr  *cmsgptr = NULL;

/* fill in msg */

/* call recvmsg() */

while ((cmsgptr = CMSG_NXTHDR(&msg, cmsgptr)) != NULL) {
    if (cmsgptr->cmsg_level == ... && cmsgptr->cmsg_type == ... ) {
        u_char  *ptr;

        ptr = CMSG_DATA(cmsgptr);
        /* process data pointed to by ptr */
    }
}
```

    One possible implementation could be:

```
    #define CMSG_NXTHDR(mhdr, cmsg) \
        ( ((cmsg) == NULL) ? CMSG_FIRSTHDR(mhdr) : \
          (((u_char *)(cmsg) + ALIGN((cmsg)->cmsg_len) \
                + ALIGN(sizeof(struct cmsghdr)) > \
           (u_char *)((mhdr)->msg_control) + (mhdr)->msg_controllen) ? \
          (struct cmsghdr *)NULL : \
          (struct cmsghdr *)((u_char *)(cmsg) + ALIGN((cmsg)->cmsg_len))) )
```

The macro ALIGN(), which is implementation dependent, rounds its
argument up to the next even multiple of whatever alignment is
required (probably a multiple of 4 or 8 bytes).

RFC 2292   Advanced Sockets API for IPv6   February 1998

4.3.3. CMSG_DATA

        unsigned char *CMSG_DATA(const struct cmsghdr *cmsg);

   CMSG_DATA() returns a pointer to the data (what is called the
   cmsg_data[] member, even though such a member is not defined in the
   structure) following a cmsghdr structure.

   One possible implementation could be:

        #define CMSG_DATA(cmsg) ((u_char *)(cmsg) + \
                               ALIGN(sizeof(struct cmsghdr)))

4.3.4. CMSG_SPACE

        unsigned int CMSG_SPACE(unsigned int length);

   This macro is new with this API. Given the length of an ancillary
   data object, CMSG_SPACE() returns the space required by the object
   and its cmsghdr structure, including any padding needed to satisfy
   alignment requirements. This macro can be used, for example, to
   allocate space dynamically for the ancillary data. This macro should
   not be used to initialize the cmsg_len member of a cmsghdr structure;
   instead use the CMSG_LEN() macro.

   One possible implementation could be:

        #define CMSG_SPACE(length) (ALIGN(sizeof(struct cmsghdr)) + \
                                 ALIGN(length))

4.3.5. CMSG_LEN

        unsigned int CMSG_LEN(unsigned int length);

   This macro is new with this API. Given the length of an ancillary
   data object, CMSG_LEN() returns the value to store in the cmsg_len
   member of the cmsghdr structure, taking into account any padding
   needed to satisfy alignment requirements.

   One possible implementation could be:

        #define CMSG_LEN(length) (ALIGN(sizeof(struct cmsghdr)) + length
)

RFC 2292   Advanced Sockets API for IPv6   February 1998

Note the difference between CMSG_SPACE() and CMSG_LEN(), shown also
in the figure in Section 4.2: the former accounts for any required
padding at the end of the ancillary data object and the latter is the
actual length to store in the cmsg_len member of the ancillary data
object.

4.4. Summary of Options Described Using Ancillary Data

There are six types of optional information described in this
document that are passed between the application and the kernel using
ancillary data:

     1.   the send/receive interface and source/destination address,
     2.   the hop limit,
     3.   next hop address,
     4.   Hop-by-Hop options,
     5.   Destination options, and
     6.   Routing header.

First, to receive any of this optional information (other than the
next hop address, which can only be set), the application must call
setsockopt() to turn on the corresponding flag:

     int on = 1;

     setsockopt(fd, IPPROTO_IPV6, IPV6_PKTINFO, &on, sizeof(on));
     setsockopt(fd, IPPROTO_IPV6, IPV6_HOPLIMIT, &on, sizeof(on));
     setsockopt(fd, IPPROTO_IPV6, IPV6_HOPOPTS, &on, sizeof(on));
     setsockopt(fd, IPPROTO_IPV6, IPV6_DSTOPTS, &on, sizeof(on));
     setsockopt(fd, IPPROTO_IPV6, IPV6_RTHDR,   &on, sizeof(on));

When any of these options are enabled, the corresponding data is
returned as control information by recvmsg(), as one or more
ancillary data objects.

Nothing special need be done to send any of this optional
information; the application just calls sendmsg() and specifies one
or more ancillary data objects as control information.

We also summarize the three cmsghdr fields that describe the
ancillary data objects:

cmsg_level	cmsg_type	cmsg_data[]	#times
IPPROTO_IPV6	IPV6_PKTINFO	in6_pktinfo structure	once
IPPROTO_IPV6	IPV6_HOPLIMIT	int	once
IPPROTO_IPV6	IPV6_NEXTHOP	socket address structure	once
IPPROTO_IPV6	IPV6_HOPOPTS	implementation dependent	mult.

RFC 2292   Advanced Sockets API for IPv6   February 1998

        IPPROTO_IPV6   IPV6_DSTOPTS   implementation dependent   mult.
        IPPROTO_IPV6   IPV6_RTHDR   implementation dependent   once

    The final column indicates how many times an ancillary data object of
    that type can appear as control information. The Hop-by-Hop and
    Destination options can appear multiple times, while all the others
    can appear only one time.

    All these options are described in detail in following sections. All
    the constants beginning with IPV6_ are defined as a result of
    including the <netinet/in.h> header.

    (Note: We intentionally use the same constant for the cmsg_level
    member as is used as the second argument to getsockopt() and
    setsockopt() (what is called the "level"), and the same constant for
    the cmsg_type member as is used as the third argument to getsockopt()
    and setsockopt() (what is called the "option name"). This is
    consistent with the existing use of ancillary data in 4.4BSD:
    returning the destination address of an IPv4 datagram.)

    (Note: It is up to the implementation what it passes as ancillary
    data for the Hop-by-Hop option, Destination option, and Routing
    header option, since the API to these features is through a set of
    inet6_option_XXX() and inet6_rthdr_XXX() functions that we define
    later. These functions serve two purposes: to simplify the interface
    to these features (instead of requiring the application to know the
    intimate details of the extension header formats), and to hide the
    actual implementation from the application. Nevertheless, we show
    some examples of these features that store the actual extension
    header as the ancillary data. Implementations need not use this
    technique.)

4.5. IPV6_PKTOPTIONS Socket Option

    The summary in the previous section assumes a UDP socket. Sending
    and receiving ancillary data is easy with UDP: the application calls
    sendmsg() and recvmsg() instead of sendto() and recvfrom().

    But there might be cases where a TCP application wants to send or
    receive this optional information. For example, a TCP client might
    want to specify a Routing header and this needs to be done before
    calling connect(). Similarly a TCP server might want to know the
    received interface after accept() returns along with any Destination
    options.

Stevens & Thomas   Informational   [Page 24]

A new socket option is defined that provides access to the optional information described in the previous section, but without using recvmsg() and sendmsg(). Setting the socket option specifies any of the optional output fields:

        setsockopt(fd, IPPROTO_IPV6, IPV6_PKTOPTIONS, &buf, len);

The fourth argument points to a buffer containing one or more ancillary data objects, and the fifth argument is the total length of all these objects. The application fills in this buffer exactly as if the buffer were being passed to sendmsg() as control information.

The options set by calling setsockopt() for IPV6_PKTOPTIONS are called "sticky" options because once set they apply to all packets sent on that socket. The application can call setsockopt() again to change all the sticky options, or it can call setsockopt() with a length of 0 to remove all the sticky options for the socket.

The corresponding receive option

        getsockopt(fd, IPPROTO_IPV6, IPV6_PKTOPTIONS, &buf, &len);

returns a buffer with one or more ancillary data objects for all the optional receive information that the application has previously specified that it wants to receive. The fourth argument points to the buffer that is filled in by the call. The fifth argument is a pointer to a value-result integer: when the function is called the integer specifies the size of the buffer pointed to by the fourth argument, and on return this integer contains the actual number of bytes that were returned. The application processes this buffer exactly as if the buffer were returned by recvmsg() as control information.

To simplify this document, in the remaining sections when we say "can be specified as ancillary data to sendmsg()" we mean "can be specified as ancillary data to sendmsg() or specified as a sticky option using setsockopt() and the IPV6_PKTOPTIONS socket option". Similarly when we say "can be returned as ancillary data by recvmsg()" we mean "can be returned as ancillary data by recvmsg() or returned by getsockopt() with the IPV6_PKTOPTIONS socket option".

4.5.1. TCP Sticky Options

When using getsockopt() with the IPV6_PKTOPTIONS option and a TCP socket, only the options from the most recently received segment are retained and returned to the caller, and only after the socket option has been set. That is, TCP need not start saving a copy of the options until the application says to do so.

RFC 2292   Advanced Sockets API for IPv6   February 1998

The application is not allowed to specify ancillary data in a call to
sendmsg() on a TCP socket, and none of the ancillary data that we
describe in this document is ever returned as control information by
recvmsg() on a TCP socket.

4.5.2. UDP and Raw Socket Sticky Options

The IPV6_PKTOPTIONS socket option can also be used with a UDP socket
or with a raw IPv6 socket, normally to set some of the options once,
instead of with each call to sendmsg().

Unlike the TCP case, the sticky options can be overridden on a per-
packet basis with ancillary data specified in a call to sendmsg() on
a UDP or raw IPv6 socket. If any ancillary data is specified in a
call to sendmsg(), none of the sticky options are sent with that
datagram.

5.   Packet Information

There are four pieces of information that an application can specify
for an outgoing packet using ancillary data:

     1.   the source IPv6 address,
     2.   the outgoing interface index,
     3.   the outgoing hop limit, and
     4.   the next hop address.

Three similar pieces of information can be returned for a received
packet as ancillary data:

     1.   the destination IPv6 address,
     2.   the arriving interface index, and
     3.   the arriving hop limit.

The first two pieces of information are contained in an in6_pktinfo
structure that is sent as ancillary data with sendmsg() and received
as ancillary data with recvmsg(). This structure is defined as a
result of including the <netinet/in.h> header.

```
struct in6_pktinfo {
  struct in6_addr ipi6_addr;    /* src/dst IPv6 address */
  unsigned int    ipi6_ifindex; /* send/recv interface index */
};
```

In the cmsghdr structure containing this ancillary data, the
cmsg_level member will be IPPROTO_IPV6, the cmsg_type member will be
IPV6_PKTINFO, and the first byte of cmsg_data[] will be the first
byte of the in6_pktinfo structure.

RFC 2292   Advanced Sockets API for IPv6   February 1998

   This information is returned as ancillary data by recvmsg() only if
   the application has enabled the IPV6_PKTINFO socket option:

        int on = 1;
        setsockopt(fd, IPPROTO_IPV6, IPV6_PKTINFO, &on, sizeof(on));

   Nothing special need be done to send this information: just specify
   the control information as ancillary data for sendmsg().

   (Note: The hop limit is not contained in the in6_pktinfo structure
   for the following reason. Some UDP servers want to respond to client
   requests by sending their reply out the same interface on which the
   request was received and with the source IPv6 address of the reply
   equal to the destination IPv6 address of the request. To do this the
   application can enable just the IPV6_PKTINFO socket option and then
   use the received control information from recvmsg() as the outgoing
   control information for sendmsg(). The application need not examine
   or modify the in6_pktinfo structure at all. But if the hop limit
   were contained in this structure, the application would have to parse
   the received control information and change the hop limit member,
   since the received hop limit is not the desired value for an outgoing
   packet.)

5.1. Specifying/Receiving the Interface

   Interfaces on an IPv6 node are identified by a small positive
   integer, as described in Section 4 of [RFC-2133]. That document also
   describes a function to map an interface name to its interface index,
   a function to map an interface index to its interface name, and a
   function to return all the interface names and indexes. Notice from
   this document that no interface is ever assigned an index of 0.

   When specifying the outgoing interface, if the ipi6_ifindex value is
   0, the kernel will choose the outgoing interface. If the application
   specifies an outgoing interface for a multicast packet, the interface
   specified by the ancillary data overrides any interface specified by
   the IPV6_MULTICAST_IF socket option (described in [RFC-2133]), for
   that call to sendmsg() only.

   When the IPV6_PKTINFO socket option is enabled, the received
   interface index is always returned as the ipi6_ifindex member of the
   in6_pktinfo structure.

5.2. Specifying/Receiving Source/Destination Address

   The source IPv6 address can be specified by calling bind() before
   each output operation, but supplying the source address together with
   the data requires less overhead (i.e., fewer system calls) and

RFC 2292   Advanced Sockets API for IPv6   February 1998

requires less state to be stored and protected in a multithreaded
application.

When specifying the source IPv6 address as ancillary data, if the
ipi6_addr member of the in6_pktinfo structure is the unspecified
address (IN6ADDR_ANY_INIT), then (a) if an address is currently bound
to the socket, it is used as the source address, or (b) if no address
is currently bound to the socket, the kernel will choose the source
address. If the ipi6_addr member is not the unspecified address, but
the socket has already bound a source address, then the ipi6_addr
value overrides the already-bound source address for this output
operation only.

The kernel must verify that the requested source address is indeed a
unicast address assigned to the node.

When the in6_pktinfo structure is returned as ancillary data by
recvmsg(), the ipi6_addr member contains the destination IPv6 address
from the received packet.

5.3. Specifying/Receiving the Hop Limit

The outgoing hop limit is normally specified with either the
IPV6_UNICAST_HOPS socket option or the IPV6_MULTICAST_HOPS socket
option, both of which are described in [RFC-2133]. Specifying the
hop limit as ancillary data lets the application override either the
kernel's default or a previously specified value, for either a
unicast destination or a multicast destination, for a single output
operation. Returning the received hop limit is useful for programs
such as Traceroute and for IPv6 applications that need to verify that
the received hop limit is 255 (e.g., that the packet has not been
forwarded).

The received hop limit is returned as ancillary data by recvmsg()
only if the application has enabled the IPV6_HOPLIMIT socket option:

```
    int  on = 1;
    setsockopt(fd, IPPROTO_IPV6, IPV6_HOPLIMIT, &on, sizeof(on));
```

In the cmsghdr structure containing this ancillary data, the
cmsg_level member will be IPPROTO_IPV6, the cmsg_type member will be
IPV6_HOPLIMIT, and the first byte of cmsg_data[] will be the first
byte of the integer hop limit.

Nothing special need be done to specify the outgoing hop limit: just
specify the control information as ancillary data for sendmsg(). As
specified in [RFC-2133], the interpretation of the integer hop limit
value is

Stevens & Thomas   Informational   [Page 28]

```
x < -1:          return an error of EINVAL
x == -1:         use kernel default
0 <= x <= 255:   use x
x >= 256:        return an error of EINVAL
```

5.4. Specifying the Next Hop Address

The IPV6_NEXTHOP ancillary data object specifies the next hop for the
datagram as a socket address structure. In the cmsghdr structure
containing this ancillary data, the cmsg_level member will be
IPPROTO_IPV6, the cmsg_type member will be IPV6_NEXTHOP, and the
first byte of cmsg_data[] will be the first byte of the socket
address structure.

This is a privileged option. (Note: It is implementation defined and
beyond the scope of this document to define what "privileged" means.
Unix systems use this term to mean the process must have an effective
user ID of 0.)

If the socket address structure contains an IPv6 address (e.g., the
sin6_family member is AF_INET6), then the node identified by that
address must be a neighbor of the sending host. If that address
equals the destination IPv6 address of the datagram, then this is
equivalent to the existing SO_DONTROUTE socket option.

5.5. Additional Errors with sendmsg()

With the IPV6_PKTINFO socket option there are no additional errors
possible with the call to recvmsg(). But when specifying the
outgoing interface or the source address, additional errors are
possible from sendmsg(). The following are examples, but some of
these may not be provided by some implementations, and some
implementations may define additional errors:

ENXIO   The interface specified by ipi6_ifindex does not exist.

ENETDOWN   The interface specified by ipi6_ifindex is not enabled
              for IPv6 use.

EADDRNOTAVAIL ipi6_ifindex specifies an interface but the address
              ipi6_addr is not available for use on that interface.

EHOSTUNREACH No route to the destination exists over the interface
              specified by ifi6_ifindex.

RFC 2292   Advanced Sockets API for IPv6   February 1998

6. Hop-By-Hop Options

   A variable number of Hop-by-Hop options can appear in a single Hop-
   by-Hop options header. Each option in the header is TLV-encoded with
   a type, length, and value.

   Today only three Hop-by-Hop options are defined for IPv6 [RFC-1883]:
   Jumbo Payload, Pad1, and PadN, although a proposal exists for a
   router-alert Hop-by-Hop option. The Jumbo Payload option should not
   be passed back to an application and an application should receive an
   error if it attempts to set it. This option is processed entirely by
   the kernel. It is indirectly specified by datagram-based
   applications as the size of the datagram to send and indirectly
   passed back to these applications as the length of the received
   datagram. The two pad options are for alignment purposes and are
   automatically inserted by a sending kernel when needed and ignored by

   the receiving kernel. This section of the API is therefore defined
   for future Hop-by-Hop options that an application may need to specify
   and receive.

   Individual Hop-by-Hop options (and Destination options, which are
   described shortly, and which are similar to the Hop-by-Hop options)
   may have specific alignment requirements. For example, the 4-byte
   Jumbo Payload length should appear on a 4-byte boundary, and IPv6
   addresses are normally aligned on an 8-byte boundary. These
   requirements and the terminology used with these options are
   discussed in Section 4.2 and Appendix A of [RFC-1883]. The alignment
   of each option is specified by two values, called x and y, written as
   "xn + y". This states that the option must appear at an integer
   multiple of x bytes from the beginning of the options header (x can
   have the values 1, 2, 4, or 8), plus y bytes (y can have a value
   between 0 and 7, inclusive). The Pad1 and PadN options are inserted
   as needed to maintain the required alignment. Whatever code builds
   either a Hop-by-Hop options header or a Destination options header
   must know the values of x and y for each option.

   Multiple Hop-by-Hop options can be specified by the application.
   Normally one ancillary data object describes all the Hop-by-Hop
   options (since each option is itself TLV-encoded) but the application
   can specify multiple ancillary data objects for the Hop-by-Hop
   options, each object specifying one or more options. Care must be
   taken designing the API for these options since

   1.   it may be possible for some future Hop-by-Hop options to be
        generated by the application and processed entirely by the
        application (e.g., the kernel may not know the alignment
        restrictions for the option),

   2.   it must be possible for the kernel to insert its own Hop-by-Hop
        options in an outgoing packet (e.g., the Jumbo Payload option),

   3.   the application can place one or more Hop-by-Hop options into a
        single ancillary data object,

   4.   if the application specifies multiple ancillary data objects,
        each containing one or more Hop-by-Hop options, the kernel must
        combine these a single Hop-by-Hop options header, and

   5.   it must be possible for the kernel to remove some Hop-by-Hop
        options from a received packet before returning the remaining
        Hop-by-Hop options to the application. (This removal might
        consist of the kernel converting the option into a pad option of
        the same length.)

Finally, we note that access to some Hop-by-Hop options or to some
Destination options, might require special privilege. That is,
normal applications (without special privilege) might be forbidden
from setting certain options in outgoing packets, and might never see
certain options in received packets.

6.1. Receiving Hop-by-Hop Options

   To receive Hop-by-Hop options the application must enable the
   IPV6_HOPOPTS socket option:

        int   on = 1;
        setsockopt(fd, IPPROTO_IPV6, IPV6_HOPOPTS, &on, sizeof(on));

   All the Hop-by-Hop options are returned as one ancillary data object
   described by a cmsghdr structure. The cmsg_level member will be
   IPPROTO_IPV6 and the cmsg_type member will be IPV6_HOPOPTS. These
   options are then processed by calling the inet6_option_next() and
   inet6_option_find() functions, described shortly.

6.2. Sending Hop-by-Hop Options

   To send one or more Hop-by-Hop options, the application just
   specifies them as ancillary data in a call to sendmsg(). No socket
   option need be set.

   Normally all the Hop-by-Hop options are specified by a single
   ancillary data object. Multiple ancillary data objects, each
   containing one or more Hop-by-Hop options, can also be specified, in
   which case the kernel will combine all the Hop-by-Hop options into a
   single Hop-by-Hop extension header. But it should be more efficient
   to use a single ancillary data object to describe all the Hop-by-Hop

options. The cmsg_level member is set to IPPROTO_IPV6 and the
cmsg_type member is set to IPV6_HOPOPTS. The option is normally
constructed using the inet6_option_init(), inet6_option_append(), and
inet6_option_alloc() functions, described shortly.

Additional errors may be possible from sendmsg() if the specified
option is in error.

6.3. Hop-by-Hop and Destination Options Processing

Building and parsing the Hop-by-Hop and Destination options is
complicated for the reasons given earlier. We therefore define a set
of functions to help the application. The function prototypes for
these functions are all in the <netinet/in.h> header.

6.3.1. inet6_option_space

```
int inet6_option_space(int nbytes);
```

This function returns the number of bytes required to hold an option
when it is stored as ancillary data, including the cmsghdr structure
at the beginning, and any padding at the end (to make its size a
multiple of 8 bytes). The argument is the size of the structure
defining the option, which must include any pad bytes at the
beginning (the value y in the alignment term "xn + y"), the type
byte, the length byte, and the option data.

(Note: If multiple options are stored in a single ancillary data
object, which is the recommended technique, this function
overestimates the amount of space required by the size of N-1 cmsghdr
structures, where N is the number of options to be stored in the
object. This is of little consequence, since it is assumed that most
Hop-by-Hop option headers and Destination option headers carry only
one option (p. 33 of [RFC-1883]).)

6.3.2. inet6_option_init

```
int inet6_option_init(void *bp, struct cmsghdr **cmsgp, int
type);
```

This function is called once per ancillary data object that will
contain either Hop-by-Hop or Destination options. It returns 0 on
success or -1 on an error.

bp is a pointer to previously allocated space that will contain the
ancillary data object. It must be large enough to contain all the
individual options to be added by later calls to
inet6_option_append() and inet6_option_alloc().

Stevens & Thomas   Informational   [Page 32]

RFC 2292   Advanced Sockets API for IPv6   February 1998

cmsgp is a pointer to a pointer to a cmsghdr structure. *cmsgp is
initialized by this function to point to the cmsghdr structure
constructed by this function in the buffer pointed to by bp.

type is either IPV6_HOPOPTS or IPV6_DSTOPTS. This type is stored in
the cmsg_type member of the cmsghdr structure pointed to by *cmsgp.

6.3.3. inet6_option_append

       int inet6_option_append(struct cmsghdr *cmsg, const uint8_t *typep,
                               int multx, int plusy);

This function appends a Hop-by-Hop option or a Destination option
into an ancillary data object that has been initialized by
inet6_option_init(). This function returns 0 if it succeeds or -1 on
an error.

cmsg is a pointer to the cmsghdr structure that must have been
initialized by inet6_option_init().

typep is a pointer to the 8-bit option type. It is assumed that this
field is immediately followed by the 8-bit option data length field,
which is then followed immediately by the option data. The caller
initializes these three fields (the type-length-value, or TLV) before
calling this function.

The option type must have a value from 2 to 255, inclusive. (0 and 1
are reserved for the Pad1 and PadN options, respectively.)

The option data length must have a value between 0 and 255,
inclusive, and is the length of the option data that follows.

multx is the value x in the alignment term "xn + y" described
earlier. It must have a value of 1, 2, 4, or 8.

plusy is the value y in the alignment term "xn + y" described
earlier. It must have a value between 0 and 7, inclusive.

6.3.4. inet6_option_alloc

       uint8_t *inet6_option_alloc(struct cmsghdr *cmsg, int datalen,
                                   int multx, int plusy);

RFC 2292   Advanced Sockets API for IPv6   February 1998

This function appends a Hop-by-Hop option or a Destination option
into an ancillary data object that has been initialized by
inet6_option_init(). This function returns a pointer to the 8-bit
option type field that starts the option on success, or NULL on an
error.

The difference between this function and inet6_option_append() is
that the latter copies the contents of a previously built option into
the ancillary data object while the current function returns a
pointer to the space in the data object where the option's TLV must
then be built by the caller.

cmsg is a pointer to the cmsghdr structure that must have been
initialized by inet6_option_init().

datalen is the value of the option data length byte for this option.
This value is required as an argument to allow the function to
determine if padding must be appended at the end of the option. (The
inet6_option_append() function does not need a data length argument
since the option data length must already be stored by the caller.)

multx is the value x in the alignment term "xn + y" described
earlier. It must have a value of 1, 2, 4, or 8.

plusy is the value y in the alignment term "xn + y" described
earlier. It must have a value between 0 and 7, inclusive.

6.3.5. inet6_option_next

      int inet6_option_next(const struct cmsghdr *cmsg, uint8_t
      **tptrp);

This function processes the next Hop-by-Hop option or Destination
option in an ancillary data object. If another option remains to be
processed, the return value of the function is 0 and *tptrp points to
the 8-bit option type field (which is followed by the 8-bit option
data length, followed by the option data). If no more options remain
to be processed, the return value is -1 and *tptrp is NULL. If an
error occurs, the return value is -1 and *tptrp is not NULL.

cmsg is a pointer to cmsghdr structure of which cmsg_level equals
IPPROTO_IPV6 and cmsg_type equals either IPV6_HOPOPTS or
IPV6_DSTOPTS.

tptrp is a pointer to a pointer to an 8-bit byte and *tptrp is used
by the function to remember its place in the ancillary data object
each time the function is called. The first time this function is
called for a given ancillary data object, *tptrp must be set to NULL.

Stevens & Thomas   Informational   [Page 34]

Each time this function returns success, *tptrp points to the 8-bit
option type field for the next option to be processed.

6.3.6. inet6_option_find

        int inet6_option_find(const struct cmsghdr *cmsg, uint8_t *tptrp,
                             int type);

This function is similar to the previously described
inet6_option_next() function, except this function lets the caller
specify the option type to be searched for, instead of always
returning the next option in the ancillary data object. cmsg is a
pointer to cmsghdr structure of which cmsg_level equals IPPROTO_IPV6
and cmsg_type equals either IPV6_HOPOPTS or IPV6_DSTOPTS.

tptrp is a pointer to a pointer to an 8-bit byte and *tptrp is used
by the function to remember its place in the ancillary data object
each time the function is called. The first time this function is
called for a given ancillary data object, *tptrp must be set to NULL.

This function starts searching for an option of the specified type
beginning after the value of *tptrp. If an option of the specified
type is located, this function returns 0 and *tptrp points to the 8-
bit option type field for the option of the specified type. If an
option of the specified type is not located, the return value is -1
and *tptrp is NULL. If an error occurs, the return value is -1 and
*tptrp is not NULL.

6.3.7. Options Examples

We now provide an example that builds two Hop-by-Hop options. First
we define two options, called X and Y, taken from the example in
Appendix A of [RFC-1883]. We assume that all options will have
structure definitions similar to what is shown below.

```
        /* option X and option Y are defined in [RFC-1883], pp. 33-34 */
#define IP6_X_OPT_TYPE        X    /* replace X with assigned value */
#define IP6_X_OPT_LEN         12
#define IP6_X_OPT_MULTX       8    /* 8n + 2 alignment */
#define IP6_X_OPT_OFFSETY     2

struct ip6_X_opt {
  uint8_t   ip6_X_opt_pad[IP6_X_OPT_OFFSETY];
  uint8_t   ip6_X_opt_type;
  uint8_t   ip6_X_opt_len;
  uint32_t  ip6_X_opt_val1;
  uint64_t  ip6_X_opt_val2;
};
```

RFC 2292   Advanced Sockets API for IPv6   February 1998

```
#define IP6_Y_OPT_TYPE        Y    /* replace Y with assigned value */
#define IP6_Y_OPT_LEN         7
#define IP6_Y_OPT_MULTX       4    /* 4n + 3 alignment */
#define IP6_Y_OPT_OFFSETY     3

struct ip6_Y_opt {
  uint8_t    ip6_Y_opt_pad[IP6_Y_OPT_OFFSETY];
  uint8_t    ip6_Y_opt_type;
  uint8_t    ip6_Y_opt_len;
  uint8_t    ip6_Y_opt_val1;
  uint16_t   ip6_Y_opt_val2;
  uint32_t   ip6_Y_opt_val3;
};
```

   We now show the code fragment to build one ancillary data object
   containing both options.

```
struct msghdr   msg;
struct cmsghdr  *cmsgptr;
struct ip6_X_opt  optX;
struct ip6_Y_opt  optY;

msg.msg_control = malloc(inet6_option_space(sizeof(optX) +
                                            sizeof(optY)));

inet6_option_init(msg.msg_control, &cmsgptr, IPV6_HOPOPTS);

optX.ip6_X_opt_type = IP6_X_OPT_TYPE;
optX.ip6_X_opt_len  = IP6_X_OPT_LEN;
optX.ip6_X_opt_val1 = <32-bit value>;
optX.ip6_X_opt_val2 = <64-bit value>;
inet6_option_append(cmsgptr, &optX.ip6_X_opt_type,
                    IP6_X_OPT_MULTX, IP6_X_OPT_OFFSETY);

optY.ip6_Y_opt_type = IP6_Y_OPT_TYPE;
optY.ip6_Y_opt_len  = IP6_Y_OPT_LEN;
optY.ip6_Y_opt_val1 = <8-bit value>;
optY.ip6_Y_opt_val2 = <16-bit value>;
optY.ip6_Y_opt_val3 = <32-bit value>;
inet6_option_append(cmsgptr, &optY.ip6_Y_opt_type,
                    IP6_Y_OPT_MULTX, IP6_Y_OPT_OFFSETY);

msg.msg_controllen = cmsgptr->cmsg_len;
```

   The call to inet6_option_init() builds the cmsghdr structure in the
   control buffer.

Stevens & Thomas   Informational   [Page 36]

RFC 2292   Advanced Sockets API for IPv6   February 1998

```
+-+-+-+-+-+-+-+-+-+-+-+-+-+-+-+-+-+-+-+-+-+-+-+-+-+-+-+-+-+-+-+-+
|          cmsg_len = CMSG_LEN(0) = 12                          |
+-+-+-+-+-+-+-+-+-+-+-+-+-+-+-+-+-+-+-+-+-+-+-+-+-+-+-+-+-+-+-+-+
|          cmsg_level = IPPROTO_IPV6                            |
+-+-+-+-+-+-+-+-+-+-+-+-+-+-+-+-+-+-+-+-+-+-+-+-+-+-+-+-+-+-+-+-+
|          cmsg_type = IPV6_HOPOPTS                             |
+-+-+-+-+-+-+-+-+-+-+-+-+-+-+-+-+-+-+-+-+-+-+-+-+-+-+-+-+-+-+-+-+
```

Here we assume a 32-bit architecture where sizeof(struct cmsghdr)
equals 12, with a desired alignment of 4-byte boundaries (that is,
the ALIGN() macro shown in the sample implementations of the
CMSG_xxx() macros rounds up to a multiple of 4).

The first call to inet6_option_append() appends the X option. Since
this is the first option in the ancillary data object, 2 bytes are
allocated for the Next Header byte and for the Hdr Ext Len byte. The
former will be set by the kernel, depending on the type of header
that follows this header, and the latter byte is set to 1. These 2
bytes form the 2 bytes of padding (IP6_X_OPT_OFFSETY) required at the
beginning of this option.

```
+-+-+-+-+-+-+-+-+-+-+-+-+-+-+-+-+-+-+-+-+-+-+-+-+-+-+-+-+-+-+-+-+
|          cmsg_len = 28                                        |
+-+-+-+-+-+-+-+-+-+-+-+-+-+-+-+-+-+-+-+-+-+-+-+-+-+-+-+-+-+-+-+-+
|          cmsg_level = IPPROTO_IPV6                            |
+-+-+-+-+-+-+-+-+-+-+-+-+-+-+-+-+-+-+-+-+-+-+-+-+-+-+-+-+-+-+-+-+
|          cmsg_type = IPV6_HOPOPTS                             |
+-+-+-+-+-+-+-+-+-+-+-+-+-+-+-+-+-+-+-+-+-+-+-+-+-+-+-+-+-+-+-+-+
| Next Header  | Hdr Ext Len=1 | Option Type=X |Opt Data Len=12|
+-+-+-+-+-+-+-+-+-+-+-+-+-+-+-+-+-+-+-+-+-+-+-+-+-+-+-+-+-+-+-+-+
|                         4-octet field                        |
+-+-+-+-+-+-+-+-+-+-+-+-+-+-+-+-+-+-+-+-+-+-+-+-+-+-+-+-+-+-+-+-+
|                                                              |
+                         8-octet field                        +
|                                                              |
+-+-+-+-+-+-+-+-+-+-+-+-+-+-+-+-+-+-+-+-+-+-+-+-+-+-+-+-+-+-+-+-+
```

The cmsg_len member of the cmsghdr structure is incremented by 16,
the size of the option.

The next call to inet6_option_append() appends the Y option to the
ancillary data object.

```
      +-+-+-+-+-+-+-+-+-+-+-+-+-+-+-+-+-+-+-+-+-+-+-+-+-+-+-+-+-+-+-+-+
      |         cmsg_len = 44                                        |
      +-+-+-+-+-+-+-+-+-+-+-+-+-+-+-+-+-+-+-+-+-+-+-+-+-+-+-+-+-+-+-+-+
      |       cmsg_level = IPPROTO_IPV6                              |
      +-|-|-|-|-|-|-|-|-|-|-+-+-+-+-+-+-+-+-+-+-+-+-+-+-+-+-+-+-+-+-+-+
      |       cmsg_type = IPV6_HOPOPTS                               |
      +-+-+-+-+-+-+-+-+-+-+-+-+-+-+-+-+-+-+-+-+-+-+-+-+-+-+-+-+-+-+-+-+
      | Next Header   | Hdr Ext Len=3 | Option Type=X |Opt Data Len=12|
      +-+-+-+-+-+-+-+-+-+-+-+-+-+-+-+-+-+-+-+-+-+-+-+-+-+-+-+-+-+-+-+-+
      |                      4-octet field                          |
      +-+-+-+-+-+-+-+-+-+-+-+-+-+-+-+-+-+-+-+-+-+-+-+-+-+-+-+-+-+-+-+-+
      |                                                             |
      +                      8-octet field                          +
      |                                                             |
      +-+-+-+-+-+-+-+-+-+-+-+-+-+-+-+-+-+-+-+-+-+-+-+-+-+-+-+-+-+-+-+-+
      | PadN Option=1 |Opt Data Len=1 |       0       | Option Type=Y |
      +-+-+-+-+-+-+-+-+-+-+-+-+-+-+-+-+-+-+-+-+-+-+-+-+-+-+-+-+-+-+-+-+
      |Opt Data Len=7 | 1-octet field |       2-octet field         |
      +-+-+-+-+-+-+-+-+-+-+-+-+-+-+-+-+-+-+-+-+-+-+-+-+-+-+-+-+-+-+-+-+
      |                      4-octet field                          |
      +-+-+-+-+-+-+-+-+-+-+-+-+-+-+-+-+-+-+-+-+-+-+-+-+-+-+-+-+-+-+-+-+
      | PadN Option=1 |Opt Data Len=2 |       0       |       0       |
      +-+-+-+-+-+-+-+-+-+-+-+-+-+-+-+-+-+-+-+-+-+-+-+-+-+-+-+-+-+-+-+-+
```

16 bytes are appended by this function, so cmsg_len becomes 44. The
inet6_option_append() function notices that the appended data
requires 4 bytes of padding at the end, to make the size of the
ancillary data object a multiple of 8, and appends the PadN option
before returning. The Hdr Ext Len byte is incremented by 2 to become
3.

Alternately, the application could build two ancillary data objects,
one per option, although this will probably be less efficient than
combining the two options into a single ancillary data object (as
just shown). The kernel must combine these into a single Hop-by-Hop
extension header in the final IPv6 packet.

```
     struct msghdr   msg;
     struct cmsghdr  *cmsgptr;
     struct ip6_X_opt  optX;
     struct ip6_Y_opt  optY;

     msg.msg_control = malloc(inet6_option_space(sizeof(optX)) +
                              inet6_option_space(sizeof(optY)));

     inet6_option_init(msg.msg_control, &cmsgptr, IPPROTO_HOPOPTS);

     optX.ip6_X_opt_type = IP6_X_OPT_TYPE;
```

```
       optX.ip6_X_opt_len  = IP6_X_OPT_LEN;
       optX.ip6_X_opt_val1 = <32-bit value>;
       optX.ip6_X_opt_val2 = <64-bit value>;
       inet6_option_append(cmsgptr, &optX.ip6_X_opt_type,
                        IP6_X_OPT_MULTX, IP6_X_OPT_OFFSETY);
       msg.msg_controllen = CMSG_SPACE(sizeof(optX));

       inet6_option_init((u_char *)msg.msg_control + msg.msg_controllen,
                     &cmsgptr, IPPROTO_HOPOPTS);

       optY.ip6_Y_opt_type = IP6_Y_OPT_TYPE;
       optY.ip6_Y_opt_len  = IP6_Y_OPT_LEN;
       optY.ip6_Y_opt_val1 = <8-bit value>;
       optY.ip6_Y_opt_val2 = <16-bit value>;
       optY.ip6_Y_opt_val3 = <32-bit value>;
       inet6_option_append(cmsgptr, &optY.ip6_Y_opt_type,
                        IP6_Y_OPT_MULTX, IP6_Y_OPT_OFFSETY);
       msg.msg_controllen += cmsgptr->cmsg_len;
```

   Each call to inet6_option_init() builds a new cmsghdr structure, and
   the final result looks like the following:

```
+-+-+-+-+-+-+-+-+-+-+-+-+-+-+-+-+-+-+-+-+-+-+-+-+-+-+-+-+-+-+-+-+
|         cmsg_len = 28                                         |
+-+-+-+-+-+-+-+-+-+-+-+-+-+-+-+-+-+-+-+-+-+-+-+-+-+-+-+-+-+-+-+-+
|       cmsg_level - IPPROTO_IPV6                               |
+-+-+-+-+-+-+-+-+-+-+-+-+-+-+-+-+-+-+-+-+-+-+-+-+-+-+-+-+-+-+-+-+
|       cmsg_type = IPV6_HOPOPTS                                |
+-+-+-+-+-+-+-+-+-+-+-+-+-+-+-+-+-+-+-+-+-+-+-+-+-+-+-+-+-+-+-+-+
| Next Header   | Hdr Ext Len=1 | Option Type=X |Opt Data Len=12|
+-+-+-+-+-+-+-+-+-+-+-+-+-+-+-+-+-+-+-+-+-+-+-+-+-+-+-+-+-+-+-+-+
|                         4-octet field                        |
+-+-+-+-+-+-+-+-+-+-+-+-+-+-+-+-+-+-+-+-+-+-+-+-+-+-+-+-+-+-+-+-+
|                                                              |
+                         8-octet field                        +
|                                                              |
+-+-+-+-+-+-+-+-+-+-+-+-+-+-+-+-+-+-+-+-+-+-+-+-+-+-+-+-+-+-+-+-+
|         cmsg_len = 28                                         |
+-+-+-+-+-+-+-+-+-+-+-+-+-+-+-+-+-+-+-+-+-+-+-+-+-+-+-+-+-+-+-+-+
|       cmsg_level = IPPROTO_IPV6                               |
+-+-+-+-+-+-+-+-+-+-+-+-+-+-+-+-+-+-+-+-+-+-+-+-+-+-+-+-+-+-+-+-+
|       cmsg_type = IPV6_HOPOPTS                                |
+-+-+-+-+-+-+-+-+-+-+-+-+-+-+-+-+-+-+-+-+-+-+-+-+-+-+-+-+-+-+-+-+
| Next Header   | Hdr Ext Len=1 | Pad1 Option=0 | Option Type=Y |
+-+-+-+-+-+-+-+-+-+-+-+-+-+-+-+-+-+-+-+-+-+-+-+-+-+-+-+-+-+-+-+-+
|Opt Data Len=7 | 1-octet field |         2-octet field         |
+-+-+-+-+-+-+-+-+-+-+-+-+-+-+-+-+-+-+-+-+-+-+-+-+-+-+-+-+-+-+-+-+
|                         4-octet field                        |
+-+-+-+-+-+-+-+-+-+-+-+-+-+-+-+-+-+-+-+-+-+-+-+-+-+-+-+-+-+-+-+-+
| PadN Option=1 |Opt Data Len=2 |       0       |       0       |
+-+-+-+-+-+-+-+-+-+-+-+-+-+-+-+-+-+-+-+-+-+-+-+-+-+-+-+-+-+-+-+-+
```

When the kernel combines these two options into a single Hop-by-Hop
extension header, the first 3 bytes of the second ancillary data
object (the Next Header byte, the Hdr Ext Len byte, and the Pad1
option) will be combined into a PadN option occupying 3 bytes.

The following code fragment is a redo of the first example shown
(building two options in a single ancillary data object) but this
time we use inet6_option_alloc().

```
uint8_t  *typep;
struct msghdr  msg;
struct cmsghdr  *cmsgptr;
struct ip6_X_opt  *optXp;  /* now a pointer, not a struct */
struct ip6_Y_opt  *optYp;  /* now a pointer, not a struct */

msg.msg_control = malloc(inet6_option_space(sizeof(*optXp) +
                                            sizeof(*optYp)));
```

Stevens & Thomas   Informational   [Page 40]

```
inet6_option_init(msg.msg_control, &cmsgptr, IPV6_HOPOPTS);

typep = inet6_option_alloc(cmsgptr, IP6_X_OPT_LEN,
                             IP6_X_OPT_MULTX, IP6_X_OPT_OFFSETY);
optXp = (struct ip6_X_opt *) (typep - IP6_X_OPT_OFFSETY);
optXp->ip6_X_opt_type = IP6_X_OPT_TYPE;
optXp->ip6_X_opt_len  = IP6_X_OPT_LEN;
optXp->ip6_X_opt_val1 = <32-bit value>;
optXp->ip6_X_opt_val2 = <64-bit value>;

typep = inet6_option_alloc(cmsgptr, IP6_Y_OPT_LEN,
                             IP6_Y_OPT_MULTX, IP6_Y_OPT_OFFSETY);
optYp = (struct ip6_Y_opt *) (typep - IP6_Y_OPT_OFFSETY);
optYp->ip6_Y_opt_type = IP6_Y_OPT_TYPE;
optYp->ip6_Y_opt_len  = IP6_Y_OPT_LEN;
optYp->ip6_Y_opt_val1 = <8-bit value>;
optYp->ip6_Y_opt_val2 = <16-bit value>;
optYp->ip6_Y_opt_val3 = <32-bit value>;

msg.msg_controllen = cmsgptr->cmsg_len;
```

   Notice that inet6_option_alloc() returns a pointer to the 8-bit
   option type field. If the program wants a pointer to an option
   structure that includes the padding at the front (as shown in our
   definitions of the ip6_X_opt and ip6_Y_opt structures), the y-offset
   at the beginning of the structure must be subtracted from the
   returned pointer.

   The following code fragment shows the processing of Hop-by-Hop
   options using the inet6_option_next() function.

```
   struct msghdr    msg;
   struct cmsghdr  *cmsgptr;

   /* fill in msg */

   /* call recvmsg() */

   for (cmsgptr = CMSG_FIRSTHDR(&msg); cmsgptr != NULL;
        cmsgptr = CMSG_NXTHDR(&msg, cmsgptr)) {
       if (cmsgptr->cmsg_level == IPPROTO_IPV6 &&
           cmsgptr->cmsg_type == IPV6_HOPOPTS) {

           uint8_t  *tptr = NULL;

           while (inet6_option_next(cmsgptr, &tptr) == 0) {
               if (*tptr == IP6_X_OPT_TYPE) {
                   struct ip6_X_opt  *optXp;
```

RFC 2292   Advanced Sockets API for IPv6   February 1998

```
                        optXp = (struct ip6_X_opt *) (tptr - IP6_X_OPT_OFFSETY);
                        <do whatever with> optXp->ip6_X_opt_val1;
                        <do whatever with> optXp->ip6_X_opt_val2;

                } else if (*tptr == IP6_Y_OPT_TYPE) {
                    struct ip6_Y_opt  *optYp;

                        optYp = (struct ip6_Y_opt *) (tptr - IP6_Y_OPT_OFFSETY);
                        <do whatever with> optYp->ip6_Y_opt_val1;
                        <do whatever with> optYp->ip6_Y_opt_val2;
                        <do whatever with> optYp->ip6_Y_opt_val3;
                }
            }
            if (tptr != NULL)
                <error encountered by inet6_option_next()>;
        }
    }
```

7. Destination Options

    A variable number of Destination options can appear in one or more
    Destination option headers. As defined in [RFC-1883], a Destination
    options header appearing before a Routing header is processed by the
    first destination plus any subsequent destinations specified in the
    Routing header, while a Destination options header appearing after a
    Routing header is processed only by the final destination. As with
    the Hop-by-Hop options, each option in a Destination options header
    is TLV-encoded with a type, length, and value.

    Today no Destination options are defined for IPv6 [RFC-1883],
    although proposals exist to use Destination options with mobility and
    anycasting.

7.1. Receiving Destination Options

    To receive Destination options the application must enable the
    IPV6_DSTOPTS socket option:

```
        int  on = 1;
        setsockopt(fd, IPPROTO_IPV6, IPV6_DSTOPTS, &on, sizeof(on));
```

    All the Destination options appearing before a Routing header are
    returned as one ancillary data object described by a cmsghdr
    structure and all the Destination options appearing after a Routing
    header are returned as another ancillary data object described by a
    cmsghdr structure. For these ancillary data objects, the cmsg_level

member will be IPPROTO_IPV6 and the cmsg_type member will be
IPV6_HOPOPTS. These options are then processed by calling the
inet6_option_next() and inet6_option_find() functions.

7.2. Sending Destination Options

To send one or more Destination options, the application just
specifies them as ancillary data in a call to sendmsg(). No socket
option need be set.

As described earlier, one set of Destination options can appear
before a Routing header, and one set can appear after a Routing
header. Each set can consist of one or more options.

Normally all the Destination options in a set are specified by a
single ancillary data object, since each option is itself TLV-
encoded. Multiple ancillary data objects, each containing one or
more Destination options, can also be specified, in which case the
kernel will combine all the Destination options in the set into a
single Destination extension header. But it should be more efficient
to use a single ancillary data object to describe all the Destination
options in a set. The cmsg_level member is set to IPPROTO_IPV6 and
the cmsg_type member is set to IPV6_DSTOPTS. The option is normally
constructed using the inet6_option_init(), inet6_option_append(), and
inet6_option_alloc() functions.

Additional errors may be possible from sendmsg() if the specified
option is in error.

8. Routing Header Option

Source routing in IPv6 is accomplished by specifying a Routing header
as an extension header. There can be different types of Routing
headers, but IPv6 currently defines only the Type 0 Routing header
[RFC-1883]. This type supports up to 23 intermediate nodes. With
this maximum number of intermediate nodes, a source, and a
destination, there are 24 hops, each of which is defined as a strict
or loose hop.

Source routing with IPv4 sockets API (the IP_OPTIONS socket option)
requires the application to build the source route in the format that
appears as the IPv4 header option, requiring intimate knowledge of
the IPv4 options format. This IPv6 API, however, defines eight
functions that the application calls to build and examine a Routing
header. Four functions build a Routing header:

inet6_rthdr_space()   - return #bytes required for ancillary data
inet6_rthdr_init()   - initialize ancillary data for Routing header

```
inet6_rthdr_add()      - add IPv6 address & flags to Routing header
inet6_rthdr_lasthop()  - specify the flags for the final hop
```

Four functions deal with a returned Routing header:

```
inet6_rthdr_reverse()  - reverse a Routing header
inet6_rthdr_segments() - return #segments in a Routing header
inet6_rthdr_getaddr()  - fetch one address from a Routing header
inet6_rthdr_getflags() - fetch one flag from a Routing header
```

The function prototypes for these functions are all in the
<netinet/in.h> header.

To receive a Routing header the application must enable the
IPV6_RTHDR socket option:

```
    int  on = 1;
    setsockopt(fd, IPPROTO_IPV6, IPV6_RTHDR, &on, sizeof(on));
```

To send a Routing header the application just specifies it as
ancillary data in a call to sendmsg().

A Routing header is passed between the application and the kernel as
an ancillary data object. The cmsg_level member has a value of
IPPROTO_IPV6 and the cmsg_type member has a value of IPV6_RTHDR. The
contents of the cmsg_data[] member is implementation dependent and
should not be accessed directly by the application, but should be
accessed using the eight functions that we are about to describe.

The following constants are defined in the <netinet/in.h> header:

```
#define IPV6_RTHDR_LOOSE    0 /* this hop need not be a neighbor */
#define IPV6_RTHDR_STRICT   1 /* this hop must be a neighbor */

#define IPV6_RTHDR_TYPE_0   0 /* IPv6 Routing header type 0 */
```

When a Routing header is specified, the destination address specified
for connect(), sendto(), or sendmsg() is the final destination
address of the datagram. The Routing header then contains the
addresses of all the intermediate nodes.

8.1. inet6_rthdr_space

```
    size_t inet6_rthdr_space(int type, int segments);
```

This function returns the number of bytes required to hold a Routing
header of the specified type containing the specified number of

Stevens & Thomas   Informational   [Page 44]

segments (addresses). For an IPv6 Type 0 Routing header, the number
of segments must be between 1 and 23, inclusive. The return value
includes the size of the cmsghdr structure that precedes the Routing
header, and any required padding.

If the return value is 0, then either the type of the Routing header
is not supported by this implementation or the number of segments is
invalid for this type of Routing header.

(Note: This function returns the size but does not allocate the space
required for the ancillary data. This allows an application to
allocate a larger buffer, if other ancillary data objects are
desired, since all the ancillary data objects must be specified to
sendmsg() as a single msg_control buffer.)

8.2. inet6_rthdr_init

        struct cmsghdr *inet6_rthdr_init(void *bp, int type);

This function initializes the buffer pointed to by bp to contain a
cmsghdr structure followed by a Routing header of the specified type.
The cmsg_len member of the cmsghdr structure is initialized to the
size of the structure plus the amount of space required by the
Routing header. The cmsg_level and cmsg_type members are also
initialized as required.

The caller must allocate the buffer and its size can be determined by
calling inet6_rthdr_space().

Upon success the return value is the pointer to the cmsghdr
structure, and this is then used as the first argument to the next
two functions. Upon an error the return value is NULL.

8.3. inet6_rthdr_add

      int inet6_rthdr_add(struct cmsghdr *cmsg,
                      const struct in6_addr *addr, unsigned int flags);

This function adds the address pointed to by addr to the end of the
Routing header being constructed and sets the type of this hop to the
value of flags. For an IPv6 Type 0 Routing header, flags must be
either IPV6_RTHDR_LOOSE or IPV6_RTHDR_STRICT.

If successful, the cmsg_len member of the cmsghdr structure is
updated to account for the new address in the Routing header and the
return value of the function is 0. Upon an error the return value of
the function is -1.

8.4.   inet6_rthdr_lasthop

        int inet6_rthdr_lasthop(struct cmsghdr *cmsg,
                              unsigned int flags);

   This function specifies the Strict/Loose flag for the final hop of a
   Routing header. For an IPv6 Type 0 Routing header, flags must be
   either IPV6_RTHDR_LOOSE or IPV6_RTHDR_STRICT.

   The return value of the function is 0 upon success, or -1 upon an
   error.

   Notice that a Routing header specifying N intermediate nodes requires
   N+1 Strict/Loose flags. This requires N calls to inet6_rthdr_add()
   followed by one call to inet6_rthdr_lasthop().

8.5.   inet6_rthdr_reverse

     int inet6_rthdr_reverse(const struct cmsghdr *in, struct cmsghdr *out);

   This function takes a Routing header that was received as ancillary
   data (pointed to by the first argument) and writes a new Routing
   header that sends datagrams along the reverse of that route. Both
   arguments are allowed to point to the same buffer (that is, the
   reversal can occur in place).

   The return value of the function is 0 on success, or -1 upon an
   error.

8.6.   inet6_rthdr_segments

      int inet6_rthdr_segments(const struct cmsghdr *cmsg);

   This function returns the number of segments (addresses) contained in
   the Routing header described by cmsg. On success the return value is
   between 1 and 23, inclusive. The return value of the function is -1
   upon an error.

8.7.   inet6_rthdr_getaddr

     struct in6_addr *inet6_rthdr_getaddr(struct cmsghdr *cmsg, int
     index);

   This function returns a pointer to the IPv6 address specified by
   index (which must have a value between 1 and the value returned by
   inet6_rthdr_segments()) in the Routing header described by cmsg. An
   application should first call inet6_rthdr_segments() to obtain the
   number of segments in the Routing header.

RFC 2292   Advanced Sockets API for IPv6   February 1998

Upon an error the return value of the function is NULL.

8.8. inet6_rthdr_getflags

        int inet6_rthdr_getflags(const struct cmsghdr *cmsg, int index);

This function returns the flags value specified by index (which must
have a value between 0 and the value returned by
inet6_rthdr_segments()) in the Routing header described by cmsg. For
an IPv6 Type 0 Routing header the return value will be either
IPV6_RTHDR_LOOSE or IPV6_RTHDR_STRICT.

Upon an error the return value of the function is -1.

(Note: Addresses are indexed starting at 1, and flags starting at 0,
to maintain consistency with the terminology and figures in [RFC-
1883].)

8.9. Routing Header Example

As an example of these Routing header functions, we go through the
function calls for the example on p. 18 of [RFC-1883]. The source is
S, the destination is D, and the three intermediate nodes are I1, I2,
and I3. f0, f1, f2, and f3 are the Strict/Loose flags for each hop.

```
                  f0          f1          f2          f3
             S -----> I1 -----> I2 -----> I3 -----> D

     src:    *    S           S           S           S    S
     dst:    D    I1          I2          I3          D    D
     A[1]:   I1   I2          I1          I1          I1   I1
     A[2]:   I2   I3          I3          I2          I2   I2
     A[3]:   I3   D           D           D           I3   I3
     #seg:   3    3           2           1           0    3

     check:  f0          f1          f2          f3
```

src and dst are the source and destination IPv6 addresses in the IPv6
header. A[1], A[2], and A[3] are the three addresses in the Routing
header. #seg is the Segments Left field in the Routing header.
check indicates which bit of the Strict/Loose Bit Map (0 through 3,
specified as f0 through f3) that node checks.

The six values in the column beneath node S are the values in the
Routing header specified by the application using sendmsg(). The
function calls by the sender would look like:

```
        void  *ptr;
        struct msghdr  msg;
        struct cmsghdr  *cmsgptr;
        struct sockaddr_in6  I1, I2, I3, D;
        unsigned int  f0, f1, f2, f3;

        ptr = malloc(inet6_rthdr_space(IPV6_RTHDR_TYPE_0, 3));
        cmsgptr = inet6_rthdr_init(ptr, IPV6_RTHDR_TYPE_0);

        inet6_rthdr_add(cmsgptr, &I1.sin6_addr, f0);
        inet6_rthdr_add(cmsgptr, &I2.sin6_addr, f1);
        inet6_rthdr_add(cmsgptr, &I3.sin6_addr, f2);
        inet6_rthdr_lasthop(cmsgptr, f3);

        msg.msg_control = ptr;
        msg.msg_controllen = cmsgptr->cmsg_len;

        /* finish filling in msg{}, msg_name = D */
        /* call sendmsg() */
```

We also assume that the source address for the socket is not
specified (i.e., the asterisk in the figure).

The four columns of six values that are then shown between the five
nodes are the values of the fields in the packet while the packet is
in transit between the two nodes. Notice that before the packet is
sent by the source node S, the source address is chosen (replacing
the asterisk), I1 becomes the destination address of the datagram,
the two addresses A[2] and A[3] are "shifted up", and D is moved to
A[3]. If f0 is IPV6_RTHDR_STRICT, then I1 must be a neighbor of S.

The columns of values that are shown beneath the destination node are
the values returned by recvmsg(), assuming the application has
enabled both the IPV6_PKTINFO and IPV6_RTHDR socket options. The
source address is S (contained in the sockaddr_in6 structure pointed
to by the msg_name member), the destination address is D (returned as
an ancillary data object in an in6_pktinfo structure), and the
ancillary data object specifying the Routing header will contain
three addresses (I1, I2, and I3) and four flags (f0, f1, f2, and f3).
The number of segments in the Routing header is known from the Hdr
Ext Len field in the Routing header (a value of 6, indicating 3
addresses).

The return value from inet6_rthdr_segments() will be 3 and
inet6_rthdr_getaddr(1) will return I1, inet6_rthdr_getaddr(2) will
return I2, and inet6_rthdr_getaddr(3) will return I3, The return

RFC 2292   Advanced Sockets API for IPv6   February 1998

value from inet6_rthdr_flags(0) will be f0, inet6_rthdr_flags(1) will
return f1, inet6_rthdr_flags(2) will return f2, and
inet6_rthdr_flags(3) will return f3.

If the receiving application then calls inet6_rthdr_reverse(), the
order of the three addresses will become I3, I2, and I1, and the
order of the four Strict/Loose flags will become f3, f2, f1, and f0.

We can also show what an implementation might store in the ancillary
data object as the Routing header is being built by the sending
process. If we assume a 32-bit architecture where sizeof(struct
cmsghdr) equals 12, with a desired alignment of 4-byte boundaries,
then the call to inet6_rthdr_space(3) returns 68: 12 bytes for the
cmsghdr structure and 56 bytes for the Routing header (8 + 3*16).

The call to inet6_rthdr_init() initializes the ancillary data object
to contain a Type 0 Routing header:

```
   +-+-+-+-+-+-+-+-+-+-+-+-+-+-+-+-+-+-+-+-+-+-+-+-+-+-+-+-+-+-+-+-+
   |          cmsg_len = 20                                        |
   +-+-+-+-+-+-+-+-+-+-+-+-+-+-+-+-+-+-+-+-+-+-+-+-+-+-+-+-+-+-+-+-+
   |          cmsg_level = IPPROTO_IPV6                            |
   +-+-+-+-+-+-+-+-+-+-+-+-+-+-+-+-+-+-+-+-+-+-+-+-+-+-+-+-+-+-+-+-+
   |          cmsg_type = IPV6_RTHDR                               |
   +-+-+-+-+-+-+-+-+-+-+-+-+-+-+-+-+-+-+-+-+-+-+-+-+-+-+-+-+-+-+-+-+
   | Next Header   | Hdr Ext Len=0 | Routing Type=0| Seg Left=0    |
   +-+-+-+-+-+-+-+-+-+-+-+-+-+-+-+-+-+-+-+-+-+-+-+-+-+-+-+-+-+-+-+-+
   |   Reserved    |                Strict/Loose Bit Map           |
   +-+-+-+-+-+-+-+-+-+-+-+-+-+-+-+-+-+-+-+-+-+-+-+-+-+-+-+-+-+-+-+-+
```

The first call to inet6_rthdr_add() adds I1 to the list.

RFC 2292   Advanced Sockets API for IPv6   February 1998

```
+-+-+-+-+-+-+-+-+-+-+-+-+-+-+-+-+-+-+-+-+-+-+-+-+-+-+-+-+-+-+-+-+
|         cmsg_len = 36                                         |
+-+-+-+-+-+-+-+-+-+-+-+-+-+-+-+-+-+-+-+-+-+-+-+-+-+-+-+-+-+-+-+-+
|       cmsg_level = IPPROTO_IPV6                               |
+-+-+-+-+-+-+-+-+-+-+-+-+-+-+-+-+-+-+-+-+-+-+-+-+-+-+-+-+-+-+-+-+
|       cmsg_type = IPV6_RTHDR                                  |
+-+-+-+-+-+-+-+-+-+-+-+-+-+-+-+-+-+-+-+-+-+-+-+-+-+-+-+-+-+-+-+-+
|  Next Header  | Hdr Ext Len=2 | Routing Type=0|  Seg Left=1   |
+-+-+-+-+-+-+-+-+-+-+-+-+-+-+-+-+-+-+-+-+-+-+-+-+-+-+-+-+-+-+-+-+
|   Reserved    |X|             Strict/Loose Bit Map            |
+-+-+-+-+-+-+-+-+-+-+-+-+-+-+-+-+-+-+-+-+-+-+-+-+-+-+-+-+-+-+-+-+
|                                                              |
+                                                              +
|                                                              |
+                     Address[1] = I1                          +
|                                                              |
+                                                              +
|                                                              |
+-+-+-+-+-+-+-+-+-+-+-+-+-+-+-+-+-+-+-+-+-+-+-+-+-+-+-+-+-+-+-+-+
```

Bit 0 of the Strict/Loose Bit Map contains the value f0, which we
just mark as X. cmsg_len is incremented by 16, the Hdr Ext Len field
is incremented by 2, and the Segments Left field is incremented by 1.

The next call to inet6_rthdr_add() adds I2 to the list.

```
+-+-+-+-+-+-+-+-+-+-+-+-+-+-+-+-+-+-+-+-+-+-+-+-+-+-+-+-+-+-+-+-+
|          cmsg_len = 52                                        |
+-+-+-+-+-+-+-+-+-+-+-+-+-+-+-+-+-+-+-+-+-+-+-+-+-+-+-+-+-+-+-+-+
|       cmsg_level = IPPROTO_IPV6                               |
+-+-+-+-+-+-+-+-+-+-+-+-+-+-+-+-+-+-+-+-+-+-+-+-+-+-+-+-+-+-+-+-+
|       cmsg_type = IPV6_RTHDR                                  |
+-+-+-+-+-+-+-+-+-+-+-+-+-+-+-+-+-+-+-+-+-+-+-+-+-+-+-+-+-+-+-+-+
|  Next Header  | Hdr Ext Len=4 | Routing Type=0| Seg Left=2    |
+-+-+-+-+-+-+-+-+-+-+-+-+-+-+-+-+-+-+-+-+-+-+-+-+-+-+-+-+-+-+-+-+
|   Reserved    |X|X|        Strict/Loose Bit Map               |
+-+-+-+-+-+-+-+-+-+-+-+-+-+-+-+-+-+-+-+-+-+-+-+-+-+-+-+-+-+-+-+-+
|                                                               |
+                                                               +
|                                                               |
+                        Address[1] = I1                        +
|                                                               |
+                                                               +
|                                                               |
+-+-+-+-+-+-+-+-+-+-+-+-+-+-+-+-+-+-+-+-+-+-+-+-+-+-+-+-+-+-+-+-+
|                                                               |
+                                                               +
|                                                               |
+                        Address[2] = I2                        +
|                                                               |
+                                                               +
|                                                               |
+-+-+-+-+-+-+-+-+-+-+-+-+-+-+-+-+-+-+-+-+-+-+-+-+-+-+-+-+-+-+-+-+
```

The next bit of the Strict/Loose Bit Map contains the value f1.
cmsg_len is incremented by 16, the Hdr Ext Len field is incremented
by 2, and the Segments Left field is incremented by 1.

The last call to inet6_rthdr_add() adds I3 to the list.

```
+-+-+-+-+-+-+-+-+-+-+-+-+-+-+-+-+-+-+-+-+-+-+-+-+-+-+-+-+-+-+-+-+
|         cmsg_len = 68                                         |
+-+-+-+-+-+-+-+-+-+-+-+-+-+-+-+-+-+-+-+-+-+-+-+-+-+-+-+-+-+-+-+-+
|       cmsg_level = IPPROTO_IPV6                               |
+-+-+-+-+-+-+-+-+-+-+-+-+-+-+-+-+-+-+-+-+-+-+-+-+-+-+-+-+-+-+-+-+
|       cmsg_type = IPV6_RTHDR                                  |
+-+-+-+-+-+-+-+-+-+-+-+-+-+-+-+-+-+-+-+-+-+-+-+-+-+-+-+-+-+-+-+-+
|  Next Header  | Hdr Ext Len=6 | Routing Type=0|  Seg Left=3   |
+-+-+-+-+-+-+-+-+-+-+-+-+-+-+-+-+-+-+-+-+-+-+-+-+-+-+-+-+-+-+-+-+
|   Reserved    |X|X|X|       Strict/Loose Bit Map              |
+-+-+-+-+-+-+-+-+-+-+-+-+-+-+-+-+-+-+-+-+-+-+-+-+-+-+-+-+-+-+-+-+
|                                                              |
+                                                              +
|                                                              |
+                    Address[1] = I1                           +
|                                                              |
+                                                              +
|                                                              |
+-+-+-+-+-+-+-+-+-+-+-+-+-+-+-+-+-+-+-+-+-+-+-+-+-+-+-+-+-+-+-+-+
|                                                              |
+                                                              +
|                                                              |
+                    Address[2] = I2                           +
|                                                              |
+                                                              +
|                                                              |
+-+-+-+-+-+-+-+-+-+-+-+-+-+-+-+-+-+-+-+-+-+-+-+-+-+-+-+-+-+-+-+-+
|                                                              |
+                                                              +
|                                                              |
+                    Address[3] = I3                           +
|                                                              |
+                                                              +
|                                                              |
+-+-+-+-+-+-+-+-+-+-+-+-+-+-+-+-+-+-+-+-+-+-+-+-+-+-+-+-+-+-+-+-+
```

The next bit of the Strict/Loose Bit Map contains the value f2.
cmsg_len is incremented by 16, the Hdr Ext Len field is incremented
by 2, and the Segments Left field is incremented by 1.

Finally, the call to inet6_rthdr_lasthop() sets the next bit of the
Strict/Loose Bit Map to the value specified by f3. All the lengths
remain unchanged.

RFC 2292   Advanced Sockets API for IPv6   February 1998

9. Ordering of Ancillary Data and IPv6 Extension Headers

   Three IPv6 extension headers can be specified by the application and
   returned to the application using ancillary data with sendmsg() and
   recvmsg(): Hop-by-Hop options, Destination options, and the Routing
   header. When multiple ancillary data objects are transferred via
   sendmsg() or recvmsg() and these objects represent any of these three
   extension headers, their placement in the control buffer is directly
   tied to their location in the corresponding IPv6 datagram. This API
   imposes some ordering constraints when using multiple ancillary data
   objects with sendmsg().

   When multiple IPv6 Hop-by-Hop options having the same option type are
   specified, these options will be inserted into the Hop-by-Hop options
   header in the same order as they appear in the control buffer. But
   when multiple Hop-by-Hop options having different option types are
   specified, these options may be reordered by the kernel to reduce
   padding in the Hop-by-Hop options header. Hop-by-Hop options may
   appear anywhere in the control buffer and will always be collected by
   the kernel and placed into a single Hop-by-Hop options header that
   immediately follows the IPv6 header.

   Similar rules apply to the Destination options: (1) those of the same
   type will appear in the same order as they are specified, and (2)
   those of differing types may be reordered. But the kernel will build
   up to two Destination options headers: one to precede the Routing
   header and one to follow the Routing header. If the application
   specifies a Routing header then all Destination options that appear
   in the control buffer before the Routing header will appear in a
   Destination options header before the Routing header and these
   options might be reordered, subject to the two rules that we just
   stated. Similarly all Destination options that appear in the control
   buffer after the Routing header will appear in a Destination options
   header after the Routing header, and these options might be
   reordered, subject to the two rules that we just stated.

   As an example, assume that an application specifies control
   information to sendmsg() containing six ancillary data objects: the
   first containing two Hop-by-Hop options, the second containing one
   Destination option, the third containing two Destination options, the
   fourth containing a Routing header, the fifth containing a Hop-by-Hop
   option, and the sixth containing two Destination options. We also
   assume that all the Hop-by-Hop options are of different types, as are
   all the Destination options. We number these options 1-9,
   corresponding to their order in the control buffer, and show them on
   the left below.

RFC 2292   Advanced Sockets API for IPv6   February 1998

In the middle we show the final arrangement of the options in the
extension headers built by the kernel. On the right we show the four
ancillary data objects returned to the receiving application.

```
        Sender's                                  Receiver's
     Ancillary Data    ->   IPv6 Extension   ->  Ancillary Data
        Objects                Headers              Objects
    ------------------      ---------------      ------------
    HOPOPT-1,2 (first)      HOPHDR(J,7,1,2)      HOPOPT-7,1,2
    DSTOPT-3                DSTHDR(4,5,3)        DSTOPT-4,5,3
    DSTOPT-4,5              RTHDR(6)             RTHDR-6
    RTHDR-6                 DSTHDR(8,9)          DSTOPT-8,9
    HOPOPT-7
    DSTOPT-8,9 (last)
```

The sender's two Hop-by-Hop ancillary data objects are reordered, as
are the first two Destination ancillary data objects. We also show a
Jumbo Payload option (denoted as J) inserted by the kernel before the
sender's three Hop-by-Hop options. The first three Destination
options must appear in a Destination header before the Routing
header, and the final two Destination options must appear in a
Destination header after the Routing header.

If Destination options are specified in the control buffer after a
Routing header, or if Destination options are specified without a
Routing header, the kernel will place those Destination options after
an authentication header and/or an encapsulating security payload
header, if present.

10.   IPv6-Specific Options with IPv4-Mapped IPv6 Addresses

The various socket options and ancillary data specifications defined
in this document apply only to true IPv6 sockets. It is possible to
create an IPv6 socket that actually sends and receives IPv4 packets,
using IPv4-mapped IPv6 addresses, but the mapping of the options
defined in this document to an IPv4 datagram is beyond the scope of
this document.

In general, attempting to specify an IPv6-only option, such as the
Hop-by-Hop options, Destination options, or Routing header on an IPv6
socket that is using IPv4-mapped IPv6 addresses, will probably result
in an error. Some implementations, however, may provide access to
the packet information (source/destination address, send/receive
interface, and hop limit) on an IPv6 socket that is using IPv4-mapped
IPv6 addresses.

Stevens & Thomas   Informational   [Page 54]

RFC 2292   Advanced Sockets API for IPv6   February 1998

11. rresvport_af

   The rresvport() function is used by the rcmd() function, and this
   function is in turn called by many of the "r" commands such as
   rlogin. While new applications are not being written to use the
   rcmd() function, legacy applications such as rlogin will continue to
   use it and these will be ported to IPv6.

   rresvport() creates an IPv4/TCP socket and binds a "reserved port" to
   the socket. Instead of defining an IPv6 version of this function we
   define a new function that takes an address family as its argument.

       #include <unistd.h>

       int   rresvport_af(int *port, int family);

   This function behaves the same as the existing rresvport() function,
   but instead of creating an IPv4/TCP socket, it can also create an
   IPv6/TCP socket. The family argument is either AF_INET or AF_INET6,
   and a new error return is EAFNOSUPPORT if the address family is not
   supported.

   (Note: There is little consensus on which header defines the
   rresvport() and rcmd() function prototypes. 4.4BSD defines it in
   <unistd.h>, others in <netdb.h>, and others don't define the function
   prototypes at all.)

   (Note: We define this function only, and do not define something like
   rcmd_af() or rcmd6(). The reason is that rcmd() calls
   gethostbyname(), which returns the type of address: AF_INET or
   AF_INET6. It should therefore be possible to modify rcmd() to
   support either IPv4 or IPv6, based on the address family returned by
   gethostbyname().)

12. Future Items

   Some additional items may require standardization, but no concrete
   proposals have been made for the API to perform these tasks. These
   may be addressed in a later document.

12.1. Flow Labels

   Earlier revisions of this document specified a set of
   inet6_flow_XXX() functions to assign, share, and free IPv6 flow
   labels. Consensus, however, indicated that it was premature to
   specify this part of the API.

Stevens & Thomas   Informational   [Page 55]

RFC 2292   Advanced Sockets API for IPv6   February 1998

12.2. Path MTU Discovery and UDP

   A standard method may be desirable for a UDP application to determine
   the "maximum send transport-message size" (Section 5.1 of [RFC-1981])
   to a given destination. This would let the UDP application send
   smaller datagrams to the destination, avoiding fragmentation.

12.3. Neighbor Reachability and UDP

   A standard method may be desirable for a UDP application to tell the
   kernel that it is making forward progress with a given peer (Section
   7.3.1 of [RFC-1970]). This could save unneeded neighbor
   solicitations and neighbor advertisements.

13. Summary of New Definitions

   The following list summarizes the constants and structure,
   definitions discussed in this memo, sorted by header.

      <netinet/icmp6.h> ICMP6_DST_UNREACH
      <netinet/icmp6.h> ICMP6_DST_UNREACH_ADDR
      <netinet/icmp6.h> ICMP6_DST_UNREACH_ADMIN
      <netinet/icmp6.h> ICMP6_DST_UNREACH_NOPORT
      <netinet/icmp6.h> ICMP6_DST_UNREACH_NOROUTE
      <netinet/icmp6.h> ICMP6_DST_UNREACH_NOTNEIGHBOR
      <netinet/icmp6.h> ICMP6_ECHO_REPLY
      <netinet/icmp6.h> ICMP6_ECHO_REQUEST
      <netinet/icmp6.h> ICMP6_INFOMSG_MASK
      <netinet/icmp6.h> ICMP6_MEMBERSHIP_QUERY
      <netinet/icmp6.h> ICMP6_MEMBERSHIP_REDUCTION
      <netinet/icmp6.h> ICMP6_MEMBERSHIP_REPORT
      <netinet/icmp6.h> ICMP6_PACKET_TOO_BIG
      <netinet/icmp6.h> ICMP6_PARAMPROB_HEADER
      <netinet/icmp6.h> ICMP6_PARAMPROB_NEXTHEADER
      <netinet/icmp6.h> ICMP6_PARAMPROB_OPTION
      <netinet/icmp6.h> ICMP6_PARAM_PROB
      <netinet/icmp6.h> ICMP6_TIME_EXCEEDED
      <netinet/icmp6.h> ICMP6_TIME_EXCEED_REASSEMBLY
      <netinet/icmp6.h> ICMP6_TIME_EXCEED_TRANSIT
      <netinet/icmp6.h> ND_NA_FLAG_OVERRIDE
      <netinet/icmp6.h> ND_NA_FLAG_ROUTER
      <netinet/icmp6.h> ND_NA_FLAG_SOLICITED
      <netinet/icmp6.h> ND_NEIGHBOR_ADVERT
      <netinet/icmp6.h> ND_NEIGHBOR_SOLICIT
      <netinet/icmp6.h> ND_OPT_MTU
      <netinet/icmp6.h> ND_OPT_PI_FLAG_AUTO
      <netinet/icmp6.h> ND_OPT_PI_FLAG_ONLINK
      <netinet/icmp6.h> ND_OPT_PREFIX_INFORMATION

```
<netinet/icmp6.h> ND_OPT_REDIRECTED_HEADER
<netinet/icmp6.h> ND_OPT_SOURCE_LINKADDR
<netinet/icmp6.h> ND_OPT_TARGET_LINKADDR
<netinet/icmp6.h> ND_RA_FLAG_MANAGED
<netinet/icmp6.h> ND_RA_FLAG_OTHER
<netinet/icmp6.h> ND_REDIRECT
<netinet/icmp6.h> ND_ROUTER_ADVERT
<netinet/icmp6.h> ND_ROUTER_SOLICIT

<netinet/icmp6.h> struct icmp6_filter{};
<netinet/icmp6.h> struct icmp6_hdr{};
<netinet/icmp6.h> struct nd_neighbor_advert{};
<netinet/icmp6.h> struct nd_neighbor_solicit{};
<netinet/icmp6.h> struct nd_opt_hdr{};
<netinet/icmp6.h> struct nd_opt_mtu{};
<netinet/icmp6.h> struct nd_opt_prefix_info{};
<netinet/icmp6.h> struct nd_opt_rd_hdr{};
<netinet/icmp6.h> struct nd_redirect{};
<netinet/icmp6.h> struct nd_router_advert{};
<netinet/icmp6.h> struct nd_router_solicit{};

<netinet/in.h>    IPPROTO_AH
<netinet/in.h>    IPPROTO_DSTOPTS
<netinet/in.h>    IPPROTO_ESP
<netinet/in.h>    IPPROTO_FRAGMENT
<netinet/in.h>    IPPROTO_HOPOPTS
<netinet/in.h>    IPPROTO_ICMPV6
<netinet/in.h>    IPPROTO_IPV6
<netinet/in.h>    IPPROTO_NONE
<netinet/in.h>    IPPROTO_ROUTING
<netinet/in.h>    IPV6_DSTOPTS
<netinet/in.h>    IPV6_HOPLIMIT
<netinet/in.h>    IPV6_HOPOPTS
<netinet/in.h>    IPV6_NEXTHOP
<netinet/in.h>    IPV6_PKTINFO
<netinet/in.h>    IPV6_PKTOPTIONS
<netinet/in.h>    IPV6_RTHDR
<netinet/in.h>    IPV6_RTHDR_LOOSE
<netinet/in.h>    IPV6_RTHDR_STRICT
<netinet/in.h>    IPV6_RTHDR_TYPE_0
<netinet/in.h>    struct in6_pktinfo{};

<netinet/ip6.h>   IP6F_OFF_MASK
<netinet/ip6.h>   IP6F_RESERVED_MASK
<netinet/ip6.h>   IP6F_MORE_FRAG
<netinet/ip6.h>   struct ip6_dest{};
<netinet/ip6.h>   struct ip6_frag{};
<netinet/ip6.h>   struct ip6_hbh{};
```

RFC 2292   Advanced Sockets API for IPv6   February 1998

```
    <netinet/ip6.h>     struct ip6_hdr{};
    <netinet/ip6.h>     struct ip6_rthdr{};
    <netinet/ip6.h>     struct ip6_rthdr0{};

    <sys/socket.h>      struct cmsghdr{};
    <sys/socket.h>      struct msghdr{};
```

   The following list summarizes the function and macro prototypes
   discussed in this memo, sorted by header.

```
<netinet/icmp6.h> void ICMP6_FILTER_SETBLOCK(int,
                                            struct icmp6_filter *);
<netinet/icmp6.h> void ICMP6_FILTER_SETBLOCKALL(struct icmp6_filter *);
<netinet/icmp6.h> void ICMP6_FILTER_SETPASS(int, struct icmp6_filter *);
<netinet/icmp6.h> void ICMP6_FILTER_SETPASSALL(struct icmp6_filter *);
<netinet/icmp6.h> int  ICMP6_FILTER_WILLBLOCK(int,
                                        const struct icmp6_filter *);
<netinet/icmp6.h> int  ICMP6_FILTER_WILLPASS(int,
                                        const struct icmp6_filter *);

<netinet/in.h>    int IN6_ARE_ADDR_EQUAL(const struct in6_addr *,
                                         const struct in6_addr *);

<netinet/in.h>    uint8_t *inet6_option_alloc(struct cmsghdr *,
                                            int, int, int);
<netinet/in.h>    int inet6_option_append(struct cmsghdr *,
                                        const uint8_t *, int, int);
<netinet/in.h>    int inet6_option_find(const struct cmsghdr *,
                                      uint8_t *, int);
<netinet/in.h>    int inet6_option_init(void *, struct cmsghdr **, int);
<netinet/in.h>    int inet6_option_next(const struct cmsghdr *,
                                      uint8_t **);
<netinet/in.h>    int inet6_option_space(int);

<netinet/in.h>    int inet6_rthdr_add(struct cmsghdr *,
                                    const struct in6_addr *,
                                    unsigned int);
<netinet/in.h>    struct in6_addr inet6_rthdr_getaddr(struct cmsghdr *,
                                                 int);
<netinet/in.h>    int inet6_rthdr_getflags(const struct cmsghdr *, int);
<netinet/in.h>    struct cmsghdr *inet6_rthdr_init(void *, int);
<netinet/in.h>    int inet6_rthdr_lasthop(struct cmsghdr *,
                                        unsigned int);
<netinet/in.h>    int inet6_rthdr_reverse(const struct cmsghdr *,
                                        struct cmsghdr *);
<netinet/in.h>    int inet6_rthdr_segments(const struct cmsghdr *);
<netinet/in.h>    size_t inet6_rthdr_space(int, int);
```

```
<sys/socket.h>     unsigned char *CMSG_DATA(const struct cmsghdr *);
<sys/socket.h>     struct cmsghdr *CMSG_FIRSTHDR(const struct msghdr *);
<sys/socket.h>     unsigned int CMSG_LEN(unsigned int);
<sys/socket.h>     struct cmsghdr *CMSG_NXTHDR(const struct msghdr *mhdr,
                                              const struct cmsghdr *);
<sys/socket.h>     unsigned int CMSG_SPACE(unsigned int);

<unistd.h>         int rresvport_af(int *, int);
```

14. Security Considerations

     The setting of certain Hop-by-Hop options and Destination options may
     be restricted to privileged processes. Similarly some Hop-by-Hop
     options and Destination options may not be returned to nonprivileged
     applications.

15. Change History

     Changes from the June 1997 Edition (-03 draft)

     -   Added a note that defined constants for multibyte fields are in
         network byte order. This affects the ip6f_offlg member of the
         Fragment header (Section 2.1.2) and the nd_na_flags_reserved
         member of the nd_neighbor_advert structure (Section 2.2.2).

     -   Section 5: the ipi6_ifindex member of the in6_pktinfo structure
         should be "unsigned int" instead of "int", for consistency with
         the interface indexes in [RFC-2133].

     -   Section 6.3.7: the three calls to inet6_option_space() in the
         examples needed to be arguments to malloc(). The final one of
         these was missing the "6" in the name "inet6_option_space".

     -   Section 8.6: the function prototype for inet6_rthdr_segments()
         was missing the ending semicolon.

     Changes from the March 1997 Edition (-02 draft)

     -   In May 1997 Draft 6.6 of Posix 1003.1g (called Posix.1g herein)
         passed ballot and will be forwarded to the IEEE Standards Board
         later in 1997 for final approval. Some changes made for this
         final Posix draft are incorporated into this Internet Draft,
         specifically the datatypes mentioned in Section 1 (and used
         throughout the text), and the socklen_t datatype used in Section
         4.1 and 4.2.

     -   Section 1: Added the intN_t signed datatypes, changed the
         datatype u_intN_t to uintN_t (no underscore after the "u"), and

removed the datatype u_intNm_t, as per Draft 6.6 of Posix.1g.

- Name space issues for structure and constant names in Section 2:
  Many of the structure member names and constant names were
  changed so that the prefixes are the same. The following
  prefixes are used for structure members: "ip6_", "icmp6_", and
  "nd_". All constants have the prefixes "ICMP6_" and "ND_".

- New definitions: Section 2.1.2: contains definitions for the IPv6
  extension headers, other than AH and ESP. Section 2.2.2:
  contains additional structures and constants for the neighbor
  discovery option header and redirected header.

- Section 2.2.2: the enum for the neighbor discovery option field
  was changed to be a set of #define constants.

- Changed the word "function" to "macro" for references to all the
  uppercase names in Sections 2.3 (IN6_ARE_ADDR_EQUAL), 3.2
  (ICMPV6_FILTER_xxx), and 4.3 (CMSG_xxx).

- Added more protocols to the /etc/protocols file (Section 2.4) and
  changed the name of "icmpv6" to "ipv6-icmp".

- Section 3: Made it more explicit that an application cannot read
  or write entire IPv6 packets, that all extension headers are
  passed as ancillary data. Added a sentence that the kernel
  fragments packets written to an IPv6 raw socket when necessary.
  Added a note that IPPROTO_RAW raw IPv6 sockets are not special.

- Section 3.1: Explicitly stated that the checksum option applies
  to both outgoing packets and received packets.

- Section 3.2: Changed the array name within the icmp6_filter
  structure from "data" to "icmp6_filt". Changes the prefix for
  the filter macros from "ICMPV6_" to "ICMP6_", for consistency
  with the names in Section 2.2. Changed the example from a ping
  program to a program that wants to receive only router
  advertisements.

- Section 4.1: Changed msg_namelen and msg_controllen from size_t
  to the Posix.1g socklen_t datatype. Updated the Note that
  follows.

- Section 4.2: Changed cmsg_len from size_t to the Posix.1g
  socklen_t datatype. Updated the Note that follows.

-   Section 4.4: Added a Note that the second and third arguments to
    getsockopt() and setsockopt() are intentionally the same as the
    cmsg_level and cmsg_type members.

-   Section 4.5: Reorganized the section into a description of the
    option, followed by the TCP semantics, and the UDP and raw socket
    semantics. Added a sentence on how to clear all the sticky
    options. Added a note that TCP need not save the options from
    the most recently received segment until the application says to
    do so. Added the statement that ancillary data is never passed
    with sendmsg() or recvmsg() on a TCP socket. Simplified the
    interaction of the sticky options with ancillary data for UDP or
    raw IP: none of the sticky options are sent if ancillary data is
    specified.

-   Final paragraph of Section 5.1: ipi6_index should be
    ipi6_ifindex.

-   Section 5.4: Added a note on the term "privileged".

-   Section 5.5: Noted that the errors listed are examples, and the
    actual errors depend on the implementation.

-   Removed Section 6 ("Flow Labels") as the consensus is that it is
    premature to try and specify an API for this feature. Access to
    the flow label field in the IPv6 header is still provided through
    the sin6_flowinfo member of the IPv6 socket address structure in
    [RFC-2133]. Added a subsection to Section 13 that this is a
    future item.

    All remaining changes are identified by their section number in
    the previous draft. With the removal of Section 6, the section
    numbers are decremented by one.

-   Section 7.3.7: the calls to malloc() in all three examples should
    be calls to inet6_option_space() instead. The two calls to
    inet6_option_append() in the third example should be calls to
    inet6_option_alloc(). The two calls to CMSG_SPACE() in the first
    and third examples should be calls to CMSG_LEN(). The second
    call to CMSG_SPACE() in the second example should be a call to
    CMSG_LEN().

-   Section 7.3.7: All the opt_X_ and opt_Y_ structure member names
    were changed to be ip6_X_opt_ and ip6_Y_opt_. The two structure
    names ipv6_opt_X and ipv6_opt_Y were changed to ip6_X_opt and
    ip6_Y_opt. The constants beginning with IPV6_OPT_X_ and
    IPV6_OPT_Y_ were changed to begin with IP6_X_OPT_ and IP6_Y_OPT_.

RFC 2292   Advanced Sockets API for IPv6   February 1998

   -   Use the term "Routing header" throughout the draft, instead of
       "source routing". Changed the names of the eight
       inet6_srcrt_XXX() functions in Section 9 to inet6_rthdr_XXX().
       Changed the name of the socket option from IPV6_SRCRT to
       IPV6_RTHDR, and the names of the three IPV6_SRCRT_xxx constants
       in Section 9 to IPV6_RTHDR_xxx.

   -   Added a paragraph to Section 9 on how to receive and send a
       Routing header.

   -   Changed inet6_rthdr_add() and inet6_rthdr_reverse() so that they
       return -1 upon an error, instead of an Exxx errno value.

   -   In the description of inet6_rthdr_space() in Section 9.1, added
       the qualifier "For an IPv6 Type 0 Routing header" to the
       restriction of between 1 and 23 segments.

   -   Refer to final function argument in Sections 9.7 and 9.8 as
       index, not offset.

   -   Updated Section 14 with new names from Section 2.

   -   Changed the References from "[n]" to "[RFC-abcd]".

   Changes from the February 1997 Edition (-01 draft)

   -   Changed the name of the ip6hdr structure to ip6_hdr (Section 2.1)
       for consistency with the icmp6hdr structure. Also changed the
       name of the ip6hdrctl structure contained within the ip6_hdr
       structure to ip6_hdrctl (Section 2.1). Finally, changed the name
       of the icmp6hdr structure to icmp6_hdr (Section 2.2). All other
       occurrences of this structure name, within the Neighbor Discovery
       structures in Section 2.2.1, already contained the underscore.

   -   The "struct nd_router_solicit" and "struct nd_router_advert"
       should both begin with "nd6_". (Section 2.2.2).

   -   Changed the name of in6_are_addr_equal to IN6_ARE_ADDR_EQUAL
       (Section 2.3) for consistency with basic API address testing
       functions. The header defining this macro is <netinet/in.h>.

   -   getprotobyname("ipv6") now returns 41, not 0 (Section 2.4).

   -   The first occurrence of "struct icmpv6_filter" in Section 3.2
       should be "struct icmp6_filter".

   -   Changed the name of the CMSG_LENGTH() macro to CMSG_LEN()
       (Section 4.3.5), since LEN is used throughout the <netinet/*.h>

Stevens & Thomas   Informational   [Page 62]

headers.

- Corrected the argument name for the sample implementations of the
  CMSG_SPACE() and CMSG_LEN() macros to be "length" (Sections 4.3.4
  and 4.3.5).

- Corrected the socket option mentioned in Section 5.1 to specify
  the interface for multicasting from IPV6_ADD_MEMBERSHIP to
  IPV6_MULTICAST_IF.

- There were numerous errors in the previous draft that specified
  <netinet/ip6.h> that should have been <netinet/in.h>. These have
  all been corrected and the locations of all definitions is now
  summarized in the new Section 14 ("Summary of New Definitions").

Changes from the October 1996 Edition (-00 draft)

- Numerous rationale added using the format (Note: ...).

- Added note that not all errors may be defined.

- Added note about ICMPv4, IGMPv4, and ARPv4 terminology.

- Changed the name of <netinet/ip6_icmp.h> to <netinet/icmp6.h>.

- Changed some names in Section 2.2.1: ICMPV6_PKT_TOOBIG to
  ICMPV6_PACKET_TOOBIG, ICMPV6_TIME_EXCEED to ICMPV6_TIME_EXCEEDED,
  ICMPV6_ECHORQST to ICMPV6_ECHOREQUEST, ICMPV6_ECHORPLY to
  ICMPV6_ECHOREPLY, ICMPV6_PARAMPROB_HDR to
  ICMPV6_PARAMPROB_HEADER, ICMPV6_PARAMPROB_NXT_HDR to
  ICMPV6_PARAMPROB_NEXTHEADER, and ICMPV6_PARAMPROB_OPTS to
  ICMPV6_PARAMPROB_OPTION.

- Prepend the prefix "icmp6_" to the three members of the
  icmp6_dataun union of the icmp6hdr structure (Section 2.2).

- Moved the neighbor discovery definitions into the
  <netinet/icmp6.h> header, instead of being in their own header
  (Section 2.2.1).

- Changed Section 2.3 ("Address Testing"). The basic macros are
  now in the basic API.

- Added the new Section 2.4 on "Protocols File".

- Added note to raw sockets description that something like BPF or
  DLPI must be used to read or write entire IPv6 packets.

- Corrected example of IPV6_CHECKSUM socket option (Section 3.1). Also defined value of -1 to disable.

- Noted that <netinet/icmp6.h> defines all the ICMPv6 filtering constants, macros, and structures (Section 3.2).

- Added note on magic number 10240 for amount of ancillary data (Section 4.1).

- Added possible padding to picture of ancillary data (Section 4.2).

- Defined <sys/socket.h> header for CMSG_xxx() functions (Section 4.2).

- Note that the data returned by getsockopt(IPV6_PKTOPTIONS) for a TCP socket is just from the optional headers, if present, of the most recently received segment. Also note that control information is never returned by recvmsg() for a TCP socket.

- Changed header for struct in6_pktinfo from <netinet.in.h> to <netinet/ip6.h> (Section 5).

- Removed the old Sections 5.1 and 5.2, because the interface identification functions went into the basic API.

- Redid Section 5 to support the hop limit field.

- New Section 5.4 ("Next Hop Address").

- New Section 6 ("Flow Labels").

- Changed all of Sections 7 and 8 dealing with Hop-by-Hop and Destination options. We now define a set of inet6_option_XXX() functions.

- Changed header for IPV6_SRCRT_xxx constants from <netinet.in.h> to <netinet/ip6.h> (Section 9).

- Add inet6_rthdr_lasthop() function, and fix errors in description of Routing header (Section 9).

- Reworded some of the Routing header descriptions to conform to the terminology in [RFC-1883].

- Added the example from [RFC-1883] for the Routing header (Section 9.9).

RFC 2292   Advanced Sockets API for IPv6   February 1998

  - Expanded the example in Section 10 to show multiple options per
    ancillary data object, and to show the receiver's ancillary data
    objects.

  - New Section 11 ("IPv6-Specific Options with IPv4-Mapped IPv6
    Addresses").

  - New Section 12 ("rresvport_af").

  - Redid old Section 10 ("Additional Items") into new Section 13
    ("Future Items").

16. References

  [RFC-1883] Deering, S., and R. Hinden, "Internet Protocol, Version 6
              (IPv6), Specification", RFC 1883, December 1995.

  [RFC-2133] Gilligan, R., Thomson, S., Bound, J., and W. Stevens,
              "Basic Socket Interface Extensions for IPv6", RFC 2133,
              April 1997.

  [RFC-1981] McCann, J., Deering, S., and J. Mogul, "Path MTU
  Discovery
              for IP version 6", RFC 1981, August 1996.

  [RFC-1970] Narten, T., Nordmark, E., and W. Simpson, "Neighbor
              Discovery for IP Version 6 (IPv6)", RFC 1970, August
              1996.

17. Acknowledgments

  Matt Thomas and Jim Bound have been working on the technical details
  in this draft for over a year. Keith Sklower is the original
  implementor of ancillary data in the BSD networking code. Craig Metz
  provided lots of feedback, suggestions, and comments based on his
  implementing many of these features as the document was being
  written.

  The following provided comments on earlier drafts: Pascal Anelli,
  Hamid Asayesh, Ran Atkinson, Karl Auerbach, Hamid Asayesh, Matt
  Crawford, Sam T. Denton, Richard Draves, Francis Dupont, Bob
  Gilligan, Tim Hartrick, Masaki Hirabaru, Yoshinobu Inoue, Mukesh
  Kacker, A. N. Kuznetsov, Pedro Marques, Jack McCann, der Mouse, John
  Moy, Thomas Narten, Erik Nordmark, Steve Parker, Charles Perkins, Tom
  Pusateri, Pedro Roque, Sameer Shah, Peter Sjodin, Stephen P.
  Spackman, Jinmei Tatuya, Karen Tracey, Quaizar Vohra, Carl Williams,
  Steve Wise, and Kazu Yamamoto.

RFC 2292   Advanced Sockets API for IPv6   February 1998

18. Authors' Addresses

   W. Richard Stevens
   1202 E. Paseo del Zorro
   Tucson, AZ   85718

   EMail: rstevens@kohala.com

   Matt Thomas
   AltaVista Internet Software
   LJO2-1/J8
   30 Porter Rd
   Littleton, MA   01460
   EMail: matt.thomas@altavista-software.com

RFC 2292   Advanced Sockets API for IPv6   February 1998

19. Full Copyright Statement

    Copyright (C) The Internet Society (1998). All Rights Reserved.

    This document and translations of it may be copied and furnished to
    others, and derivative works that comment on or otherwise explain it
    or assist in its implementation may be prepared, copied, published
    and distributed, in whole or in part, without restriction of any
    kind, provided that the above copyright notice and this paragraph are
    included on all such copies and derivative works. However, this
    document itself may not be modified in any way, such as by removing
    the copyright notice or references to the Internet Society or other
    Internet organizations, except as needed for the purpose of
    developing Internet standards in which case the procedures for
    copyrights defined in the Internet Standards process must be
    followed, or as required to translate it into languages other than
    English.

    The limited permissions granted above are perpetual and will not be
    revoked by the Internet Society or its successors or assigns.

    This document and the information contained herein is provided on an
    "AS IS" basis and THE INTERNET SOCIETY AND THE INTERNET ENGINEERING
    TASK FORCE DISCLAIMS ALL WARRANTIES, EXPRESS OR IMPLIED, INCLUDING
    BUT NOT LIMITED TO ANY WARRANTY THAT THE USE OF THE INFORMATION
    HEREIN WILL NOT INFRINGE ANY RIGHTS OR ANY IMPLIED WARRANTIES OF
    MERCHANTABILITY OR FITNESS FOR A PARTICULAR PURPOSE.

E

RFC3542 "Advanced Sockets Application Program Interface (API) for IPv6"

Network Working Group   W. Stevens
Request for Comments: 3542   M. Thomas
Obsoletes: 2292   Consultant
Category: Informational   E. Nordmark
                                                                    Sun
                                                              T. Jinmei
                                                                Toshiba
                                                               May 2003

          Advanced Sockets Application Program Interface (API) for IPv6

Status of this Memo

   This memo provides information for the Internet community. It does
   not specify an Internet standard of any kind. Distribution of this
   memo is unlimited.

Abstract

   This document provides sockets Application Program Interface (API) to
   support "advanced" IPv6 applications, as a supplement to a separate
   specification, RFC 3493. The expected applications include Ping,
   Traceroute, routing daemons and the like, which typically use raw
   sockets to access IPv6 or ICMPv6 header fields. This document
   proposes some portable interfaces for applications that use raw
   sockets under IPv6. There are other features of IPv6 that some
   applications will need to access: interface identification
   (specifying the outgoing interface and determining the incoming
   interface), IPv6 extension headers, and path Maximum Transmission
   Unit (MTU) information. This document provides API access to these
   features too. Additionally, some extended interfaces to libraries
   for the "r" commands are defined. The extension will provide better
   backward compatibility to existing implementations that are not
   IPv6-capable.

RFC 3542   Advanced Sockets API for IPv6   May 2003

Table of Contents

RFC 3542   Advanced Sockets API for IPv6   May 2003

1. Introduction

    A separate specification [RFC-3493] contains changes to the sockets
    API to support IP version 6. Those changes are for TCP and UDP-based
    applications. This document defines some of the "advanced" features
    of the sockets API that are required for applications to take
    advantage of additional features of IPv6.

Stevens, et al.   Informational   [Page 3]

Today, the portability of applications using IPv4 raw sockets is quite high, but this is mainly because most IPv4 implementations started from a common base (the Berkeley source code) or at least started with the Berkeley header files. This allows programs such as Ping and Traceroute, for example, to compile with minimal effort on many hosts that support the sockets API. With IPv6, however, there is no common source code base that implementors are starting from, and the possibility for divergence at this level between different implementations is high. To avoid a complete lack of portability amongst applications that use raw IPv6 sockets, some standardization is necessary.

There are also features from the basic IPv6 specification that are not addressed in [RFC-3493]: sending and receiving Routing headers, Hop-by-Hop options, and Destination options, specifying the outgoing interface, being told of the receiving interface, and control of path MTU information.

This document updates and replaces RFC 2292. This revision is based on implementation experience of RFC 2292, as well as some additional extensions that have been found to be useful through the IPv6 deployment. Note, however, that further work on this document may still be needed. Once the API specification becomes mature and is deployed among implementations, it may be formally standardized by a more appropriate body, such as has been done with the Basic API [RFC-3493].

This document can be divided into the following main sections.

1. Definitions of the basic constants and structures required for applications to use raw IPv6 sockets. This includes structure definitions for the IPv6 and ICMPv6 headers and all associated constants (e.g., values for the Next Header field).

2. Some basic semantic definitions for IPv6 raw sockets. For example, a raw ICMPv4 socket requires the application to calculate and store the ICMPv4 header checksum. But with IPv6 this would require the application to choose the source IPv6 address because the source address is part of the pseudo header that ICMPv6 now uses for its checksum computation. It should be defined that with a raw ICMPv6 socket the kernel always calculates and stores the ICMPv6 header checksum.

3. Packet information: how applications can obtain the received interface, destination address, and received hop limit, along with specifying these values on a per-packet basis. There are a class of applications that need this capability and the technique should be portable.

RFC 3542   Advanced Sockets API for IPv6   May 2003

    4. Access to the optional Routing header, Hop-by-Hop options, and
       Destination options extension headers.

    5. Additional features required for improved IPv6 application
       portability.

    The packet information along with access to the extension headers
    (Routing header, Hop-by-Hop options, and Destination options) are
    specified using the "ancillary data" fields that were added to the
    4.3BSD Reno sockets API in 1990. The reason is that these ancillary
    data fields are part of the Posix standard [POSIX] and should
    therefore be adopted by most vendors.

    This document does not address application access to either the
    authentication header or the encapsulating security payload header.

    Many examples in this document omit error checking in favor of
    brevity and clarity.

    We note that some of the functions and socket options defined in this
    document may have error returns that are not defined in this
    document. Some of these possible error returns will be recognized
    only as implementations proceed.

    Datatypes in this document follow the Posix format: intN_t means a
    signed integer of exactly N bits (e.g., int16_t) and uintN_t means an
    unsigned integer of exactly N bits (e.g., uint32_t).

    Note that we use the (unofficial) terminology ICMPv4, IGMPv4, and
    ARPv4 to avoid any confusion with the newer ICMPv6 protocol.

2. Common Structures and Definitions

    Many advanced applications examine fields in the IPv6 header and set
    and examine fields in the various ICMPv6 headers. Common structure
    definitions for these protocol headers are required, along with
    common constant definitions for the structure members.

    This API assumes that the fields in the protocol headers are left in
    the network byte order, which is big-endian for the Internet
    protocols. If not, then either these constants or the fields being
    tested must be converted at run-time, using something like htons() or
    htonl().

    Two new header files are defined: <netinet/ip6.h> and
    <netinet/icmp6.h>.

When an include file is specified, that include file is allowed to
include other files that do the actual declaration or definition.

2.1. The ip6_hdr Structure

The following structure is defined as a result of including
<netinet/ip6.h>. Note that this is a new header.

```
struct ip6_hdr {
  union {
    struct ip6_hdrctl {
      uint32_t ip6_un1_flow; /* 4 bits version, 8 bits TC, 20 bits
                                flow-ID */
      uint16_t ip6_un1_plen; /* payload length */
      uint8_t  ip6_un1_nxt;  /* next header */
      uint8_t  ip6_un1_hlim; /* hop limit */
    } ip6_un1;
    uint8_t ip6_un2_vfc;     /* 4 bits version, top 4 bits
                                tclass */
  } ip6_ctlun;
  struct in6_addr ip6_src;   /* source address */
  struct in6_addr ip6_dst;   /* destination address */
};

#define ip6_vfc    ip6_ctlun.ip6_un2_vfc
#define ip6_flow   ip6_ctlun.ip6_un1.ip6_un1_flow
#define ip6_plen   ip6_ctlun.ip6_un1.ip6_un1_plen
#define ip6_nxt    ip6_ctlun.ip6_un1.ip6_un1_nxt
#define ip6_hlim   ip6_ctlun.ip6_un1.ip6_un1_hlim
#define ip6_hops   ip6_ctlun.ip6_un1.ip6_un1_hlim
```

2.1.1. IPv6 Next Header Values

IPv6 defines many new values for the Next Header field. The
following constants are defined as a result of including
<netinet/in.h>.

```
#define IPPROTO_HOPOPTS   0    /* IPv6 Hop-by-Hop options */
#define IPPROTO_IPV6     41    /* IPv6 header */
#define IPPROTO_ROUTING  43    /* IPv6 Routing header */
#define IPPROTO_FRAGMENT 44    /* IPv6 fragment header */
#define IPPROTO_ESP      50    /* encapsulating security payload */
#define IPPROTO_AH       51    /* authentication header */
#define IPPROTO_ICMPV6   58    /* ICMPv6 */
#define IPPROTO_NONE     59    /* IPv6 no next header */
#define IPPROTO_DSTOPTS  60    /* IPv6 Destination options */
```

RFC 3542   Advanced Sockets API for IPv6   May 2003

    Berkeley-derived IPv4 implementations also define IPPROTO_IP to be 0.
    This should not be a problem since IPPROTO_IP is used only with IPv4
    sockets and IPPROTO_HOPOPTS only with IPv6 sockets.

2.1.2. IPv6 Extension Headers

    Six extension headers are defined for IPv6. We define structures for
    all except the Authentication header and Encapsulating Security
    Payload header, both of which are beyond the scope of this document.
    The following structures are defined as a result of including
    <netinet/ip6.h>.

```
        /* Hop-by-Hop options header */
        struct ip6_hbh {
          uint8_t   ip6h_nxt;          /* next header */
          uint8_t   ip6h_len;          /* length in units of 8 octets */
            /* followed by options */
        };

        /* Destination options header */
        struct ip6_dest {
          uint8_t   ip6d_nxt;          /* next header */
          uint8_t   ip6d_len;          /* length in units of 8 octets */
            /* followed by options */
        };

        /* Routing header */
        struct ip6_rthdr {
          uint8_t   ip6r_nxt;          /* next header */
          uint8_t   ip6r_len;          /* length in units of 8 octets */
          uint8_t   ip6r_type;         /* routing type */
          uint8_t   ip6r_segleft;      /* segments left */
            /* followed by routing type specific data */
        };

        /* Type 0 Routing header */
        struct ip6_rthdr0 {
          uint8_t   ip6r0_nxt;         /* next header */
          uint8_t   ip6r0_len;         /* length in units of 8 octets */
          uint8_t   ip6r0_type;        /* always zero */
          uint8_t   ip6r0_segleft;     /* segments left */
          uint32_t  ip6r0_reserved;    /* reserved field */
            /* followed by up to 127 struct in6_addr */
        };
```

```
      /* Fragment header */
      struct ip6_frag {
        uint8_t    ip6f_nxt;       /* next header */
        uint8_t    ip6f_reserved;  /* reserved field */
        uint16_t   ip6f_offlg;     /* offset, reserved, and flag */
        uint32_t   ip6f_ident;     /* identification */
      };

      #if     BYTE_ORDER == BIG_ENDIAN
      #define IP6F_OFF_MASK         0xfff8  /* mask out offset from
                                               ip6f_offlg */
      #define IP6F_RESERVED_MASK  0x0006  /* reserved bits in
                                               ip6f_offlg */
      #define IP6F_MORE_FRAG        0x0001  /* more-fragments flag */
      #else   /* BYTE_ORDER == LITTLE_ENDIAN */
      #define IP6F_OFF_MASK         0xf8ff  /* mask out offset from
                                               ip6f_offlg */
      #define IP6F_RESERVED_MASK  0x0600  /* reserved bits in
                                               ip6f_offlg */
      #define IP6F_MORE_FRAG        0x0100  /* more-fragments flag */
      #endif
```

2.1.3. IPv6 Options

   Several options are defined for IPv6, and we define structures and
   macro definitions for some of them below. The following structures
   are defined as a result of including <netinet/ip6.h>.

```
      /* IPv6 options */
      struct ip6_opt {
        uint8_t  ip6o_type;
        uint8_t  ip6o_len;
      };

      /*
       * The high-order 3 bits of the option type define the behavior
       * when processing an unknown option and whether or not the option
       * content changes in flight.
       */
      #define IP6OPT_TYPE(o)            ((o) & 0xc0)
      #define IP6OPT_TYPE_SKIP          0x00
      #define IP6OPT_TYPE_DISCARD       0x40
      #define IP6OPT_TYPE_FORCEICMP     0x80
      #define IP6OPT_TYPE_ICMP          0xc0
      #define IP6OPT_MUTABLE            0x20

      #define IP6OPT_PAD1               0x00 /* 00 0 00000 */
      #define IP6OPT_PADN               0x01 /* 00 0 00001 */
```

```
#define IP6OPT_JUMBO          0xc2  /* 11 0 00010 */
#define IP6OPT_NSAP_ADDR      0xc3  /* 11 0 00011 */
#define IP6OPT_TUNNEL_LIMIT   0x04  /* 00 0 00100 */
#define IP6OPT_ROUTER_ALERT   0x05  /* 00 0 00101 */

/* Jumbo Payload Option */
struct ip6_opt_jumbo {
  uint8_t  ip6oj_type;
  uint8_t  ip6oj_len;
  uint8_t  ip6oj_jumbo_len[4];
};
#define IP6OPT_JUMBO_LEN   6

/* NSAP Address Option */
struct ip6_opt_nsap {
  uint8_t  ip6on_type;
  uint8_t  ip6on_len;
  uint8_t  ip6on_src_nsap_len;
  uint8_t  ip6on_dst_nsap_len;
    /* followed by source NSAP */
    /* followed by destination NSAP */
};

/* Tunnel Limit Option */
struct ip6_opt_tunnel {
  uint8_t  ip6ot_type;
  uint8_t  ip6ot_len;
  uint8_t  ip6ot_encap_limit;
};

/* Router Alert Option */
struct ip6_opt_router {
  uint8_t  ip6or_type;
  uint8_t  ip6or_len;
  uint8_t  ip6or_value[2];
};

/* Router alert values (in network byte order) */
#ifdef _BIG_ENDIAN
#define IP6_ALERT_MLD     0x0000
#define IP6_ALERT_RSVP    0x0001
#define  IP6_ALERT_AN     0x0002
#else
#define IP6_ALERT_MLD     0x0000
#define IP6_ALERT_RSVP    0x0100
#define IP6_ALERT_AN      0x0200
#endif
```

2.2. The icmp6_hdr Structure

The ICMPv6 header is needed by numerous IPv6 applications including
Ping, Traceroute, router discovery daemons, and neighbor discovery
daemons. The following structure is defined as a result of including
<netinet/icmp6.h>. Note that this is a new header.

```
struct icmp6_hdr {
  uint8_t      icmp6_type;    /* type field */
  uint8_t      icmp6_code;    /* code field */
  uint16_t     icmp6_cksum;   /* checksum field */
  union {
    uint32_t   icmp6_un_data32[1]; /* type-specific field */
    uint16_t   icmp6_un_data16[2]; /* type-specific field */
    uint8_t    icmp6_un_data8[4];  /* type-specific field */
  } icmp6_dataun;
};

#define icmp6_data32    icmp6_dataun.icmp6_un_data32
#define icmp6_data16    icmp6_dataun.icmp6_un_data16
#define icmp6_data8     icmp6_dataun.icmp6_un_data8
#define icmp6_pptr      icmp6_data32[0]  /* parameter prob */
#define icmp6_mtu       icmp6_data32[0]  /* packet too big */
#define icmp6_id        icmp6_data16[0]  /* echo request/reply */
#define icmp6_seq       icmp6_data16[1]  /* echo request/reply */
#define icmp6_maxdelay  icmp6_data16[0]  /* mcast group
                                            membership */
```

2.2.1. ICMPv6 Type and Code Values

In addition to a common structure for the ICMPv6 header, common
definitions are required for the ICMPv6 type and code fields. The
following constants are also defined as a result of including
<netinet/icmp6.h>.

```
#define ICMP6_DST_UNREACH            1
#define ICMP6_PACKET_TOO_BIG         2
#define ICMP6_TIME_EXCEEDED          3
#define ICMP6_PARAM_PROB             4

#define ICMP6_INFOMSG_MASK  0x80     /* all informational
                                        messages */

#define ICMP6_ECHO_REQUEST          128
#define ICMP6_ECHO_REPLY            129

#define ICMP6_DST_UNREACH_NOROUTE    0 /* no route to
                                          destination */
```

RFC 3542   Advanced Sockets API for IPv6   May 2003

```
    #define ICMP6_DST_UNREACH_ADMIN        1 /* communication with
                                                  destination */
                                             /* admin. prohibited */
    #define ICMP6_DST_UNREACH_BEYONDSCOPE 2 /* beyond scope of source
                                                  address */
    #define ICMP6_DST_UNREACH_ADDR         3 /* address unreachable */
    #define ICMP6_DST_UNREACH_NOPORT       4 /* bad port */

    #define ICMP6_TIME_EXCEED_TRANSIT      0 /* Hop Limit == 0 in
                                                  transit */
    #define ICMP6_TIME_EXCEED_REASSEMBLY   1 /* Reassembly time out */

    #define ICMP6_PARAMPROB_HEADER         0 /* erroneous header
                                                  field */
    #define ICMP6_PARAMPROB_NEXTHEADER     1 /* unrecognized
                                                  Next Header */
    #define ICMP6_PARAMPROB_OPTION         2 /* unrecognized
                                                  IPv6 option */
```

   The five ICMP message types defined by IPv6 neighbor discovery (133-
   137) are defined in the next section.

2.2.2. ICMPv6 Neighbor Discovery Definitions

   The following structures and definitions are defined as a result of
   including <netinet/icmp6.h>.

```
    #define ND_ROUTER_SOLICIT          133
    #define ND_ROUTER_ADVERT           134
    #define ND_NEIGHBOR_SOLICIT        135
    #define ND_NEIGHBOR_ADVERT         136
    #define ND_REDIRECT                137

    struct nd_router_solicit {     /* router solicitation */
      struct icmp6_hdr  nd_rs_hdr;
        /* could be followed by options */
    };

    #define nd_rs_type              nd_rs_hdr.icmp6_type
    #define nd_rs_code              nd_rs_hdr.icmp6_code
    #define nd_rs_cksum             nd_rs_hdr.icmp6_cksum
    #define nd_rs_reserved          nd_rs_hdr.icmp6_data32[0]
```

```
struct nd_router_advert {        /* router advertisement */
  struct icmp6_hdr  nd_ra_hdr;
  uint32_t    nd_ra_reachable;  /* reachable time */
  uint32_t    nd_ra_retransmit; /* retransmit timer */
    /* could be followed by options */
};

#define nd_ra_type              nd_ra_hdr.icmp6_type
#define nd_ra_code              nd_ra_hdr.icmp6_code
#define nd_ra_cksum             nd_ra_hdr.icmp6_cksum
#define nd_ra_curhoplimit       nd_ra_hdr.icmp6_data8[0]
#define nd_ra_flags_reserved    nd_ra_hdr.icmp6_data8[1]
#define ND_RA_FLAG_MANAGED      0x80
#define ND_RA_FLAG_OTHER        0x40
#define nd_ra_router_lifetime   nd_ra_hdr.icmp6_data16[1]

struct nd_neighbor_solicit {   /* neighbor solicitation */
  struct icmp6_hdr  nd_ns_hdr;
  struct in6_addr   nd_ns_target; /* target address */
    /* could be followed by options */
};

#define nd_ns_type              nd_ns_hdr.icmp6_type
#define nd_ns_code              nd_ns_hdr.icmp6_code
#define nd_ns_cksum             nd_ns_hdr.icmp6_cksum
#define nd_ns_reserved          nd_ns_hdr.icmp6_data32[0]

struct nd_neighbor_advert {     /* neighbor advertisement */
  struct icmp6_hdr  nd_na_hdr;
  struct in6_addr   nd_na_target; /* target address */
    /* could be followed by options */
};

#define nd_na_type              nd_na_hdr.icmp6_type
#define nd_na_code              nd_na_hdr.icmp6_code
#define nd_na_cksum             nd_na_hdr.icmp6_cksum
#define nd_na_flags_reserved    nd_na_hdr.icmp6_data32[0]
#if     BYTE_ORDER == BIG_ENDIAN
#define ND_NA_FLAG_ROUTER       0x80000000
#define ND_NA_FLAG_SOLICITED    0x40000000
#define ND_NA_FLAG_OVERRIDE     0x20000000
#else   /* BYTE_ORDER == LITTLE_ENDIAN */
#define ND_NA_FLAG_ROUTER       0x00000080
#define ND_NA_FLAG_SOLICITED    0x00000040
#define ND_NA_FLAG_OVERRIDE     0x00000020
#endif
```

```
struct nd_redirect {              /* redirect */
  struct icmp6_hdr  nd_rd_hdr;
  struct in6_addr   nd_rd_target; /* target address */
  struct in6_addr   nd_rd_dst;    /* destination address */
    /* could be followed by options */
};

#define nd_rd_type                nd_rd_hdr.icmp6_type
#define nd_rd_code                nd_rd_hdr.icmp6_code
#define nd_rd_cksum               nd_rd_hdr.icmp6_cksum
#define nd_rd_reserved            nd_rd_hdr.icmp6_data32[0]

struct nd_opt_hdr {              /* Neighbor discovery option header */
  uint8_t  nd_opt_type;
  uint8_t  nd_opt_len;           /* in units of 8 octets */
    /* followed by option specific data */
};

#define   ND_OPT_SOURCE_LINKADDR      1
#define   ND_OPT_TARGET_LINKADDR      2
#define   ND_OPT_PREFIX_INFORMATION   3
#define   ND_OPT_REDIRECTED_HEADER    4
#define   ND_OPT_MTU                  5

struct nd_opt_prefix_info {     /* prefix information */
  uint8_t   nd_opt_pi_type;
  uint8_t   nd_opt_pi_len;
  uint8_t   nd_opt_pi_prefix_len;
  uint8_t   nd_opt_pi_flags_reserved;
  uint32_t  nd_opt_pi_valid_time;
  uint32_t  nd_opt_pi_preferred_time;
  uint32_t  nd_opt_pi_reserved2;
  struct in6_addr  nd_opt_pi_prefix;
};

#define ND_OPT_PI_FLAG_ONLINK       0x80
#define ND_OPT_PI_FLAG_AUTO         0x40

struct nd_opt_rd_hdr {          /* redirected header */
  uint8_t   nd_opt_rh_type;
  uint8_t   nd_opt_rh_len;
  uint16_t  nd_opt_rh_reserved1;
  uint32_t  nd_opt_rh_reserved2;
    /* followed by IP header and data */
};
```

```
struct nd_opt_mtu {                 /* MTU option */
  uint8_t    nd_opt_mtu_type;
  uint8_t    nd_opt_mtu_len;
  uint16_t   nd_opt_mtu_reserved;
  uint32_t   nd_opt_mtu_mtu;
};
```

We note that the nd_na_flags_reserved flags have the same byte
ordering problems as we showed with ip6f_offlg.

2.2.3. Multicast Listener Discovery Definitions

The following structures and definitions are defined as a result of
including <netinet/icmp6.h>.

```
#define MLD_LISTENER_QUERY          130
#define MLD_LISTENER_REPORT         131
#define MLD_LISTENER_REDUCTION      132

struct mld_hdr {
  struct icmp6_hdr  mld_icmp6_hdr;
  struct in6_addr   mld_addr; /* multicast address */
};
#define mld_type                  mld_icmp6_hdr.icmp6_type
#define mld_code                  mld_icmp6_hdr.icmp6_code
#define mld_cksum                 mld_icmp6_hdr.icmp6_cksum
#define mld_maxdelay              mld_icmp6_hdr.icmp6_data16[0]
#define mld_reserved              mld_icmp6_hdr.icmp6_data16[1]
```

2.2.4. ICMPv6 Router Renumbering Definitions

The following structures and definitions are defined as a result of
including <netinet/icmp6.h>.

```
#define ICMP6_ROUTER_RENUMBERING    138   /* router renumbering */

struct icmp6_router_renum {  /* router renumbering header */
  struct icmp6_hdr  rr_hdr;
  uint8_t           rr_segnum;
  uint8_t           rr_flags;
  uint16_t          rr_maxdelay;
  uint32_t          rr_reserved;
};
#define rr_type                   rr_hdr.icmp6_type
#define rr_code                   rr_hdr.icmp6_code
#define rr_cksum                  rr_hdr.icmp6_cksum
#define rr_segnum                 rr_hdr.icmp6_data32[0]
```

```
      /* Router renumbering flags */
      #define ICMP6_RR_FLAGS_TEST         0x80
      #define ICMP6_RR_FLAGS_REQRESULT    0x40
      #define ICMP6_RR_FLAGS_FORCEAPPLY   0x20
      #define ICMP6_RR_FLAGS_SPECSITE     0x10
      #define ICMP6_RR_FLAGS_PREVDONE     0x08


      struct rr_pco_match {      /* match prefix part */
        uint8_t            rpm_code;
        uint8_t            rpm_len;
        uint8_t            rpm_ordinal;
        uint8_t            rpm_matchlen;
        uint8_t            rpm_minlen;
        uint8_t            rpm_maxlen;
        uint16_t           rpm_reserved;
        struct in6_addr    rpm_prefix;
      };

      /* PCO code values */
      #define RPM_PCO_ADD              1
      #define RPM_PCO_CHANGE           2
      #define RPM_PCO_SETGLOBAL        3

      struct rr_pco_use {      /* use prefix part */
        uint8_t            rpu_uselen;
        uint8_t            rpu_keeplen;
        uint8_t            rpu_ramask;
        uint8_t            rpu_raflags;
        uint32_t           rpu_vltime;
        uint32_t           rpu_pltime;
        uint32_t           rpu_flags;
        struct in6_addr    rpu_prefix;
      };
      #define ICMP6_RR_PCOUSE_RAFLAGS_ONLINK   0x20
      #define ICMP6_RR_PCOUSE_RAFLAGS_AUTO     0x10

      #if BYTE_ORDER == BIG_ENDIAN
      #define ICMP6_RR_PCOUSE_FLAGS_DECRVLTIME 0x80000000
      #define ICMP6_RR_PCOUSE_FLAGS_DECRPLTIME 0x40000000
      #elif BYTE_ORDER == LITTLE_ENDIAN
      #define ICMP6_RR_PCOUSE_FLAGS_DECRVLTIME 0x80
      #define ICMP6_RR_PCOUSE_FLAGS_DECRPLTIME 0x40
      #endif
```

```
struct rr_result {      /* router renumbering result message */
  uint16_t        rrr_flags;
  uint8_t         rrr_ordinal;
  uint8_t         rrr_matchedlen;
  uint32_t        rrr_ifid;
  struct in6_addr rrr_prefix;
};

#if BYTE_ORDER == BIG_ENDIAN
#define ICMP6_RR_RESULT_FLAGS_OOB         0x0002
#define ICMP6_RR_RESULT_FLAGS_FORBIDDEN   0x0001
#elif BYTE_ORDER == LITTLE_ENDIAN
#define ICMP6_RR_RESULT_FLAGS_OOB         0x0200
#define ICMP6_RR_RESULT_FLAGS_FORBIDDEN   0x0100
#endif
```

2.3. Address Testing Macros

   The basic API ([RFC-3493]) defines some macros for testing an IPv6
   address for certain properties. This API extends those definitions
   with additional address testing macros, defined as a result of
   including <netinet/in.h>.

```
int  IN6_ARE_ADDR_EQUAL(const struct in6_addr *,
                        const struct in6_addr *);
```

   This macro returns non-zero if the addresses are equal; otherwise it
   returns zero.

2.4. Protocols File

   Many hosts provide the file /etc/protocols that contains the names of
   the various IP protocols and their protocol number (e.g., the value
   of the protocol field in the IPv4 header for that protocol, such as 1
   for ICMP). Some programs then call the function getprotobyname() to
   obtain the protocol value that is then specified as the third
   argument to the socket() function. For example, the Ping program
   contains code of the form

```
struct protoent  *proto;

proto = getprotobyname("icmp");

s = socket(AF_INET, SOCK_RAW, proto->p_proto);
```

   Common names are required for the new IPv6 protocols in this file, to
   provide portability of applications that call the getprotoXXX()
   functions.

RFC 3542   Advanced Sockets API for IPv6   May 2003

We define the following protocol names with the values shown. These
are taken under http://www.iana.org/numbers.html.

```
hopopt            0    # hop-by-hop options for ipv6
ipv6             41    # ipv6
ipv6-route       43    # routing header for ipv6
ipv6-frag        44    # fragment header for ipv6
esp              50    # encapsulating security payload for ipv6
ah               51    # authentication header for ipv6
ipv6-icmp        58    # icmp for ipv6
ipv6-nonxt       59    # no next header for ipv6
ipv6-opts        60    # destination options for ipv6
```

3. IPv6 Raw Sockets

   Raw sockets bypass the transport layer (TCP or UDP). With IPv4, raw
   sockets are used to access ICMPv4, IGMPv4, and to read and write IPv4
   datagrams containing a protocol field that the kernel does not
   process. An example of the latter is a routing daemon for OSPF,
   since it uses IPv4 protocol field 89. With IPv6 raw sockets will be
   used for ICMPv6 and to read and write IPv6 datagrams containing a
   Next Header field that the kernel does not process. Examples of the
   latter are a routing daemon for OSPF for IPv6 and RSVP (protocol
   field 46).

   All data sent via raw sockets must be in network byte order and all
   data received via raw sockets will be in network byte order. This
   differs from the IPv4 raw sockets, which did not specify a byte
   ordering and used the host's byte order for certain IP header fields.

   Another difference from IPv4 raw sockets is that complete packets
   (that is, IPv6 packets with extension headers) cannot be sent or
   received using the IPv6 raw sockets API. Instead, ancillary data
   objects are used to transfer the extension headers and hoplimit
   information, as described in Section 6. Should an application need
   access to the complete IPv6 packet, some other technique, such as the
   datalink interfaces BPF or DLPI, must be used.

   All fields except the flow label in the IPv6 header that an
   application might want to change (i.e., everything other than the
   version number) can be modified using ancillary data and/or socket
   options by the application for output. All fields except the flow
   label in a received IPv6 header (other than the version number and
   Next Header fields) and all extension headers that an application
   might want to know are also made available to the application as
   ancillary data on input. Hence there is no need for a socket option

RFC 3542   Advanced Sockets API for IPv6   May 2003

similar to the IPv4 IP_HDRINCL socket option and on receipt the
application will only receive the payload i.e., the data after the
IPv6 header and all the extension headers.

This API does not define access to the flow label field, because
today there is no standard usage of the field.

When writing to a raw socket the kernel will automatically fragment
the packet if its size exceeds the path MTU, inserting the required
fragment headers. On input the kernel reassembles received
fragments, so the reader of a raw socket never sees any fragment
headers.

When we say "an ICMPv6 raw socket" we mean a socket created by
calling the socket function with the three arguments AF_INET6,
SOCK_RAW, and IPPROTO_ICMPV6.

Most IPv4 implementations give special treatment to a raw socket
created with a third argument to socket() of IPPROTO_RAW, whose value
is normally 255, to have it mean that the application will send down
complete packets including the IPv4 header. (Note: This feature was
added to IPv4 in 1988 by Van Jacobson to support traceroute, allowing
a complete IP header to be passed by the application, before the
IP_HDRINCL socket option was added.) We note that IPPROTO_RAW has no
special meaning to an IPv6 raw socket (and the IANA currently
reserves the value of 255 when used as a next-header field).

3.1. Checksums

The kernel will calculate and insert the ICMPv6 checksum for ICMPv6
raw sockets, since this checksum is mandatory.

For other raw IPv6 sockets (that is, for raw IPv6 sockets created
with a third argument other than IPPROTO_ICMPV6), the application
must set the new IPV6_CHECKSUM socket option to have the kernel (1)
compute and store a checksum for output, and (2) verify the received
checksum on input, discarding the packet if the checksum is in error.
This option prevents applications from having to perform source
address selection on the packets they send. The checksum will
incorporate the IPv6 pseudo-header, defined in Section 8.1 of [RFC-
2460]. This new socket option also specifies an integer offset into
the user data of where the checksum is located.

```
    int  offset = 2;
    setsockopt(fd, IPPROTO_IPV6, IPV6_CHECKSUM, &offset,
            sizeof(offset));
```

Stevens, et al.   Informational   [Page 18]

By default, this socket option is disabled. Setting the offset to -1
also disables the option. By disabled we mean (1) the kernel will
not calculate and store a checksum for outgoing packets, and (2) the
kernel will not verify a checksum for received packets.

This option assumes the use of the 16-bit one's complement of the
one's complement sum as the checksum algorithm and that the checksum
field is aligned on a 16-bit boundary. Thus, specifying a positive
odd value as offset is invalid, and setsockopt() will fail for such
offset values.

An attempt to set IPV6_CHECKSUM for an ICMPv6 socket will fail.
Also, an attempt to set or get IPV6_CHECKSUM for a non-raw IPv6
socket will fail.

(Note: Since the checksum is always calculated by the kernel for an
ICMPv6 socket, applications are not able to generate ICMPv6 packets
with incorrect checksums (presumably for testing purposes) using this
API.)

3.2. ICMPv6 Type Filtering

ICMPv4 raw sockets receive most ICMPv4 messages received by the
kernel. (We say "most" and not "all" because Berkeley-derived
kernels never pass echo requests, timestamp requests, or address mask
requests to a raw socket. Instead these three messages are processed
entirely by the kernel.) But ICMPv6 is a superset of ICMPv4, also
including the functionality of IGMPv4 and ARPv4. This means that an
ICMPv6 raw socket can potentially receive many more messages than
would be received with an ICMPv4 raw socket: ICMP messages similar to
ICMPv4, along with neighbor solicitations, neighbor advertisements,
and the three multicast listener discovery messages.

Most applications using an ICMPv6 raw socket care about only a small
subset of the ICMPv6 message types. To transfer extraneous ICMPv6
messages from the kernel to user can incur a significant overhead.
Therefore this API includes a method of filtering ICMPv6 messages by
the ICMPv6 type field.

Each ICMPv6 raw socket has an associated filter whose datatype is
defined as

    struct icmp6_filter;

This structure, along with the macros and constants defined later in
this section, are defined as a result of including the
<netinet/icmp6.h>.

The current filter is fetched and stored using getsockopt() and
setsockopt() with a level of IPPROTO_ICMPV6 and an option name of
ICMP6_FILTER.

Six macros operate on an icmp6_filter structure:

```
void ICMP6_FILTER_SETPASSALL (struct icmp6_filter *);
void ICMP6_FILTER_SETBLOCKALL(struct icmp6_filter *);

void ICMP6_FILTER_SETPASS ( int, struct icmp6_filter *);
void ICMP6_FILTER_SETBLOCK( int, struct icmp6_filter *);

int  ICMP6_FILTER_WILLPASS (int,
                              const struct icmp6_filter *);
int  ICMP6_FILTER_WILLBLOCK(int,
                              const struct icmp6_filter *);
```

The first argument to the last four macros (an integer) is an ICMPv6
message type, between 0 and 255. The pointer argument to all six
macros is a pointer to a filter that is modified by the first four
macros and is examined by the last two macros.

The first two macros, SETPASSALL and SETBLOCKALL, let us specify that
all ICMPv6 messages are passed to the application or that all ICMPv6
messages are blocked from being passed to the application.

The next two macros, SETPASS and SETBLOCK, let us specify that
messages of a given ICMPv6 type should be passed to the application
or not passed to the application (blocked).

The final two macros, WILLPASS and WILLBLOCK, return true or false
depending whether the specified message type is passed to the
application or blocked from being passed to the application by the
filter pointed to by the second argument.

When an ICMPv6 raw socket is created, it will by default pass all
ICMPv6 message types to the application.

As an example, a program that wants to receive only router
advertisements could execute the following:

```
struct icmp6_filter  myfilt;

fd = socket(AF_INET6, SOCK_RAW, IPPROTO_ICMPV6);

ICMP6_FILTER_SETBLOCKALL(&myfilt);
ICMP6_FILTER_SETPASS(ND_ROUTER_ADVERT, &myfilt);
setsockopt(fd, IPPROTO_ICMPV6, ICMP6_FILTER, &myfilt,
```

RFC 3542   Advanced Sockets API for IPv6   May 2003

```
                  sizeof(myfilt));
```

The filter structure is declared and then initialized to block all
messages types. The filter structure is then changed to allow router
advertisement messages to be passed to the application and the filter
is installed using setsockopt().

In order to clear an installed filter the application can issue a
setsockopt for ICMP6_FILTER with a zero length. When no such filter
has been installed, getsockopt() will return the kernel default
filter.

The icmp6_filter structure is similar to the fd_set datatype used
with the select() function in the sockets API. The icmp6_filter
structure is an opaque datatype and the application should not care
how it is implemented. All the application does with this datatype
is allocate a variable of this type, pass a pointer to a variable of
this type to getsockopt() and setsockopt(), and operate on a variable
of this type using the six macros that we just defined.

Nevertheless, it is worth showing a simple implementation of this
datatype and the six macros.

```
   struct icmp6_filter {
     uint32_t  icmp6_filt[8];   /* 8*32 = 256 bits */
   };

   #define ICMP6_FILTER_WILLPASS(type, filterp) \
     ((((filterp)->icmp6_filt[(type) >> 5]) & \
       (1 << ((type) & 31))) != 0)
   #define ICMP6_FILTER_WILLBLOCK(type, filterp) \
     ((((filterp)->icmp6_filt[(type) >> 5]) & \
       (1 << ((type) & 31))) == 0)
   #define ICMP6_FILTER_SETPASS(type, filterp) \
     ((((filterp)->icmp6_filt[(type) >> 5]) |= \
       (1 << ((type) & 31))))
   #define ICMP6_FILTER_SETBLOCK(type, filterp) \
     ((((filterp)->icmp6_filt[(type) >> 5]) &= \
       ~(1 << ((type) & 31))))
   #define ICMP6_FILTER_SETPASSALL(filterp) \
     memset((filterp), 0xFF, sizeof(struct icmp6_filter))
   #define ICMP6_FILTER_SETBLOCKALL(filterp) \
     memset((filterp), 0, sizeof(struct icmp6_filter))
```

(Note: These sample definitions have two limitations that an
implementation may want to change. The first four macros evaluate
their first argument two times. The second two macros require the
inclusion of the <string.h> header for the memset() function.)

Stevens, et al.   Informational   [Page 21]

3.3. ICMPv6 Verification of Received Packets

   The protocol stack will verify the ICMPv6 checksum and discard any
   packets with invalid checksums.

   An implementation might perform additional validity checks on the
   ICMPv6 message content and discard malformed packets. However, a
   portable application must not assume that such validity checks have
   been performed.

   The protocol stack should not automatically discard packets if the
   ICMP type is unknown to the stack. For extensibility reasons
   received ICMP packets with any type (informational or error) must be
   passed to the applications (subject to ICMP6_FILTER filtering on the
   type value and the checksum verification).

4. Access to IPv6 and Extension Headers

   Applications need to be able to control IPv6 header and extension
   header content when sending as well as being able to receive the
   content of these headers. This is done by defining socket option
   types which can be used both with setsockopt and with ancillary data.
   Ancillary data is discussed in Appendix A. The following optional
   information can be exchanged between the application and the kernel:

   1. The send/receive interface and source/destination address,
   2. The hop limit,
   3. Next hop address,
   4. The traffic class,
   5. Routing header,
   6. Hop-by-Hop options header, and
   7. Destination options header.

   First, to receive any of this optional information (other than the
   next hop address, which can only be set) on a UDP or raw socket, the
   application must call setsockopt() to turn on the corresponding flag:

```
    int  on = 1;

    setsockopt(fd, IPPROTO_IPV6, IPV6_RECVPKTINFO,  &on, sizeof(on));
    setsockopt(fd, IPPROTO_IPV6, IPV6_RECVHOPLIMIT, &on, sizeof(on));
    setsockopt(fd, IPPROTO_IPV6, IPV6_RECVRTHDR,    &on, sizeof(on));
    setsockopt(fd, IPPROTO_IPV6, IPV6_RECVHOPOPTS,  &on, sizeof(on));
    setsockopt(fd, IPPROTO_IPV6, IPV6_RECVDSTOPTS,  &on, sizeof(on));
    setsockopt(fd, IPPROTO_IPV6, IPV6_RECVTCLASS,   &on, sizeof(on));
```

RFC 3542   Advanced Sockets API for IPv6   May 2003

    When any of these options are enabled, the corresponding data is
    returned as control information by recvmsg(), as one or more
    ancillary data objects.

    This document does not define how to receive the optional information
    on a TCP socket. See Section 4.1 for more details.

    Two different mechanisms exist for sending this optional information:

    1. Using setsockopt to specify the option content for a socket.
       These are known "sticky" options since they affect all transmitted
       packets on the socket until either a new setsockopt is done or the
       options are overridden using ancillary data.

    2. Using ancillary data to specify the option content for a single
       datagram. This only applies to datagram and raw sockets; not to
       TCP sockets.

    The three socket option parameters and the three cmsghdr fields that
    describe the options/ancillary data objects are summarized as:

        opt level/   optname/   optval/
        cmsg_level   cmsg_type   cmsg_data[]
        -----------   -----------   ---------------------
        IPPROTO_IPV6   IPV6_PKTINFO   in6_pktinfo structure
        IPPROTO_IPV6   IPV6_HOPLIMIT   int
        IPPROTO_IPV6   IPV6_NEXTHOP   socket address structure
        IPPROTO_IPV6   IPV6_RTHDR   ip6_rthdr structure
        IPPROTO_IPV6   IPV6_HOPOPTS   ip6_hbh structure
        IPPROTO_IPV6   IPV6_DSTOPTS   ip6_dest structure
        IPPROTO_IPV6   IPV6_RTHDRDSTOPTS   ip6_dest structure
        IPPROTO_IPV6   IPV6_TCLASS   int

        (Note: IPV6_HOPLIMIT can be used as ancillary data items only)

    All these options are described in detail in Section 6, 7, 8 and 9.
    All the constants beginning with IPV6_ are defined as a result of
    including <netinet/in.h>.

    Note: We intentionally use the same constant for the cmsg_level
    member as is used as the second argument to getsockopt() and
    setsockopt() (what is called the "level"), and the same constant for
    the cmsg_type member as is used as the third argument to getsockopt()
    and setsockopt() (what is called the "option name").

RFC 3542   Advanced Sockets API for IPv6   May 2003

Issuing getsockopt() for the above options will return the sticky
option value i.e., the value set with setsockopt(). If no sticky
option value has been set getsockopt() will return the following
values:

-   For the IPV6_PKTINFO option, it will return an in6_pktinfo
    structure with ipi6_addr being in6addr_any and ipi6_ifindex being
    zero.

-   For the IPV6_TCLASS option, it will return the kernel default
    value.

-   For other options, it will indicate the lack of the option value
    with optlen being zero.

The application does not explicitly need to access the data
structures for the Routing header, Hop-by-Hop options header, and
Destination options header, since the API to these features is
through a set of inet6_rth_XXX() and inet6_opt_XXX() functions that
we define in Section 7 and Section 10. Those functions simplify the
interface to these features instead of requiring the application to
know the intimate details of the extension header formats.

When specifying extension headers, this API assumes the header
ordering and the number of occurrences of each header as described in
[RFC-2460]. More details about the ordering issue will be discussed
in Section 12.

4.1. TCP Implications

It is not possible to use ancillary data to transmit the above
options for TCP since there is not a one-to-one mapping between send
operations and the TCP segments being transmitted. Instead an
application can use setsockopt to specify them as sticky options.
When the application uses setsockopt to specify the above options it
is expected that TCP will start using the new information when
sending segments. However, TCP may or may not use the new
information when retransmitting segments that were originally sent
when the old sticky options were in effect.

It is unclear how a TCP application can use received information
(such as extension headers) due to the lack of mapping between
received TCP segments and receive operations. In particular, the
received information could not be used for access control purposes
like on UDP and raw sockets.

Stevens, et al.   Informational   [Page 24]

RFC 3542   Advanced Sockets API for IPv6   May 2003

This specification therefore does not define how to get the received
information on TCP sockets. The result of the IPV6_RECVxxx options
on a TCP socket is undefined as well.

4.2. UDP and Raw Socket Implications

The receive behavior for UDP and raw sockets is quite
straightforward. After the application has enabled an IPV6_RECVxxx
socket option it will receive ancillary data items for every
recvmsg() call containing the requested information. However, if the
information is not present in the packet the ancillary data item will
not be included. For example, if the application enables
IPV6_RECVRTHDR and a received datagram does not contain a Routing
header there will not be an IPV6_RTHDR ancillary data item. Note
that due to buffering in the socket implementation there might be
some packets queued when an IPV6_RECVxxx option is enabled and they
might not have the ancillary data information.

For sending the application has the choice between using sticky
options and ancillary data. The application can also use both having
the sticky options specify the "default" and using ancillary data to
override the default options.

When an ancillary data item is specified in a call to sendmsg(), the
item will override an existing sticky option of the same name (if
previously specified). For example, if the application has set
IPV6_RTHDR using a sticky option and later passes IPV6_RTHDR as
ancillary data this will override the IPV6_RTHDR sticky option and
the routing header of the outgoing packet will be from the ancillary
data item, not from the sticky option. Note, however, that other
sticky options than IPV6_RTHDR will not be affected by the IPV6_RTHDR
ancillary data item; the overriding mechanism only works for the same
type of sticky options and ancillary data items.

(Note: the overriding rule is different from the one in RFC 2292. In
RFC 2292, an ancillary data item overrode all sticky options
previously defined. This was reasonable, because sticky options
could only be specified as a set by a single socket option. However,
in this API, each option is separated so that it can be specified as
a single sticky option. Additionally, there are much more ancillary
data items and sticky options than in RFC 2292, including ancillary-
only one. Thus, it should be natural for application programmers to
separate the overriding rule as well.)

An application can also temporarily disable a particular sticky
option by specifying a corresponding ancillary data item that could
disable the sticky option when being used as an argument for a socket
option. For example, if the application has set IPV6_HOPOPTS as a

sticky option and later passes IPV6_HOPOPTS with a zero length as an
ancillary data item, the packet will not have a Hop-by-Hop options
header.

5. Extensions to Socket Ancillary Data

This specification uses ancillary data as defined in Posix with some
compatible extensions, which are described in the following
subsections. Section 20 will provide a detailed overview of
ancillary data and related structures and macros, including the
extensions.

5.1. CMSG_NXTHDR

        struct cmsghdr *CMSG_NXTHDR(const struct msghdr *mhdr,
                                    const struct cmsghdr *cmsg);

CMSG_NXTHDR() returns a pointer to the cmsghdr structure describing
the next ancillary data object. Mhdr is a pointer to a msghdr
structure and cmsg is a pointer to a cmsghdr structure. If there is
not another ancillary data object, the return value is NULL.

The following behavior of this macro is new to this API: if the value
of the cmsg pointer is NULL, a pointer to the cmsghdr structure
describing the first ancillary data object is returned. That is,
CMSG_NXTHDR(mhdr, NULL) is equivalent to CMSG_FIRSTHDR(mhdr). If
there are no ancillary data objects, the return value is NULL.

5.2. CMSG_SPACE

socklen_t CMSG_SPACE(socklen_t length);

This macro is new with this API. Given the length of an ancillary
data object, CMSG_SPACE() returns an upper bound on the space
required by the object and its cmsghdr structure, including any
padding needed to satisfy alignment requirements. This macro can be
used, for example, when allocating space dynamically for the
ancillary data. This macro should not be used to initialize the
cmsg_len member of a cmsghdr structure; instead use the CMSG_LEN()
macro.

5.3. CMSG_LEN

    socklen_t CMSG_LEN(socklen_t length);

    This macro is new with this API. Given the length of an ancillary
    data object, CMSG_LEN() returns the value to store in the cmsg_len
    member of the cmsghdr structure, taking into account any padding
    needed to satisfy alignment requirements.

    Note the difference between CMSG_SPACE() and CMSG_LEN(), shown also
    in the figure in Section 20.2: the former accounts for any required
    padding at the end of the ancillary data object and the latter is the
    actual length to store in the cmsg_len member of the ancillary data
    object.

6. Packet Information

    There are five pieces of information that an application can specify
    for an outgoing packet using ancillary data:

        1.   the source IPv6 address,
        2.   the outgoing interface index,
        3.   the outgoing hop limit,
        4.   the next hop address, and
        5.   the outgoing traffic class value.

    Four similar pieces of information can be returned for a received
    packet as ancillary data:

        1.   the destination IPv6 address,
        2.   the arriving interface index,
        3.   the arriving hop limit, and
        4.   the arriving traffic class value.

    The first two pieces of information are contained in an in6_pktinfo
    structure that is set with setsockopt() or sent as ancillary data
    with sendmsg() and received as ancillary data with recvmsg(). This
    structure is defined as a result of including <netinet/in.h>.

        struct in6_pktinfo {
          struct in6_addr ipi6_addr;   /* src/dst IPv6 address */
          unsigned int   ipi6_ifindex; /* send/recv interface index */
        };

    In the socket option and cmsghdr level will be IPPROTO_IPV6, the type
    will be IPV6_PKTINFO, and the first byte of the option value and
    cmsg_data[] will be the first byte of the in6_pktinfo structure. An
    application can clear any sticky IPV6_PKTINFO option by doing a

"regular" setsockopt with ipi6_addr being in6addr_any and
ipi6_ifindex being zero.

This information is returned as ancillary data by recvmsg() only if
the application has enabled the IPV6_RECVPKTINFO socket option:

```
int  on = 1;
setsockopt(fd, IPPROTO_IPV6, IPV6_RECVPKTINFO, &on, sizeof(on));
```

(Note: The hop limit is not contained in the in6_pktinfo structure
for the following reason. Some UDP servers want to respond to client
requests by sending their reply out the same interface on which the
request was received and with the source IPv6 address of the reply
equal to the destination IPv6 address of the request. To do this the
application can enable just the IPV6_RECVPKTINFO socket option and
then use the received control information from recvmsg() as the
outgoing control information for sendmsg(). The application need not
examine or modify the in6_pktinfo structure at all. But if the hop
limit were contained in this structure, the application would have to
parse the received control information and change the hop limit
member, since the received hop limit is not the desired value for an
outgoing packet.)

6.1. Specifying/Receiving the Interface

Interfaces on an IPv6 node are identified by a small positive
integer, as described in Section 4 of [RFC-3493]. That document also
describes a function to map an interface name to its interface index,
a function to map an interface index to its interface name, and a
function to return all the interface names and indexes. Notice from
this document that no interface is ever assigned an index of 0.

When specifying the outgoing interface, if the ipi6_ifindex value is
0, the kernel will choose the outgoing interface.

The ordering among various options that can specify the outgoing
interface, including IPV6_PKTINFO, is defined in Section 6.7.

When the IPV6_RECVPKTINFO socket option is enabled, the received
interface index is always returned as the ipi6_ifindex member of the
in6_pktinfo structure.

6.2. Specifying/Receiving Source/Destination Address

The source IPv6 address can be specified by calling bind() before
each output operation, but supplying the source address together with
the data requires less overhead (i.e., fewer system calls) and
requires less state to be stored and protected in a multithreaded
application.

When specifying the source IPv6 address as ancillary data, if the
ipi6_addr member of the in6_pktinfo structure is the unspecified
address (IN6ADDR_ANY_INIT or in6addr_any), then (a) if an address is
currently bound to the socket, it is used as the source address, or
(b) if no address is currently bound to the socket, the kernel will
choose the source address. If the ipi6_addr member is not the
unspecified address, but the socket has already bound a source
address, then the ipi6_addr value overrides the already-bound source
address for this output operation only.

The kernel must verify that the requested source address is indeed a
unicast address assigned to the node. When the address is a scoped
one, there may be ambiguity about its scope zone. This is
particularly the case for link-local addresses. In such a case, the
kernel must first determine the appropriate scope zone based on the
zone of the destination address or the outgoing interface (if known),
then qualify the address. This also means that it is not feasible to
specify the source address for a non-binding socket by the
IPV6_PKTINFO sticky option, unless the outgoing interface is also
specified. The application should simply use bind() for such
purposes.

IPV6_PKTINFO can also be used as a sticky option for specifying the
socket's default source address. However, the ipi6_addr member must
be the unspecified address for TCP sockets, because it is not
possible to dynamically change the source address of a TCP
connection. When the IPV6_PKTINFO option is specified for a TCP
socket with a non-unspecified address, the call will fail. This
restriction should be applied even before the socket binds a specific
address.

When the in6_pktinfo structure is returned as ancillary data by
recvmsg(), the ipi6_addr member contains the destination IPv6 address
from the received packet.

6.3. Specifying/Receiving the Hop Limit

The outgoing hop limit is normally specified with either the
IPV6_UNICAST_HOPS socket option or the IPV6_MULTICAST_HOPS socket
option, both of which are described in [RFC-3493]. Specifying the

hop limit as ancillary data lets the application override either the
kernel's default or a previously specified value, for either a
unicast destination or a multicast destination, for a single output
operation. Returning the received hop limit is useful for IPv6
applications that need to verify that the received hop limit is 255
(e.g., that the packet has not been forwarded).

The received hop limit is returned as ancillary data by recvmsg()
only if the application has enabled the IPV6_RECVHOPLIMIT socket
option:

```
int  on = 1;
setsockopt(fd, IPPROTO_IPV6, IPV6_RECVHOPLIMIT, &on, sizeof(on));
```

In the cmsghdr structure containing this ancillary data, the
cmsg_level member will be IPPROTO_IPV6, the cmsg_type member will be
IPV6_HOPLIMIT, and the first byte of cmsg_data[] will be the first
byte of the integer hop limit.

Nothing special need be done to specify the outgoing hop limit: just
specify the control information as ancillary data for sendmsg(). As
specified in [RFC-3493], the interpretation of the integer hop limit
value is

```
x < -1:          return an error of EINVAL
x == -1:         use kernel default
0 <= x <= 255:   use x
x >= 256:        return an error of EINVAL
```

This API defines IPV6_HOPLIMIT as an ancillary-only option, that is,
the option name cannot be used as a socket option. This is because
[RFC-3493] has more fine-grained socket options; IPV6_UNICAST_HOPS
and IPV6_MULTICAST_HOPS.

6.4. Specifying the Next Hop Address

The IPV6_NEXTHOP ancillary data object specifies the next hop for the
datagram as a socket address structure. In the cmsghdr structure
containing this ancillary data, the cmsg_level member will be
IPPROTO_IPV6, the cmsg_type member will be IPV6_NEXTHOP, and the
first byte of cmsg_data[] will be the first byte of the socket
address structure.

This is a privileged option. (Note: It is implementation defined and
beyond the scope of this document to define what "privileged" means.
Unix systems use this term to mean the process must have an effective
user ID of 0.)

RFC 3542   Advanced Sockets API for IPv6   May 2003

This API only defines the case where the socket address contains an
IPv6 address (i.e., the sa_family member is AF_INET6). And, in this
case, the node identified by that address must be a neighbor of the
sending host. If that address equals the destination IPv6 address of
the datagram, then this is equivalent to the existing SO_DONTROUTE
socket option.

This option does not have any meaning for multicast destinations. In
such a case, the specified next hop will be ignored.

When the outgoing interface is specified by IPV6_PKTINFO as well, the
next hop specified by this option must be reachable via the specified
interface.

In order to clear a sticky IPV6_NEXTHOP option the application must
issue a setsockopt for IPV6_NEXTHOP with a zero length.

6.5. Specifying/Receiving the Traffic Class value

The outgoing traffic class is normally set to 0. Specifying the
traffic class as ancillary data lets the application override either
the kernel's default or a previously specified value, for either a
unicast destination or a multicast destination, for a single output
operation. Returning the received traffic class is useful for
programs such as a diffserv debugging tool and for user level ECN
(explicit congestion notification) implementation.

The received traffic class is returned as ancillary data by recvmsg()
only if the application has enabled the IPV6_RECVTCLASS socket
option:

    int on = 1;
    setsockopt(fd, IPPROTO_IPV6, IPV6_RECVTCLASS, &on, sizeof(on));

In the cmsghdr structure containing this ancillary data, the
cmsg_level member will be IPPROTO_IPV6, the cmsg_type member will be
IPV6_TCLASS, and the first byte of cmsg_data[] will be the first byte
of the integer traffic class.

To specify the outgoing traffic class value, just specify the control
information as ancillary data for sendmsg() or using setsockopt().
Just like the hop limit value, the interpretation of the integer
traffic class value is

    x < -1:   return an error of EINVAL
    x == -1:   use kernel default
    0 <= x <= 255: use x
    x >= 256:   return an error of EINVAL

In order to clear a sticky IPV6_TCLASS option the application can
specify -1 as the value.

There are cases where the kernel needs to control the traffic class
value and conflicts with the user-specified value on the outgoing
traffic. An example is an implementation of ECN in the kernel,
setting 2 bits of the traffic class value. In such cases, the kernel
should override the user-specified value. On the incoming traffic,
the kernel may mask some of the bits in the traffic class field.

6.6. Additional Errors with sendmsg() and setsockopt()

With the IPV6_PKTINFO socket option there are no additional errors
possible with the call to recvmsg(). But when specifying the
outgoing interface or the source address, additional errors are
possible from sendmsg() or setsockopt(). Note that some
implementations might only be able to return this type of errors for
setsockopt(). The following are examples, but some of these may not
be provided by some implementations, and some implementations may
define additional errors:

ENXIO   The interface specified by ipi6_ifindex does not exist.

ENETDOWN   The interface specified by ipi6_ifindex is not enabled
               for IPv6 use.

EADDRNOTAVAIL ipi6_ifindex specifies an interface but the address
               ipi6_addr is not available for use on that interface.

EHOSTUNREACH   No route to the destination exists over the interface
               specified by ipi6_ifindex.

6.7. Summary of Outgoing Interface Selection

This document and [RFC-3493] specify various methods that affect the
selection of the packet's outgoing interface. This subsection
summarizes the ordering among those in order to ensure deterministic
behavior.

For a given outgoing packet on a given socket, the outgoing interface
is determined in the following order:

1. if an interface is specified in an IPV6_PKTINFO ancillary data
   item, the interface is used.

2. otherwise, if an interface is specified in an IPV6_PKTINFO sticky
   option, the interface is used.

RFC 3542   Advanced Sockets API for IPv6   May 2003

   3. otherwise, if the destination address is a multicast address and
      the IPV6_MULTICAST_IF socket option is specified for the socket,
      the interface is used.

   4. otherwise, if an IPV6_NEXTHOP ancillary data item is specified,
      the interface to the next hop is used.

   5. otherwise, if an IPV6_NEXTHOP sticky option is specified, the
      interface to the next hop is used.

   6. otherwise, the outgoing interface should be determined in an
      implementation dependent manner.

   The ordering above particularly means if the application specifies an
   interface by the IPV6_MULTICAST_IF socket option (described in [RFC-
   3493]) as well as specifying a different interface by the
   IPV6_PKTINFO sticky option, the latter will override the former for
   every multicast packet on the corresponding socket. The reason for
   the ordering comes from expectation that the source address is
   specified as well and that the pair of the address and the outgoing
   interface should be preferred.

   In any case, the kernel must also verify that the source and
   destination addresses do not break their scope zones with regard to
   the outgoing interface.

7. Routing Header Option

   Source routing in IPv6 is accomplished by specifying a Routing header
   as an extension header. There can be different types of Routing
   headers, but IPv6 currently defines only the Type 0 Routing header
   [RFC-2460]. This type supports up to 127 intermediate nodes (limited
   by the length field in the extension header). With this maximum
   number of intermediate nodes, a source, and a destination, there are
   128 hops.

   Source routing with the IPv4 sockets API (the IP_OPTIONS socket
   option) requires the application to build the source route in the
   format that appears as the IPv4 header option, requiring intimate
   knowledge of the IPv4 options format. This IPv6 API, however,
   defines six functions that the application calls to build and examine
   a Routing header, and the ability to use sticky options or ancillary
   data to communicate this information between the application and the
   kernel using the IPV6_RTHDR option.

RFC 3542   Advanced Sockets API for IPv6   May 2003

    Three functions build a Routing header:

        inet6_rth_space()   - return #bytes required for Routing header
        inet6_rth_init()   - initialize buffer data for Routing header
        inet6_rth_add()   - add one IPv6 address to the Routing header

    Three functions deal with a returned Routing header:

        inet6_rth_reverse() - reverse a Routing header
        inet6_rth_segments() - return #segments in a Routing header
        inet6_rth_getaddr() - fetch one address from a Routing header

    The function prototypes for these functions are defined as a result
    of including <netinet/in.h>.

    To receive a Routing header the application must enable the
    IPV6_RECVRTHDR socket option:

        int on = 1;
        setsockopt(fd, IPPROTO_IPV6, IPV6_RECVRTHDR, &on, sizeof(on));

    Each received Routing header is returned as one ancillary data object
    described by a cmsghdr structure with cmsg_type set to IPV6_RTHDR.
    When multiple Routing headers are received, multiple ancillary data
    objects (with cmsg_type set to IPV6_RTHDR) will be returned to the
    application.

    To send a Routing header the application specifies it either as
    ancillary data in a call to sendmsg() or using setsockopt(). For the
    sending side, this API assumes the number of occurrences of the
    Routing header as described in [RFC-2460]. That is, applications can
    only specify at most one outgoing Routing header.

    The application can remove any sticky Routing header by calling
    setsockopt() for IPV6_RTHDR with a zero option length.

    When using ancillary data a Routing header is passed between the
    application and the kernel as follows: The cmsg_level member has a
    value of IPPROTO_IPV6 and the cmsg_type member has a value of
    IPV6_RTHDR. The contents of the cmsg_data[] member is implementation
    dependent and should not be accessed directly by the application, but
    should be accessed using the six functions that we are about to
    describe.

    The following constant is defined as a result of including the
    <netinet/in.h>:

        #define IPV6_RTHDR_TYPE_0   0 /* IPv6 Routing header type 0 */

Stevens, et al.   Informational   [Page 34]

RFC 3542   Advanced Sockets API for IPv6   May 2003

   When a Routing header is specified, the destination address specified
   for connect(), sendto(), or sendmsg() is the final destination
   address of the datagram. The Routing header then contains the
   addresses of all the intermediate nodes.

7.1.   inet6_rth_space

      socklen_t inet6_rth_space(int type, int segments);

   This function returns the number of bytes required to hold a Routing
   header of the specified type containing the specified number of
   segments (addresses). For an IPv6 Type 0 Routing header, the number
   of segments must be between 0 and 127, inclusive. The return value
   is just the space for the Routing header. When the application uses
   ancillary data it must pass the returned length to CMSG_SPACE() to
   determine how much memory is needed for the ancillary data object
   (including the cmsghdr structure).

   If the return value is 0, then either the type of the Routing header
   is not supported by this implementation or the number of segments is
   invalid for this type of Routing header.

   (Note: This function returns the size but does not allocate the space
   required for the ancillary data. This allows an application to
   allocate a larger buffer, if other ancillary data objects are
   desired, since all the ancillary data objects must be specified to
   sendmsg() as a single msg_control buffer.)

7.2.   inet6_rth_init

      void *inet6_rth_init(void *bp, socklen_t bp_len, int type,
                           int segments);

   This function initializes the buffer pointed to by bp to contain a
   Routing header of the specified type and sets ip6r_len based on the
   segments parameter. bp_len is only used to verify that the buffer is
   large enough. The ip6r_segleft field is set to zero; inet6_rth_add()
   will increment it.

   When the application uses ancillary data the application must
   initialize any cmsghdr fields.

   The caller must allocate the buffer and its size can be determined by
   calling inet6_rth_space().

   Upon success the return value is the pointer to the buffer (bp), and
   this is then used as the first argument to the inet6_rth_add()
   function. Upon an error the return value is NULL.

Stevens, et al.   Informational   [Page 35]

RFC 3542   Advanced Sockets API for IPv6   May 2003

7.3. inet6_rth_add

        int inet6_rth_add(void *bp, const struct in6_addr *addr);

   This function adds the IPv6 address pointed to by addr to the end of
   the Routing header being constructed.

   If successful, the segleft member of the Routing Header is updated to
   account for the new address in the Routing header and the return
   value of the function is 0. Upon an error the return value of the
   function is -1.

7.4. inet6_rth_reverse

        int inet6_rth_reverse(const void *in, void *out);

   This function takes a Routing header extension header (pointed to by
   the first argument) and writes a new Routing header that sends
   datagrams along the reverse of that route. The function reverses the
   order of the addresses and sets the segleft member in the new Routing
   header to the number of segments. Both arguments are allowed to
   point to the same buffer (that is, the reversal can occur in place).

   The return value of the function is 0 on success, or -1 upon an
   error.

7.5. inet6_rth_segments

        int inet6_rth_segments(const void *bp);

   This function returns the number of segments (addresses) contained in
   the Routing header described by bp. On success the return value is
   zero or greater. The return value of the function is -1 upon an
   error.

7.6. inet6_rth_getaddr

        struct in6_addr *inet6_rth_getaddr(const void *bp, int index);

   This function returns a pointer to the IPv6 address specified by
   index (which must have a value between 0 and one less than the value
   returned by inet6_rth_segments()) in the Routing header described by
   bp. An application should first call inet6_rth_segments() to obtain
   the number of segments in the Routing header.

   Upon an error the return value of the function is NULL.

Stevens, et al.   Informational   [Page 36]

RFC 3542   Advanced Sockets API for IPv6   May 2003

8. Hop-By-Hop Options

    A variable number of Hop-by-Hop options can appear in a single Hop-
    by-Hop options header. Each option in the header is TLV-encoded with
    a type, length, and value. This IPv6 API defines seven functions
    that the application calls to build and examine a Hop-by_Hop options
    header, and the ability to use sticky options or ancillary data to
    communicate this information between the application and the kernel.
    This uses the IPV6_HOPOPTS for a Hop-by-Hop options header.

    Today several Hop-by-Hop options are defined for IPv6. Two pad
    options, Pad1 and PadN, are for alignment purposes and are
    automatically inserted by the inet6_opt_XXX() routines and ignored by
    the inet6_opt_XXX() routines on the receive side. This section of
    the API is therefore defined for other (and future) Hop-by-Hop
    options that an application may need to specify and receive.

    Four functions build an options header:

        inet6_opt_init()   - initialize buffer data for options header
        inet6_opt_append()   - add one TLV option to the options header
        inet6_opt_finish()   - finish adding TLV options to the options
                                header
        inet6_opt_set_val()   - add one component of the option content to
                                the option

    Three functions deal with a returned options header:

        inet6_opt_next()   - extract the next option from the options
                                header
        inet6_opt_find()   - extract an option of a specified type from
                                the header
        inet6_opt_get_val()   - retrieve one component of the option
                                content

    Individual Hop-by-Hop options (and Destination options, which are
    described in Section 9 and are very similar to the Hop-by-Hop
    options) may have specific alignment requirements. For example, the
    4-byte Jumbo Payload length should appear on a 4-byte boundary, and
    IPv6 addresses are normally aligned on an 8-byte boundary. These
    requirements and the terminology used with these options are
    discussed in Section 4.2 and Appendix B of [RFC-2460]. The alignment
    of first byte of each option is specified by two values, called x and
    y, written as "xn + y". This states that the option must appear at
    an integer multiple of x bytes from the beginning of the options
    header (x can have the values 1, 2, 4, or 8), plus y bytes (y can
    have a value between 0 and 7, inclusive). The Pad1 and PadN options
    are inserted as needed to maintain the required alignment. The

Stevens, et al.   Informational   [Page 37]

functions below need to know the alignment of the end of the option
(which is always in the form "xn," where x can have the values 1, 2,
4, or 8) and the total size of the data portion of the option. These
are passed as the "align" and "len" arguments to inet6_opt_append().

Multiple Hop-by-Hop options must be specified by the application by
placing them in a single extension header.

Finally, we note that use of some Hop-by-Hop options or some
Destination options, might require special privilege. That is,
normal applications (without special privilege) might be forbidden
from setting certain options in outgoing packets, and might never see
certain options in received packets.

8.1. Receiving Hop-by-Hop Options

To receive a Hop-by-Hop options header the application must enable
the IPV6_RECVHOPOPTS socket option:

```
int  on - 1;
setsockopt(fd, IPPROTO_IPV6, IPV6_RECVHOPOPTS, &on, sizeof(on));
```

When using ancillary data a Hop-by-hop options header is passed
between the application and the kernel as follows: The cmsg_level
member will be IPPROTO_IPV6 and the cmsg_type member will be
IPV6_HOPOPTS. These options are then processed by calling the
inet6_opt_next(), inet6_opt_find(), and inet6_opt_get_val()
functions, described in Section 10.

8.2. Sending Hop-by-Hop Options

To send a Hop-by-Hop options header, the application specifies the
header either as ancillary data in a call to sendmsg() or using
setsockopt().

The application can remove any sticky Hop-by-Hop options header by
calling setsockopt() for IPV6_HOPOPTS with a zero option length.

All the Hop-by-Hop options must be specified by a single ancillary
data object. The cmsg_level member is set to IPPROTO_IPV6 and the
cmsg_type member is set to IPV6_HOPOPTS. The option is normally
constructed using the inet6_opt_init(), inet6_opt_append(),
inet6_opt_finish(), and inet6_opt_set_val() functions, described in
Section 10.

Additional errors may be possible from sendmsg() and setsockopt() if
the specified option is in error.

RFC 3542   Advanced Sockets API for IPv6   May 2003

9. Destination Options

    A variable number of Destination options can appear in one or more
    Destination options headers. As defined in [RFC-2460], a Destination
    options header appearing before a Routing header is processed by the
    first destination plus any subsequent destinations specified in the
    Routing header, while a Destination options header that is not
    followed by a Routing header is processed only by the final
    destination. As with the Hop-by-Hop options, each option in a
    Destination options header is TLV-encoded with a type, length, and
    value.

9.1. Receiving Destination Options

    To receive Destination options header the application must enable the
    IPV6_RECVDSTOPTS socket option:

        int on = 1;
        setsockopt(fd, IPPROTO_IPV6, IPV6_RECVDSTOPTS, &on, sizeof(on));

    Each Destination options header is returned as one ancillary data
    object described by a cmsghdr structure with cmsg_level set to
    IPPROTO_IPV6 and cmsg_type set to IPV6_DSTOPTS.

    These options are then processed by calling the inet6_opt_next(),
    inet6_opt_find(), and inet6_opt_get_value() functions.

9.2. Sending Destination Options

    To send a Destination options header, the application specifies it
    either as ancillary data in a call to sendmsg() or using
    setsockopt().

    The application can remove any sticky Destination options header by
    calling setsockopt() for IPV6_RTHDRDSTOPTS/IPV6_DSTOPTS with a zero
    option length.

    This API assumes the ordering about extension headers as described in
    [RFC-2460]. Thus, one set of Destination options can only appear
    before a Routing header, and one set can only appear after a Routing
    header (or in a packet with no Routing header). Each set can consist
    of one or more options but each set is a single extension header.

    Today all destination options that an application may want to specify
    can be put after (or without) a Routing header. Thus, applications
    should usually need IPV6_DSTOPTS only and should avoid using
    IPV6_RTHDRDSTOPTS whenever possible.

When using ancillary data a Destination options header is passed
between the application and the kernel as follows: The set preceding
a Routing header are specified with the cmsg level member set to
IPPROTO_IPV6 and the cmsg_type member set to IPV6_RTHDRDSTOPTS. Any
setsockopt or ancillary data for IPV6_RTHDRDSTOPTS is silently
ignored when sending packets unless a Routing header is also
specified. Note that the "Routing header" here means the one
specified by this API. Even when the kernel inserts a routing header
in its internal routine (e.g., in a mobile IPv6 stack), the
Destination options header specified by IPV6_RTHDRDSTOPTS will still
be ignored unless the application explicitly specifies its own
Routing header.

The set of Destination options after a Routing header, which are also
used when no Routing header is present, are specified with the
cmsg_level member is set to IPPROTO_IPV6 and the cmsg_type member is
set to IPV6_DSTOPTS.

The Destination options are normally constructed using the
inet6_opt_init(), inet6_opt_append(), inet6_opt_finish(), and
inet6_opt_set_val() functions, described in Section 10.

Additional errors may be possible from sendmsg() and setsockopt() if
the specified option is in error.

10. Hop-by-Hop and Destination Options Processing

Building and parsing the Hop-by-Hop and Destination options is
complicated for the reasons given earlier. We therefore define a set
of functions to help the application. These functions assume the
formatting rules specified in Appendix B in [RFC-2460] i.e., that the
largest field is placed last in the option.

The function prototypes for these functions are defined as a result
of including <netinet/in.h>.

The first 3 functions (init, append, and finish) are used both to
calculate the needed buffer size for the options, and to actually
encode the options once the application has allocated a buffer for
the header. In order to only calculate the size the application must
pass a NULL extbuf and a zero extlen to those functions.

RFC 3542   Advanced Sockets API for IPv6   May 2003

10.1. inet6_opt_init

        int inet6_opt_init(void *extbuf, socklen_t extlen);

   This function returns the number of bytes needed for the empty
   extension header i.e., without any options. If extbuf is not NULL it
   also initializes the extension header to have the correct length
   field. In that case if the extlen value is not a positive (i.e.,
   non-zero) multiple of 8 the function fails and returns -1.

   (Note: since the return value on success is based on a "constant"
   parameter, i.e., the empty extension header, an implementation may
   return a constant value. However, this specification does not
   require the value be constant, and leaves it as implementation
   dependent. The application should not assume a particular constant
   value as a successful return value of this function.)

10.2. inet6_opt_append

        int inet6_opt_append(void *extbuf, socklen_t extlen, int offset,
                             uint8_t type, socklen_t len, uint_t align,
                             void **databufp);

   Offset should be the length returned by inet6_opt_init() or a
   previous inet6_opt_append(). This function returns the updated total
   length taking into account adding an option with length 'len' and
   alignment 'align'. If extbuf is not NULL then, in addition to
   returning the length, the function inserts any needed pad option,
   initializes the option (setting the type and length fields) and
   returns a pointer to the location for the option content in databufp.
   If the option does not fit in the extension header buffer the
   function returns -1.

   Type is the 8-bit option type. Len is the length of the option data
   (i.e., excluding the option type and option length fields).

   Once inet6_opt_append() has been called the application can use the
   databuf directly, or use inet6_opt_set_val() to specify the content
   of the option.

   The option type must have a value from 2 to 255, inclusive. (0 and 1
   are reserved for the Pad1 and PadN options, respectively.)

   The option data length must have a value between 0 and 255,
   inclusive, and is the length of the option data that follows.

   The align parameter must have a value of 1, 2, 4, or 8. The align
   value can not exceed the value of len.

10.3. inet6_opt_finish

        int inet6_opt_finish(void *extbuf, socklen_t extlen, int offset);

   Offset should be the length returned by inet6_opt_init() or
   inet6_opt_append(). This function returns the updated total length
   taking into account the final padding of the extension header to make
   it a multiple of 8 bytes. If extbuf is not NULL the function also
   initializes the option by inserting a Pad1 or PadN option of the
   proper length.

   If the necessary pad does not fit in the extension header buffer the
   function returns -1.

10.4. inet6_opt_set_val

        int inet6_opt_set_val(void *databuf, int offset, void *val,
                         socklen_t vallen);

   Databuf should be a pointer returned by inet6_opt_append(). This
   function inserts data items of various sizes in the data portion of
   the option. Val should point to the data to be inserted. Offset
   specifies where in the data portion of the option the value should be
   inserted; the first byte after the option type and length is accessed
   by specifying an offset of zero.

   The caller should ensure that each field is aligned on its natural
   boundaries as described in Appendix B of [RFC-2460], but the function
   must not rely on the caller's behavior. Even when the alignment
   requirement is not satisfied, inet6_opt_set_val should just copy the
   data as required.

   The function returns the offset for the next field (i.e., offset +
   vallen) which can be used when composing option content with multiple
   fields.

10.5. inet6_opt_next

        int inet6_opt_next(void *extbuf, socklen_t extlen, int offset,
                      uint8_t *typep, socklen_t *lenp,
                      void **databufp);

   This function parses received option extension headers returning the
   next option. Extbuf and extlen specifies the extension header.
   Offset should either be zero (for the first option) or the length
   returned by a previous call to inet6_opt_next() or inet6_opt_find().
   It specifies the position where to continue scanning the extension
   buffer. The next option is returned by updating typep, lenp, and

RFC 3542   Advanced Sockets API for IPv6   May 2003

databufp. Typep stores the option type, lenp stores the length of
the option data (i.e., excluding the option type and option length
fields), and databufp points the data field of the option. This
function returns the updated "previous" length computed by advancing
past the option that was returned. This returned "previous" length
can then be passed to subsequent calls to inet6_opt_next(). This
function does not return any PAD1 or PADN options. When there are no
more options or if the option extension header is malformed the
return value is -1.

10.6. inet6_opt_find

       int inet6_opt_find(void *extbuf, socklen_t extlen, int offset,
                          uint8_t type, socklen_t *lenp,
                          void **databufp);

This function is similar to the previously described inet6_opt_next()
function, except this function lets the caller specify the option
type to be searched for, instead of always returning the next option
in the extension header.

If an option of the specified type is located, the function returns
the updated "previous" total length computed by advancing past the
option that was returned and past any options that didn't match the
type. This returned "previous" length can then be passed to
subsequent calls to inet6_opt_find() for finding the next occurrence
of the same option type.

If an option of the specified type is not located, the return value
is -1. If the option extension header is malformed, the return value
is -1.

10.7. inet6_opt_get_val

       int inet6_opt_get_val(void *databuf, int offset, void *val,
                             socklen_t vallen);

Databuf should be a pointer returned by inet6_opt_next() or
inet6_opt_find(). This function extracts data items of various sizes
in the data portion of the option. Val should point to the
destination for the extracted data. Offset specifies from where in
the data portion of the option the value should be extracted; the
first byte after the option type and length is accessed by specifying
an offset of zero.

It is expected that each field is aligned on its natural boundaries
as described in Appendix B of [RFC-2460], but the function must not
rely on the alignment.

The function returns the offset for the next field (i.e., offset + vallen) which can be used when extracting option content with multiple fields.

11. Additional Advanced API Functions

11.1. Sending with the Minimum MTU

Unicast applications should usually let the kernel perform path MTU discovery [RFC-1981], as long as the kernel supports it, and should not care about the path MTU. Some applications, however, might not want to incur the overhead of path MTU discovery, especially if the applications only send a single datagram to a destination. A potential example is a DNS server.

[RFC-1981] describes how path MTU discovery works for multicast destinations. From practice in using IPv4 multicast, however, many careless applications that send large multicast packets on the wire have caused implosion of ICMPv4 error messages. The situation can be worse when there is a filtering node that blocks the ICMPv4 messages. Though the filtering issue applies to unicast as well, the impact is much larger in the multicast cases.

Thus, applications sending multicast traffic should explicitly enable path MTU discovery only when they understand that the benefit of possibly larger MTU usage outweighs the possible impact of MTU discovery for active sources across the delivery tree(s). This default behavior is based on the today's practice with IPv4 multicast and path MTU discovery. The behavior may change in the future once it is found that path MTU discovery effectively works with actual multicast applications and network configurations.

This specification defines a mechanism to avoid path MTU discovery by sending at the minimum IPv6 MTU [RFC-2460]. If the packet is larger than the minimum MTU and this feature has been enabled the IP layer will fragment to the minimum MTU. To control the policy about path MTU discovery, applications can use the IPV6_USE_MIN_MTU socket option.

As described above, the default policy should depend on whether the destination is unicast or multicast. For unicast destinations path MTU discovery should be performed by default. For multicast destinations path MTU discovery should be disabled by default. This option thus takes the following three types of integer arguments:

-1: perform path MTU discovery for unicast destinations but do not perform it for multicast destinations. Packets to multicast destinations are therefore sent with the minimum MTU.

Stevens, et al.   Informational   [Page 44]

RFC 3542   Advanced Sockets API for IPv6   May 2003

   0: always perform path MTU discovery.

   1: always disable path MTU discovery and send packets at the minimum
      MTU.

   The default value of this option is -1. Values other than -1, 0, and
   1 are invalid, and an error EINVAL will be returned for those values.

   As an example, if a unicast application intentionally wants to
   disable path MTU discovery, it will add the following lines:

      int on = 1;
      setsockopt(fd, IPPROTO_IPV6, IPV6_USE_MIN_MTU, &on, sizeof(on));

   Note that this API intentionally excludes the case where the
   application wants to perform path MTU discovery for multicast but to
   disable it for unicast. This is because such usage is not feasible
   considering a scale of performance issues around whether to do path
   MTU discovery or not. When path MTU discovery makes sense to a
   destination but not to a different destination, regardless of whether
   the destination is unicast or multicast, applications either need to
   toggle the option between sending such packets on the same socket, or
   use different sockets for the two classes of destinations.

   This option can also be sent as ancillary data. In the cmsghdr
   structure containing this ancillary data, the cmsg_level member will
   be IPPROTO_IPV6, the cmsg_type member will be IPV6_USE_MIN_MTU, and
   the first byte of cmsg_data[] will be the first byte of the integer.

11.2. Sending without Fragmentation

   In order to provide for easy porting of existing UDP and raw socket
   applications IPv6 implementations will, when originating packets,
   automatically insert a fragment header in the packet if the packet is
   too big for the path MTU.

   Some applications might not want this behavior. An example is
   traceroute which might want to discover the actual path MTU.

   This specification defines a mechanism to turn off the automatic
   inserting of a fragment header for UDP and raw sockets. This can be
   enabled using the IPV6_DONTFRAG socket option.

      int on = 1;
      setsockopt(fd, IPPROTO_IPV6, IPV6_DONTFRAG, &on, sizeof(on));

RFC 3542   Advanced Sockets API for IPv6   May 2003

By default, this socket option is disabled. Setting the value to 0
also disables the option i.e., reverts to the default behavior of
automatic inserting. This option can also be sent as ancillary data.
In the cmsghdr structure containing this ancillary data, the
cmsg_level member will be IPPROTO_IPV6, the cmsg_type member will be
IPV6_DONTFRAG, and the first byte of cmsg_data[] will be the first
byte of the integer. This API only specifies the use of this option
for UDP and raw sockets, and does not define the usage for TCP
sockets.

When the data size is larger than the MTU of the outgoing interface,
the packet will be discarded. Applications can know the result by
enabling the IPV6_RECVPATHMTU option described below and receiving
the corresponding ancillary data items. An additional error EMSGSIZE
may also be returned in some implementations. Note, however, that
some other implementations might not be able to return this
additional error when sending a message.

11.3. Path MTU Discovery and UDP

UDP and raw socket applications need to be able to determine the
"maximum send transport-message size" (Section 5.1 of [RFC-1981]) to
a given destination so that those applications can participate in
path MTU discovery. This lets those applications send smaller
datagrams to the destination, avoiding fragmentation.

This is accomplished using a new ancillary data item (IPV6_PATHMTU)
which is delivered to recvmsg() without any actual data. The
application can enable the receipt of IPV6_PATHMTU ancillary data
items by setting the IPV6_RECVPATHMTU socket option.

    int on = 1;
    setsockopt(fd, IPPROTO_IPV6, IPV6_RECVPATHMTU, &on, sizeof(on));

By default, this socket option is disabled. Setting the value to 0
also disables the option. This API only specifies the use of this
option for UDP and raw sockets, and does not define the usage for TCP
sockets.

When the application is sending packets too big for the path MTU
recvmsg() will return zero (indicating no data) but there will be a
cmsghdr with cmsg_type set to IPV6_PATHMTU, and cmsg_len will
indicate that cmsg_data is sizeof(struct ip6_mtuinfo) bytes long.
This can happen when the sending node receives a corresponding ICMPv6
packet too big error, or when the packet is sent from a socket with
the IPV6_DONTFRAG option being on and the packet size is larger than
the MTU of the outgoing interface. This indication is considered as
an ancillary data item for a separate (empty) message. Thus, when

Stevens, et al.   Informational   [Page 46]

there are buffered messages (i.e., messages that the application has
not received yet) on the socket the application will first receive
the buffered messages and then receive the indication.

The first byte of cmsg_data[] will point to a struct ip6_mtuinfo
carrying the path MTU to use together with the IPv6 destination
address.

```
    struct ip6_mtuinfo {
      struct sockaddr_in6 ip6m_addr; /* dst address including
                                          zone ID */
      uint32_t            ip6m_mtu;  /* path MTU in host byte order */
    };
```

This cmsghdr will be passed to every socket that sets the
IPV6_RECVPATHMTU socket option, even if the socket is non-connected.
Note that this also means an application that sets the option may
receive an IPV6_MTU ancillary data item for each ICMP too big error
the node receives, including such ICMP errors caused by other
applications on the node. Thus, an application that wants to perform
the path MTU discovery by itself needs to keep history of
destinations that it has actually sent to and to compare the address
returned in the ip6_mtuinfo structure to the history. An
implementation may choose not to delivery data to a connected socket
that has a foreign address that is different than the address
specified in the ip6m_addr structure.

When an application sends a packet with a routing header, the final
destination stored in the ip6m_addr member does not necessarily
contain complete information of the entire path.

11.4. Determining the Current Path MTU

Some applications might need to determine the current path MTU e.g.,
applications using IPV6_RECVPATHMTU might want to pick a good
starting value.

This specification defines a get-only socket option to retrieve the
current path MTU value for the destination of a given connected
socket. If the IP layer does not have a cached path MTU value it
will return the interface MTU for the interface that will be used
when sending to the destination address.

This information is retrieved using the IPV6_PATHMTU socket option.
This option takes a pointer to the ip6_mtuinfo structure as the
fourth argument, and the size of the structure should be passed as a
value-result parameter in the fifth argument.

```
    struct ip6_mtuinfo mtuinfo;
    socklen_t infolen = sizeof(mtuinfo);

    getsockopt(fd, IPPROTO_IPV6, IPV6_PATHMTU, &mtuinfo, &infolen);
```

When the call succeeds, the path MTU value is stored in the ip6m_mtu
member of the ip6_mtuinfo structure. Since the socket is connected,
the ip6m_addr member is meaningless and should not be referred to by
the application.

This option can only be used for a connected socket, because a non-
connected socket does not have the information of the destination and
there is no way to pass the destination via getsockopt(). When
getsockopt() for this option is issued on a non-connected socket, the
call will fail. Despite this limitation, this option is still useful
from a practical point of view, because applications that care about
the path MTU tend to send a lot of packets to a single destination
and to connect the socket to the destination for performance reasons.
If the application needs to get the MTU value in a more generic way,
it should use a more generic interface, such as routing sockets
[TCPIPILLUST].

12. Ordering of Ancillary Data and IPv6 Extension Headers

   Three IPv6 extension headers can be specified by the application and
   returned to the application using ancillary data with sendmsg() and
   recvmsg(): the Routing header, Hop-by-Hop options header, and
   Destination options header. When multiple ancillary data objects are
   transferred via recvmsg() and these objects represent any of these
   three extension headers, their placement in the control buffer is
   directly tied to their location in the corresponding IPv6 datagram.
   For example, when the application has enabled the IPV6_RECVRTHDR and
   IPV6_RECVDSTOPTS options and later receives an IPv6 packet with
   extension headers in the following order:

      The IPv6 header
      A Hop-by-Hop options header
      A Destination options header (1)
      A Routing header
      An Authentication header
      A Destination options header (2)
      A UDP header and UDP data

then the application will receive three ancillary data objects in the
following order:

        an object with cmsg_type set to IPV6_DSTOPTS, which represents
        the destination options header (1)
        an object with cmsg_type set to IPV6_RTHDR, which represents the
        Routing header
        an object with cmsg_type set to IPV6_DSTOPTS, which represents the
        destination options header (2)

This example follows the header ordering described in [RFC-2460], but
the receiving side of this specification does not assume the
ordering. Applications may receive any numbers of objects in any
order according to the ordering of the received IPv6 datagram.

For the sending side, however, this API imposes some ordering
constraints according to [RFC-2460]. Applications using this API
cannot make a packet with extension headers that do not follow the
ordering. Note, however, that this does not mean applications must
always follow the restriction. This is just a limitation in this API
in order to give application programmers a guideline to construct
headers in a practical manner. Should an application need to make an
outgoing packet in an arbitrary order about the extension headers,
some other technique, such as the datalink interfaces BPF or DLPI,
must be used.

The followings are more details about the constraints:

-   Each IPV6_xxx ancillary data object for a particular type of
    extension header can be specified at most once in a single control
    buffer.

-   IPV6_xxx ancillary data objects can appear in any order in a
    control buffer, because there is no ambiguity of the ordering.

-   Each set of IPV6_xxx ancillary data objects and sticky options
    will be put in the outgoing packet along with the header ordering
    described in [RFC-2460].

-   An ancillary data object or a sticky option of IPV6_RTHDRDSTOPTS
    will affect the outgoing packet only when a Routing header is
    specified as an ancillary data object or a sticky option.
    Otherwise, the specified value for IPV6_RTHDRDSTOPTS will be
    ignored.

RFC 3542   Advanced Sockets API for IPv6   May 2003

For example, when an application sends a UDP datagram with a control
data buffer containing ancillary data objects in the following order:

    an object with cmsg_type set to IPV6_DSTOPTS
    an object with cmsg_type set to IPV6_RTHDRDSTOPTS
    an object with cmsg_type set to IPV6_HOPOPTS

and the sending socket does not have any sticky options, then the
outgoing packet would be constructed as follows:

    The IPv6 header
    A Hop-by-Hop options header
    A Destination options header
    A UDP header and UDP data

where the destination options header corresponds to the ancillary
data object with the type IPV6_DSTOPTS.

Note that the constraints above do not necessarily mean that the
outgoing packet sent on the wire always follows the header ordering
specified in this API document. The kernel may insert additional
headers that break the ordering as a result. For example, if the
kernel supports Mobile IPv6, an additional destination options header
may be inserted before an authentication header, even without a
routing header.

This API does not provide access to any other extension headers than
the supported three types of headers. In particular, no information
is provided about the IP security headers on an incoming packet, nor
can be specified for an outgoing packet. This API is for
applications that do not care about the existence of IP security
headers.

13.   IPv6-Specific Options with IPv4-Mapped IPv6 Addresses

The various socket options and ancillary data specifications defined
in this document apply only to true IPv6 sockets. It is possible to
create an IPv6 socket that actually sends and receives IPv4 packets,
using IPv4-mapped IPv6 addresses, but the mapping of the options
defined in this document to an IPv4 datagram is beyond the scope of
this document.

In general, attempting to specify an IPv6-only option, such as the
Hop-by-Hop options, Destination options, or Routing header on an IPv6
socket that is using IPv4-mapped IPv6 addresses, will probably result
in an error. Some implementations, however, may provide access to

Stevens, et al.   Informational   [Page 50]

RFC 3542   Advanced Sockets API for IPv6   May 2003

the packet information (source/destination address, send/receive
interface, and hop limit) on an IPv6 socket that is using IPv4-mapped
IPv6 addresses.

14. Extended interfaces for rresvport, rcmd and rexec

Library functions that support the "r" commands hide the creation of
a socket and the name resolution procedure from an application. When
the libraries return an AF_INET6 socket to an application that do not
support the address family, the application may encounter an
unexpected result when, e.g., calling getpeername() for the socket.
In order to support AF_INET6 sockets for the "r" commands while
keeping backward compatibility, this section defines some extensions
to the libraries.

14.1. rresvport_af

The rresvport() function is used by the rcmd() function, and this
function is in turn called by many of the "r" commands such as
rlogin. While new applications are not being written to use the
rcmd() function, legacy applications such as rlogin will continue to
use it and these will be ported to IPv6.

rresvport() creates an IPv4/TCP socket and binds a "reserved port" to
the socket. Instead of defining an IPv6 version of this function we
define a new function that takes an address family as its argument.

    #include <unistd.h>

    int rresvport_af(int *port, int family);

This function behaves the same as the existing rresvport() function,
but instead of creating an AF_INET TCP socket, it can also create an
AF_INET6 TCP socket. The family argument is either AF_INET or
AF_INET6, and a new error return is EAFNOSUPPORT if the address
family is not supported.

(Note: There is little consensus on which header defines the
rresvport() and rcmd() function prototypes. 4.4BSD defines it in
<unistd.h>, others in <netdb.h>, and others don't define the function
prototypes at all.)

14.2. rcmd_af

The existing rcmd() function can not transparently use AF_INET6
sockets since an application would not be prepared to handle AF_INET6
addresses returned by e.g., getpeername() on the file descriptor
created by rcmd(). Thus a new function is needed.

Stevens, et al.   Informational   [Page 51]

```
int rcmd_af(char **ahost, unsigned short rport,
            const char *locuser, const char *remuser,
            const char *cmd, int *fd2p, int af)
```

This function behaves the same as the existing rcmd() function, but
instead of creating an AF_INET TCP socket, it can also create an
AF_INET6 TCP socket. The family argument is AF_INET, AF_INET6, or
AF_UNSPEC. When either AF_INET or AF_INET6 is specified, this
function will create a socket of the specified address family. When
AF_UNSPEC is specified, it will try all possible address families
until a connection can be established, and will return the associated
socket of the connection. A new error EAFNOSUPPORT will be returned
if the address family is not supported.

14.3. rexec_af

The existing rexec() function can not transparently use AF_INET6
sockets since an application would not be prepared to handle AF_INET6
addresses returned by e.g., getpeername() on the file descriptor
created by rexec(). Thus a new function is needed.

```
int rexec_af(char **ahost, unsigned short rport, const char *name,
             const char *pass, const char *cmd, int *fd2p, int af)
```

This function behaves the same as the existing rexec() function, but
instead of creating an AF_INET TCP socket, it can also create an
AF_INET6 TCP socket. The family argument is AF_INET, AF_INET6, or
AF_UNSPEC. When either AF_INET or AF_INET6 is specified, this
function will create a socket of the specified address family. When
AF_UNSPEC is specified, it will try all possible address families
until a connection can be established, and will return the associated
socket of the connection. A new error EAFNOSUPPORT will be returned
if the address family is not supported.

15. Summary of New Definitions

The following list summarizes the constants and structure,
definitions discussed in this memo, sorted by header.

```
<netinet/icmp6.h> ICMP6_DST_UNREACH
<netinet/icmp6.h> ICMP6_DST_UNREACH_ADDR
<netinet/icmp6.h> ICMP6_DST_UNREACH_ADMIN
<netinet/icmp6.h> ICMP6_DST_UNREACH_BEYONDSCOPE
<netinet/icmp6.h> ICMP6_DST_UNREACH_NOPORT
<netinet/icmp6.h> ICMP6_DST_UNREACH_NOROUTE
<netinet/icmp6.h> ICMP6_ECHO_REPLY
<netinet/icmp6.h> ICMP6_ECHO_REQUEST
<netinet/icmp6.h> ICMP6_INFOMSG_MASK
```

```
<netinet/icmp6.h> ICMP6_PACKET_TOO_BIG
<netinet/icmp6.h> ICMP6_PARAMPROB_HEADER
<netinet/icmp6.h> ICMP6_PARAMPROB_NEXTHEADER
<netinet/icmp6.h> ICMP6_PARAMPROB_OPTION
<netinet/icmp6.h> ICMP6_PARAM_PROB
<netinet/icmp6.h> ICMP6_ROUTER_RENUMBERING
<netinet/icmp6.h> ICMP6_RR_FLAGS_FORCEAPPLY
<netinet/icmp6.h> ICMP6_RR_FLAGS_PREVDONE
<netinet/icmp6.h> ICMP6_RR_FLAGS_REQRESULT
<netinet/icmp6.h> ICMP6_RR_FLAGS_SPECSITE
<netinet/icmp6.h> ICMP6_RR_FLAGS_TEST
<netinet/icmp6.h> ICMP6_RR_PCOUSE_FLAGS_DECRPLTIME
<netinet/icmp6.h> ICMP6_RR_PCOUSE_FLAGS_DECRVLTIME
<netinet/icmp6.h> ICMP6_RR_PCOUSE_RAFLAGS_AUTO
<netinet/icmp6.h> ICMP6_RR_PCOUSE_RAFLAGS_ONLINK
<netinet/icmp6.h> ICMP6_RR_RESULT_FLAGS_FORBIDDEN
<netinet/icmp6.h> ICMP6_RR_RESULT_FLAGS_OOB
<netinet/icmp6.h> ICMP6_TIME_EXCEEDED
<netinet/icmp6.h> ICMP6_TIME_EXCEED_REASSEMBLY
<netinet/icmp6.h> ICMP6_TIME_EXCEED_TRANSIT
<netinet/icmp6.h> MLD_LISTENER_QUERY
<netinet/icmp6.h> MLD_LISTENER_REDUCTION
<netinet/icmp6.h> MLD_LISTENER_REPORT
<netinet/icmp6.h> ND_NA_FLAG_OVERRIDE
<netinet/icmp6.h> ND_NA_FLAG_ROUTER
<netinet/icmp6.h> ND_NA_FLAG_SOLICITED
<netinet/icmp6.h> ND_NEIGHBOR_ADVERT
<netinet/icmp6.h> ND_NEIGHBOR_SOLICIT
<netinet/icmp6.h> ND_OPT_MTU
<netinet/icmp6.h> ND_OPT_PI_FLAG_AUTO
<netinet/icmp6.h> ND_OPT_PI_FLAG_ONLINK
<netinet/icmp6.h> ND_OPT_PREFIX_INFORMATION
<netinet/icmp6.h> ND_OPT_REDIRECTED_HEADER
<netinet/icmp6.h> ND_OPT_SOURCE_LINKADDR
<netinet/icmp6.h> ND_OPT_TARGET_LINKADDR
<netinet/icmp6.h> ND_RA_FLAG_MANAGED
<netinet/icmp6.h> ND_RA_FLAG_OTHER
<netinet/icmp6.h> ND_REDIRECT
<netinet/icmp6.h> ND_ROUTER_ADVERT
<netinet/icmp6.h> ND_ROUTER_SOLICIT

<netinet/icmp6.h> struct icmp6_filter{};
<netinet/icmp6.h> struct icmp6_hdr{};
<netinet/icmp6.h> struct icmp6_router_renum{};
<netinet/icmp6.h> struct mld_hdr{};
<netinet/icmp6.h> struct nd_neighbor_advert{};
<netinet/icmp6.h> struct nd_neighbor_solicit{};
<netinet/icmp6.h> struct nd_opt_hdr{};
```

```
<netinet/icmp6.h> struct nd_opt_mtu{};
<netinet/icmp6.h> struct nd_opt_prefix_info{};
<netinet/icmp6.h> struct nd_opt_rd_hdr{};
<netinet/icmp6.h> struct nd_redirect{};
<netinet/icmp6.h> struct nd_router_advert{};
<netinet/icmp6.h> struct nd_router_solicit{};
<netinet/icmp6.h> struct rr_pco_match{};
<netinet/icmp6.h> struct rr_pco_use{};
<netinet/icmp6.h> struct rr_result{};

<netinet/in.h>    IPPROTO_AH
<netinet/in.h>    IPPROTO_DSTOPTS
<netinet/in.h>    IPPROTO_ESP
<netinet/in.h>    IPPROTO_FRAGMENT
<netinet/in.h>    IPPROTO_HOPOPTS
<netinet/in.h>    IPPROTO_ICMPV6
<netinet/in.h>    IPPROTO_IPV6
<netinet/in.h>    IPPROTO_NONE
<netinet/in.h>    IPPROTO_ROUTING
<netinet/in.h>    IPV6_CHECKSUM
<netinet/in.h>    IPV6_DONTFRAG
<netinet/in.h>    IPV6_DSTOPTS
<netinet/in.h>    IPV6_HOPLIMIT
<netinet/in.h>    IPV6_HOPOPTS

<netinet/in.h>    IPV6_NEXTHOP
<netinet/in.h>    IPV6_PATHMTU
<netinet/in.h>    IPV6_PKTINFO
<netinet/in.h>    IPV6_RECVDSTOPTS
<netinet/in.h>    IPV6_RECVHOPLIMIT
<netinet/in.h>    IPV6_RECVHOPOPTS
<netinet/in.h>    IPV6_RECVPKTINFO
<netinet/in.h>    IPV6_RECVRTHDR
<netinet/in.h>    IPV6_RECVTCLASS
<netinet/in.h>    IPV6_RTHDR
<netinet/in.h>    IPV6_RTHDRDSTOPTS
<netinet/in.h>    IPV6_RTHDR_TYPE_0
<netinet/in.h>    IPV6_RECVPATHMTU
<netinet/in.h>    IPV6_TCLASS
<netinet/in.h>    IPV6_USE_MIN_MTU
<netinet/in.h>    struct in6_pktinfo{};
<netinet/in.h>    struct ip6_mtuinfo{};

<netinet/ip6.h>   IP6F_MORE_FRAG
<netinet/ip6.h>   IP6F_OFF_MASK
<netinet/ip6.h>   IP6F_RESERVED_MASK
<netinet/ip6.h>   IP6OPT_JUMBO
<netinet/ip6.h>   IP6OPT_JUMBO_LEN
```

Stevens, et al.   Informational   [Page 54]

```
<netinet/ip6.h>    IP6OPT_MUTABLE
<netinet/ip6.h>    IP6OPT_NSAP_ADDR
<netinet/ip6.h>    IP6OPT_PAD1
<netinet/ip6.h>    IP6OPT_PADN
<netinet/ip6.h>    IP6OPT_ROUTER_ALERT
<netinet/ip6.h>    IP6OPT_TUNNEL_LIMIT
<netinet/ip6.h>    IP6OPT_TYPE_DISCARD
<netinet/ip6.h>    IP6OPT_TYPE_FORCEICMP
<netinet/ip6.h>    IP6OPT_TYPE_ICMP
<netinet/ip6.h>    IP6OPT_TYPE_SKIP
<netinet/ip6.h>    IP6_ALERT_AN
<netinet/ip6.h>    IP6_ALERT_MLD
<netinet/ip6.h>    IP6_ALERT_RSVP
<netinet/ip6.h>    struct ip6_dest{};
<netinet/ip6.h>    struct ip6_frag{};
<netinet/ip6.h>    struct ip6_hbh{};
<netinet/ip6.h>    struct ip6_hdr{};
<netinet/ip6.h>    struct ip6_opt{};
<netinet/ip6.h>    struct ip6_opt_jumbo{};
<netinet/ip6.h>    struct ip6_opt_nsap{};
<netinet/ip6.h>    struct ip6_opt_router{};
<netinet/ip6.h>    struct ip6_opt_tunnel{};
<netinet/ip6.h>    struct ip6_rthdr{};
<netinet/ip6.h>    struct ip6_rthdr0{};
```

The following list summarizes the function and macro prototypes
discussed in this memo, sorted by header.

```
<netinet/icmp6.h> void ICMP6_FILTER_SETBLOCK(int, struct
                                        icmp6_filter *);
<netinet/icmp6.h> void
                  ICMP6_FILTER_SETBLOCKALL(struct icmp6_filter *);
<netinet/icmp6.h> void
                  ICMP6_FILTER_SETPASS(int,
                                        struct icmp6_filter *);
<netinet/icmp6.h> void
                  ICMP6_FILTER_SETPASSALL(struct icmp6_filter *);
<netinet/icmp6.h> int   ICMP6_FILTER_WILLBLOCK(int,
                                        const struct icmp6_filter *);
<netinet/icmp6.h> int   ICMP6_FILTER_WILLPASS(int,
                                        const struct icmp6_filter *);

<netinet/in.h>      int IN6_ARE_ADDR_EQUAL(const struct in6_addr *,
                                        const struct in6_addr *);

<netinet/in.h>      int inet6_opt_append(void *, socklen_t, int,
                                        uint8_t, socklen_t, uint_t,
                                        void **);
```

```
    <netinet/in.h>      int inet6_opt_get_val(void *, int, void *,
                                        socklen_t);
    <netinet/in.h>      int inet6_opt_find(void *, socklen_t,
                                        int, uint8_t ,
                                        socklen_t *, void **);
    <netinet/in.h>      int inet6_opt_finish(void *, socklen_t, int);
    <netinet/in.h>      int inet6_opt_init(void *, socklen_t);
    <netinet/in.h>      int inet6_opt_next(void *, socklen_t,
                                        int, uint8_t *,
                                        socklen_t *, void **);
    <netinet/in.h>      int inet6_opt_set_val(void *, int,
                                        void *, socklen_t);

    <netinet/in.h>      int inet6_rth_add(void *,
                                        const struct in6_addr *);
    <netinet/in.h>      struct in6_addr inet6_rth_getaddr(const void *,
                                                        int);
    <netinet/in.h>      void *inet6_rth_init(void *, socklen_t,
                                        int, int);
    <netinet/in.h>      int inet6_rth_reverse(const void *, void *);
    <netinet/in.h>      int inet6_rth_segments(const void *);
    <netinet/in.h>      soccklen_t inet6_rth_space(int, int);

    <netinet/ip6.h>     int  IP6OPT_TYPE(uint8_t);

    <sys/socket.h>      socklen_t CMSG_LEN(socklen_t);
    <sys/socket.h>      socklen_t CMSG_SPACE(socklen_t);

    <unistd.h>          int rresvport_af(int *, int);
    <unistd.h>          int rcmd_af(char **, unsigned short,
                                const char *, const char *,
                                const char *, int *, int);
    <unistd.h>          int rexec_af(char **, unsigned short,
                                    const char *, const char *,
                                    const char *, int *, int);
```

16. Security Considerations

   The setting of certain Hop-by-Hop options and Destination options may
   be restricted to privileged processes. Similarly some Hop-by-Hop
   options and Destination options may not be returned to non-privileged
   applications.

   The ability to specify an arbitrary source address using IPV6_PKTINFO
   must be prevented; at least for non-privileged processes.

RFC 3542   Advanced Sockets API for IPv6   May 2003

17. Changes from RFC 2292

    Significant changes that affect the compatibility to RFC 2292:

    - Removed the IPV6_PKTOPTIONS socket option by allowing sticky
       options to be set with individual setsockopt() calls.

    - Removed the ability to be able to specify Hop-by-Hop and
       Destination options using multiple ancillary data items. The
       application, using the inet6_opt_xxx() routines (see below), is
       responsible for formatting the whole extension header.

    - Removed the support for the loose/strict Routing header since that
       has been removed from the IPv6 specification.

    - Loosened the constraints for jumbo payload option that this option
       was always hidden from applications.

    - Disabled the use of the IPV6_HOPLIMIT sticky option.

    - Removed ip6r0_addr field from the ip6_rthdr structure.

    - Intentionally unspecified how to get received packet's information
       on TCP sockets.

    New features:

    - Added IPV6_RTHDRDSTOPTS to specify a Destination Options header
       before the Routing header.

    - Added separate IPV6_RECVxxx options to enable the receipt of the
       corresponding ancillary data items.

    - Added inet6_rth_xxx() and inet6_opt_xxx() functions to deal with
       routing or IPv6 options headers.

    - Added extensions of libraries for the "r" commands.

    - Introduced additional IPv6 option definitions such as IP6OPT_PAD1.

    - Added MLD and router renumbering definitions.

    - Added MTU-related socket options and ancillary data items.

    - Added options and ancillary data items to manipulate the traffic
       class field.

- Changed the name of ICMPv6 unreachable code 2 to be "beyond scope of source address." ICMP6_DST_UNREACH_NOTNEIGHBOR was removed with this change.

Clarifications:

- Added clarifications on extension headers ordering; for the sending side, assume the recommended ordering described in RFC 2460. For the receiving side, do not assume any ordering and pass all headers to the application in the received order.

- Added a summary about the interface selection rule.

- Clarified the ordering between IPV6_MULTICAST_IF and the IPV6_PKTINFO sticky option for multicast packets.

- Clarified how sticky options and the ICMPv6 filter are turned off and that getsockopt() of a sticky option returns what was set with setsockopt().

- Clarified that IPV6_NEXTHOP should be ignored for a multicast destination, that it should not contradict with the specified outgoing interface, and that the next hop should be a sockaddr_in6 structure.

- Clarified corner cases of IPV6_CHECKSUM.

- Aligned with the POSIX standard.

Editorial changes:

- Replaced MUST with must (since this is an informational document).

- Revised abstract to be more clear and concise, particularly concentrating on differences from RFC 2292.

- Made the URL of assigned numbers less specific so that it would be more robust for future changes.

- Updated the reference to the basic API.

- Added a reference to the latest POSIX standard.

- Moved general specifications of ancillary data and CMSG macros to the appendix.

RFC 3542   Advanced Sockets API for IPv6   May 2003

18. References

   [RFC-1981]   McCann, J., Deering, S. and J. Mogul, "Path MTU
                 Discovery for IP version 6", RFC 1981, August 1996.

   [RFC-2460]   Deering, S. and R. Hinden, "Internet Protocol, Version
                 6 (IPv6) Specification", RFC 2460, December 1998.

   [RFC-3493]   Gilligan, R., Thomson, S., Bound, J., McCann, J. and
                 W. Stevens, "Basic Socket Interface Extensions for
                 IPv6", RFC 3493, March 2003.

   [POSIX]   IEEE Std. 1003.1-2001 Standard for Information
                 Technology — Portable Operating System Interface
                 (POSIX). Open group Technical Standard: Base
                 Specifications, Issue 6, December 2001. ISO/IEC
                 9945:2002. http://www.opengroup.org/austin

   [TCPIPILLUST] Wright, G., Stevens, W., "TCP/IP Illustrated, Volume 2:
                 The Implementation", Addison Wesley, 1994.

19. Acknowledgments

   Matt Thomas and Jim Bound have been working on the technical details
   in this document for over a year. Keith Sklower is the original
   implementor of ancillary data in the BSD networking code. Craig Metz
   provided lots of feedback, suggestions, and comments based on his
   implementing many of these features as the document was being
   written. Mark Andrews first proposed the idea of the
   IPV6_USE_MIN_MTU option. Jun-ichiro Hagino contributed text for the
   traffic class API from a document of his own.

   The following provided comments on earlier drafts: Pascal Anelli,
   Hamid Asayesh, Ran Atkinson, Karl Auerbach, Hamid Asayesh, Don
   Coolidge, Matt Crawford, Sam T. Denton, Richard Draves, Francis
   Dupont, Toerless Eckert, Lilian Fernandes, Bob Gilligan, Gerri
   Harter, Tim Hartrick, Bob Halley, Masaki Hirabaru, Michael Hunter,
   Yoshinobu Inoue, Mukesh Kacker, A. N. Kuznetsov, Sam Manthorpe, Pedro
   Marques, Jack McCann, der Mouse, John Moy, Lori Napoli, Thomas
   Narten, Atsushi Onoe, Steve Parker, Charles Perkins, Ken Powell, Tom
   Pusateri, Pedro Roque, Sameer Shah, Peter Sjodin, Stephen P.
   Spackman, Jinmei Tatuya, Karen Tracey, Sowmini Varadhan, Quaizar
   Vohra, Carl Williams, Steve Wise, Eric Wong, Farrell Woods, Kazu
   Yamamoto, Vladislav Yasevich, and Yoshifuji Hideaki.

RFC 3542   Advanced Sockets API for IPv6   May 2003

20.   Appendix A: Ancillary Data Overview

4.2BSD allowed file descriptors to be transferred between separate
processes across a UNIX domain socket using the sendmsg() and
recvmsg() functions. Two members of the msghdr structure,
msg_accrights and msg_accrightslen, were used to send and receive the
descriptors. When the OSI protocols were added to 4.3BSD Reno in
1990 the names of these two fields in the msghdr structure were
changed to msg_control and msg_controllen, because they were used by
the OSI protocols for "control information", although the comments in
the source code call this "ancillary data".

Other than the OSI protocols, the use of ancillary data has been
rare. In 4.4BSD, for example, the only use of ancillary data with
IPv4 is to return the destination address of a received UDP datagram
if the IP_RECVDSTADDR socket option is set. With Unix domain sockets
ancillary data is still used to send and receive descriptors.

Nevertheless the ancillary data fields of the msghdr structure
provide a clean way to pass information in addition to the data that
is being read or written. The inclusion of the msg_control and
msg_controllen members of the msghdr structure along with the cmsghdr
structure that is pointed to by the msg_control member is required by
the Posix sockets API standard.

20.1.   The msghdr Structure

The msghdr structure is used by the recvmsg() and sendmsg()
functions. Its Posix definition is:

```
    struct msghdr {
      void        *msg_name;        /* ptr to socket address
                                       structure */
      socklen_t   msg_namelen;      /* size of socket address
                                       structure */
      struct iovec  *msg_iov;       /* scatter/gather array */
      int         msg_iovlen;       /* # elements in msg_iov */
      void        *msg_control;     /* ancillary data */
      socklen_t   msg_controllen;   /* ancillary data buffer length */
      int         msg_flags;        /* flags on received message */
    };
```

The structure is declared as a result of including <sys/socket.h>.

(Note: Before Posix the two "void *" pointers were typically "char
*", and the two socklen_t members were typically integers. Earlier
drafts of Posix had the two socklen_t members as size_t, but it then
changed these to socklen_t to simplify binary portability for 64-bit

implementations and to align Posix with X/Open's Networking Services,
Issue 5. The change in msg_control to a "void *" pointer affects any
code that increments this pointer.)

Most Berkeley-derived implementations limit the amount of ancillary
data in a call to sendmsg() to no more than 108 bytes (an mbuf).
This API requires a minimum of 10240 bytes of ancillary data, but it
is recommended that the amount be limited only by the buffer space
reserved by the socket (which can be modified by the SO_SNDBUF socket
option). (Note: This magic number 10240 was picked as a value that
should always be large enough. 108 bytes is clearly too small as the
maximum size of a Routing header is 2048 bytes.)

20.2. The cmsghdr Structure

The cmsghdr structure describes ancillary data objects transferred by
recvmsg() and sendmsg(). Its Posix definition is:

```
struct cmsghdr {
  socklen_t  cmsg_len;   /* #bytes, including this header */
  int        cmsg_level; /* originating protocol */
  int        cmsg_type;  /* protocol-specific type */
             /* followed by unsigned char cmsg_data[]; */
};
```

This structure is declared as a result of including <sys/socket.h>.

(Note: Before Posix the cmsg_len member was an integer, and not a
socklen_t. See the Note in the previous section for why socklen_t is
used here.)

As shown in this definition, normally there is no member with the
name cmsg_data[]. Instead, the data portion is accessed using the
CMSG_xxx() macros, as described in Section 20.3. Nevertheless, it is
common to refer to the cmsg_data[] member.

When ancillary data is sent or received, any number of ancillary data
objects can be specified by the msg_control and msg_controllen
members of the msghdr structure, because each object is preceded by a
cmsghdr structure defining the object's length (the cmsg_len member).
Historically Berkeley-derived implementations have passed only one
object at a time, but this API allows multiple objects to be passed
in a single call to sendmsg() or recvmsg(). The following example
shows two ancillary data objects in a control buffer.

RFC 3542   Advanced Sockets API for IPv6   May 2003

```
|<------------------------- msg_controllen ------------------------>|
|                                   OR                              |
|<------------------------- msg_controllen ------------------------>|
|                                                                   |
|<----- ancillary data object ----->|<---- ancillary data object ----->|
|<------ min CMSG_SPACE() --------->|<----- min CMSG_SPACE() --------->|
|                                   |                               |
|<--------- cmsg_len ---------->|   |<-------- cmsg_len ---------->|   |
|<--------- CMSG_LEN() -------->|   |<------- CMSG_LEN() --------->|   |
|                               |   |                             |   |
+-----+-----+-----+--+----------+--+-----+-----+-----+--+----------+--+
|cmsg_|cmsg_|cmsg_|XX|   cmsg_   |XX|cmsg_|cmsg_|cmsg_|XX|   cmsg_   |XX|
|len  |level|type |XX|   data[]  |XX|len  |level|type |XX|   data[]  |XX|
+-----+-----+-----+--+----------+--+-----+-----+-----+--+----------+--+
^
|
msg_control
points here
```

The fields shown as "XX" are possible padding, between the cmsghdr
structure and the data, and between the data and the next cmsghdr
structure, if required by the implementation. While sending an
application may or may not include padding at the end of last
ancillary data in msg_controllen and implementations must accept both
as valid. On receiving a portable application must provide space for
padding at the end of the last ancillary data as implementations may
copy out the padding at the end of the control message buffer and
include it in the received msg_controllen. When recvmsg() is called
if msg_controllen is too small for all the ancillary data items
including any trailing padding after the last item an implementation
may set MSG_CTRUNC.

20.3. Ancillary Data Object Macros

To aid in the manipulation of ancillary data objects, three macros
from 4.4BSD are defined by Posix: CMSG_DATA(), CMSG_NXTHDR(), and
CMSG_FIRSTHDR(). Before describing these macros, we show the
following example of how they might be used with a call to recvmsg().

```
struct msghdr    msg;
struct cmsghdr   *cmsgptr;

/* fill in msg */

/* call recvmsg() */
```

```
    for (cmsgptr = CMSG_FIRSTHDR(&msg); cmsgptr != NULL;
         cmsgptr = CMSG_NXTHDR(&msg, cmsgptr)) {
        if (cmsgptr->cmsg_len == 0) {
            /* Error handling */
          break;
        }
        if (cmsgptr->cmsg_level == ... &&
            cmsgptr->cmsg_type == ... ) {
            u_char  *ptr;

            ptr = CMSG_DATA(cmsgptr);
            /* process data pointed to by ptr */
        }
    }
```

We now describe the three Posix macros, followed by two more that are
new with this API: CMSG_SPACE() and CMSG_LEN(). All these macros are
defined as a result of including <sys/socket.h>.

20.3.1. CMSG_FIRSTHDR

    struct cmsghdr *CMSG_FIRSTHDR(const struct msghdr *mhdr);

CMSG_FIRSTHDR() returns a pointer to the first cmsghdr structure in
the msghdr structure pointed to by mhdr. The macro returns NULL if
there is no ancillary data pointed to by the msghdr structure (that
is, if either msg_control is NULL or if msg_controllen is less than
the size of a cmsghdr structure).

One possible implementation could be

```
    #define CMSG_FIRSTHDR(mhdr) \
        ( (mhdr)->msg_controllen >= sizeof(struct cmsghdr) ? \
          (struct cmsghdr *)(mhdr)->msg_control : \
          (struct cmsghdr *)NULL )
```

(Note: Most existing implementations do not test the value of
msg_controllen, and just return the value of msg_control. The value
of msg_controllen must be tested, because if the application asks
recvmsg() to return ancillary data, by setting msg_control to point
to the application's buffer and setting msg_controllen to the length
of this buffer, the kernel indicates that no ancillary data is
available by setting msg_controllen to 0 on return. It is also
easier to put this test into this macro, than making the application
perform the test.)

20.3.2. CMSG_NXTHDR

As described in Section 5.1, CMSG_NXTHDR has been extended to handle
a NULL 2nd argument to mean "get the first header". This provides an
alternative way of coding the processing loop shown earlier:

```
struct msghdr   msg;
struct cmsghdr  *cmsgptr = NULL;

/* fill in msg */

/* call recvmsg() */

while ((cmsgptr = CMSG_NXTHDR(&msg, cmsgptr)) != NULL) {
    if (cmsgptr->cmsg_len == 0) {
        /* Error handling */
     break;
    }
    if (cmsgptr->cmsg_level == ... &&
        cmsgptr->cmsg_type -- ... ) {
        u_char  *ptr;

        ptr = CMSG_DATA(cmsgptr);
        /* process data pointed to by ptr */
    }
}
```

One possible implementation could be:

```
#define CMSG_NXTHDR(mhdr, cmsg) \
  (((cmsg) == NULL) ? CMSG_FIRSTHDR(mhdr) : \
   (((u_char *)(cmsg) + ALIGN_H((cmsg)->cmsg_len) \
                  + ALIGN_D(sizeof(struct cmsghdr)) > \
    (u_char *)((mhdr)->msg_control) + (mhdr)->msg_controllen) ? \
    (struct cmsghdr *)NULL : \
    (struct cmsghdr *)((u_char *)(cmsg) + \
                              ALIGN_H((cmsg)->cmsg_len))))
```

The macros ALIGN_H() and ALIGN_D(), which are implementation
dependent, round their arguments up to the next even multiple of
whatever alignment is required for the start of the cmsghdr structure
and the data, respectively. (This is probably a multiple of 4 or 8
bytes.) They are often the same macro in implementations platforms
where alignment requirement for header and data is chosen to be
identical.

RFC 3542   Advanced Sockets API for IPv6   May 2003

20.3.3. CMSG_DATA

    unsigned char *CMSG_DATA(const struct cmsghdr *cmsg);

CMSG_DATA() returns a pointer to the data (what is called the
cmsg_data[] member, even though such a member is not defined in the
structure) following a cmsghdr structure.

One possible implementation could be:

    #define CMSG_DATA(cmsg) ((u_char *)(cmsg) + \
                        ALIGN_D(sizeof(struct cmsghdr)))

20.3.4. CMSG_SPACE

CMSG_SPACE is new with this API (see Section 5.2). It is used to
determine how much space needs to be allocated for an ancillary data
item.

One possible implementation could be:

    #define CMSG_SPACE(length) (ALIGN_D(sizeof(struct cmsghdr)) + \
                        ALIGN_H(length))

20.3.5. CMSG_LEN

CMSG_LEN is new with this API (see Section 5.3). It returns the
value to store in the cmsg_len member of the cmsghdr structure,
taking into account any padding needed to satisfy alignment
requirements.

One possible implementation could be:

    #define CMSG_LEN(length) (ALIGN_D(sizeof(struct cmsghdr)) + \
                        length)

21. Appendix B: Examples Using the inet6_rth_XXX() Functions

Here we show an example for both sending Routing headers and
processing and reversing a received Routing header.

21.1. Sending a Routing Header

As an example of these Routing header functions defined in this
document, we go through the function calls for the example on p. 17
of [RFC-2460]. The source is S, the destination is D, and the three
intermediate nodes are I1, I2, and I3.

```
          S -----> I1 -----> I2 -----> I3 -----> D

   src:    *    S         S         S         S   S
   dst:    D    I1        I2        I3        D   D
   A[1]:   I1   I2        I1        I1        I1  I1
   A[2]:   I2   I3        I3        I2        I2  I2
   A[3]:   I3   D         D         D         I3  I3
   #seg:   3    3         2         1         0   3
```

src and dst are the source and destination IPv6 addresses in the IPv6
header. A[1], A[2], and A[3] are the three addresses in the Routing
header. #seg is the Segments Left field in the Routing header.

The six values in the column beneath node S are the values in the
Routing header specified by the sending application using sendmsg()
of setsockopt(). The function calls by the sender would look like:

```
    void  *extptr;
    socklen_t   extlen;
    struct msghdr  msg;
    struct cmsghdr  *cmsgptr;
    int   cmsglen;
    struct sockaddr_in6   I1, I2, I3, D;

    extlen = inet6_rth_space(IPV6_RTHDR_TYPE_0, 3);
    cmsglen = CMSG_SPACE(extlen);
    cmsgptr = malloc(cmsglen);
    cmsgptr->cmsg_len = CMSG_LEN(extlen);
    cmsgptr->cmsg_level = IPPROTO_IPV6;
    cmsgptr->cmsg_type = IPV6_RTHDR;

    extptr = CMSG_DATA(cmsgptr);
    extptr = inet6_rth_init(extptr, extlen, IPV6_RTHDR_TYPE_0, 3);

    inet6_rth_add(extptr, &I1.sin6_addr);
    inet6_rth_add(extptr, &I2.sin6_addr);
    inet6_rth_add(extptr, &I3.sin6_addr);

    msg.msg_control = cmsgptr;
    msg.msg_controllen = cmsglen;

    /* finish filling in msg{}, msg_name = D */
    /* call sendmsg() */
```

We also assume that the source address for the socket is not
specified (i.e., the asterisk in the figure).

The four columns of six values that are then shown between the five
nodes are the values of the fields in the packet while the packet is
in transit between the two nodes. Notice that before the packet is
sent by the source node S, the source address is chosen (replacing
the asterisk), I1 becomes the destination address of the datagram,
the two addresses A[2] and A[3] are "shifted up", and D is moved to
A[3].

The columns of values that are shown beneath the destination node are
the values returned by recvmsg(), assuming the application has
enabled both the IPV6_RECVPKTINFO and IPV6_RECVRTHDR socket options.
The source address is S (contained in the sockaddr_in6 structure
pointed to by the msg_name member), the destination address is D
(returned as an ancillary data object in an in6_pktinfo structure),
and the ancillary data object specifying the Routing header will
contain three addresses (I1, I2, and I3). The number of segments in
the Routing header is known from the Hdr Ext Len field in the Routing
header (a value of 6, indicating 3 addresses).

The return value from inet6_rth_segments() will be 3 and
inet6_rth_getaddr(0) will return I1, inet6_rth_getaddr(1) will return
I2, and inet6_rth_getaddr(2) will return I3,

If the receiving application then calls inet6_rth_reverse(), the
order of the three addresses will become I3, I2, and I1.

We can also show what an implementation might store in the ancillary
data object as the Routing header is being built by the sending
process. If we assume a 32-bit architecture where sizeof(struct
cmsghdr) equals 12, with a desired alignment of 4-byte boundaries,
then the call to inet6_rth_space(3) returns 68: 12 bytes for the
cmsghdr structure and 56 bytes for the Routing header (8 + 3*16).

The call to inet6_rth_init() initializes the ancillary data object to
contain a Type 0 Routing header:

```
+-+-+-+-+-+-+-+-+-+-+-+-+-+-+-+-+-+-+-+-+-+-+-+-+-+-+-+-+-+-+-+-+
|          cmsg_len = 20                                        |
+-+-+-+-+-+-+-+-+-+-+-+-+-+-+-+-+-+-+-+-+-+-+-+-+-+-+-+-+-+-+-+-+
|       cmsg_level = IPPROTO_IPV6                               |
+-+-+-+-+-+-+-+-+-+-+-+-+-+-+-+-+-+-+-+-+-+-+-+-+-+-+-+-+-+-+-+-+
|       cmsg_type = IPV6_RTHDR                                  |
+-+-+-+-+-+-+-+-+-+-+-+-+-+-+-+-+-+-+-+-+-+-+-+-+-+-+-+-+-+-+-+-+
|  Next Header  | Hdr Ext Len=6 | Routing Type=0| Seg Left=0    |
+-+-+-+-+-+-+-+-+-+-+-+-+-+-+-+-+-+-+-+-+-+-+-+-+-+-+-+-+-+-+-+-+
|                          Reserved                             |
+-+-+-+-+-+-+-+-+-+-+-+-+-+-+-+-+-+-+-+-+-+-+-+-+-+-+-+-+-+-+-+-+
```

RFC 3542   Advanced Sockets API for IPv6   May 2003

    The first call to inet6_rth_add() adds I1 to the list.

```
     +-+-+-+-+-+-+-+-+-+-+-+-+-+-+-+-+-+-+-+-+-+-+-+-+-+-+-+-+-+-+-+-+
     |          cmsg_len = 36                                        |
     +-+-+-+-+-+-+-+-+-+-+-+-+-+-+-+-+-+-+-+-+-+-+-+-+-+-+-+-+-+-+-+-+
     |        cmsg_level = IPPROTO_IPV6                              |
     +-+-+-+-+-+-+-+-+-+-+-+-+-+-+-+-+-+-+-+-+-+-+-+-+-+-+-+-+-+-+-+-+
     |        cmsg_type = IPV6_RTHDR                                 |
     +-+-+-+-+-+-+-+-+-+-+-+-+-+-+-+-+-+-+-+-+-+-+-+-+-+-+-+-+-+-+-+-+
     |  Next Header  | Hdr Ext Len=6 | Routing Type=0| Seg Left=1   |
     +-+-+-+-+-+-+-+-+-+-+-+-+-+-+-+-+-+-+-+-+-+-+-+-+-+-+-+-+-+-+-+-+
     |                         Reserved                             |
     +-+-+-+-+-+-+-+-+-+-+-+-+-+-+-+-+-+-+-+-+-+-+-+-+-+-+-+-+-+-+-+-+
     |                                                              |
     +                                                              +
     |                                                              |
     +                     Address[1] = I1                          +
     |                                                              |
     +                                                              +
     |                                                              |
     +-+-+-+-+-+-+-+-+-+-+-+-+-+-+-+-+-+-+-+-+-+-+-+-+-+-+-+-+-+-+-+-+
```

    cmsg_len is incremented by 16, and the Segments Left field is
    incremented by 1.

Stevens, et al.   Informational   [Page 68]

The next call to inet6_rth_add() adds I2 to the list.

```
+-+-+-+-+-+-+-+-+-+-+-+-+-+-+-+-+-+-+-+-+-+-+-+-+-+-+-+-+-+-+-+-+
|          cmsg_len = 52                                       |
+-+-+-+-+-+-+-+-+-+-+-+-+-+-+-+-+-+-+-+-+-+-+-+-+-+-+-+-+-+-+-+-+
|        cmsg_level = IPPROTO_IPV6                             |
+-+-+-+-+-+-+-+-+-+-+-+-+-+-+-+-+-+-+-+-+-+-+-+-+-+-+-+-+-+-+-+-+
|        cmsg_type = IPV6_RTHDR                                |
+-+-+-+-+-+-+-+-+-+-+-+-+-+-+-+-+-+-+-+-+-+-+-+-+-+-+-+-+-+-+-+-+
| Next Header  | Hdr Ext Len=6 | Routing Type=0| Seg Left=2   |
+-+-+-+-+-+-+-+-+-+-+-+-+-+-+-+-+-+-+-+-+-+-+-+-+-+-+-+-+-+-+-+-+
|                            Reserved                          |
+-+-+-+-+-+-+-+-+-+-+-+-+-+-+-+-+-+-+-+-+-+-+-+-+-+-+-+-+-+-+-+-+
|                                                              |
+                                                              +
|                                                              |
+                     Address[1] = I1                          +
|                                                              |
+                                                              +
|                                                              |
+-+-+-+-+-+-+-+-+-+-+-+-+-+-+-+-+-+-+-+-+-+-+-+-+-+-+-+-+-+-+-+-+
|                                                              |
+                                                              +
|                                                              |
+                     Address[2] = I2                          +
|                                                              |
+                                                              +
|                                                              |
+-+-+-+-+-+-+-+-+-+-+-+-+-+-+-+-+-+-+-+-+-+-+-+-+-+-+-+-+-+-+-+-+
```

cmsg_len is incremented by 16, and the Segments Left field is
incremented by 1.

The last call to inet6_rth_add() adds I3 to the list.

```
+-+-+-+-+-+-+-+-+-+-+-+-+-+-+-+-+-+-+-+-+-+-+-+-+-+-+-+-+-+-+-+-+
|          cmsg_len = 68                                        |
+-+-+-+-+-+-+-+-+-+-+-+-+-+-+-+-+-+-+-+-+-+-+-+-+-+-+-+-+-+-+-+-+
|          cmsg_level = IPPROTO_IPV6                            |
+-+-+-+-+-+-+-+-+-+-+-+-+-+-+-+-+-+-+-+-+-+-+-+-+-+-+-+-+-+-+-+-+
|          cmsg_type = IPV6_RTHDR                               |
+-+-+-+-+-+-+-+-+-+-+-+-+-+-+-+-+-+-+-+-+-+-+-+-+-+-+-+-+-+-+-+-+
| Next Header  | Hdr Ext Len=6 | Routing Type=0| Seg Left=3     |
+-+-+-+-+-+-+-+-+-+-+-+-+-+-+-+-+-+-+-+-+-+-+-+-+-+-+-+-+-+-+-+-+
|                           Reserved                            |
+-+-+-+-+-+-+-+-+-+-+-+-+-+-+-+-+-+-+-+-+-+-+-+-+-+-+-+-+-+-+-+-+
|                                                               |
+                                                               +
|                                                               |
+                       Address[1] = I1                         +
|                                                               |
+                                                               +
|                                                               |
+-+-+-+-+-+-+-+-+-+-+-+-+-+-+-+-+-+-+-+-+-+-+-+-+-+-+-+-+-+-+-+-+
|                                                               |
+                                                               +
|                                                               |
+                       Address[2] = I2                         +
|                                                               |
+                                                               +
|                                                               |
+-+-+-+-+-+-+-+-+-+-+-+-+-+-+-+-+-+-+-+-+-+-+-+-+-+-+-+-+-+-+-+-+
|                                                               |
+                                                               +
|                                                               |
+                       Address[3] = I3                         +
|                                                               |
+                                                               +
|                                                               |
+-+-+-+-+-+-+-+-+-+-+-+-+-+-+-+-+-+-+-+-+-+-+-+-+-+-+-+-+-+-+-+-+
```

cmsg_len is incremented by 16, and the Segments Left field is
incremented by 1.

21.2. Receiving Routing Headers

This example assumes that the application has enabled IPV6_RECVRTHDR
socket option. The application prints and reverses a source route
and uses that to echo the received data.

Stevens, et al.   Informational   [Page 70]

```
        struct sockaddr_in6     addr;
        struct msghdr           msg;
        struct iovec            iov;
        struct cmsghdr          *cmsgptr;
        socklen_t               cmsgspace;
        void                    *extptr;
        int                     extlen;

        int                     segments;
        int                     i;
        char                    databuf[8192];

        segments = 100;         /* Enough */
        extlen = inet6_rth_space(IPV6_RTHDR_TYPE_0, segments);
        cmsgspace = CMSG_SPACE(extlen);
        cmsgptr = malloc(cmsgspace);
        if (cmsgptr == NULL) {
                perror("malloc");
                exit(1);
        }
        extptr = CMSG_DATA(cmsgptr);

        msg.msg_control = cmsgptr;
        msg.msg_controllen = cmsgspace;
        msg.msg_name = (struct sockaddr *)&addr;
        msg.msg_namelen = sizeof (addr);
        msg.msg_iov = &iov;
        msg.msg_iovlen = 1;
        iov.iov_base = databuf;
        iov.iov_len = sizeof (databuf);
        msg.msg_flags = 0;
        if (recvmsg(s, &msg, 0) == -1) {
                perror("recvmsg");
                return;
        }
        if (msg.msg_controllen != 0 &&
            cmsgptr->cmsg_level == IPPROTO_IPV6 &&
            cmsgptr->cmsg_type == IPV6_RTHDR) {
                struct in6_addr *in6;
                char asciiname[INET6_ADDRSTRLEN];
                struct ip6_rthdr *rthdr;

                rthdr = (struct ip6_rthdr *)extptr;
                segments = inet6_rth_segments(extptr);
                printf("route (%d segments, %d left): ",
                    segments, rthdr->ip6r_segleft);
                for (i = 0; i < segments; i++) {
                        in6 = inet6_rth_getaddr(extptr, i);
```

```
                        if (in6 == NULL)
                                printf("<NULL> ");
                        else
                                printf("%s ", inet_ntop(AF_INET6,
                                    (void *)in6->s6_addr,
                                    asciiname, INET6_ADDRSTRLEN));
                }
                if (inet6_rth_reverse(extptr, extptr) == -1) {
                        printf("reverse failed");
                        return;
                }
        }
        iov.iov_base = databuf;
        iov.iov_len = strlen(databuf);
        if (sendmsg(s, &msg, 0) == -1)
                perror("sendmsg");
        if (cmsgptr != NULL)
                free(cmsgptr);
```

Note: The above example is a simple illustration. It skips some
error checks, including those involving the MSG_TRUNC and MSG_CTRUNC
flags. It also leaves some type mismatches in favor of brevity.

22. Appendix C: Examples Using the inet6_opt_XXX() Functions

This shows how Hop-by-Hop and Destination options can be both built
as well as parsed using the inet6_opt_XXX() functions. These
examples assume that there are defined values for OPT_X and OPT_Y.

Note: The example is a simple illustration. It skips some error
checks and leaves some type mismatches in favor of brevity.

22.1. Building Options

We now provide an example that builds two Hop-by-Hop options using
the example in Appendix B of [RFC-2460].

```
        void *extbuf;
        socklen_t extlen;
        int currentlen;
        void *databuf;
        int offset;
        uint8_t value1;
        uint16_t value2;
        uint32_t value4;
        uint64_t value8;

        /* Estimate the length */
```

```
        currentlen = inet6_opt_init(NULL, 0);
        if (currentlen == -1)
                return (-1);
        currentlen = inet6_opt_append(NULL, 0, currentlen, OPT_X,
                                      12, 8, NULL);
        if (currentlen == -1)
                return (-1);
        currentlen = inet6_opt_append(NULL, 0, currentlen, OPT_Y,
                                      7, 4, NULL);
        if (currentlen == -1)
                return (-1);
        currentlen = inet6_opt_finish(NULL, 0, currentlen);
        if (currentlen == -1)
                return (-1);
        extlen = currentlen;

        extbuf = malloc(extlen);
        if (extbuf == NULL) {
                perror("malloc");
                return (-1);
        }
        currentlen = inet6_opt_init(extbuf, extlen);
        if (currentlen == -1)
                return (-1);

        currentlen = inet6_opt_append(extbuf, extlen, currentlen,
            OPT_X, 12, 8, &databuf);
        if (currentlen == -1)
                return (-1);
        /* Insert value 0x12345678 for 4-octet field */
        offset = 0;
        value4 = 0x12345678;
        offset = inet6_opt_set_val(databuf, offset,
                                   &value4, sizeof (value4));
        /* Insert value 0x0102030405060708 for 8-octet field */
        value8 = 0x0102030405060708;
        offset = inet6_opt_set_val(databuf, offset,
                                   &value8, sizeof (value8));

        currentlen = inet6_opt_append(extbuf, extlen, currentlen,
            OPT_Y, 7, 4, &databuf);
        if (currentlen == -1)
                return (-1);
        /* Insert value 0x01 for 1-octet field */
        offset = 0;
        value1 = 0x01;
        offset = inet6_opt_set_val(databuf, offset,
                                   &value1, sizeof (value1));
```

```
      /* Insert value 0x1331 for 2-octet field */
      value2 = 0x1331;
      offset = inet6_opt_set_val(databuf, offset,
                                 &value2, sizeof (value2));
      /* Insert value 0x01020304 for 4-octet field */
      value4 = 0x01020304;
      offset = inet6_opt_set_val(databuf, offset,
                                 &value4, sizeof (value4));

      currentlen = inet6_opt_finish(extbuf, extlen, currentlen);
      if (currentlen == -1)
              return (-1);
      /* extbuf and extlen are now completely formatted */
```

22.2. Parsing Received Options

   This example parses and prints the content of the two options in the
   previous example.

```
      int
      print_opt(void *extbuf, socklen_t extlen)
      {
              struct ip6_dest *ext;
              int currentlen;
              uint8_t type;
              socklen_t len;
              void *databuf;
              int offset;
              uint8_t value1;
              uint16_t value2;
              uint32_t value4;
              uint64_t value8;

              ext = (struct ip6_dest *)extbuf;
              printf("nxt %u, len %u (bytes %d)\n", ext->ip6d_nxt,
                  ext->ip6d_len, (ext->ip6d_len + 1) * 8);

              currentlen = 0;
              while (1) {
                      currentlen = inet6_opt_next(extbuf, extlen,
                                                  currentlen, &type,
                                                  &len, &databuf);
                      if (currentlen == -1)
                              break;
                      printf("Received opt %u len %u\n",
                          type, len);
                      switch (type) {
                      case OPT_X:
```

```
                        offset = 0;
                        offset =
                            inet6_opt_get_val(databuf, offset,
                                              &value4,
                                              sizeof (value4));
                        printf("X 4-byte field %x\n", value4);
                        offset =
                            inet6_opt_get_val(databuf, offset,
                                              &value8,
                                              sizeof (value8));
                        printf("X 8-byte field %llx\n", value8);
                        break;
                case OPT_Y:
                        offset = 0;
                        offset =
                            inet6_opt_get_val(databuf, offset,
                                              &value1,
                                              sizeof (value1));
                        printf("Y 1-byte field %x\n", value1);
                        offset =
                            inet6_opt_get_val(databuf, offset,
                                              &value2,
                                              sizeof (value2));
                        printf("Y 2-byte field %x\n", value2);
                        offset =
                            inet6_opt_get_val(databuf, offset,
                                              &value4,
                                              sizeof (value4));
                        printf("Y 4-byte field %x\n", value4);
                        break;
                default:
                        printf("Unknown option %u\n", type);
                        break;
                }
        }
        return (0);
    }
```

RFC 3542   Advanced Sockets API for IPv6   May 2003

23. Authors' Addresses

   W. Richard Stevens (deceased)

   Matt Thomas
   3am Software Foundry
   8053 Park Villa Circle
   Cupertino, CA 95014

   EMail: matt@3am-software.com

   Erik Nordmark
   Sun Microsystems Laboratories, Europe
   180, avenue de l'Europe
   38334 SAINT ISMIER Cedex, France

   Phone: +33 (0)4 74 18 88 03
   Fax: +33 (0)4 76 18 88 88
   EMail: Erik.Nordmark@sun.com

   Tatuya JINMEI
   Corporate Research & Development Center, Toshiba Corporation
   1 Komukai Toshiba-cho, Kawasaki-shi
   Kanagawa 212-8582, Japan

   EMail: jinmei@isl.rdc.toshiba.co.jp

RFC 3542   Advanced Sockets API for IPv6   May 2003

24. Full Copyright Statement

    Copyright (C) The Internet Society (2003). All Rights Reserved.

    This document and translations of it may be copied and furnished to
    others, and derivative works that comment on or otherwise explain it
    or assist in its implementation may be prepared, copied, published
    and distributed, in whole or in part, without restriction of any
    kind, provided that the above copyright notice and this paragraph are
    included on all such copies and derivative works. However, this
    document itself may not be modified in any way, such as by removing
    the copyright notice or references to the Internet Society or other
    Internet organizations, except as needed for the purpose of
    developing Internet standards in which case the procedures for
    copyrights defined in the Internet Standards process must be
    followed, or as required to translate it into languages other than
    English.

    The limited permissions granted above are perpetual and will not be
    revoked by the Internet Society or its successors or assigns.

    This document and the information contained herein is provided on an
    "AS IS" basis and THE INTERNET SOCIETY AND THE INTERNET ENGINEERING
    TASK FORCE DISCLAIMS ALL WARRANTIES, EXPRESS OR IMPLIED, INCLUDING
    BUT NOT LIMITED TO ANY WARRANTY THAT THE USE OF THE INFORMATION
    HEREIN WILL NOT INFRINGE ANY RIGHTS OR ANY IMPLIED WARRANTIES OF
    MERCHANTABILITY OR FITNESS FOR A PARTICULAR PURPOSE.

Acknowledgement

    Funding for the RFC Editor function is currently provided by the
    Internet Society.

F

IPv4-Mapped Address API Considered Harmful

Draft-cmetz-v6ops-v4mapped-api-harmful-00.txt

Internet Engineering Task Force   Craig Metz
INTERNET-DRAFT   Extreme Networks
Expires: Apr 27, 2003   Jun-ichiro itojun Hagino
                                                      Research Lab, IIJ
                                                         Oct 27, 2002

             IPv4-Mapped Address API Considered Harmful
            draft-cmetz-v6ops-v4mapped-api-harmful-00.txt

Status of this Memo

This document is an Internet-Draft and is in full conformance with all
provisions of Section 10 of RFC2026.

Internet-Drafts are working documents of the Internet Engineering Task
Force (IETF), its areas, and its working groups. Note that other groups
may also distribute working documents as Internet-Drafts.

Internet-Drafts are draft documents valid for a maximum of six months
and may be updated, replaced, or obsoleted by other documents at any
time. It is inappropriate to use Internet-Drafts as reference material
or to cite them other than as ''work in progress.''

To view the list Internet-Draft Shadow Directories, see
http://www.ietf.org/shadow.html.

Distribution of this memo is unlimited.

The internet-draft will expire in 6 months. The date of expiration will
be Apr 27, 2003.

Abstract

The IPv6 Addressing Architecture [Hinden, 1998] defines the "IPv4-mapped
IPv6 address." This representation is used in the IPv6 basic API
[Gilligan, 1999] to denote IPv4 addresses using AF_INET6 sockets. The
use of IPv4-mapped addresses on AF_INET6 sockets degrades portability,
complicates IPv6 systems, and is likely to create security problems.
This document discusses each issue in turn. Finally, it proposes to
resolve these problems by recommending deprecation of this mechanism.

1. Drawbacks due to IPv4 mapped address support

1.1. Degraded portability

RFC2553 section 3.7 specifies the behavior of IPv4-mapped addresses with
an AF_INET6 socket. However, the description fails to specify important
details that are necessary for good portability. Specifically, the

DRAFT   IPv4-mapped Addr. API Considered Harmful   Oct 2002

specification needs to define:

(1) The interaction between multiple bind(2) attempts to the same port,
    with different addresses. What happens when an application does and
    does not call setsockopt(..., SO_REUSEPORT, ...) in order to bind(2)
    to the same port on AF_INET and AF_INET6? What happens when an
    application calls bind(2) on AF_INET socket, and an application
    calls bind(2) on an AF_INET6 socket with IPv4-mapped address? Note
    that there are many more issues here that need specification.

(2) The selection/interaction of port numbers between AF_INET and
    AF_INET6 sockets on bind(2) and/or connect(2) system calls. This is
    related to (1).

(3) The treatment of socket options (setsockopt(2) and getsockopt(2))
    with IPv4-mapped addresses on AF_INET6 sockets. What happens when
    an application calls setsockopt(2) for IPv4 options or IPv6 options
    on an AF_INET6 socket that is not yet bound (and, therefore, the
    host does not know if IPv4 or IPv6 communication will be used)?
    What happens when an application calls setsockopt(2) for IPv4
    options or IPv6 options on an AF_INET6 socket that is bound to
    IPv4-mapped addresses?

(4) The delivery of multicast packets to AF_INET and AF_INET6 sockets.
    What happens when an application binds to the IPv6 unspecified
    address (::) with a certain port — does it receive IPv4 multicast
    traffic as well? What will be the relationship between
    IP_MULTICAST_IF and IPV6_MULTICAST_IF socket options? What happens
    when an application calls sendto(2) to an IPv4-mapped address for an
    IPv4 multicast address? How will the source address will be
    selected?

Due to these ambiguities, developers of applications that use
IPv4-mapped addresses on AF_INET6 sockets might encounter portability
problems.

1.2. Increased implementation complexity

Implementation of IPv4-mapped addresses has a real and significant cost,
both in the system software (e.g., network stack, kernel, and system
libraries) and in the application software (ALL of which must now
correctly handle IPv4-mapped addresses). The combined man-time for
developers, testers, document writers, and support staff is a real and
potentially tangible added cost of this particular feature. Because
applications are affected, the number of implementations for which this
cost will apply has the potential to be huge.

Implementation of IPv4-mapped addresses increases the complexity of all
IPv6 implementations, both in the system software and in the application
software. Increased complexity is bad for software engineering reasons
beyond the scope of this document. Technology market forces and
Internet history have demonstrated that simpler protocols and simpler

Metz and Hagino   Expires: Apr 27, 2003   [Page 2]

DRAFT   IPv4-mapped Addr. API Considered Harmful   Oct 2002

systems have a tendency to be more successful than complex alternatives.

If the community wishes to see IPv6 achieve successful deployment, it is
important that the resource costs and complexity costs associated with
IPv6 be as low as possible. Where opportunities exist to decrease these
costs, the community should seriously consider doing so in order to
nurture deployment.

1.3. Access control complexity

RFC2553 section 3.7 adds extra complexity to address-based access
controls. It is likely that there will be many errors introduced by of
this.

Due to RFC2553 section 3.7, AF_INET6 sockets will accept IPv4 packets.
On an IPv4/v6 dual stack node, if there is no AF_INET listening socket,
most users would believe that there will be no access from IPv4 peers.
However, if an AF_INET6 listening socket is present, IPv4 peers will be
able to access the service. This is likely to confuse users and result
in configuration errors that can be exploited by malicious parties. (It
is violating the security principle of least surprise)

AF_INET6 sockets will accept IPv4 packets even (and especially) if the
application is not expecting them. Every application that uses AF_INET6
sockets MUST correctly handle reception of IPv4 packets. Failure of a
developer to consider every relevant case might lead to a security
problem. This is likely to be overlooked by developers — especially
those new to IPv6 development (as most are). This is likely to result
in applications with flaws that can be exploited by malicious parties.
(Again, this is violating the security principle of least surprise)

Systems that support IPv4 communications on AF_INET6 sockets using
IPv4-mapped addresses have a greater potential to have security problems
than they would if they did not have this feature.

2. Recommended solution

o Deprecate RFC2553 section 3.7. By doing so, IPv6 implementations will
  be greatly simplified, both in the system software and in all IPv6
  application software.

3. Alternative solution

o Expand RFC2553 section 3.7 to fully define the behavior of AF_INET6
  sockets using IPv4-mapped addresses.

o Change the default value for IPV6_V6ONLY socket option defined in
  [Gilligan, 2002] to "on." With this approach, systems must still
  implement the complex interactions between AF_INET and AF_INET6
  socket, which can lead to security problems. Also, once a application

Metz and Hagino   Expires: Apr 27, 2003   [Page 3]

turns the socket option off, it MUST correctly handle all cases where
an IPv4-mapped address might be used or it may have security problems.

4. Implementation tips to application developers

o In EVERY application, check for IPv4-mapped addresses wherever
  addresses enter code paths under your control (i.e., are returned from
  system calls, or from library calls, or are input from the user or a
  file), and handle them in an appropriate manner. This approach is
  difficult in reality, and there is no way to determine whether it has
  been followed fully.

o Do not intentionally use RFC2553 section 3.7 (IPv4 traffic on AF_INET6
  socket). Implement server applications by using separate AF_INET and
  AF_INET6 listening sockets. Explicitly set the IPV6_V6ONLY socket
  option to on, whenever the socket option is available on the system.

    NOTE: Due to the lack of standard behavior in bind(2) semantics,
    this may not be possible on some systems. Some IPv6 stack does not
    permit bind(2) to 0.0.0.0, after bind(2) to ::. Also, there is no
    standard on how IPv4 traffic will be routed when both 0.0.0.0 and
    :: listening sockets are available on the same port.

o Implement programs in a protocol-independent manner using
  getaddrinfo(3) and getnameinfo(3), instead of hard-coding AF_INET6.
  RFC2553 section 3.7 leads people to port IPv4 application to IPv6 by
  replacing AF_INET into AF_INET6. However, by hard-coding AF_INET6
  into the program, developers are failing to correct their dependencies
  on particular protocol families. As a consequence, any future
  protocol support will again require the application to be modified.
  Applications that hard-code AF_INET6 require IPv6-capable systems and
  will fail on a system that only has IPv4 support. It is critical to
  implement programs in a protocol-independent manner if you want to
  ship a single program (binary/source) that runs on IPv4-only,
  IPv6-only, as well as IPv4/v6 dual stack systems.

5. Security considerations

This document discusses security issues with the use of IPv4-mapped
address. A recommended and alternate solution is provided.

6. Change History

None yet.

DRAFT   IPv4-mapped Addr. API Considered Harmful   Oct 2002

References

Hinden, 1998.
R. Hinden and S. Deering, "IP Version 6 Addressing Architecture" in
RFC2373 (July 1998). ftp://ftp.isi.edu/in-notes/rfc2373.txt.

Gilligan, 1999.
R. Gilligan, S. Thomson, J. Bound, and W. Stevens, "Basic Socket
Interface Extensions for IPv6" in RFC2553 (March 1999).
ftp://ftp.isi.edu/in-notes/rfc2553.txt.

Gilligan, 2002.
R. Gilligan, S. Thomson, J. Bound, J. McCann, and W. R. Stevens, "Basic
Socket Interface Extensions for IPv6" in draft-ietf-ipngwg-
rfc2553bis-06.txt (July 2002). work in progress material.

Author's address

     Craig Metz
     Extreme Networks
     220 Spring Street, Suite 100
     Herndon, VA 20170-5209, USA
     Tel: +1 703 885 6721
     email: cmetz@inner.net

     Jun-ichiro itojun Hagino
     Research Laboratory, Internet Initiative Japan Inc.
     Takebashi Yasuda Bldg.,
     3-13 Kanda Nishiki-cho,
     Chiyoda-ku,Tokyo 101-0054, JAPAN
     Tel: +81-3-5259-6350
     Fax: +81-3-5259-6351
     email: itojun@iijlab.net

G

IPv4-Mapped Addresses on the Wire Considered Harmful

Draft-itojun-v6ops-v4mapped-harmful-01.txt

Internet Engineering Task Force   Craig Metz
INTERNET-DRAFT   Extreme Networks
Expires: Apr 27, 2003   Jun-ichiro itojun Hagino
                                               Research Lab, IIJ
                                                    Oct 27, 2002

           IPv4-Mapped Addresses on the Wire Considered Harmful
                draft-itojun-v6ops-v4mapped-harmful-01.txt

Status of this Memo

Abstract

The IPv6 Addressing Architecture [Hinden, 1998] defines the "IPv4-mapped
IPv6 address." These addresses are used in the IPv6 basic API
[Gilligan, 1999] to denote IPv4 addresses using AF_INET6 sockets. These
addresses are used in protocol proposals such as SIIT [Nordmark, 2000]
to denote IPv6 communication using AF_INET6 sockets. Therefore,
IPv4-mapped addresses have two different meanings, and they are not
distinguishable from the user-land applications.

This draft discusses security threats due to this ambiguity of
IPv4-mapped address. It also discusses threats due to the additional
complexities introduced by IPv4-mapped addresses. Finally, it proposes
to resolve these problems by forbidding protocols from using IPv4-mapped
addresses for IPv6 communications.

1. Dual meaning of IPv4-mapped address

Basic Socket Interface Extensions for IPv6 [Gilligan, 1999] defines the
use of IPv4-mapped address with AF_INET6 sockets. IPv4-mapped addresses
are used to represent IPv4 addresses using the IPv6 API (e.g., on
AF_INET6 sockets). The API is designed with IPv4/v6 dual stack nodes in
mind. When an IPv4 packet reaches an IPv4/v6 dual stack node, the
node's IPv4 layer will process it, then pass it to the transport layer.
When the transport layer finds an AF_INET6 listening socket, it will
pass the packet to the listening socket as if it was from the
corresponding IPv4-mapped address. In this document, we will refer to
this as the "basic API behavior."

Some of the IPv6 translation protocols, such as SIIT [Nordmark, 2000] ,
use IPv4-mapped addresses actual IPv6 packets on the wire. These
protocols are designed for use with IPv6-only nodes. When an IPv6
packet containing these addresses reaches a node, the node's IPv6 layer
will process it, then pass it to the transport layer. When the
transport layer finds an AF_INET6 listening socket, it will pass the
packet to the listening socket with the IPv4-mapped address intact. In
this document, we will refer to this as the "SIIT behavior."

2. Threats due to the use of IPv4-mapped address on wire

When an application using the AF_INET6 API receives an IPv4-mapped
addresses (for example, returned by getpeername(2) or recvfrom(2)), it
cannot detect if the packet received by the node actually used IPv4
(basic API behavior) or IPv6 (SIIT behavior).

This ambiguity creates an opportunity that a malicious party can exploit
in order to deceive victim nodes. For example:

o If an attacker transmits an IPv6 packet with ::ffff:127.0.0.1 in the
  IPv6 source address field, he might be able to bypass a node's access
  controls by deceiving applications into believing that the packet is
  from the node itself (e.g., the IPv4 loopback address, 127.0.0.1).
  The same attack might be performed using the node's IPv4 interface
  address instead.

o If an attacker transmits an IPv6 packet with IPv4-mapped addresses in
  the IPv6 destination address field corresponding to IPv4 addresses
  inside a site's security perimeter (e.g., ::ffff:10.1.1.1), he might
  be able to bypass IPv4 packet filtering rules and traverse a site's
  firewall.

o If an attacker transmits an IPv6 packet with IPv4-mapped addresses in
  the IPv6 source and destination fields to a protocol that swaps IPv6
  source and destination addresses, he might be able to use a node as a
  proxy for certain types of attacks. For example, this might be used
  to construct broadcast multiplication and proxy TCP port scan attacks.

DRAFT   IPv4-mapped Addr. on Wire Considered Harmful   Oct 2002

3. Recommended solution

Forbid the use of IPv4-mapped address on wire.

The IPv6 node requirements:

o IPv6 nodes MUST NOT generate packets that contain IPv4-mapped
  addresses in any network layer field. Specifically, the IPv6 header,
  routing header, options headers, and any other chained headers MUST
  NOT contain IPv4-mapped addresses.

o IPv6 nodes SHOULD NOT generate packets that contain IPv4-mapped
  addresses in any field. (As a particular exception, it MAY be
  acceptable for fields referring to third-party nodes to contain
  IPv4-mapped addresses. Implementors must ensure that, where this is
  allowed, it is done with great care.)

o IPv6 nodes MUST silently discard packets that contain IPv4-mapped
  address in IPv6 header fields, or IPv6 extension header fields.

The IPv6 router requirements:

o IPv6 routers MUST NOT forward packets that contain IPv4-mapped
  addresses in any field the router processes. Specifically, the IPv6
  header, routing header, and the hop-by-hop options headers parsed by
  the router MUST NOT contain IPv4-mapped addresses.

o IPv6 routers MUST NOT advertise any prefixes into a routing protocol
  that are within the IPv4-mapped address space. Further, IPv6 routers
  MUST appropriately discard and/or ignore any received prefixes within
  the IPv4-mapped address space.

Standards requirements:

o The IPv6 address architecture document [Hinden, 1998] MUST explicitly
  state that IPv4-mapped addresses are exclusively for uses local to a
  node as specified in the basic API [Gilligan, 1999] and MUST never
  appear in the wire.

o Any document that suggests the use of IPv4-mapped addresses in packets
  on the wire SHOULD be modified to remove such usage. This will remove
  the threat due to the use of IPv4-mapped address on wire.

An alternate solution is to deprecate IPv4-mapped addresses from the
basic API. Due to the wide deployment of applications that use IPv6
basic API, further study of this option's feasibility is required. This
solution is not mutually exclusive with the recommended solution.

DRAFT   IPv4-mapped Addr. on Wire Considered Harmful   Oct 2002

4. Suggested implementation tips

4.1. System (e.g., kernel and library) developers

o Drop any IPv6 native packet with IPv4-mapped addresses in any of IPv6
  header fields as well as IPv6 extension header fields. (N.B., this
  will make the system incompatible with the current version of SIIT
  [Nordmark, 2000])

o Drop any IPv6 DNS response that contains IPv4-mapped addresses.

5. Security considerations

This document discusses security issues with the use of IPv4-mapped
address. A recommended and alternate solution is provided.

6. Change History

00 -> 01
    Craig Metz joins the team. Updates based on feedback given at
    v6ops interim meeting fall 2002. Move API issues to a separate
    draft.

References

Hinden, 1998.
R. Hinden and S. Deering, "IP Version 6 Addressing Architecture" in
RFC2373 (July 1998). ftp://ftp.isi.edu/in-notes/rfc2373.txt.

Gilligan, 1999.
R. Gilligan, S. Thomson, J. Bound, and W. Stevens, "Basic Socket
Interface Extensions for IPv6" in RFC2553 (March 1999).
ftp://ftp.isi.edu/in-notes/rfc2553.txt.

Nordmark, 2000.
E. Nordmark, "Stateless IP/ICMP Translator (SIIT)" in RFC2765 (February,
2000). ftp://ftp.isi.edu/in-notes/rfc2765.txt.

Author's addresses

DRAFT   IPv4-mapped Addr. on Wire Considered Harmful   Oct 2002

Craig Metz
Extreme Networks
220 Spring Street, Suite 100
Herndon, VA 20170-5209, USA
Tel: +1 703 885 6721
email: cmetz@inner.net

Jun-ichiro itojun Hagino
Research Laboratory, Internet Initiative Japan Inc.
Takebashi Yasuda Bldg.,
3-13 Kanda Nishiki-cho,
Chiyoda-ku,Tokyo 101-0054, JAPAN
Tel: +81-3-5259-6350
Fax: +81-3-5259-6351
email: itojun@iijlab.net

Possible Abuse Against IPv6 Transition Technologies

Draft-itojun-ipv6-transition-abuse-01.txt

Internet Engineering Task Force   Jun-ichiro itojun Hagino
INTERNET-DRAFT   Research Lab, IIJ
Expires: January 10, 2001   July 10, 2000

                Possible abuse against IPv6 transition technologies
                    draft-itojun-ipv6-transition-abuse-01.txt

Status of this Memo

This document is an Internet-Draft and is in full conformance with all
provisions of Section 10 of RFC2026.

Internet-Drafts are working documents of the Internet Engineering Task
Force (IETF), its areas, and its working groups. Note that other groups
may also distribute working documents as Internet-Drafts.

Internet-Drafts are draft documents valid for a maximum of six months
and may be updated, replaced, or obsoleted by other documents at any
time. It is inappropriate to use Internet-Drafts as reference material
or to cite them other than as "work in progress."

    The list of current Internet-Drafts can be accessed at
    http://www.ietf.org/ietf/1id-abstracts.txt

    The list of Internet-Draft Shadow Directories can be accessed at
    http://www.ietf.org/shadow.html.

Distribution of this memo is unlimited.

The internet-draft will expire in 6 months. The date of expiration will
be January 10, 2001.

Abstract

The document talks about possible abuse of IPv6 transition technologies,
which may lead to denial-of-service (DoS) attacks and other problems.
IPv6 transition technologies, namely IPv6 over IPv4 tunnelling
specifications and some others, have room for abuse by malicious
parties. Detailed descriptions and possible workarounds are supplied.

1. Abuse of IPv4 compatible address

1.1. Problem

To implement automatic tunnelling described in RFC1933 [Gilligan, 1996]
, IPv4 compatible addresses (like ::123.4.5.6) are used. From IPv6
stack point of view, an IPv4 compatible address is considered to be a
normal unicast address. If an IPv6 packet has IPv4 compatible addresses
in the header, the packet will be encapsulated automatically into an
IPv4 packet, with IPv4 address taken from lowermost 4 bytes of the IPv4
compatible addresses. Since there is no good way to check if embedded

DRAFT   Abuse against IPv6 transition technologies   July 2000

IPv4 address is sane, improper IPv4 packet can be generated as a result.
Malicious party can abuse it, by injecting IPv6 packets to an IPv4/v6
dual stack node with certain IPv6 source address, to cause transmission
of unexpected IPv4 packets. Consider the following scenario:

o You have an IPv6 transport-capable DNS server, running on top of
  IPv4/v6 dual stack node. The node is on IPv4 subnet 10.1.1.0/24.

o Malicious party transmits an IPv6 UDP packet to port 53 (DNS), with
  source address ::10.1.1.255. It does not make difference if it is
  encapsulated into an IPv4 packet, or is transmitted as a native IPv6
  packet.

o IPv6 transport-capable DNS server will transmit an IPv6 packet as a
  reply, copying the original source address into the destination
  address. Note that the IPv6 DNS server will treat IPv6 compatible
  address as normal IPv6 unicast address.

o The reply packet will automatically be encapsulated into IPv4 packet,
  based on RFC1933 automatic tunnelling. As a result, IPv4 packet
  toward 10.1.1.255 will be transmitted. This is the subnet broadcast
  address for your IPv4 subnet, and will (improperly) reach every node
  on the IPv4 subnet.

1.2. Possible solutions

For the following sections, possible solutions are presented in the
order of preference (the author recommends to implement solutions that
appear earlier). Note that some of the following are partial solution
to the problem. Some of the solutions may overwrap, or be able to
coexist, with other solutions. Solutions marked with (*) are already
incorporated into [Gilligan, 2000] which is an updated version of
RFC1933. Note that, however, solutions incorporated into [Gilligan,
2000] do not make a complete protection against malicious parties.

o Disable automatic tunnelling support.

o Reject IPv6 packets with IPv4 compatible address in IPv6 header
  fields. Note that we may need to check extension headers as well.

o Perform ingress filter against IPv6 packet and tunnelled IPv6 packet.
  Ingress filter should let the packets with IPv4 compatible source
  address through, only if the source address embeds an IPv4 address
  belongs to the organization. The approach is a partial solution for
  avoiding possible transmission of malicious packet, from the
  organization to the outside. (*)

o Whenever possible, check if the addresses on the packet meet the
  topology you have. For example, if the IPv4 address block for your
  site is 43.0.0.0/8, and you have a packet from IPv4-wise outside with
  encapsulated IPv6 source matches ::43.0.0.0/104, it is likely that
  someone is doing something nasty. This may not be possible to make

Hagino   Expires: January 10, 2001   [Page 2]

DRAFT   Abuse against IPv6 transition technologies   July 2000

the filter complete, so consider it as a partial solution. (*)

o Require use of IPv4 IPsec, namely authentication header [Kent, 1998] ,
  for encapsulated packet. Even with IPv4 IPsec, reject the packet if
  the IPv6 compatible address in the IPv6 header does not embed the IPv4
  address in the IPv4 header. We cannot blindly trust the inner IPv6
  packet based on the existence of IPv4 IPsec association, since the
  inner IPv6 packet may be originated by other nodes and forwarded by
  the authenticated peer. The solution may be impractical, since it
  only solves very small part of the problem with too many requirements.

o Reject inbound/outgoing IPv6 packets, if it has certain IPv4
  compatible address in IPv6 header fields. Note that we may need to
  check extension headers as well. The author recommends to check any
  IPv4 compatible address that is mapped from/to IPv4 address not
  suitable as IPv4 peer. They include 0.0.0.0/8, 127.0.0.0/8,
  224.0.0.0/4, 255.255.255.255/32, and subnet broadcast addresses.
  Since the check can never be perfect (we cannot check for subnet
  broadcast address in remote site, for example) the direction is not
  recommend. (*)

2. Abuse of 6to4 address

6to4 [Carpenter, 2000] is another proposal for IPv6-over-IPv4 packet
encapsulation, and is very similar to RFC1933 automatic tunneling
mentioned in the previous section. 6to4 address embeds IPv4 address in
the middle (2nd byte to 5th byte). If an IPv6 packet has a 6to4 address
as destination address, it will be encapsulated into IPv4 packet with
the embedded IPv4 address as IPv4 destination.

IPv6 packets with 6to4 address have the same problems as those with IPv4
compatible address. See the previous section for the details of the
problems, and possible solutions.

The latest 6to4 draft [Carpenter, 2000] do incoporate some of the
solutions presented in the previous section, however, they do not make a
complete protection against malicious parties.

3. Abuse of IPv4 mapped address

3.1. Problems

IPv6 basic socket API [Gilligan, 1999] defines the use of IPv4 mapped
address with AF_INET6 sockets. IPv4 mapped address is used to handle
inbound IPv4 traffic toward AF_INET6 sockets, and outbound IPv4 traffic
from AF_INET6 sockets. Inbound case has higher probability of abuse,
while outbound case contributes to the abuse as well. Here we briefly
describe the kernel behavior in inbound case. When we have an AF_INET6
socket bound to IPv6 unspecified address (::), IPv4 traffic, as well as
IPv6 traffic, will be captured by the socket. The kernel will present

the address of the IPv4 peer to the userland program by using IPv4
mapped address. For example, if an IPv4 traffic from 10.1.1.1 is
captured by an AF_INET6 socket, the userland program will think that the
peer is at ::ffff:10.1.1.1. The userland program can manipulate IPv4
mapped address just like it would do against normal IPv6 unicast
address.

We have three problems with the specification. First, IPv4 mapped
address support complicates IPv4 access control mechanisms. For
example, if you would like to reject accesses from IPv4 clients to a
certain transport layer service, it is not enough to reject accesses to
AF_INET socket. You will need to check AF_INET6 socket for accesses
from IPv4 clients (seen as accesses from IPv4 mapped address) as well.

Secondly, malicious party may be able to use IPv6 packets with IPv4
mapped address, to bypass access control. Consider the following
scenario:

o Attacker throws unencapsulated IPv6 packets, with ::ffff:127.0.0.1 as
  source address.

o The access control code in the server thinks that this is from
  localhost, and grants accesses.

Lastly, malicious party can make servers generate unexpected IPv4
traffic. This can be accomplished by sending IPv6 packet with IPv4
mapped address as a source (similar to abuse of IPv4 compatible
address), or by presenting IPv4 mapped address to servers (like FTP
bounce attack [Allman, 1999] from IPv6 to IPv4). The problem is
slightly different from the problems with IPv4 compatible addresses and
6to4 addresses, since it does not make use of tunnels. It makes use of
certain behavior of userland applications.

The confusion came from the dual use of IPv4 mapped address, for node-
internal representation for remote IPv4 destination/source, and for real
IPv6 destination/source.

3.2. Possible solutions

o In IPv6 addressing architecutre document [Hinden, 1998] , disallow the
  use of IPv4 mapped addresses on the wire. The change will conflict
  with SIIT [Nordmark, 2000] , which is the only protocol which tries to
  use IPv4 mapped address on IPv6 native packet. The dual use of IPv4
  mapped address (as a host-internal representation of IPv4
  destinations, and as a real IPv6 address) is the prime source of the
  problem.

o Reject IPv6 packets, if it has IPv4 mapped address in IPv6 header
  fields. Note that we may need to check extension headers such as
  routing headers, as well. IPv4 mapped address is internal
  representation in a node, so doing this will raise no conflicts with
  existing protocols. We recommend to check the condition in IPv6 input

DRAFT   Abuse against IPv6 transition technologies   July 2000

packet processing, and transport layer processing (TCP input and UDP
input) to be sure.

o Reject DNS replies, or other host name database replies, which contain
  IPv4 mapped address. Again, IPv4 mapped address is internal
  represntation in a node and should never appear on external host name
  databases.

o Do not route inbound IPv4 traffic to AF_INET6 sockets. When an
  application would like to accept IPv4 traffic, it should explicitly
  open AF_INET sockets. You may want to run two applications instead,
  one for an AF_INET socket, and another for an AF_INET6 socket. Or you
  may want to make the functionality optional, off by default, and let
  the userland applications explicitly enable it. This greatly
  simplifies access control issues. This approach conflicts with what
  IPv6 basic API document says, however, it should raise no problem with
  properly-written IPv6 applications. It only affects server programs,
  ported by assuming the behavior of AF_INET6 listening socket against
  IPv4 traffic.

o When implementing TCP or UDP stack, explicitly record the wire packet
  format (IPv4 or IPv6) into connection table. It is unwise to guess
  the wire packet format, by existence of IPv6 mapped address in the
  address pair.

o We should separately fix problems like FTP bounce attack.

o Applications should always check if the connection to AF_INET6 socket
  is from an IPv4 node (IPv4 mapped address), or IPv6 node. It should
  then treat the connection as from IPv4 node (not from IPv6 node with
  special adderss), or reject the connection. This is, however,
  dangerous to assume that every application implementers are aware of
  the issue. The solution is not recommended (this is not a solution
  actually).

4. Attacks by combining different address formats

Malicious party can use different address formats simultaneously, in a
single packet. For example, suppose you have implemented checks for
abuse against IPv4 compatible address in automatic tunnel egress module.
Bad guys may try to send a native IPv6 packet with 6to4 destination
address with IPv4 compatible source address, to bypass security checks
against IPv4 compatible address in tunnel decapsulation module. Your
implementation will not be able to detect it, since the packet will not
visit egress module for automatic tunnels.

Analyze code path with great care, and reject any packets that does not
look sane.

DRAFT   Abuse against IPv6 transition technologies   July 2000

5. Attacks using source address-based authentication

5.1. Problems

IPv6-to-IPv4 translators [Nordmark, 2000; Tsirtsis, 2000; Hagino, 2000]
usually relay, or rewrite, IPv6 packet into IPv4 packet. The IPv4
source address in the IPv4 packet will not represent the ultimate source
node (IPv6 node). Usually the IPv4 source address represents translator
box instead. If we use the IPv4 source address for authentication at
the destination IPv4 node, all traffic relayed/translated by the
translator box will mistakenly be considered as authentic.

The problem applies to IPv4-to-IPv6 translators as well. The problem is
similar to proxied services, like HTTP proxy.

5.2. Possible solutions

o Do not use translators, for protocols that use IP source address as
  authentication credental (for example, rlogin [Kantor, 1991]).

o translators must implement some sort of access control, to reject any
  IPv6 traffic from malicious IPv6 nodes.

o Do not use source address based authentication. IP source address
  should not be used as an authentication credental from the first
  place, since it is very easy for malicious parties to spoof IP source
  address.

6. Conclusions

IPv6 transition technologies have been proposed, however, some of them
looks immune against abuse. The document presented possible ways of
abuse, and possible solutions against them. The presented solutions
should be reflected to the revision of specifications referenced.

For coming protocols, the author would like to propose a set of
guilelines for IPv6 transition technologies:

o Tunnels must explicitly be configured. Manual configuration, or
  automatic configuration with proper authentication, should be okay.

o Do not embed IPv4 addresses into IPv6 addresses, for tunnels or other
  cases. It leaves room for abuse, since we cannot practically check if
  embedded IPv4 address is sane.

o Do not define an IPv6 address format that does not appear on the wire.
  It complicates access control issues.

The author hopes to see more deployment of native IPv6 networks, where
tunnelling technologies become unnecessary.

Hagino   Expires: January 10, 2001   [Page 6]

DRAFT   Abuse against IPv6 transition technologies   July 2000

7. Security considerations

The document talks about security issues in existing IPv6 related
protocol specifications. Possible solutions are provided.

References

Gilligan, 1996.
R. Gilligan and E. Nordmark, "Transition Mechanisms for IPv6 Hosts and
Routers" in RFC1933 (April 1996). ftp://ftp.isi.edu/in-
notes/rfc1933.txt.

Gilligan, 2000.
R. Gilligan and E. Nordmark, "Transition Mechanisms for IPv6 Hosts and
Routers" in draft-ietf-ngtrans-mech-06.txt (April 2000). work in
progress.

Kent, 1998.
S. Kent and R. Atkinson, "IP Authentication Header" in RFC2402 (November
1998). ftp://ftp.isi.edu/in-notes/rfc2402.txt.

Carpenter, 2000.
Brian Carpenter and Keith Moore, "Connection of IPv6 Domains via IPv4
Clouds without Explicit Tunnels" in draft-ietf-ngtrans-6to4-06.txt (June
2000). work in progress.

Gilligan, 1999.
R. Gilligan, S. Thomson, J. Bound, and W. Stevens, "Basic Socket
Interface Extensions for IPv6" in RFC2553 (March 1999).
ftp://ftp.isi.edu/in-notes/rfc2553.txt.

Allman, 1999.
M. Allman and S. Ostermann, "FTP Security Considerations" in RFC2577
(May 1999). ftp://ftp.isi.edu/in-notes/rfc2577.txt.

Hinden, 1998.
R. Hinden and S. Deering, "IP Version 6 Addressing Architecture" in
RFC2373 (July 1998). ftp://ftp.isi.edu/in-notes/rfc2373.txt.

Nordmark, 2000.
E. Nordmark, "Stateless IP/ICMP Translator (SIIT)" in RFC2765 (February,
2000). ftp://ftp.isi.edu/in-notes/rfc2765.txt.

Tsirtsis, 2000.
G. Tsirtsis and P. Srisuresh, "Network Address Translation - Protocol
Translation (NAT-PT)" in RFC2766 (February 2000). ftp://ftp.isi.edu/in-
notes/rfc2766.txt.

Hagino, 2000.
Jun-ichiro Hagino and Kazu Yamamoto, "An IPv6-to-IPv4 transport relay
translator" in draft-ietf-ngtrans-tcpudp-relay-01.txt (May 2000). work

DRAFT   Abuse against IPv6 transition technologies   July 2000

in progress material.

Kantor, 1991.
B. Kantor, "BSD Rlogin" in RFC1282 (December 1991).
ftp://ftp.isi.edu/in-notes/rfc1282.txt.

Author's address

        Jun-ichiro itojun Hagino
        Research Laboratory, Internet Initiative Japan Inc.
        Takebashi Yasuda Bldg.,
        3-13 Kanda Nishiki-cho,
        Chiyoda-ku,Tokyo 101-0054, JAPAN
        Tel: +81-3-5259-6350
        Fax: +81-3-5259-6351
        email: itojun@iijlab.net

An Extension of format for IPv6 Scoped Addresses

Draft-ietf-ipngwg-scopedaddr-format-02.txt

INTERNET-DRAFT   T. Jinmei, Toshiba
June 28, 2000   A. Onoe,   Sony

                  An Extension of Format for IPv6 Scoped Addresses

                  <draft-ietf-ipngwg-scopedaddr-format-02.txt>

Status of this Memo

    This document is an Internet-Draft and is in full conformance with
    all provisions of Section 10 of RFC 2026 [STD-PROC].

    Internet-Drafts are working documents of the Internet Engineering
    Task Force (IETF), its areas, and its working groups. Note that
    other groups may also distribute working documents as Internet-
    Drafts.

    Internet-Drafts are draft documents valid for a maximum of six months
    and may be updated, replaced, or obsoleted by other documents at any
    time. It is inappropriate to use Internet-Drafts as reference
    material or to cite them other than as "work in progress."

    The list of current Internet-Drafts can be accessed at
    http://www.ietf.org/ietf/1id-abstracts.txt

    The list of Internet-Draft Shadow Directories can be accessed at
    http://www.ietf.org/shadow.html.

    This Internet Draft will expire on December 28, 2000.

Abstract

    This document defines an extension of the format for IPv6 scoped
    addresses. In the format, a zone identifier is attached to a scoped
    address in order to supplement ambiguity of the semantics of the
    address. Using the format with some library routines will make
    scope-aware applications simpler.

1. Introduction

    There are several types of scoped addresses defined in the "IPv6
    Addressing Architecture" [ADDRARCH]. Since uniqueness of a scoped
    address is guaranteed only within a corresponding zone [SCOPEARCH],
    the semantics for a scoped address is ambiguous on a zone
    boundary. For example, when a user specifies to send a packet from
    a node to a link-local address of another node, the user must
    specify the link of the destination as well, if the node is
    attached to more than one link.

    This characteristic of scoped addresses may introduce additional
    cost to scope-aware applications; a scope-aware application may
    have to provide a way to specify a scope zone for each scoped
    address (e.g. a specific link for a link-local address) that the
    application uses. Also, it is hard for a user to "cut and paste" a
    scoped address due to the ambiguity of its scope.

draft-ietf-ipngwg-scopedaddr-format-02.txt   [Page 1]

Applications that are supposed to be used in end hosts
like telnet, ftp, and ssh, are not usually aware of scoped
addresses, especially of link-local addresses. However, an expert
user (e.g. a network administrator) sometimes has to give even
link-local addresses to such applications.

Here is a concrete example. Consider a multi-linked router, called
"R1", that has at least two point-to-point interfaces. Each of the
interfaces is connected to another router, called "R2" and "R3".
Also assume that the point-to-point interfaces are "unnumbered",
that is, they have link-local addresses only.

Now suppose that the routing system on R2 hangs up and has to be
reinvoked. In this situation, we may not be able to use a global
address of R2, because this is a routing trouble and we cannot
expect that we have enough routes for global reachability to R2.

Hence, we have to login R1 first, and then try to login R2 using
link-local addresses. In such a case, we have to give the
link-local address of R2 to, for example, telnet. Here we assume
the address is fe80::2.

Note that we cannot just type like
% telnet fe80::2
here, since R1 has more than one interface (i.e. link) and hence
the telnet command cannot detect which link it should try to
connect.

Although R1 could spray neighbor solicitations for fe80::2 on all
links that R1 attaches in order to detect an appropriate link, we
cannot completely rely on the result. This is because R3 might also
assign fe80::2 to its point-to-point interface and might return a
neighbor advertisement faster than R2. There is currently no
mechanism to (automatically) resolve such conflict. Even if we had
one, the administrator of R3 might not accept to change the
link-local address especially when R3 belongs to a different
organization from R1's.

Another example is an EBGP peering. When two IPv6 ISPs establish an
EBGP peering, using a particular ISP's global addresses for the
peer would be unfair, and using their link-local addresses would be
better in a neutral IX. In such a case, link-local addresses should
be specified in a router's configuration file and the link for the
addresses should be disambiguated, since a router usually connects
to multiple links.

This document defines an extension of the format for scoped addresses
in order to overcome this inconvenience. Using the extended format
with some appropriate library routines will make scope-aware
applications simpler.

2. Assumptions and Definitions

In this document we adopt the same assumption of characteristics of scopes as described in the scoped routing document [SCOPEDROUTING].

The keywords MUST, MUST NOT, REQUIRED, SHALL, SHALL NOT, SHOULD, SHOULD NOT, RECOMMENDED, MAY, and OPTIONAL, if and where they appear in this document, are to be interpreted as described in [KEYWORDS].

3. Proposal

The proposed format for scoped addresses is as follows:

        <scoped_address>%<zone_id>

where
    <scoped_address> is a literal IPv6 address,
    <zone_id> is a string to identify the scope zone of the address, and
    '%' is a delimiter character to distinguish between
    <scoped_address> and <zone_id>.

The following subsections describe detail definitions and concrete examples of the format.

3.1 Scoped Addresses

The proposed format is applied to all kinds of unicast and multicast scoped addresses, that is, all non-global unicast and multicast addresses.

The format should not be used for global addresses. However, an implementation which handles addresses (c.g. name to address mapping functions) MAY allow users to use such a notation (see also Appendix C).

3.2 Zone Identifiers

An implementation SHOULD support at least numerical identifiers as <zone_id>, which are non-negative decimal numbers. Positive identifiers MUST uniquely specify a single zone for a given scoped address. An implementation MAY use zero to have a special meaning, for example, a meaning that no scope zone is specified.

An implementation MAY support other kinds of non-null strings as <zone_id> unless the strings conflict with the delimiter character. The precise semantics of such additional strings is implementation dependent.

One possible candidate of such strings would be interface names, since interfaces uniquely disambiguate any type of scopes [SCOPEDROUTING]. In particular, if an implementation can assume that there is a one-to-one mapping between links and interfaces (and the assumption is usually reasonable,) using interface names as link identifiers would be natural.

An implementation could also use interface names as <zone_id> for larger scopes than links, but there might be some confusion in such use. For example, when more than one interface belongs to a same site, a user would be confused about which interface should be used. Also, a mapping function from an address to a name would encounter a same kind of problem when it prints a scoped address with an interface name as a zone identifier. This document does not specify how these cases should be treated and leaves it implementation dependent.

It cannot be assumed that a same identifier is common to all nodes in a zone. Hence, the proposed format MUST be used only within a node and MUST NOT be sent on a wire.

3.3 Examples
Here are examples. The following addresses

        fe80::1234 (whose link identifier is 1)
        fec0::5678 (whose site identifier is 2)
        ff02::9abc (whose link identifier is 5)
        ff08::def0 (whose organization identifier is 10)

would be represented as follows:

        fe80::1234%1
        fec0::5678%2
        ff02::9abc%5
        ff08::def0%10

If we use interface names as <zone_id>, those addresses could also be represented as follows:

        fe80::1234%ne0
        fec0::5678%ether2
        ff02::9abc%pvc1.3
        ff08::def0%interface10

where the interface "ne0" belongs to link 1, "ether2" belongs to site 2, and so on.

3.4 Omitting Zone Identifiers
This document does not intend to invalidate the original format for scoped addresses, that is, the format without the scope identifier portion. An implementation SHOULD rather provide a user with a "default" zone of each scope and allow the user to omit zone identifiers.

Also, when an implementation can assume that there is no ambiguity of any type of scopes on a node, it MAY even omit the whole functionality to handle the proposed format. An end host with a single interface would be an example of such a case.

4. Combinations of Delimiter Characters

draft-ietf-ipngwg-scopedaddr-format-02.txt   [Page 4]

There are other kinds of delimiter characters defined for IPv6
addresses. In this section, we describe how they should be combined
with the proposed format for scoped addresses.

The IPv6 addressing architecture [ADDRARCH] also defines the syntax
of IPv6 prefixes. If the address portion of a prefix is scoped one
and the scope should be disambiguated, the address portion SHOULD
be in the proposed format. For example, the prefix fec0:0:0:1::/64
on a site whose identifier is 2 should be represented as follows:

         fec0:0:0:1::%2/64

In this combination, it is important to place the zone identifier
portion before the prefix length, when we consider parsing the
format by a name-to-address library function (see Appendix A). That
is, we can first separate the address with the zone identifier from
the prefix length, and just pass the former to the library function.

The preferred format for literal IPv6 addresses in URL's are also
defined [URLFORMAT]. When a user types the preferred format for an
IPv6 scoped address whose zone should be explicitly specified, the
user could use the proposed format combined with the preferred
format.

However, the typed URL is often sent on a wire, and it would cause
confusion if an application did not strip the <zone_id> portion
before sending. Also, the proposed format might conflict with the
URI syntax [URI], since the syntax defines the delimiter chracter
('%') as the escape character.

Hence, this document does not specify how the proposed format
should be combined with the preferred format for literal IPv6
addresses. As for the conflict issue with the URI format, it would
be better to wait until the relationship between the preferred
format and the URI syntax is clarified. Actually, the preferred
format for IPv6 literal addresses itself has same kind of conflict.
In any case, it is recommended to use an FQDN instead of a literal
IPv6 address in a URL, whenever an FQDN is available.

5. Related Issues
   In this document, it is assumed that a zone identifier is not
   necessarily common in a single zone. However, it would be useful if
   a common notation is introduced (e.g. an organization name for a
   site). In such a case, the proposed format could be commonly used
   to designate a single interface (or a set of interfaces for a
   multicast address) in a scope zone.

   When the network configuration of a node changes, the change may
   affect <zone_id>. Suppose that the case where numerical
   identifiers are sequentially used as <zone_id>. When a network
   interface card is newly inserted in the node, some identifiers may
   have to be renumbered accordingly. This would be inconvenient,

INTERNET-DRAFT   Format for IPv6 Scoped Addresses   June 2000

especially when addresses with the numerical identifiers are stored
in non-volatile storage and reused after rebooting.

6. Security Considerations
    Since the use of this approach to represent IPv6 scoped addresses
    is restricted within a single node, it does not cause a security
    atack from the outside of the node.

    However, a malicious node might send a packet that contains a
    textual IPv6 scoped address in the proposed format, intending to
    deceive the receiving node about the zone of the scoped
    address. Thus, an implementation should be careful when it
    receives packets that contain IPv6 scoped addresses as data.

Appendix A. Interaction with API
    The proposed format would be useful with some library functions
    defined in the "Basic Socket API" [BASICAPI], the functions which
    translate a nodename to an address, or vice versa.

    For example, if getaddrinfo() parses a literal IPv6 address in the
    proposed format and fills an identifier according to <zone_id> in
    the sin6_scope_id field of a sockaddr_in6 structure, then an
    application would be able to just call getaddrinfo() and would not
    have to care about scopes.

    Also, if getnameinfo() returns IPv6 scoped addresses in the proposed
    format, a user or an application would be able to reuse the result by
    a simple "cut and paste" method.

    The kernel should interpret the sin6_scope_id field properly in
    order to make these extensions feasible. For example, if an
    application passes a sockaddr_in6 structure that has a non-zero
    sin6_scope_id value to the sendto() system call, the kernel should
    send the packet to the appropriate zone according to the
    sin6_scope_id field. Similarly, when a packet arrives from a scoped
    address, the kernel should detect the correct zone identifier based
    on the address and the receiving interface, fill the identifier in
    the sin6_scope_id field of a sockaddr_in6 structure, and then pass
    the packet to an application via the recvfrom() system call, etc.

    Note that the ipng working group is now revising the basic socket
    API in order to support scoped addresses appropriately. When the
    revised version is available, it should be preferred to the
    description of this section.

Appendix B. Implementation Experiences
    The WIDE KAME IPv6 stack implements the extension to the
    getaddrinfo() and the getnameinfo() functions described in Appendix
    A of this document. The source code is available as free software,
    bundled in the KAME IPv6 stack kit.

draft-ietf-ipngwg-scopedaddr-format-02.txt   [Page 6]

The current implementation assumes a one-to-one mapping between
links and interfaces, and hence it uses interface names as
<zone_id> for links.

For instance, the implementation shows its routing table as
follows:
```
    Internet6:
    Destination         Gateway                    Flags  Intface
    default             fe80::fe32:93d1%ef0        UG     ef0
```

This means that the default router is fe80::fe32:93d1 on the link
identified by the interface "ef0". A user can "cut and paste" the
result in order to telnet to the default router like this:

```
    % telnet fe80::fe32:93d1%ef0
```

even on a multi-linked node.

As another example, we show how the implementation can be used for
the problem described in Section 1.

We first confirm the link-local address assigned to the
point-to-point interface of R2:
```
    (on R1)% ping ff02::1%pvc0

    PING(56=40+8+8 bytes) fe80::1 --> ff02::1
    16 bytes from fe80::1%lo0, icmp_seq=0 hlim=64 time=0.474 ms
    16 bytes from fe80::2%pvc0, icmp_seq=0 hlim=64 time=0.374 ms(DUP!)
    ...
    (we assume here that the name of the point-to-point interface
    on R1 toward R2 is "pvc0" and that the link-local address on
    the interface is "fe80::1".)
```

So the address should be fe80::2. Then we can login R2 using the
address by the telnet command without ambiguity:

```
    % telnet fe80::2%pvc0
```

Though the implementation supports the extended format for all type
of scoped addresses, our current experience is limited to link-local
addresses. For other type of scopes, we need more experience.

The implementation also supports the notion of "default" scope zone
as described in Section 3.4. If a user specified "pvc0" as the
default link in the above example, the user can just type

```
    % telnet fe80::2
```

then the kernel will automatically use the link identified by
"pvc0" as the link of the address fe80::2.

Appendix C. A Comprehensive Description of KAME's getXXXinfo Functions

The following tables describe the behavior of the KAME's
implementation we mentioned in Appendix B using concrete
examples. Note that those tables are not intended to be standard
specifications of the extensions but are references for other
implementors.

Those tables summarize what value the getXXXinfo functions return
against various arguments. For each of two functions we first
explain typical cases and then show non-typical ones.

The tables for getaddrinfo() have four columns. The first two are
arguments for the function, and the last two are the results. The
tables for getnameinfo() also have four columns. The first three
are arguments, and the last one is the results.

Columns "Hostname" contain strings that are numeric or non-numeric
IPv6 hostnames.

Columns "NI_NUMERICHOST" or "NHOST" show if the NI_NUMERICHOST is
set to flags for the corresponding getXXXinfo function. Columns
"NSCOPE" show if the NI_NUMERICSCOPE is set to flags for the
corresponding getnameinfo function. The value "1" means the flag
is set, and "0" means the flag is clear. "-" means that the field
does not affect the result.

Columns "sin6_addr" contain IPv6 binary addresses in the textual
format, which mean the values of the sin6_addr field of the
corresponding sockaddr_in6 structure.

Columns "sin6_scope_id" contain numeric numbers, which mean the
values of the sin6_scope_id field of the corresponding sockaddr_in6
structure.

If necessary, we use an additional column titled "N/B" to note
something special.

If an entry of a result column has the value "Error", it means the
corresponding function fails.

In the examples, we assume the followings:
- The hostname "foo.kame.net" has a AAAA DNS record
  "3ffe:501::1". We also assume the reverse map is configured
  correctly.
- There is no FQDN representation for scoped addresses.
- The numeric link identifier for the interface "ne0" is 5.
- We have an interface belonging to a site whose numeric identifier
  is 10.
- The numeric identifier "20" is invalid for any type of scopes.
- We use the string "none" as an invalid non-numeric zone identifier.

Typical cases for getaddrinfo():

Hostname NI_NUMERICHOSTsin6_addr   sin6_scope_id

```
INTERNET-DRAFT            Format for IPv6 Scoped Addresses          June 2000
"foo.kame.net"   0              3ffe:501::1   0
"3ffe:501::1"    -              3ffe:501::1   0
"fec0::1%10"     -              fec0::1       10
"fe80::1%ne0"    -              fe80::1       5
"fe80::1%5"      -              fe80::1       5
```

Typical cases for getnameinfo():

sin6_addr	sin6_scope_id	NHOST	NSCOPE	Hostname
3ffe:501::1	0	0	-	"foo.kame.net"
3ffe:501::1	0	1	-	"3ffe:501::1"
fec0::1	10	-	-	"fec0::1%10"
fe80::1	5	-	0	"fe80::1%ne0"
fe80::1	5	-	1	"fe80::1%5"

Non-typical cases for getaddrinfo():

Hostname	NI_NUMERICHOST	sin6_addr	sin6_scope_id	N/B
"foo.kame.net"	1	Error		
"foo.kame.net%20"	-	Error		(*1)
"foo.kame.net%none"	-	Error		(*1)
"3ffe:501::1%none"	-	Error		
"3ffe:501::1%0"	-	3ffe:501::1	0	(*2)
"3ffe:501::1%20"	-	3ffe:501::1	20	(*2)
"fec0::1%none"	-	Error		
"fec0::1"	-	fec0::1	0	(*3)
"fec0::1%0"	-	fec0::1	0	(*4)
"fec0::1%20"	-	fec0::1	20	(*5)
"fe80::1%none"	-	Error		
"fe80::1"	-	fe80::1	0	(*3)
"fe80::1%0"	-	fe80::1	0	(*4)
"fe80::1%20"	-	fe80::1	20	(*5)

(*1) <zone_id> against an FQDN is invalid.
(*2) We do not expect that <zone_id> is specified for a global
     address, but we don't regard it as invalid.
(*3) We usually expect that a scoped address is specified with
     <zone_id>, but if no identifier is specified we just set 0 to
     the sin6_scope_id field.
(*4) Explicitly specifying 0 as <zone_id> is not meaningful, but
     we just treat the value as opaque.
(*5) The <zone_id> portion is opaque to getaddrinfo() even if it
     is invalid. It is kernel's responsibility to raise errors, if
     there is any connection attempt that the kernel cannot handle.

Non-typical cases for getnameinfo():

sin6_addr	sin6_scope_id	NHOST	NSCOPE	Hostname	N/B
3ffe:501::1	20	1	-	"3ffe:501::1%20"	(*6)
3ffe:501::1	20	0	-	"foo.kame.net"	(*7)
fec0::1	20	-	-	"fec0::1%20"	
fec0::1	0	-	-	"fec0::1"	(*8)
fe80::1	20	-	-	"fe80::1%20"	
fe80::1	0	-	-	"fe80::1"	(*8)

INTERNET-DRAFT   Format for IPv6 Scoped Addresses   June 2000

>   (*6) We do not expect that a global IPv6 address has a non-zero
>   zone identifier. But if it is the case, we just treat it as
>   opaque.
>   (*7) Despite the above, if the NI_NUMERICHOST is clear, we resolve
>   the address to a hostname and print the name without scope
>   zone information. We might have to reconsider this behavior.
>   (*8) We usually expect that a scoped address has a non-zero zone
>   identifier. But if the identifier is 0, we simply print the
>   address portion without scope zone information.

Acknowledgments
    We authors are indebted to Brian Zill, Richard Draves, and Francis
    Dupont for their careful comments and suggestions in a discussion
    to define a unified format among early implementations.

    Jim Bound also gave us valuable comments and clarifications through
    discussions about API extensions for scoped addresses in the ipngwg
    mailing list.

    Hideaki YOSHIFUJI commented on relationship between the URI syntax
    and the proposed format, and helped us improve the related section.

    Jun-ichiro Hagino has been helping us through all the discussions
    and his implementation efforts.

Authors' Addresses
    Tatuya JINMEI
    Research and Development Center, Toshiba Corporation
    1 Komukai Toshiba-cho, Kawasaki-shi
    Kanagawa 212-8582, JAPAN
    Tel: +81-44-549-2230
    Fax: +81-44-520-1841
    Email: jinmei@isl.rdc.toshiba.co.jp

    Atsushi Onoe
    Internet Systems Laboratory, IN Laboratories, Sony Corporation
    6-7-35 Kitashinagawa, Shinagawa-ku, Tokyo 141-0001, JAPAN
    Tel: +81-3-5448-4620
    Fax: +81-3-5448-4622
    Email: onoe@sm.sony.co.jp

References
    [ADDRARCH] Hinden, R., Deering, S., "IP Version 6 Addressing
               Architecture", RFC 2373, July 1998.

    [BASICAPI] Gilligan, R. E., Thomson, S., Bound, J., Stevens, W.,
               "Basic Socket Interface Extensions for IPv6", Internet-Draft,
               May 2000, <draft-ietf-ipngwg-rfc2553bis-00.txt>.

    [KEYWORDS] Bradner, S., "Key words for use in RFCs to Indicate

          Requirement Levels", BCP 14, RFC 2119, March 1997.

   [SCOPEARCH] S. Deering, B. Haberman, B. Zill, "IP Version 6 Scoped
               Address Architecture", Internet-Draft, March 2000,
               <draft-ietf-ipngwg-scoping-arch-00.txt>.

   [SCOPEDROUTING] Haberman, B., "Routing of Scoped Addresses in the
               Internet Protocol Version 6 (IPv6)", Internet-Draft,
               March 2000, <draft-ietf-ipngwg-scoped-routing-03.txt>.

   [STD-PROC] Bradner, S., The Internet Standards Process — Revision 3,
               RFC 2026, October 1996.

   [URLFORMAT] Hinden, R., Carpenter, B., Masinter, L., "Preferred
               Format for Literal IPv6 Addresses in URL's", RFC 2732,
               December 1999.

   [URI] T. Berners-Lee, R. Fielding, and L. Masinter, "Uniform
   Resource Identifiers (URI): Generic Syntax", RFC 2396, August
   1998.

J

Protocol Independence Using the Sockets API

Proceedings of FREENIX Track:
2000 USENIX Annual Technical Conference

San Diego, California, USA, June 18–23, 2000

PROTOCOL INDEPENDENCE
USING THE SOCKETS API

Craig Metz

Protocol Independence Using the Sockets API

Craig Metz
Department of Computer Science
University of Virginia
Charlottesville, VA 22904
`cmetz@inner.net`

Abstract

The BSD sockets API provides abstractions and
other features that help applications be protocol-
independent. Unfortunately, not all of the API is abstract and generic, and many programs do not use the
APIs in a protocol- independent way. This means that
most network programs, in practice, only work with
one layered set of communications protocols – usually
TCP over IP. This hinders compatibility with older
protocols and deployment of new ones, and is making
IP a victim of its own success.

During the course of next-generation IP development, implementors worked to convert protocol-
dependent applications into protocol-independent applications. Along the way, they defined new interfaces
to fix some problems and they found a number of usage
problems that lead to protocol dependencies.

This paper explains many of the problems encountered, using examples from freely available software,
and how to solve them. It also explains many of the
new protocol-independent interfaces.

1 Introduction

The single most painful lesson learned by implementors of next generation IP proposals (such as IPv6) was
how deeply most network programs are dependent on
the network protocol that they were originally written
to use. The widespread success of the IP Internet has
put it into the position of being the only network protocol that matters for most network applications, and
so there is currently little incentive to support anything else.

Even today, this is a problem. There are other network protocols that are in use today – such as Appletalk, ATM, AX.25, DECnet, Frame Relay, IPX,
and OSI – and few applications actually support them.
This is also a serious problem for the future, as any
research into new network protocols is greatly con-
strained by the lesson of IPv6: that anything not IP

will not be supported by the applications people want
to use, and that anything that is not supported by existing applications will encounter great difficulty gain-
ing acceptance.

The core of the BSD sockets API, especially the actual system calls, is not tied to any particular protocol. The problems fall in two major categories: supporting APIs that are protocol-dependent, and poor
programming practices that are common. There have
been great advances made in fixing the networking
APIs in the system libraries though the efforts of the
IETF's IPng working group[1] and the IEEE's POSIX
p1003.1g (networking API) working group. New library functions, data structures, and pre-processor
symbols together allow addresses and other network
properties to be treated as variable-length abstract objects whose internal format can be changed without
the application's involvement. But there is still a serious problem of programmer education, which in turn
requires good documentation of the problems and how
to solve them. To date, this documentation still does
not exist.

In the NRL IPv6 implementation[2], standard networking applications from BSD and from the Internet
were taken and modified to support protocol independence. For most applications, this was straightforward
once we had done a few applications and knew what to
look for. The end result was not only a conversion to
allow the applications to support almost any protocol,
but also a significant cleanup of the applications' code.

In this paper, I will first discuss the problems
that need to be solved to make programs protocol-
independent: what is wrong, why it is wrong, and
how it can be done right. I will then discuss the
new protocol-independent API functions and compare
them with older BSD networking API functions in
light of the problems that need to be solved. I will also
present in more detail some additional functions that
we found necessary to solve certain problems that have
not yet been standardized. Specific examples from

freely available networking programs will be used.

2   Protocol Independence Problems

Fundamentally, the problem with protocol independence is that software has not been written with the intent of being protocol-independent. Some common programs, such as Sendmail, support multiple protocols, but are still only capable of operating with certain protocols that they know about (and usually only one protocol really works). A protocol-independent application hides away knowledge of particular protocols into run-time abstractions that allow the same operations to apply regardless of what actual protocols happen to be in use. In some cases, it is not possible to make operations completely generic, in which case protocol-dependent code needs to be carefully guarded and some reasonable default actions must be available for other protocols. But most importantly, programs must be tested with several different protocols to prove that they can handle them. The jump from supporting one protocol to two is the biggest hurdle, and clearing that in a reasonable way makes supporting other protocols much easier.

2.1   Hard Coding

The most obvious protocol dependence problem seen in network programs is to hard-code the use of one protocol. Figure 1 shows an example from 4.4BSD-Lite2[3]'s telnet program. There are three major problems here. First, the protocol family to be used is hard-coded as AF_INET. That basically prevents protocols other than IP from being used. The family needs to be chosen based on the name resolution information, as will be discussed later. Second, the socket address used is a protocol-dependent address, in this case sockaddr_in. This structure is not big enough to hold addresses for some protocols, and in any case manipulating the fields in the structure itself is a protocol-dependent activity. Sockaddrs need to be treated as an opaque buffer manipulated by protocol-independent library functions or carefully guarded code. Third, IP-specific socket options are being used without any guards. That is, if the first two problems were fixed, the IP-specific setsockopt calls would still be done and they should always fail. Depending on the particular option being set, the socket option call needs to be replaced with an abstract equivalent or needs to be surrounded by a guard that skips the call if the protocol in use is not IP.

This particular bit of code also carries a common bug: it tries to be slightly protocol-independent and ends up worse off for the effort. It uses the protocol family returned by gethostbyname() and copies addresses in a variable-length way, but copies that into a field within a sockaddr_in and later tries to connect() to that address using an AF_INET socket while specifying the length of the sockaddr_in as the length of the address information. If the family was something other than AF_INET, the sockaddr_in would probably not be filled in with something meaningful, and connect() call would probably fail regardless because the protocol family of the target address was not the same as that of the socket. As long as the only addresses that ever get returned by gethostbyname() are IP addresses, this practice will actually work. If addresses other than IP addresses were returned, programs written this way would break. This creates an interesting problem: interfaces that might be made protocol independent cannot be, because legacy programs don't use them correctly and changing what they return would break software. Using a new interface designed for protocol independence (like getaddrinfo()) and using it correctly will solve this problem.

A variation of this problem is hard coding addressing information, such as addresses and ports. Figure 2 shows an example from Sendmail 8.7.6[4]. There are three major problems here. First, the code always treats the address as a sockaddr_in without any guards. As in the example above, this is bad for protocol independence. Second, the code hard-codes an address and a port. While this is sometimes useful, it is usually bad practice and always bad practice when not combined with a test to check the protocol family. Third, the code explicitly specifies TCP as the transport protocol being used. This hard-codes a transport protocol and implies that only a small number of network protocols are usable (those that TCP has been made to run over). The second and third problems can be solved by using protocol-independent name resolution functions correctly.

2.2   Inflexible Storage

Another class of problems comes about when storing information needed by various protocols. This was already mentioned in the discussion of Figure 1, where not only does the use of sockaddr_in hardcode the address format of a particular protocol, but it also does not provide enough space to store the addresses of many protocols. The most common place where this problem comes into play is when used with getpeername(). Figure 3 shows an example of this from the 4.4BSD-Lite2's fingerd source; similar code sequences can be found in almost any server program. This code example also shows the assumption that the returned socket will be an IP socket; while originally a fair assumption, this needs to be fixed in order to be protocol-independent.

```
            temp = inet_addr(hostp);
            if (temp != (unsigned long) -1) {
                sin.sin_addr.s_addr = temp;
                sin.sin_family = AF_INET;
                (void) strcpy(_hostname, hostp);
                hostname = _hostname;
            } else {
                host = gethostbyname(hostp);
                if (host) {
                    sin.sin_family = host->h_addrtype;
#if     defined(h_addr)              /* In 4.3, this is a #define */
                    memmove((caddr_t)&sin.sin_addr,
                                    host->h_addr_list[0], host->h_length);

...

            net = socket(AF_INET, SOCK_STREAM, 0);
            setuid(getuid());
            if (net < 0) {
                perror("telnet: socket");
                return 0;
            }
#if     defined(IP_OPTIONS) && defined(IPPROTO_IP)
            if (srp && setsockopt(net, IPPROTO_IP, IP_OPTIONS, (char *)srp, srlen) <
 0)
                    perror("setsockopt (IP_OPTIONS)");
#endif

...

            if (connect(net, (struct sockaddr *)&sin, sizeof (sin)) < 0) {
```

Figure 1: Hard-Coding the Network Protocol (4.4BSD Telnet)

```
            if (DaemonAddr.sin.sin_family == 0)
                    DaemonAddr.sin.sin_family = AF_INET;
            if (DaemonAddr.sin.sin_addr.s_addr == 0)
                    DaemonAddr.sin.sin_addr.s_addr = INADDR_ANY;
            if (DaemonAddr.sin.sin_port == 0)
            {
                    register struct servent *sp;

                    sp = getservbyname("smtp", "tcp");
                    if (sp == NULL)
                    {
                            syserr("554 service \"smtp\" unknown");
                            DaemonAddr.sin.sin_port = htons(25);
                    }
                    else
                            DaemonAddr.sin.sin_port = sp->s_port;
            }
```

Figure 2: Hard Coding Addresses and Ports (Sendmail 8.7.6)

```
            struct sockaddr_in sin;
    ...
            if (logging) {
                    sval = sizeof(sin);
                    if (getpeername(0, (struct sockaddr *)&sin, &sval) < 0)
                            err("getpeername: %s", strerror(errno));
                    if (hp = gethostbyaddr((char *)&sin.sin_addr.s_addr,
                        sizeof(sin.sin_addr.s_addr), AF_INET))
                            lp = hp->h_name;
                    else
                            lp = inet_ntoa(sin.sin_addr);
                    syslog(LOG_NOTICE, "query from %s", lp);
            }
```

Figure 3: Use of a sockaddr_in to Store Arbitrary Addresses (4.4BSD fingerd)

A similar problem is also seen frequently in servers: the use of a generic **sockaddr** to store address information. Like the IP protocol specific structure, it is not big enough to hold addresses for many protocols (on most systems, the two structures are actually the same size). When the size of the address to be stored is known, a buffer of that size can be allocated. When it is not, a maximal-length buffer can be allocated using a **sockaddr_storage**, which will be discussed later.

A particularly bad special case of this problem comes about in some IP-only programs. Because IP addresses happen to be 32 bit unsigned integers and many modern systems have that as a native data type, some programs simply use integers to store IP addresses. Figure 4 shows an example from vat 4.0b2[5], which uses **u_int32_ts** internally to store network addresses (this is a bit less bad than using more generic integer types, but still hopelessly IP- dependent). Due to a particularly common example of this in earlier versions of BSD, this is sometimes referred to as the "all the world's a **u_long**" problem, and has a lot in common with the old "all the world's a VAX" problem. Optimizing assumptions are being made about the size and form of an address that happen to work on most currently interesting systems and protocols. But they're still poor assumptions that break portability, both in terms of supporting different systems and supporting different protocols. 4.4BSD-Lite2 has fixed this problem in many places by using **in_addr** instead, which is still protocol-dependent but at least is the correct type. In general, raw addresses should not be stored – socket addresses should be used instead.

Also, some protocols have variable-length addresses. Most existing programs treat addresses as fixed-length objects and do not store the real length as provided by run-time functions. Programs must store the length of addresses along with the addresses themselves – as with the address type, this can be necessary information for interpreting the address. This also means that the sizes of buffers used to hold addresses should not be arbitrarily bounded.

Using the generic **sockaddr** or the wrong protocol-specific structure also creates problems with alignment. Most network protocols have some alignment requirement for their protocol-specific address structures that may not be satisfied by other structures. Care must be taken to either use the correct protocol specific address structure or to arrange for the buffer used to store addresses to be properly aligned.

The generic **sockaddr** *should* be used as a structure to which an arbitrary socket address can be cast in order to access the **sa_family** and **sa_len** fields. While those fields should have the same type no matter what protocol specific structure is used to access the buffer, it is still good use of types to use the generic **sockaddr** for access where the network protocol in use are not yet known, rather than to using the wrong protocol-specific type.

Finally, many programs assume that a "port" is an integer. The concept of an integer port number is not universal. Some protocols use string service names instead, or use other formats that are at least convertable to a string. Service endpoints should be represented as strings that may or may not end up converted to another format for representation in a socket address.

2.3 Inflexible User Interface

Many programs get address information through some sort of user interface or user parameter syntax. For example, web clients get resource information through URLs, free network programs such as **tcp_wrappers** [6] read configuration files, and some GUI network programs use four three-digit entry blanks to enter a numeric address. In many cases, the user interface or syntax that these clients use is dependent on the syntax of particular kinds of addresses. The use of colons and slashes in URLs, for example, makes it difficult to use those characters in network addresses (colons are the delimiter for IPv6 addresses, so this is a real problem). Similarly, the configuration files for `tcp_wrappers` 7.6 uses colons as the field separator. The generic solution to this problem is to provide support for escaping and/or quoting so that somewhat arbitrary characters can be used in address information. In many cases, a quick-fix solution can be made by changing the fields or delimiters, but this is not backwards compatible and only fixes things until the next new address syntax comes along.

Another problem is that more information may need to be provided to a program in order for it to know how to correctly interpret an address. For example, a host name may be valid in multiple protocol families. If the user wants to use a specific protocol, then this needs to be somehow specified. Programs need to have enough flexibility in their user interfaces to add these sort of options.

2.4   Not Handling Multiple Addresses

Multi-homed IP support in programs is still not as common as it should be. The problem of multi-homing support – supporting multiple interfaces with one or more IP address – is similar to the problem of supporting multiple addresses for different network protocols. In both cases, some subset of the available addresses may need to be listened on (for a server) or be available for an outgoing connection. The selection of these addresses creates interesting problems. In particular, it sometimes (esp. in the case of servers) creates the need to have multiple network sockets open at once and to handle traffic on any of them. Most networking programs are written to use only one network socket, and changing that requires significant work.

Both multi-homing and multi-protocol support requires extra user interface capability. For example, both will cause multiple addresses to be returned from some name lookups, of which a subset might be reachable endpoints. The user should be either be given a choice among this set or some attempt should be made to progress in a reasonable way (for example, trying each in sequence until one succeeds). Whatever actually happens, the user should be made aware of what's happening.

2.5   Protocols Carrying Address Information

Some IP application protocols, such as FTP and talk, pass address information over the network. This means that the application protocol will need to be modified to be multi-protocol, which generally means

adding flexibility similar to what has to be done inside a network program. Exactly how to do this is outside the scope of this document, but an example is the approach used for FTP[7]. In general, the best solution to this problem is to change the application protocol to not send address information over the network, because this practice causes problems for many network/protocol translation devices.

3   New Interfaces

The IETF's IPng working group and the POSIX p1003.1g working group have made a good bit of progress in identifying and standardizing new APIs needed to develop protocol-independent programs. Beyond this, the NRL IPv6 implementation found several other interfaces that we felt needed to be present in order to develop fully functional protocol-independent applications. In many cases, the BSD sockets interfaces were almost good enough but in practice misused. The new interfaces extend many BSD interfaces and supersede others.

The new interfaces break down into roughly two categories. The first are functions to perform name resolution operations (name to addresses, address to name) in a clean way. The second are operations to help use socket addresses (sockaddrs) in a clean way.

3.1   Name Resolution

Figure 5 shows a brief summary of the new name resolution interfaces.

The `getaddrinfo()` and `getnameinfo()` functions provide a protocol-independent way of mapping names to addresses information and of mapping address information back to names. Given a host name, a service name, and other information to constrain the lookup, `getaddrinfo()` returns either an integer error or a list of filled in `addrinfo` structures. Each contains the information that needs to be passed to `socket()` to open a socket as well as the information that needs to be passed to `connect()` or `sendmsg()` to reach the named endpoint.

Many programs can simply take the returned list and iterate through it, executing `socket()` and `connect()` calls with the information in each list element, until one attempt succeeds completely or the list has been exhausted. Figure 6 gives an example of how to do this. Notice how the program never needs to manipulate addresses directly. The program only needs to take information out of the `addrinfo` structure and feed it into other functions. This simple block of code is capable of obtaining a connected socket with any stream protocol that is supported in both the kernel and in the runtime library. If the runtime library

```
int Network::dorecv(u_char* buf, int len, u_int32_t& from, int fd)
{
        sockaddr_in sfrom;
        int fromlen = sizeof(sfrom);
        int cc = ::recvfrom(fd, (char*)buf, len, 0,
                            (sockaddr*)&sfrom, &fromlen);
        if (cc < 0) {
                if (errno != EWOULDBLOCK)
                        perror("recvfrom");
                return (-1);
        }
        from = sfrom.sin_addr.s_addr;
```

Figure 4: Using an Integer for an Address (from vat 4.0b2)

```
#define AI_PASSIVE     /* Socket address is intended for bind() */
#define AI_CANONNAME   /* Request for canonical name */
#define AI_NUMERICHOST /* Don't ever try nameservice */

struct addrinfo {
  int ai_flags;              /* input flags */
  int ai_family;             /* protocol family for socket */
  int ai_socktype;           /* socket type */
  int ai_protocol;           /* protocol for socket */
  int ai_addrlen;            /* length of socket-address */
  struct sockaddr *ai_addr;  /* socket-address for socket */
  char *ai_canonname;        /* canonical name for service location (iff req) */
  struct addrinfo *ai_next;  /* pointer to next in list */
};

int getaddrinfo(const char *name, const char *service,
                const struct addrinfo *req, struct addrinfo **pai);

void freeaddrinfo(struct addrinfo *ai);

char *gai_strerror(int ecode);

#define NI_MAXHOST         /* Maximum host name buffer length needed */
#define NI_MAXSERV         /* Max. service name buffer length needed */
#define NI_NUMERICHOST     /* Don't do name resolution for the host */
#define NI_NUMERICSERV     /* Don't do name resolution for the service */
#define NI_NOFQDN          /* Don't fully qualify host names */
#define NI_NAMEREQD        /* Fail if name resolution for the host fails */
#define NI_DGRAM           /* Service is for a DGRAM socket (not a STREAM) */

int getnameinfo(const struct sockaddr *sa, size_t addrlen, char *host,
                size_t hostlen, char *serv, size_t servlen, int flags);

int nrl_afnametonum(const char *name);       /* (Nonstandard) */
const char *nrl_afnumtoname(int num);        /* (Nonstandard) */
int nrl_socktypenametonum(const char *name); /* (Nonstandard) */
const char *nrl_socktypenumtoname(int num);  /* (Nonstandard) */
```

Figure 5: Summary of New Name Resolution APIs

does not support a protocol, it will not be returned by
getaddrinfo(). If the kernel does not support a protocol, this function will print an error for those sockets
and skip that protocol. This is especially important for
binaries to be shipped on systems where the protocols
available in the runtime library and/or kernel can be
configured by the end user; one binary will be able to
work as long as the system is configured so that there
is one protocol that the entire system supports.

Note that **getaddrinfo()** and **getnameinfo()** handle both host names and printable numeric addresses,
as appropriate. One historical problem with functions
like **gethostbyname()** and **gethostbyaddr()** is that
on some systems they handle printable numeric addresses and on some systems they do not. Portable
programs must be written to attempt printable-
numeric conversion separately, just in case – programs
that assume the system handles these have encountered portability problems. Some programs have bugs
caused by the old printable numeric conversion functions, making this even more of a problem. These new
functions should hopefully put these problem to rest.

As shown in the example, the **gai_strerror()** function converts the errors returned by **getaddrinfo()**
and **getnameinfo()** into human-printable form.
There are also constants for the error values, but few
programs need to distinguish between the types of failures beyond giving an appropriate error message. The
freeaddrinfo() function releases the memory used
by the result list, and *must* be called when the result
is no longer needed.

The functions **nrl_afnametonum()** and
nrl_afnumtoname() convert address family names
(inet, inet6, local, etc.) to numbers and back. This
is needed in order to support user entry of an address family to constrain **getaddrinfo()** lookups.
For example, many NRL IPv6-enabled applications
support a command line flag that the user can use
to specify a family, such as "inet" or "inet6," that
selects what protocol to use. The number-to-name
function is also helpful for diagnostic output. Similarly, the functions **nrl_socktypenametonum()** and
nrl_socktypenumtoname convert socket type names
(stream, dgram, seqpacket, etc.) to numbers and
back. These are less useful for user input, but are still
useful for diagnostic purposes.

3.2 Socket Addresses

Figure 7 shows a brief summary of the new socket
address interfaces. The major new addition is the
sockaddr_storage, which is defined as a structure
that is big enough to hold any socket address that
the system supports or might support in the future,
and provides sufficient alignment for any socket address that the system supports or might support in

the future. In practice, the size of the structure is
bounded on many systems by the capacity of the eight
bit integer used in the **sa_len** field of all socket addresses. On other systems, the bound might be provided by other structures' fields. The bound actually chosen can be selected by the systems' authors,
but the **sockaddr_storage** is defined to have whatever size is needed. The alignment provided by the
sockaddr_storage will typically be the largest alignment available on the system, though again the exact
choice is up to the systems' implementors.

Note that the **sockaddr_storage** is required to
have fields of the same type and in the same place
as the **sa_len** and **sa_family** fields in the systems'
sockaddrs, but that the standards that specify this
data structure don not actually require those fields to
have a known name and give examples with names that
makes them "hidden." While it is hoped that the long
term solution will be to fix this problem in the standards, the short term most portable way to use these
fields is to cast a **sockaddr_storage** to a **sockaddr**
and to use the fields through the latter type.

The **sockaddr_storage** is used where a socket address needs to be stored before its exact length is
known. Figure 8 shows some of the example in Figure 3, changed to take advantage of this structure as
well as **getnameinfo()**. The code is not very different, but the use of the **sockaddr_storage** guarantees
that any protocol-specific socket address can be safely
stored in the buffer.

A controversial API extension that was used heav-
ily in the NRL code is the **SA_LEN()** macro. On
systems whose **sockaddr** has a **sa_len** field, this ex-
pands to return the contents of that field and has the
same semantics except that it is only defined to be an
rvalue. On systems whose **sockaddr** does not, this ex-
pands into an operation that returns the correct value
based on the value of the **sa_family** field. This macro
solves the problem of needing a sockaddr's length for
many function calls well after existing code has lost
the length information. It is frequently far easier to
replace a hard coded value such as **sizeof(struct
sockaddr_in)** with a macro use like **SA_LEN(sa)** than
it is to gut an entire program and fix this. Using the
macro, this technique is portable to systems with and
without **sa_len** support. Authors who have used this
technique extensively have been quite supportive of it,
while authors of systems that don't have **sa_len** fields
have been opposed to it.

3.3 State of Deployment

New API functions are fine as long as they are available everywhere, but deployment does not happen
quickly. The interfaces described as non-standard
are just that, and are unlikely to be present any-

```
int get_stream(char *host, *service)
{
  int error, fd;
  struct addrinfo req, *ai, *ai2;
  char hbuf[NI_MAXHOST], sbuf[NI_MAXSERV];

  memset(&req, 0, sizeof(struct addrinfo));
  req.ai_socktype = SOCK_STREAM;

  if (error = getaddrinfo(host, service, NULL, &ai)) {
    fprintf(stderr, "getaddrinfo(%s, %s, ...): %s(%d)", gai_strerror(error),
      error);
    return -1;
  }

  for (ai2 = ai; ai = ai->ai_next) {
    if (error = getnameinfo(ai->ai_addr, ai->ai_addrlen, hbuf, sizeof(hbuf),
        sbuf, sizeof(sbuf), NI_NUMERICHOST | NI_NUMERICSERV)) {
      fprintf(stderr, "getnameinfo(%p, %d, %p, %d, %p, %d, %d): %s(%d)\n",
        ai->ai_addr, ai->ai_addrlen, hbuf, sizeof(hbuf), sbuf, sizeof(sbuf),
        NI_NUMERICHOST | NI_NUMERICSERV, gai_strerror(error), error);
      continue;
    }

    fprintf(stdout, "Trying %s.%s...\n", hbuf, sbuf);

    if ((fd = socket(ai->ai_family, ai->ai_socktype, ai->ai_protocol)) < 0) {
      fprintf(stderr, "socket(%d, %d, %d): %s(%d)\n", ai->ai_family,
        ai->ai_socktype, ai->ai_protocol, strerror(errno), errno);
      continue;
    }

    if (connect(fd, ai->ai_addr, ai->ai_addrlen) < 0) {
      fprintf(stderr, "connect(%d, %p, %d): %s(%d)\n", fd, ai->ai_addr,
        ai->ai_addrlen, strerror(errno), errno);
      close(fd);
      continue;
    }

    freeaddrinfo(ai2);
    return fd;
  }

  freeaddrinfo(ai2);
  fprintf(stderr, "No connections result.\n");
  return -1;
}
```

Figure 6: Using `getaddrinfo()` to Get one Stream Connection

References

IPv6:

IPv6: The New Internet Protocol (2nd edition)

Christian Huitema

ISBN 0138505055

A comprehensive book on the history of IPv6 design, development, and the specification itself. It was published in 1997, so, it is based on the old IPv6 specification (RFC 1883) rather than the lastest one (RFC 2460).

Network Programming Using Socket API:

UNIX Network Programming, Volume 1: Networking APIs—Sockets and XTI (2nd edition)

W. Richard Stevens

ISBN 013490012X

A definitive book on programming using socket API. Note, however, that the description of IPv6 API is out-of-date, so don't refer to it. Refer to this book and/or RFC 2553.

TCP/IP Illustrated, Volume 1: The Protocols

W. Richard Stevens

ISBN 0201633469

Describes the design of TCP/IP protocols, as well as actual packet flows. It will help you understand what will happen after you make certain socket API calls.

IPv6-Related RFCs:

RFC 2373 IP Version 6 Addressing Architecture

R. Hinden, S. Deering. July 1998. (Format: TXT = 52,526 bytes) (Obsoletes RFC 1884) (Status: PROPOSED STANDARD)

Defines various types of IPv6 addresses, such as multicast addresses or link-local addresses. The document also defines textual notation for the IPv6 address (hexadecimals separated by colons).

RFC 2460 Internet Protocol, Version 6 (IPv6) Specification

S. Deering, R. Hinden. December 1998. (Format: TXT = 85,490 bytes) (Obsoletes RFC 1883) (Status: DRAFT STANDARD)

The base specification of IPv6. Defines IPv6 header and various extension headers.

RFC 2461 Neighbor Discovery for IP Version 6 (IPv6)

T. Narten, E. Nordmark, W. Simpson. December 1998. (Format: TXT = 22,2516 bytes) (Obsoletes RFC 1970) (Status: DRAFT STANDARD)

Defines Neighbor Discovery (ND) protocol, which is necessary for IPv6 communication over the Ethernet. ND is the the IPv6 counterpart for IPv4 ARP.

RFC 2462 IPv6 Stateless Address Autoconfiguration

S. Thomson, T. Narten. December 1998. (Format: TXT = 61,210 bytes) (Obsoletes RFC 1971) (Status: DRAFT STANDARD)

Specification on address autoconfiguration, which is an important feature of IPv6.

RFC 2463 Internet Control Message Protocol (ICMPv6) for the Internet Proto col Version 6 (IPv6) Specification

A. Conta, S. Deering. December 1998. (Format: TXT = 34,190 bytes) (Obsoletes RFC 1885) (Status: DRAFT STANDARD)

Defines ICMP for IPv6. RFCs can be downloaded from ftp://ftp.ietf.org/rfc/.

Index